ALBANIA AND THE BALKANS

ESSAYS IN HONOUR OF SIR REGINALD HIBBERT

For Julia and Alexander

ALBANIA AND THE BALKANS

ESSAYS IN HONOUR OF SIR REGINALD HIBBERT

EDITED BY JAMES PETTIFER

Elbow Publishing
Cornwall

Contents

Some Historical Perspectives

Post-Communist Realities

Biography
Reginald Hibbert

Born 21st February 1922 in Essex, brought up in Barnet,
North London. Educated at Queen Elizabeth's School, Barnet.

1940   Scholarship to Worcester College Oxford to read History

1943   Officer training, Royal Military Academy, Sandhurst

1943   Volunteered for SOE and parachuted into Albania

November 1943 – October 1944
        British Liaison Officer with the Communist Partisans in
        Albania

December 1944
        Re-joined the 4th Queen's Own Hussars, ending the war
        in the autumn of 1945 as a tank commander in the Italian
        campaign

1946   Joined the Foreign and Commonwealth Office, Secretary
        to the British delegation to the Paris Conference, the New
        York Conference, member of Bevin's delegation to the
        Council of Foreign Ministers in Moscow

1947   First overseas posting to Bucharest, Romania

1949   Married Ann Pugh

1949   South East Asia Department, FCO London

1951   Second Secretary Vienna

1954   Northern Department FCO London

1957-64   Guatemala, Turkey, Brussels

1964-66   Chargé d'Affaires in Ulan Bator, first British diplomat
        posted to Outer Mongolia

1966-67   Research Fellow University of Leeds

1967-69   Political Adviser's Office Singapore

1970-71   Political Adviser to the Commander-in-Chief, Far East

1972-75   Minister, Bonn

1975-76   Assistant Under-Secretary of State, FCO

1976-79   Deputy Under-Secretary of State;

1979-82   Ambassador to France;

1982-87   Director, Ditchley Foundation;

1984-88   Visiting Fellow, St Antony's College, Oxford

1990-95   Chairman, Franco-British Society

1996-2000 President, Albania Society of Britain,

1997-99   President, Fédération Britannique des Alliances Françaises

Died 5 October 2002

Senior Associate Member, St Antony's College, CMG 1966, KCMG 1979, GCMG 1982

Source: CIA World Factbook

Introduction
James Pettifer

Sir Reginald (Reg) Hibbert was a man of many parts, a World War Two soldier and Special Operations Executive (SOE) operative, a prominent diplomat who ended his career as British Ambassador in Paris and a writer, activist and historian. He was a warm, generous and faithful friend, a strong family man, with an acute practical intelligence, a wonderful dry wit, and an exhaustive knowledge of international affairs.

His main publication Albania's National Liberation: The Bitter Victory, based on his World War II SOE experiences appeared in 1991 after his retirement from the Foreign Office. In normal circumstances it would have been seen as a valuable memoir and historical work by scholars, but would have attracted little attention in the wider world. But when it appeared, in 1991, it was not 'normal times'. Albanian communism was collapsing and war was breaking out in the northern Balkans in Yugoslavia. Intense debate developed about the crisis in the second Yugoslavia in the Foreign and Commonwealth Office and in the Royal Insttute of International Affairs, at Chatham House, where Reg and I were active members. There were many bitter divisions of opinion about the origins of the conflicts. Many of those involved also had World War II experience in the Balkans, and were soon involved in controversy about the true history of events in which they had taken part in their youth. For many participants the war involved a rediscovery of 'lost' national histories which Yugoslav and Albanian communism had sought to suppress and the reemergence of Albanian history was no exception to this process.

This volume is intended to be a tribute, eleven or more years after his death in 2002 to a man who was central to those debates and devoted much of the last period of his life to the understanding and progress of Albania and Kosova, as he had earlier been an influential advocate of international intervention in Bosnia. He was often a critic of the United Nations and was a strong supporter of US primacy and leadership, not simply on ideological grounds but with the view that without the US on board in an initiative, little or nothing would happen, particularly in the Balkans. Unlike some diplomats he was always ready to see the need for a military component in the policy armory, and he was a vigorous advocate of military action against the Milosevic regime in Serbia when in the mid-1990's many of his Foreign Office ex-colleagues and other contemporaries rejected it.

If this collection has a unifying theme, it is the perspective and experience of such diverse outsiders in the region that Reginald Hibbert risked his life in, in conditions of considerable hardship, and never forgot. By way of background, Nada Boškovska re-tells an extraordinary kidnap of 1903 as an illustration of western perceptions of the region. The Second World War brings Basil Kondis on an early attempted intervention by the British in northern Albania, and Gani Perolli's passionate exploration of the 1945 Herec massacre involving his family. Inez Muzarku considers the Albanian experiences of diverse outsiders – travellers, SOE officers and missionaries. Moving into the post-war period and the evolution of Hoxha's Albania, Tom Winnifrith re-examines Kim Philby's responsibility for the failure of British and American attempts to topple Hoxha. Michael Schmidt-Neke discusses the Sigurimi and Stephen Nash reviews religious history under the dictatorship. Xhervat Lloshi re-considers Hibbert's Albania's National Liberation Struggle as a contribution to the rebirth of Albanian historiography.

With the death of Hoxha and the subsequent collapse of his regime, Albania and the outside world began to re-experience each other. Michael Kaser addresses the economic aspects of Albania's transition, and Bernd Fischer assesses the role played by the country's intelligentsia in the collapse of the dictatorship. While Albania was re-emerging, its neighbours were enduring collapse, war, and then protracted international intervention. A series of authors considers different aspects of the international role: while Bob Churcher gives one of the first serious accounts of the Preshevo Valley crisis, Shaun Byrnes analyses the Kosovo Diplomatic Observer Mission and C. Dennison-Lane does the same for the post-1999 UN Mission there. Robert Wilton's essay considers the international interventions as a pattern, showing how the lessons of Reginald Hibbert's experiences in Albania could have, but generally haven't, been learned by more recent official visitors. Three very different essays close the collection: Nurcan Ozgur Baklacioglu analyses the relationship between Turkey and the Albanians; Miranda Vickers completes the range of external perspectives with a history of the roles and relations of the two Albanian Societies active in the UK; and, looking to traditional Albania's future, Antonia Young and Erin Marchington study the impact of tourism in a remote north Albanian village.

The deliberate diversity of these pieces reflects Reginald Hibbert's breadth of interest and activity. The book is a colloquium, and the voices of this unusual mixture of authors – academics of different disciplines and practitioners of rich experience, from half a dozen nations – have been left largely unedited, to speak for themselves. We have welcomed the variety of opinions, literary and academic conventions and standpoints reflected, responsibility for which rests solely with the authors.

In terms of his own historical writing, Hibbert was working firmly in the Thucydidean problematic, like many other ex-SOE authors like Nicholas Hammond, Julian Amery, Basil Davidson, and C.M. Woodhouse who had been involved in the different Balkan nations' resistance against the Axis occupation and then the ensuing internal conflicts. He was a gentleman and scholar who donned military uniform to do what had to be done in fraught times, and he then wrote the history of those times as a participant. Along with most of the other ex-SOE officers, he kept a strong interest in Albanian affairs while in the usual variety of foreign postings in his post-war diplomatic career. He was an active member and then President of the Albania Society and sought to modernize the society and later was involved in early merger discussions with the Anglo-Albanian Society. He was a great educator of the younger generation of scholars, publicists and activists in the wartime period when the Yugoslav/Serbian lobby in government and much of the political elite in London remained very strong. In the wider world he supported numerous progressive causes, particularly those concerned with environmental conservation and tree planting in the vicinity of Machynlleth in north Wales where he made his home for many years.

As the Albanian proverb goes, you can take the man out of Albania but you cannot take Albania out of the man, and there is no doubt that as a historian, polemicist and political activist Reg played an influential role in the emergence of Albania from the cloistered isolation of the final years of the one-party state and into a new future. It was perhaps fitting that his final visit with Miranda Vickers and I to the region was in the winter of 1999-2000, soon after the end of the Kosova war in which he had been as active as ever in London as an advocate and lobbyist for the Kosova

Albanian cause. He was a brave and humorous travelling companion in the wilds of the Dibra highlands, making a last visit to the scenes of the Partisan warfare of his youth where he was still held in great esteem by local people we met, and then travelling in Macedonia and newly free Kosova, even though already in some pain and discomfort from the onset of what was to be his final illness.

I am very grateful to the Contributors, many of whom knew Hibbert personally, for their patient work and to Jane Nicholov (Nee Hibbert), Reg's daughter, for all her help, and to Elbow Publishing.

James Pettifer, St Cross College, Oxford, 2013

Reginald Hibbert: In my memory
Jane Hibbert

The experiences of my father, Reginald Hibbert, as a British Liaison Officer in Albania during World War II and his later involvement in commenting on the future development of Albania and the surrounding Balkan political region provide several key considerations for anyone with a special interest in this area. His diary and his later analysis of the deeper background to the events he experienced in his book 'Albania's National Liberation Struggle, The Bitter Victory' illustrate how the presence of the BLO's and their subsequent retelling of events have helped shape British Balkan studies and British foreign policy towards Albania, Kosovo and Macedonia, giving Albania a prominence that its size might belie and respecting its social and geo-political significance in Europe. At the same time his personal account in his letters and diary offer insights into what happens to young people when subjected to extraordinary experiences 'In Albania I learned much about people and society and politics. It must have contributed something to my character and mind and faculties. This something is all that I carry away with me.'[1] This 'something', is the experience that enriches some people enabling them to make valuable contributions throughout their lives and it was certainly so in my father's case.

His wartime experiences in Albania pursued my father throughout his life, both psychologically and in his career. His life illustrated his own view that many BLOs felt responsibility for the subsequent political isolation of Albania and the later events in Kosovo, knowing that they had played a part in the 'chance encounters, narrow margins, narrowly missed opportunities and extraordinary turns of luck'[2] which laid the grounds for how that corner of the Balkans developed both before and after the fall of communism and the dissolution of Yugoslavia. In his personal life, Albania was the key to my father's life-long interest in South-Eastern Europe and the nature of Communism, prompting his return to Oxford after the war to read Russian, drawing his own children

[1]Diary entry 12 October – 4 November 1944
[2]Hibbert 1991 p243

into that interest and now influencing the next generation of his family as well. 'The men who served as BLOs were marked by Albania in the sense that they all carried away strong feelings about the events in which they had taken part. Albania's relative insignificance and its self-imposed isolation from the rest of Europe have provided no normal channels for the expression of those feelings such as have existed for those that who worked with the resistance forces in other countries. The strong feelings have persisted none the less for over forty years.'[3] On his retirement from the Foreign Service, however, he was free finally to find a forum in which to express those feelings, speaking up for the country which had been his 'university', doing so with great energy, writing articles and letters, giving talks, and in a sense carrying on where he had left off in 1944.

My father was one of many BLOs who subsequently wrote of their experiences and also kept diaries which have all been important resources for scholars of Albania. He treasured the diary he kept in the field, quite illegally, 'It was against regulations but, for a young man fresh from university, it was a way of absorbing the experiences of a very strange world'.[4] His diary was his main record but he also left his early letters written both before his assignment to Albania and after his evacuation to Cairo in 1944, with a long gap for the ten months spent in the Albanian mountains. Reading both the diaries and the letters not only tell us about the events of the time but give us an insight into the mind of a young man who set off believing 'as one still could and did in those days that it was fairly safe to do nearly anything if you were British'[5] and came back deeply affected with his tone of discourse significantly changed.

One of the very few comments my father made about his experience in Albania in the letters home which he was finally allowed to write after his evacuation from Albania was 'Don't pay any attention to what the papers tell you about guerrillas and resistance movements. They blind you with glamour and romance – the facts tell a very different story.'[6] He was evacuated from Albania arriving back in Italy on 8 October 1944 and his letters are full of accounts of the frantic social life he and his fellow-BLO, Richard Riddell, flung themselves into to make up for the ten months

---

[3]Hibbert 1991 p242

[4]Hibbert 1991 p87

[5]Hibbert 1991 p88

[6]Letter to Reg's parents, Bari December 5 1944

'in the mountains' rushing from 'lunches to dinners, from cocktail parties to dances'. Their experience was not one they could easily share with people who had been completely uninvolved in his life in Albania, cut off by Army censorship, but his enthusiastic details about the drinking, the parties, the love affairs with nurses and secretaries betray the deprivation of the previous months if his readers had understood the implication of his words. In a letter to his parents he thanks them for sending parcels and tells them 'My teeth have been in a bad condition, due chiefly to unavoidable neglect. My hayfever has been negligible, due I think to the altitudes at which we have been living. All my kit has been lost, some of it several times over.'[7]

This is a man who has not been able to clean his teeth for ten months and has been living on a mountainside without the basics of everyday living who explains his thrill at seeing Rome as excusable because he had not seen a city of any sort for so long. Could his family and non-combatant friends really imagine what all this meant in terms of physical discomfort to someone who, when they had known him, had been a North London grammar school boy, rather a swot and then an Oxford undergraduate fond of poetry and Scottish dancing? One of his first requests in fact from his friend and fellow-undergraduate, Ann Pugh, was for 'something slim and full of poetry.'[8] Although he often tried to debunk romantic ideas of partisan warfare, inevitably, romantic recollections intruded, however. Christmas with his new regiment draws out one memory which, while seeming to make light of the scene, nevertheless reveals the emotional hold his experiences were already beginning to have over him and which was to last the rest of his life: 'Our Christmas promises to be as festive as possible, though probably not so gay as last year, which was very picturesque. There were plenty of us of all nationalities crowded in a ramshackle house in the mountains, drinking local firewater and eating barbaric meals of wild pig, chicken, fruit and goatsmilk cheese. Our specialities were some precious Italian chianti, beer and cognac. You can guess that we had a wild and fantastic party by fire and candle-light, with songs and speeches in every language available, and with Moslems making huge efforts to help a Christian feast on its way with much firing of weapons and shouting and public speech-making. This Christmas will

---

[7]Letter to Reg's parents, Bari 2 November 1944
[8]Letter to Ann Pugh, Bari 21 November 1944

be very sober by comparison.'[9] This is his only contemporary description of the 'facts', apart from his diary written in the field, and they are closer to the romantic view of the guerrilla life that his family and friends in England might have had and perhaps chosen by him for that reason, to entertain and amuse but also to share because his letters reveal how desperate he and Riddell were to share and review their experiences.

His family and Ann Pugh probably longed to know what he had been doing in Albania but it was with fellow officers that he and Riddell wanted to share their experiences and debrief themselves. In Albania they had lived intensively 'in a society of enthusiasts', caught up in the creation of a new state, and had 'returned from the Balkans wiser but far less sober men'[10] but what appeared to them to be deeply significant both personally and in terms of the war was brushed aside by the very people whose interest and approval they valued, their senior officers, the specialists and their fellow officers. In his diary he writes; 'No one in the office seems very interested in what we have to say.'[11] By the end of October the novelty of 'civilised' life in Bari with beds with bedsprings and shops full of goods was wearing off. 'We are only too anxious to talk about our experiences; our lives have consisted of nothing else for a year. But no one is very interested to hear them. People seem a bit afraid of us, as if we were mad or 'bolshy' or just too enthusiastic. Disillusion grows on us. The war which we have been fighting does not seem to exist any more. In Albania we were fighting to create a state. Here that does not count. The criteria here are what will destroy Germany quickest and what will spread British influence furthest. The two planes of experience and thought ought to be inter-related but are not.'[12] He was already up against the paradox of reconciling experience on the ground with the detachment of planners who had their eye on tactics and were uninterested in Albania's eventual political destiny, while the BLOs had thought that was precisely what they had been caught up in. Albania's internal political fate would be the long-term side-effect of their involvement although Reg commented in one of his final diary entries 'the B.L.O.s know that it is not they who decide the

---

[9]Letter to Reg's parents, Ancona, 23 December 1944

[10]Letter to Reg's parents, Bari 19 October 1944

[11]Diary entry 11 October 1944

[12]Diary entry 12 October – 4 November 1944

future of Albania and that it is the blind force of events which is causing a tremendous pattern of change to unfold in Europe.'[13] Later he becomes resigned and by the beginning of November he writes 'I think that the B.L.O.s who stay on in the firm in the hope of influencing them [the planners] for good are mistaken. It is better to leave them to get it wrong, as they are at present doing. The Partisans will in any case get what they want, without reference to Bari'[14] as indeed they did.

I was born five years after my father's arrival in Bari from Albania. By the time I was six or seven Albanian stories were part of my and my small brother's meal time entertainment. Occasionally the precious little black diary was brought out at my request and my father's cramped and loopy handwriting peered at as if we were examining cuneiform or Egyptian hieroglyphics. How I liked the story of the funny Italians who led the mules, cooked meals, shaved the English officers. I imagined them giving themselves up in a wood for some reason. That story had a happy ending because after the war the cook became a chef in Venice and my father and mother went to see him there. Then there was the tense story of the broken fork. A chieftain proudly brought out his aluminium knives and forks in honour of the English visitors at a ceremonial meal and my father's fork bent and broke. In order not to insult his host's pride in his cutlery my father had to carry on eating while holding the parts together in his palm. Of course we children had to pretend to do the same. We listened goggle eyed to the tale of the two dinners when on another occasion my father and his men had to hide in an upstairs room peering down through the rafters at a group of German soldiers being entertained to the very meal they themselves had been eating a few minutes earlier. Supposing the Germans had looked up or heard a cough? We were disgusted at the thought of eating sheep's eyes and my father exaggerated the taste and consistency for his own amusement but years later I still could not bring myself to eat one when offered sheep's head in another Balkan country. And then there were the gold coins in money belts to pay the local people, just like pieces of eight, and the secret maps, the parachutes that were buried and the camp fires and the man with the broken leg. When we asked whether we could go and dig up the parachutes and money one day, my father laughed and said they were

---

[13] Diary entry 12 October – 4 November 1944
[14] Diary entry 12 October – 4 November 1944

probably under a cement factory. For his children, Reg made Albania into a place of romance and drama that he knew was not the whole story but was all he could convey to small minds eleven or twelve years after the events which had left such a strong impression on him. The truth was that he felt the need to keep Albania alive in his mind. Although there were other funny stories about war time exploits, in training at Sandhurst, and during the Italian campaign, I was very aware that Albania was in a different category. On the bookshelf was a copy of Peter Kemp's 'No Colours or Crest' with its flamboyant jacket showing a cloak and dagger. In the 1980s on a visit to the Dalmatian coast I hired a car and drove down to Skutari with the sole purpose of seeing Albania from the Montenegrin side of the border. From certain vantage points on the road you could look down onto the plain and know you were looking at the forbidden land, secret and inaccessible, although I was disappointed not to see any of the dramatic mountains I had learned about as a child.

The darker side of my father's Albanian experience directly affected our lives as a family, however. His diplomatic career included a series of strange postings often one after another usually coinciding with local crises: Guatemala and the Belize conflict, Outer Mongolia as first British chargé d'affaires in residence in Ulan Bator, Singapore as political advisor to the C in C Far East at the time of the complete withdrawal of British army, air force and naval bases. My mother confided in us that the absence of any ambassadorial posting late into his career was because 'people' had accused him of being a Communist sympathiser in Albania and of being involved with Enver Hoxha, with his chief accuser being a fellow officer whom he had helped, the famous man with the broken leg from our childhood stories. His subsequent appointment by David Owen to the great prize of the Paris Embassy gave the family a huge amount of satisfaction that his qualities had been finally recognised and that the rumour mongers had not affected David Owen's judgment of him.

With the break-up of Yugoslavia and the later events in Kosovo, however, all things Albanian came back into his life. At this point he decided to write his own account, far later than any of the others, with the benefit of later historical insight and against the background of political events in an Albania in transition from one of the harshest Communist regimes in the world. It also meant that Albania was no longer a secret language shared by those who had been there and those responsible for sending them. His written account and interpretation of war time events became part of the transition itself when it was translated and published in Tirana. The years between his return to Bari were bridged with his own return to Albania. Reg became politically active for the first time since the war. Now retired, he wrote papers and letters expressing his strongly held views about the fate and post war history of Albania and the future of Kosovo and Albania.

For me, however, Albania has been a constant in my relations with my father. The most fascinating thing has been how the wild Ruritania of childhood stories and of my childhood imagination has been given a real historical setting with the publication of his book. Yet even more important has been to finally read his diary, carefully typed up by my mother and his letters home from Bari, and to enter the mind of a twenty two year old officer and to understand that 'The war which we have been fighting', which he felt was ignored by the people he wanted to debrief to in Bari at the time and did 'not seem to exist an more'[15],did after all come to exist because people uninvolved with the war wanted to know about it and understand it. 'In Albania were conscious all the time that the Partisans were fighting to create a state.'[16] The nature of that state and its later consequences has become the matter of regular political debate and academic research.

In 2011, the website of one London publisher listed seventeen titles relating directly to Albania but only fifteen titles devoted to all the other Balkan countries together, including Kosovo, the former Yugoslav republics, Bulgaria, Macedonia and Romania. Where does this fascination come from for a country whose image for the British public up until World War Two has been described by Roderick Bailey as one 'of a wild and mountainous country far away and best avoided'[17]? Britain like every other country at the time had declined to intervene when the Italians invaded in April 1939 'as none wanted war over a place so remote'[18] yet in the years after the war and in spite of the real, self-imposed, remoteness of Albania under Enver Xoxha, instead of returning to the status of a land where the likes of John Buchan's adventurer Richard Hannay might

---

[15]Diary entry 12 October – 4 November 1944
[16]Diary entry 12 October – 4 November
[17]Bailey 2008 p 13
[18]Bailey 2008 p 13

find a way of passing the time without yawning, Albania has had book after book published about her in Britain, to start with mainly by former British Liaison Officers or others associated with planning and executing SOE's activities in Albania during World War Two and later by academics.

This wealth of publications after the war has created the sense of a special British relationship with Albania because, while the break-up of Yugoslavia and the subsequent Kosovo crisis have undoubtedly breathed new life into Albanian studies, prior to that, an active interest had already developed not only in examining the former history of Albania and Britain's relationship with her but also in satisfying a persistent need to understand the events leading up to the assertion of communist dominance in 1944 and the fatal path taken by Albania for which the BLOs and their planners felt a level of responsibility or at least involvement because of 'the intensity of the Albanian experience.'[19] This intensity of the personal experience, of the physical hardships and the dangers of dealing with a little understood people and their system of local loyalties combined with the direct experience and interpretation of events by the BLOs themselves with their varying personal, political and social backgrounds. These in turn were affected by the limitations on knowledge and understanding of the country on the part of the planners and commanding officers and with the bigger picture of the interests of the war time powers Italy, Germany, Britain, the USSR. My father's diary with its daily record of events 'when put against the broader narrative told in this book [Albania's National Liberation Struggle, the Bitter Victory], shows what a gulf existed between our experience on the ground and the thinking about Albania at higher military and political levels.'[20] As a result, the personal experience of Albania could be seen as critical to understanding the history of the aftermath of the triumph of Enver Hoxha's faction.

Military memoirs pour out during and after every conflict as many a ghost-writer can confirm in this last decade with the Iraq and Afghan wars. A veteran of the Vietnam War, a former lieutenant in the 1st Battalion (Airborne) of the 8th Cavalry Regiment explains the compulsion of former soldiers to write about their wartime exploits 'I decided that I had something to say. Vanity and egoism…played a part but I wanted to

[19]Bailey 2008 p 327
[20]Hibbert 1991 p 88

comment, not least for those young lieutenants out there who might be assisted by my 'lessons learned.'[21] In this case the 'lessons learned' were less to do with details of combat and life under arms than with clarifying, in Patrick Leigh Fermor's words, the 'matter of rumour and surmise' that was wartime Albania by an examination of the actions of these one hundred or so men, by the untangling of the complex relationships between the different Albanian groups and individuals and, let it be said, by being frank about the placing of blame on this or that individual or group for Albania's painful post war history, the 'bitter victory' referred to in the title of Reg's account of his experiences. Because so many of the British officers took on positions of influence in their post-war life, their interpretation of their Albanian experiences has had a direct influence on British foreign policy and later they were able to articulate their differences in a public forum they had easy personal access to. David Smiley makes direct reference to this in the last chapter of his 'Albanian Assignment' listing MPs, MI6 and Foreign Office officials, journalists and authors.

However, the greatest legacy of this fifty year battle to determine whose was the true interpretation of those complex events has been the creation of a strong school of Albanian studies which has led Balkan studies in the United Kingdom for half a century and to which this book is another valuable contribution. While other officers were sent to other Balkan theatres of war none returned home with the same sense of unfinished business and a personal commitment to the country which provided them with such an intense personal experience as did the BLOs in Albania, who had felt 'all the tension of sharing and living Albania's fate.'[22] We should be highly grateful to all the SOE men, whatever their stance, for bringing Albania into the light of academic investigation.

References

Reginald Hibbert's wartime diary written in the field in Albania 19 December 1943-4 November 1944

Reginald Hibbert's personal letters October /November 1944

---

[21] William Crisp letter January 2012 commenting on his reason for writing an account of his experiences in Vietnam between 1966-1967, 'Air Assault' (unpublished)

[22] Diary entry 12 October – 4 November 1944

Hibbert, R. *Albania's National Liberation Struggle, The Bitter Victory* (1991) London, Pinter Publishers

Bailey, R. *The Wildest Province, SOE in the Land of the Eagle* (2008) London, Jonathan Cape

The Kidnapping of Miss Stone: The Balkans in 1903 in Western Perspective
Nada Boškovska

Around 1900 the Ottoman Empire had already lost most of its possessions in the Balkans. Several independent or at least autonomous small states had left the Empire during the 19th century: Serbia, Greece, Romania, Montenegro and Bulgaria. Bosnia-Herzegovina had been occupied by Austria-Hungary in 1878. The remaining parts of the Ottoman Empire in Europe were Macedonia, Thrace, Epirus, Albania and Kosovo. It was mainly the interests of the great powers which prevented the Empire disintegrating even further. Each of the powers kept a close watch so that none of the others gained in territory or influence. The young Balkan states with their strong interest in the remains of the Ottoman Empire were also to be kept at bay. For these reasons the powers preferred the maintaining of the status quo as the lesser of two evils. The governments could not turn a blind eye however to the defects of the Ottoman Empire. It was the legal uncertainty above all which caused repeated outrage in sections of the public in the west. The Englishwoman Mary E. Durham, travelling in the Ottoman Balkans several times at the beginning of the 20th century, denounced anarchy and lawlessness there: 'Law, like salaries, exists mainly on paper. Whether it is enforced depends entirely upon who has broken it. Every man, if he is strong enough, can be his own policeman.'[1] Under these conditions it was the Christian population – the majority in the Balkans – who suffered most, since they did not bear arms and were exposed without protection to attacks by armed Muslims, whether soldiers or civilians.[2] According to a British journalist, the privilege of bearing arms formed an unbridgeable divide between the Muslims and the 'unbelievers'[3]. This is how the American Frederick Moore describes the contrast in behaviour between Christians and Muslims encountered on the country road from Bitola to Prilep, Macedonia, in summer 1903: 'We passed Christian caravans which took

---

[1] *Mary Edith Durham*, The Burden of the Balkans, London 1905, 87.
[2] *Victor Bérard*, Pro Macedonia, Paris 1904, 4-5.
[3] *John MacDonald* in: The Daily News (London), April 1, 1903.

the fields to give us the road, and Mohamedan carts which made us give them the right of way. The former were unarmed and most meek, doffing their dejected fezzes and standing abject with hands clasped on their stomachs as we passed. The others, down to the half-grown boys, carried pistols and guns, and bore themselves like a ruling race. The Turks, however, appeared to be as poor as the Christians, and once two veiled women, gathering their faded rags about them, even to covering their henna-tipped fingers, came up to our horses to beg. Nevertheless, their husband, riding a dwarfed donkey, carried a revolver.' [4]

Under pressure from the great powers, the Ottoman Porte repeatedly promised to improve the situation of the Christian population, but in practice hardly anything was done. At the end of the 19th century, the English journalist Harry C. Thomson summarised conditions in Macedonia as follows: 'The country is in almost absolute anarchy. The troops are in a state of semi-mutiny, owing to not being regularly paid, and there is no security anywhere for either life or the property of the rayahs.' [5] 'Fear is the dominant, the ever-present motive', concluded the Briton Henry Brailsford on an extended visit to Macedonia in 1903. Massacres and murders were not especially frequent, but were always possible, so that a feeling of security could not prevail. [6]

Against this background, the Macedonian border region of the Ottoman Empire towards Bulgaria witnessed the spectacular kidnapping of an American missionary in late summer 1901. What became known as 'the Miss Stone affair' kept the public in Europe and the United States in suspense for quite a while. It offers a splendid example of how historic developments can become concentrated in a single event which in turn plays its part in history. Closely connected with the political and social situation of the time in Macedonia, the kidnapping had bearings on international relations and the activity of church organisations. Moreover, it forms part of the history of liberation movements and uprisings and is an early instance of the politically motivated kidnapping and hostage-taking which became highly significant in the 20th century. In an era when various factors including innovative broadcasting and

---

[4] Frederick Moore, The Balkan Trail [New York 1906], New York 1971, 163.
[5] 'Rayahs' refers to the Christian population. *Harry C. Thomson*, The outgoing Turk. Impressions of a journey through the Western Balkans, London 1897, 235f.
[6] *Henry N. Brailsford*, Macedonia. Its races and their future, London 1906, 36-38.

reproducing technologies contributed to the development of the press as a mass medium[7], the 'Miss Stone affair' became a media event. This lent transnational significance in Europe and the United States to goings-on in a little-known, marginal area of the European continent and contributed considerably to the consolidating of negative stereotypes of the Balkans.

Both kidnappers and victims provided reports on the events, and these ego documents make it possible to analyse the personal and politico-cultural encounter between a female American Protestant missionary and Macedonian 'brigands'.

Events began to unfold on September 3, 1901, when the American Methodist Ellen Stone, accompanied by twelve other people, was travelling from Bansko to Gorna Dzhumaya (now Blagoevgrad in Bulgaria). In Bansko, Stone had been teaching a class of eight elementary school teachers and 'Bible women' in a summer course lasting several weeks. [8]

Ellen Maria Stone was born in Roxbury, Massachusetts in 1846. Her deeply religious Protestant family had early plans for her to become a missionary. After ten years working as an editor on the journal The *Boston Congregationalist*, Stone was sent in September 1878 by the missionary society American Board of Commissioners for Foreign Missions to the Bulgarian town of Samokov. Following centuries of Ottoman rule, Bulgaria had just been granted the status of an autonomous principality at the Berlin Congress. In her new field of activity, Stone was expected to devote herself primarily to the 'emancipation of Oriental womanhood.'[9] Protestant missionary societies frequently placed the education and Christian instruction of women in the hands of female missionaries. It was they who ran schools for girls, taught mothers western ideas of hygiene and healthy eating, and propagated the ideal of the Christian home in which husband and wife showed mutual respect and children received both food and welfare. The underlying philosophy was formulated by

---

[7] *Habbo Knoch / Daniel Morat*, Medienwandel und Gesellschaftsbilder 1880-1960. Zur historischen Kommunikologie der massenmedialen Sattelzeit, in: Id. (eds.), Kommunikation als Beobachtung. Medienwandel und Gesellschaftsbilder 1880-1960, München 2003, 9-33, here 21.

[8] *Ellen M. Stone*, Six months among brigands, in: McClure's Magazine 19 (1902), 2-14, 99-109, 222-232, 464-471, 562-570, here 2f.

[9] *Teresa Carpenter*, The Miss Stone affair. America's first modern hostage crisis, New York et al. 2003, 6f.

Nannie Gaines, who spent many years as a missionary in Japan: 'No country can rise higher than her women. The kind of home decides the kind of country.'[10] The women missionaries, whose work was to a large degree practical rather than spiritual, and was aimed at the family as an institution, were thus operating at the interface of religious charitable activity and cultural imperialism.

The missionary endeavours of American and British Protestants in the Ottoman Empire began in the early 19th century. As the conversion of Muslims was strictly forbidden, their efforts were directed above all at the Greek and Slav Christians of the Eastern Church as well as Christian Armenians.[11] From the mid-19th century the American Board of Commissioners for Foreign Missions, representing the Congregational and Presbyterian churches, stepped up its efforts by joining forces with the Methodist Episcopal Church.[12]

In the eyes of both Protestants and Roman Catholics the adherents of the Eastern Churches were not genuine Christians. They had to be converted so that their souls could be saved. This becomes apparent in the words of a missionary in Bulgaria who wrote in 1870 on the occasion of the building of a Bulgarian Orthodox church next to the existing Greek Orthodox one: 'Is there not reason to hope that this nominal division of the Bulgarians from the Greek Church, may ultimately contribute to the conversion of the nation to Christ?'[13] The mission field was thorny, however. The Christians who had preserved their faith during several centuries of Ottoman domination vehemently rejected the missionising. They had been Christians for over a thousand years, they pointed out, whereas Protestantism was a heretical doctrine dating from the 16th century. The Orthodox Christians for their part regarded the Protestants as 'godless', especially when they discovered that these

---

[10]Cited from: *Dana Lee Robert*, American women in mission. A social history of their thought and practice, Macon/Georgia, 1996, 410f.

[11]*Carpenter*, The Miss Stone affair, 4; *Patrick Ph. Streiff*, Der Methodismus in Europa im 19. und 20. Jahrhundert. Mit einem Geleitwort von Manfred Marquardt, Stuttgart 2003, 59.

[12]*Tatyana Nestorova*, American missionaries among the Bulgarians (1858-1912), New York 1987, 5-8.

[13]*Henry C. Haskell*, 11th annual report of the Philipoppolis Station 1869-1870, Philippopolis May 5th, 1870, Clare Papers, cited from *Nestorova*, American missionaries, 9.

neither fasted nor crossed themselves. In 1909, despite years of missionary work, the Protestant church in the European part of Turkey had only 1456 members.[14]

One offer made by the missionaries was very welcome, however: they founded schools. The poorly developed secular school system in the Ottoman Empire provided for the Muslim population and used only the Turkish language.[15] Most of the schools attended by Balkan Christians in the Ottoman Empire were run by the neighbouring states of Greece, Bulgaria, Serbia and Romania, which pursued primarily their own national aims. Thus the Protestant mission was immediately confronted with the longing for education among its target group. Some expressed concrete wishes such as the provision of schools for girls. The missionaries were irritated and not a little disappointed to find that the people were chiefly interested in secular education and had hardly any desire for religious instruction. They liked to buy the Bible, but mainly because it was a book for reading in their own language and easy to obtain. It was not religious matters which preoccupied the Macedonian Christians, but the political situation. In 1880 the missionary J.W.Baird wrote from Monastir (the Macedonian Bitola) that people there 'are so much in fear of the gov't and so angry at it for its tyranny, that it is hard to interest them in any other subject.'[16]

Ellen Stone, who learned the Bulgarian language during her long stay in the country, taught at first in the girls' school in Samokov. From 1883 she was in charge of the training of indigenous 'Bible women'. Part of their task, in accordance with the efforts on behalf of women as described above, was to visit remote villages where they would distribute Christian literature as well as instructing women in childcare and hygiene. They also ran literacy courses and organised sewing circles and training in nursing.[17] When the first Protestant branch was set up in Thessaloniki in Ottoman Macedonia in 1894, Ellen Stone was sent there as an experienced missionary.[18] For 50-150 days a year she was out travelling. 'Like a true frontierswoman, she travels through the rough country on

[14] *Nestorova*, American missionaries, 31, 119-123.

[15] *Selçuk Akşin Somel*, The modernization of public education in the Ottoman empire, 1839-1908. Islamization, autocracy and discipline, Leiden 2001, 240, 272-274.

[16] Nestorova, American missionaries, 56-58, 85, 115 (citation).

[17] Nestorova, American missionaries, 56-58, 85, 115 (citation).

[18] Carpenter, The Miss Stone affair, 9.

horseback and inspects the schools', a newspaper reported.[19] Three times
before she was kidnapped, Stone encountered brigands without ever
being seriously in danger. The fourth encounter on September 3, 1901
was very different, however. Stone and her travelling companions were
ambushed and encircled by about twenty heavily armed men. It quickly
became apparent that this was not a robbery. The men were after the
missionary Ellen Stone, who together with one of her companions,
Katerina Tsilka, was separated from the rest of the group and led away.
Later, Stone wrote in her report of the kidnapping that if the men had
known what difficulties awaited them with the two women, she was
certain they would have freed them without delay. Escaping with the
prey took almost six months. The women had nothing with them but
the summer dresses they were wearing, a cape, an umbrella and a Bible.
Before long, Ottoman troops were hot on the heels of the kidnappers.
The group hid in the Pirin Mountains, moving around mainly at night in
silent convoy in punishing conditions, and spending the days in darkened,
smoke-filled huts and sheepstalls.[20]

Stone's companion Katerina Stefanova Tsilka (1868?-1952) was a local
woman from Bansko who had been trained as a nurse by the missionary
society in the United States. There she had also met her husband Gregor
Tsilka, a Christian Albanian. The couple lived in Korça, Albania, where
Tsilka was the priest of a small Protestant parish and a teacher at the
only school for girls in the town which taught in Albanian. The Tsilkas
were well trained indigenous Protestants who spoke several languages. As
well as Bulgarian, Katerina spoke Albanian, Turkish, Greek, Aromanian
and English.[21]

Ellen Stone was aware that her travelling companion was five months
pregnant. She informed the kidnappers of this fact within the first few
days, but they showed little concern. Their plan was to obtain a ransom
of 25,000 Turkish pounds within the next 20 days.[22] Their optimistic

---

[19] Eugene P. Lyle, Jr., An American woman captured by brigands, in: Everybody's
Magazine 6 (1902), 44-54.

http://library.ferris.edu/~cochranr/stone/stone2b1.htm (25.1.2008).

[20] Stone, Six months, 2-11.

[21] Stone, Six months, 2f. In general, western languages were spoken only by the
highly educated, whereas knowledge of more than one Balkan language was quite
common.

[22] Stone, Six months, 14f.

assessment of the situation was possibly advanced by an incident in the summer of 1899. The Frenchman Louis Chevalier, director of the Isvoro mines on Chalkidiki, was kidnapped and then rapidly freed following the payment of a ransom of 15,000 Turkish pounds.[23] Stone calculated that the sum demanded by her kidnappers was the equivalent of 110,000 dollars, and this thoroughly disheartened her. She was certain that such a high sum would never be paid.[24] The fact that the payment was demanded in gold caused a newspaper journalist to comment: 'In their rustic simplicity, the outlaws had doubtless never thought but that it could be put into the pockets of one's trousers.'[25]

The kidnappers' optimism proved unjustified. A number of attempts to make contact with appropriate persons failed. Next, it was indeed difficult to get together the sum demanded. The Board had informed its missionaries in advance that if they were taken hostage no ransoms would be paid. In the end it was Ellen Stone's family in the United States who managed to amass part of the money, 14,500 Turkish pounds, by making public appeals. Meanwhile exhausted, the kidnappers accepted this sum, but various delays in attempting to hand over the ransom followed. Not until January 18 did the gold change hands, after which the two women were freed on February 23 1902 near the small town of Strumica.[26]

What was the background of this kidnapping, and what went on between hostage-takers and hostages in the Pirin mountains in those wintry six months? Following their release, both Ellen Stone and Katerina Tsilka wrote a report for the well-known American monthly *McClure's Magazine*. Stone described the whole of the kidnapping, whereas Tsilka focussed entirely on the events surrounding the birth of her child. The

---

[23] *CKKhristophe Chiclet*, Les prodromes du terrorisme moderne. Fédais et Komitadjis à l'aube du XXème siècle, in: Confluences, Hiver 1996-1997, 25-29, here 28. Curtis on the other hand gives a sum of 15,000 dollars, approximately the equivalent of 3,500 pounds. His publication includes a list – by no means complete, as Curtis emphasises – of nineteen foreigners kidnapped for ransom since 1880. *William Eleroy Curtis*, The Turk and his lost provinces Greece, Bulgaria, Serbia, Bosnia, New York/Chicago 1903. For chapter XI, The Kidnapping of Miss Stone, cf. http://library.ferris.edu/~cochranr/stone/stone2c1.htm (28.1.2008).

[24] *Stone*, Six months, 12f.

[25] *Lyle*, An American woman, 44-54.

[26] *Stone*, Six months, 563; *Spomeni. I.H. Nikolov, D. Gruev, B. Sarafov, J. Sandanski, M. Gedžikov, d-r H. Tatarčev*, Transl. by Cvetko Martinovski. Foreword by Ivan Katardžiev, Skopje 1995, 212.

texts are multifaceted constructs; Stone's much longer report in particular is an impressive model of how, accompanied by fluctuating emotions, the dynamics of a relationship between hostage-takers and hostages develops. At first, the women's fear is foregrounded. The kidnappers are described by Stone as 'fierce of face, and wild of dress.'[27] They were resolute, and proved this early on by killing a passing 'Turk' who happened to witness the kidnapping. They intimidated the women in order to enforce their compliance with instructions, and they threatened to kill them should the ransom not be paid.[28] Under this threat, the problems of obtaining and handing over the money gave rise to constant tension and fear for the hostages.

It soon becomes apparent from the reports however that the women were never treated badly or denied respect. The reports even contain some irritatingly romanticising elements, such as Stone's description of how, in the early stages, one of the brigands brought her a bunch of wild cyclamen. This quieted her fears considerably.[29] In other ways too the kidnappers adhered to customary social conventions. Their aim had been to kidnap Ellen Stone. Katerina Tsilka shared her fate only so that the missionary would not be alone with a group of men out in the wilds. This would have offended against good behaviour in any part of Europe at that time. Originally, the oldest woman in the group of hostages was to have accompanied Ellen Stone, but she fell ill.[30] Katerina Tsilka was then chosen as the only married woman in the group. A specific Balkan or southern European patriarchy is evident in the fact that the kidnappers would not have considered taking one of the young girls. This would have damaged the girl's own reputation and shown the kidnappers in a bad light.[31]

The men looked after the two women as best they could. They tried to provide adequate food, and when winter set in they obtained thick material for making winter clothing. Stone and Tsilka worked with a will, finally enjoying some variety in their daily routine. Katerina Tsilka

[27] *Stone*, Six months, 6.

[28] *Spomeni*, 208; *Stone*, Six months, 7, 13.

[29] *Stone*, Six months, 10f.

[30] *Stone*, Six months, 99ff; *Spomeni*, 208.

[31] 'There were a lot of young girls in the party, but we were afraid of the gossip [...]. We paid heavily for conventions', in the words of Chernopeev, one of the leaders. *Albert Sonnichsen*, Confessions of a Macedonian bandit, New York 1909, 260.

was treated solicitously, 'her pregnancy awakening the men's soft side', as Stone emphasised. Hostages and hostage-takers gradually converged in a common fate with similar interests. They shared the things of everyday life – combs, needles, threads – and the hope that the ransom would soon be handed over. Together they feared and fled from the Ottoman security forces, as is clear from Tsilka's report: 'After two days we had to run away, for the *potera* [pursuers] were upon us.'[32] Together they endured the strain of the silent nocturnal marches through the snowbound mountains, the winter cold and the monotony of endless days in cramped, darkened hideouts. Once, when a different group wanted to take over the hostages, Stone and Tsilka decided they would rather be killed by their captors than fall into the hands of the others.[33]

Stone's descriptions paint a picture of alternating emotional ups and downs, closeness and distance, sympathy and hostility. She reports for instance how on the day before Thanksgiving she was sad and absorbed with thoughts of her family. One of the kidnappers noticed her sadness, whereupon Tsilka explained the festival and how it is celebrated. Next morning, the kidnappers served a turkey. So as not to spoil the day for the women, they kept to themselves for the moment the bad news that the ransom negotiations in Sofia had failed. But after this they took their victims on long night walks in the cold into even more remote regions, threatening to hold on to them for five years if necessary in order to obtain the ransom. Tsilka, heavily pregnant, had her own moments of sadness and depression. Almost at breaking point during the stressful flight, she begged more than once: 'Leave me here to die. I cannot go any farther.' According to Stone, the men then encouraged and supported her even more.[34]

The birth of Tsilka's baby was in several respects a highlight and a turning point –both in the kidnapping itself and in the dramaturgy of the report. Everyone had awaited the event with trepidation – above all

---

[32]*Katerina Stefanova Tsilka*, Born among brigands. Mrs Tsilka's story of her baby, in: McClure's Magazine 19 (1902), 291-300. Since the hostage taking of August 1973 in a Stockholm bank, the phenomenon of hostages showing solidarity with their captors against the police has been known as the 'Stockholm syndrome'. The question of whether aspects of this syndrome are apparent in the case of Stone and Tsilka cannot be pursued here.

[33]*Stone*, Six months, 109.

[34]*Stone*, Six months, 106-109, 223f.

Katerina herself, who wondered what would become of her child.[35] She could well imagine that there was nothing a band of outlaws on the run needed less than a howling infant. Her baby, a girl, was born without difficulties on January 4th, after the mother had spent 10 hours of the previous night in the saddle. Tsilka's fears for her baby proved unfounded: little Elena was accepted as a new member of the group, and with her arrival monotony and boredom were banished.[36]

An elderly woman had been brought in to help with the birth. Tsilka and Stone, who for months had had only the company of men, were very glad to see her. It is striking however that in her description of the midwife Tsilka focuses on her superstition and lack of cleanliness. The wrinkles in the woman's face were allegedly full of dirt – 'accumulated there for months, and perhaps years.' As a Protestant and trained nurse, Tsilka was no by no means taken with the activities of the midwife, whom she describes as full of superstition. Tsilka had no desire to be sprinkled with holy water or to blow into a tin. The old woman gave the newborn a dark red cap decorated with a coin and a piece of garlic. The garlic was to protect the baby from the evil gaze.

Then the woman spat on to her finger and stuck it in the baby's mouth. Tsilka does not explain this act but leaves it to take effect on her readers.[37] Given that the reports by Tsilka and Stone rarely contain negative stereotypes of the native population, this passage is striking. A possible interpretation is that the comment on dirt and superstition – this latter also treated more than once by Ellen Stone – both explains and legitimises the efforts of missionaries to bring such people true religion and western civilisation.

The day after the birth, the whole group visited mother and child. The men were smart, dressed in full gear and armed. According to Stone, their hands and faces were exceptionally clean – a further reference to what was seen as their usual lack of hygiene. The kidnappers offered congratulations and murmured blessings 'as is their custom'. Tsilka and Stone for their part thanked God for softening the hearts of the 'cruel

---

[35] *Tsilka*, Born among brigands, 292.

[36] *Stone*, Six months, 224.

[37] *Tsilka*, Born among brigands, 294f., 298. Clearly this was intended to protect the child from evil. Belief in the healing and preventive properties of saliva is widespread. Cf. e.g. *Hanns Bächtold-Stäubli* (ed.), Handwörterbuch des deutschen Aberglaubens, Augsburg 2005, Vol. 8, 149-153.

brigands.'[38] The leader of the group paid especial attention to the baby, evoking a quite romantic outburst in Tsilka's report: 'He was no more a brigand to me, but a brother, a father, a protector to my baby.' The mood was cheerful and lively. The leader is reported to have announced proudly that never before had a child been born in such a group: her name should be engraved on the guns. Another in the group compared Tsilka with Mary, who like her had given birth on straw in the winter. No, said another, no one had ever suffered like this woman. According to Tsilka, this was the moment from which they were no longer treated as prisoners but as free people.

The baby's position as a member of this group with its shared fate is symbolised in a further gesture with romantic overtones. The brigands clothed the baby, handing over to the women the gauze they used to clean their weapons, and the wool from which they made their footwear.[39] The women enthusiastically set to work on making clothes as intricate as possible so that they would have plenty to do. 'Oh, the blessedness of work!' was the telling comment by the Protestant Ellen Stone.[40]

The women referred to the kidnappers in their reports as 'brigands.' The European and American press however generally used the expressions 'robbers', 'villains', 'outlaws' and 'bandits'.[41] The correspondent of the *New York Post* was more differentiated in pointing out that there were 'brigands and brigands', with a certain aristocracy even among such people. He expressed the hope that Miss Stone had fallen into the hands of Bulgarian rather than Turkish 'bandits', as the first tended to be robbers with political motives.[42]

The kidnappers of Ellen Stone and Katerina Tsilka were not robbers, however. They regarded themselves as revolutionaries and freedom fighters. They were members of the Internal Macedonian Revolutionary Organisation (IMRO)[43] fighting for Macedonian autonomy. Around

---

[38] *Stone*, Six months, 227f.; *Tsilka*, Born among brigands, 296.

[39] *Tsilka*, Born among brigands, 295-297.

[40] *Stone*, Six months, 223.

[41] The St James Gazette, 21.11.01; NZZ, 4.10.1901/Abendblatt, 17.10.1901/ Morgenblatt, 18.10.1901/Beilage; *Lyle*, An American woman, 44-54; New York Times, 9.10.1901.

[42] New York Post, 7.10.1901.

[43] The name of the organisation, founded in 1893, changed several times. For reasons of clarity and simplicity the best-known designation is used here.

1900, Macedonia was the only sizeable Balkan province that remained under Turkish rule. Its neighbours Greece, Bulgaria and Serbia, each a small nation state looking for expansion, cast a covetous eye on the strategically important region. They exercised influence through the church and by founding schools. They attempted to convince the Slav Christians of the area, who for the most part defined themselves by their religious allegiance, that they were in fact Greeks, Serbs or Bulgarians. In the school year 1899/1900 the neighbouring countries were running a total of 2116 schools in Macedonia with 71,000 male and female pupils.[44] On the one hand, these schools poisoned the atmosphere with their aggressive attempts to implant varying national identities in a homogenous ethnic group. On the other hand, they created the first indigenous educated elite in Macedonia. When organised resistance to Ottoman rule began to form in the 1890s, it was the graduates of these schools who led the way. In Thessaloniki in 1893, a group of six young men, five of them teachers and the sixth a doctor who had studied in Zurich and Berlin, founded the secret revolutionary organisation named above. Its aim was to work for the fulfilling of Article 23 of the Berlin Treaty of 1878, which provided for Macedonian autonomy within the Ottoman Empire. Gotse Delchev, certainly the most charismatic of this group of leaders, saw Macedonia as an enslaved country which would have to liberate itself from within. For this purpose it was necessary to prepare people in every village for the great uprising. Until the time for the uprising arrived, Ottoman authority was to be undermined by means of guerrilla tactics and the establishing of parallel structures.[45] This strategy is a familiar one in very recent Balkan history. In the 1990s, Albanian groups in Kosovo acted similarly. They succeeded where the Macedonian organisation had failed a century earlier, by internationalising the conflict and thus winning with external help. At the end of the 20th century, the status quo was not in accordance with the interests of the Western powers. Rather, as the disintegration of the Communist system in Eastern Europe took its course, they affirmed the secessionist movements in Yugoslavia.

---

[44]Istorija na makedonskiot narod. Vol. 2: Od po etokot na XIX vek do krajot na prvata svetska vojna. Eds. *Mihailo Apostolski* et al., Skopje 1969, 153.

[45]*Duncan M. Perry*, The Macedonian Cause. A critical history of the Macedonian Revolutionary Organisation 1893-1903, Ann Arbor 1981, 77-106.

The IMRO saw itself as a liberation movement, but it needed an armed branch. From 1897 it gradually built up small, mobile fighting units known as Cheti, each consisting of a few dozen fighters. The central committee of the organisation, based in Thessaloniki, divided Macedonia into areas of military operations, each under the command of a Cheta. These had not only military functions: other responsibilities meant that the leaders required a certain level of education. Political agitation was one of their tasks, as well as police and court functions and tax-collecting.[46] Last but not least, the Cheti were expected to exterminate from the population any hated representatives of the regime or other persons regarded as oppressors.[47]

As is often the case with resistance movements, several rival groups developed. Besides the Internal Organisation, named because it was founded and operated within Macedonia itself, a group among the numerous Macedonian refugees and emigres living in Bulgaria formed the 'Macedonian Committee' in March 1895. From December of that year it was called 'Supreme Macedonian Committee', claiming primacy over all Macedonian organisations, wherever they might be. This included the Internal Organisation in Macedonia. The Supreme Committee, with its seat in Sofia, aimed to see Macedonia and Thrace annexed to Bulgaria.[48] Despite their contrasting aims, the IMRO and the Supreme Committee worked together at first. The IMRO, short of funds from the start, was financially supported by the Supreme Committee. At the end of 1900 however relations between the two deteriorated. They disagreed in particular on the question of when the uprising that was to liberate Macedonia should take place. The IMRO wanted to wait, whereas the Supreme Committee wanted to strike sooner. Its financial support for the Internal Organisation ended in January 1901.

---

[46] *Perry*, The Macedonian Cause, 252-258, 261-263.

[47] For example, according to Chernopeev, the 'Turk' murdered during the kidnapping was in fact an Albanian, the administrator of a landowner, whose abuse and assaults – including rape – had long been a cause of complaint for the peasants. They had demanded that the organisation should kill him. *Sonnichsen*, Confessions, 260.

[48] *Stefan Troebst*, Mussolini, Makedonien und die Mächte 1922-1930. Die 'Innere Makedonische Revolutionäre Organisation' in der Südosteuropapolitik des faschistischen Italien, Köln 1987, 88f.

Also in January 1901, the Ottoman authorities arrested the whole
of the central committee of the IMRO and dozens of its supporters in
Thessaloniki and banished them to Asia Minor, leaving the organisation
virtually without leadership.[49] Taking advantage of this situation, the
Supreme Committee immediately sent its own Cheti to Macedonia to
take over from the weakened IMRO.[50] Their need for money became
even more pressing. One of the few IMRO leaders left was Iane Sandanski,
who operated in the Ottoman-Bulgarian border region with his group.
Born in Vlahi in Ottoman East Macedonia in 1872, he had grown up
mostly with his uncle in Bulgaria, helping out in his legal practice. He had
an interest in revolutionary literature and was inspired by the Bulgarian
national revolutionary Vasil Levski (1837-1872). He also read widely on
the Macedonian question. Sandanski became active for the first time
in 1895, when he joined a Cheta operating in the Bulgarian-Ottoman
border region. He knew the Supreme Committee in Sofia, but it was only
in 1896 that he learned of the revolutionary organisation in Macedonia
itself and gradually got to know its leading members. When the conflict
with the Supreme Committee in Sofia began in 1900, Sandanski sided
with the Internal Organisation. In spring 1901 he became the leader
(voivoda) of his own Cheta, operating for IMRO with it in the border
region and setting up self-administration in the villages. In the course of
the conflict with the Supreme Committee, Sandanski was commissioned
to raise money in the population for the purchase of guns. Realising there
would be little to collect from an impoverished people, he and Khristo
Chernopeev developed a plan for a lucrative kidnapping.[51] At that time,
kidnappings with demands for ransom money were widespread in the
Balkans. They were carried out by bands of robbers of varying ethnic

---

[49] *Laura Beth Sherman*, Fires on the Mountain. The Macedonian revolutionary
movement and the kidnapping of Ellen Stone, Boulder 1980, 18-21.
[50] *Sonnichsen*, Confessions, 256-261.
[51] Spomeni, 201-206.

backgrounds,[52] or by several Albanian tribes who secured part of their income in this way.[53]

It is not known how often the IMRO had already made use of this form of money-making. The kidnapping of Louis Chevalier mentioned above seems to have been such a case. Gotse Delchev, the icon of the Macedonian liberation movement, was said to have kidnapped a Turk and a Greek on different occasions, both of whom escaped because they were not closely guarded.[54] According to Sandanski and his group, this was their first kidnapping.[55] They examined various alternatives and then chose Ellen Stone, hearing that she was an important missionary and expected in the area soon. Sandanski made careful preparation, securing the agreement of the local committee of IMRO, including its Protestant members, whose help would be needed.[56] Some leading members of the movement who were in prison at the time, such as Dame Gruev, roundly condemned the kidnapping when they heard of it.[57] It may be assumed that they recognised the risks involved for the image of the organisation.

The two women and around twenty men – their number decreased considerably over time – spent almost six months together. It was a time of great hardship which they all in the end survived remarkably well. Possibly the observable similarities between hostages and hostage-takers played a part in this. Each will have owed their physical stamina and psychological strength to their conviction of fulfilling an important mission in their lives and their deeds.

Ellen Stone wanted to bring to Orthodox Christians in the Ottoman Empire a proper understanding of the gospel, enabling them to live better lives and become Protestants. She worked on this even during the kidnapping, engaging in conversations about the Bible with her

---

[52]Examples include: the demand for 5000 pounds for the release of a Jew by a band of robbers (New York Times, June 29, 1891); a kidnapped group of Germans ransomed for 500 Turkish pounds (New York Times, June 28, 1891); the sum of 10,000 pounds paid for the release of two Frenchwomen (New York Times, July 12, 1896).

[53]Brailsford, Macedonia, 48f.

[54]Mercia MacDermott, For freedom and perfection. The life of Yané Sandansky, London 1988, 67.

[55]Sonnichsen, Confessions, 259.

[56]Spomeni, 206-208.

[57]Sonnichsen, Confessions, 264.

kidnappers.[58] She was familiar with physical hardship and used to dealing with the indigenous population. In her self-presentation for the American public she comes across as a highly self-controlled woman, remaining externally calm and trusting God even in times of great fear.[59] The situation was difficult for Katerina Tsilka, who was physically under increasing strain because of her pregnancy, and who feared for the child in her womb. Only three weeks before her departure, her only child had died.[60] In her report she describes herself as terrified and exhausted on the one hand, yet steadfast and self-confident on the other.

No less than Ellen Stone, Yane Sandanski was fulfilling a mission: that of liberating Macedonia from Turkish rule. This meant that when necessary he had to ensure the survival of his organisation and provide for its funding. His execution of this money-making plan – which took on quite unexpected dimensions – was circumspect, consistent and resolute. His strong will was evident in details such as the fact that although he had injured his ankle on the second day of the kidnapping and could hardly put his foot on the ground for three months, he led the action from beginning to end, not taking time off like most of the other members.[61]

Ellen Stone too displayed endurance, a determined will and great self-assurance. These qualities made life difficult for her captors. According to Albert Sonnichsen, Khristo Chernopeev complained bitterly about this pugnacious missionary: 'If you were older, and long married – have you ever found yourself in a position of strong opposition to a middle-aged woman with a determined will of her own? She assuming the attitude that you are a brute, and you feeling it? Firm opposition, not with physical violence; that would be a relief, hour by hour, day by day.' On one occasion he actually did have the impression that she wanted to hit him: 'Once she made a sudden move with her umbrella – she always carried that umbrella and her Bible and the old bonnet – well, it may have been imagination on my part, that move with the umbrella, but I stumbled backward through the doorway of the hut, to save my dignity. But I didn't save much of it.' A constant issue was smoking, which Ellen Stone disapproved of: 'She wouldn't allow smoking. She didn't forbid

[58] *Stone*, Six months, 102.

[59] Cf. e.g. *Stone*, Six months, 7f.

[60] *Stone*, Six months, 4.

[61] *Spomeni*, 208.

it by actual injunction, you know, but so: 'Have you human hearts, or have you absolutely no regard for helpless women?' In a shrill voice, you know. You couldn't smoke in her presence after such a scene.'[62] Clearly Sonnichsen has clothed Chernopeev's statements in his own words, but the content is consistent with Stone's and Sandanski's reports.

Ellen Stone's constant attempts to interest her kidnappers in the Bible and in Protestantism were not well received. Evidently this was made public even at the time, the *New York Times* reporting on December 13, 1901: 'It appears that the brigands are now complaining that Miss Stone is attempting to convert them.'[63] This demonstrates how good the lines of communication with the outside world were, when the kidnappers so desired. In fact the whole 'affair' shows how extensive and well-functioning the IMRO's organisational network was. The kidnappers, presented in parts of the press as simple peasants, proved themselves capable, during the whole of the kidnapping and under conspiratorial circumstances, of acquiring everything needed for survival. They arranged accommodation – which sometimes even meant building huts in the forest in advance –,[64] organised a midwife, made contact with the relevant authorities in the Ottoman Empire and in Bulgaria, sent letters and, at the end, outwitted the Ottoman security forces when the ransom was handed over. All this points to their having plenty of helpers and sympathisers among the local population. Sonnichsen, who spent six months with guerrilla, notes that the peasants were by no means afraid even to send young girls to the guerrilla in the forest, since women were always well treated. The diary of a *voivoda* reveals that women were very often used as couriers,[65] presumably because they were less frequently checked by the Ottoman security forces.

Chernopeev complained bitterly to Sonnichsen that the world regarded them as brigands. He sharply accused the western world of hypocrisy: 'They allow our women and small babies to be outraged and slaughtered, and when we ask them for help, only to stop it, in the name of Christ, they give us soft, lying words. And then, when we give one of

---

[62] *Sonnichsen*, Confessions, 256, 261f.
[63] The New York Times, 13.12.1901.
[64] *Stone*, Six months, 108.
[65] *Sonnichsen*, Confessions, 151-152; *Dnevnikot na vojvodata Vasil Čakalarov*. Ed. by Dejan Pavlevski, Skopje 2007.

their women a few months' worry and discomfort, which we more than
share with her, only to give us the means to save a million women from
death, or worse, we are brigands. Because it was one of their women, they
didn't worry about poor Mrs Tsilka, no, it was only Miss Stone. For that
we are brigands, outlaws, criminals. No, damn such a civilisation. It isn't
real.'[66] Most of the foreign newspapers did indeed only mention Ellen
Stone in their reports.

We know from Stone herself that the legitimacy of the kidnapping was
an issue in the group. She reports on a furious row breaking out when
the ransom had once again not been paid and she had remarked that
they could not simply kill two women who had done them no harm.
The leader Iane Sandanski, normally described as friendly and called 'the
good man' by Stone and Tsilka, was enraged and replied in words similar
to those of Chernopeev: 'Why shame and reproach to take the life of
two women, when unnumbered women and children in Turkey suffer
nameless outrages, and are put to death daily!'[67]

The women's fears that they and later the baby might be killed were
not unfounded. Sandanski and Chernopeev argued heatedly in this
matter. The latter was afraid that a crying baby would draw the pursuers'
attention to the group, or that the women might betray too much after
their release. He was not averse to taking the extreme step of killing
the women. Sandanski on the other hand, as the leader of the group,
contended that such a murder would be incompatible with their self-
image as revolutionaries and highly damaging to the reputation of the
organisation.[68]

In both Europe and the United States the kidnapping became a major
media event.[69] The Vienna paper *Illustrierte Wiener Extrablatt* noted on

---

[66] Sonnichsen, Confessions, 266.

[67] *Stone*, Six months, 104.

[68] *MacDermott*, For freedom, 87f.

[69] According to Dayan/Katz, only planned and announced events and their
respectful direct transmission are 'media events' (such as the funeral of John F.
Kennedy). Unexpected events on the other hand are termed 'news events' (such
as the assassination of John F. Kennedy). *Daniel Dayan/Elihu Katz*, Media events.
The live broadcasting of history, Cambridge, Ma./London 1992, 9. Since this
publication the term has been broadened considerably, however. The Giessen
Graduate Lectures 'Transnationale Medienereignisse von der Frühen Neuzeit
bis zur Gegenwart' for example defines its object of research in general as events
characterised by 'a high degree of medial attention and a noticeable intensification

the title page of its evening edition on February 7, 1902 that the Miss Stone affair was rolling through the columns of the world press like an endless snake. For the United States this was the first experience of a kidnapping in a foreign country. This, together with the fact that it involved women and was taking place in a little known area on the margins of Europe, made it especially newsworthy. The papers published dramatic appeals for money from Ellen Stone's family and friends, addressed to 'Christian America' and emphasising the threatened killing of this 'American Christian patriot.'[70] This fanned the flames of public interest. If the ransom had been immediately available, this kidnapping would probably – like many others – have made waves only among those directly affected and in diplomatic circles. As it was, however, large numbers of newspaper correspondents appeared on the scene, taking up the trail of the hostages, making contact with mediators and, towards the end, following the ransom money. When there was nothing new to report in the case, neither facts nor rumours, attention turned to the country and its people. Some newspapers had illustrators on the spot, others made use of photographs. Postcards showing the women with their captors were printed as souvenirs.[71] For the first time the general public in Europe and the United States experienced quite comprehensive, continuous and sustained reporting on the Balkans, an area they could only vaguely imagine. The picture offered by the press was what now formed their ideas, and for the most part it presented a strange, backward and wild region. In the illustrations, deep gorges and torrential streams dominated the landscape.[72] Paths appeared to be non-existent or were shown as marshy, with buffalo-drawn carts sinking into them. The kidnappers were presented in exotic costume or as grim figures.[73] On January 25, 1902, the *New York Times* described – with reference to the *London Daily Graphic*, whose correspondent had allegedly interviewed Katerina Tsilka (the women were not released until February 23, however) – the murder of the 'Turk' as an act of brutality: '[they] beat him with the butt ends of their

---

of the communication processes.' http://www.uni-giessen.de/gkmedienereignisse/home/gk-forschungsprogramm.php (15.6.2008).

[70]For example in the New York Times of 5.10.1901.

[71]*Stone*, Six months, 103f.

[72]Cf. e.g. The Graphic, 15.12.1901; The Daily Graphic, 31.1.1902.

[73]As in the Illustriertes Wiener Extrablatt, 13.10.1901 and 3.11.1901.

rifles, shot him dead, and then plunged their knives into his body.'[74] The roughness of the inhabitants and the confusing mixture of ethnicities and religions in the area where the kidnapping took place correlated with the picturesque wildness of the Pirin Mountains. As a correspondent wrote, '[it] has for ages been a happy hunting ground of brigands of the most extraordinary mixture of races.'[75]

The rumours which reached the media concerning the fate of the two women only served to reinforce the exotic flair of the story and illustrate the uncivilised nature of the region. Once it was reported that Tsilka had died as a result of a miscarriage;[76] another time, the women were said to be in the harem of a Turkish beg near Nevrokop.[77] The *Illustriertes Wiener Extrablatt* noted that Stone's companion was a 'fine-looking Bulgarian girl', suggesting the danger of sexual assault by the men.[78] An American magazine informed its readers that among bandits it was customary to send the family one of the kidnapped victim's ears, with a warning that the head would follow if the ransom were not paid. The magazine emphasised that 'the Balkan outlaws observe these conventionalities religiously.'[79] Several times the death of the two women was announced and denied; similarly their alleged release.[80]

The commission charged with delivery of the ransom was closely pursued by the illustrated London paper *Daily Graphic*. One of its high-profile journalists, William T. Maud, also designated 'artist correspondent', was on the scene. It was he who succeeded time and again in fanning the declining public interest in a long-drawn-out affair. When the women were released however, he came off worst. Sam S. McClure, the proprietor of the American *McClure's Magazine*, made his way to the Balkans to secure an exclusive contract for the printing of the sensational story at a price of 5,000 dollars. On her way home, Ellen Stone was accompanied by a representative of the magazine and, with his assistance, began to

---

[74]The New York Times, 25.1.1902.

[75]The St James's Gazette, 21.11. 1901.

[76]Daily News, 29.11.1901; Standard, 29.11.1901; Allgemeine Zeitung (Munich), 29.11.1901.

[77]*Lyle*, An American woman, 44-54.

[78]Illustriertes Wiener Extrablatt, No. 281, 13.10.1901.

[79]Lyle, An American woman, 44-54.

[80]Cf. NZZ, 20.10.1901, 1. Abendblatt; 29.11. 1901, Morgenblatt, Denial in 1. Abendblatt. Cf. also Daily News, 29.11.1901, NZZ, 8.1.1902, 1. Abendblatt.

write her report.[81] In England she received numerous invitations to give talks and lectures on her experiences, all of which she declined. Health reasons were given,[82] but it seems likely she was meeting the terms of her exclusive contract with McClure.

Crowds awaited the famous traveller at the railway stations between Thessaloniki and Vienna, and when her ship docked in Jersey City on April 10, 1902, Stone was awaited by a huge crowd and a large number of reporters. Public interest was so great that as well as McClure the well-known agent Major J.B. Pond hoped to gain commercial success by inviting Ellen Stone to give 54 talks for a fee of 29,000 dollars.[83] Her first talk was in her home town on April 15, 1902. Surprisingly, the series was a failure. Ellen Stone did not fulfil the expectations of the press or the public. She did not recount barbaric, gruesome details of her imprisonment, nor did she accuse her kidnappers. On the contrary, she reported Turkish atrocities in Macedonia and called for the liberation of the province. Finally the American Board of Commissioners threatened to break with her if she should continue her anti-Turkish and pro-Macedonian talks. She completed the series as arranged, but not without moderating her tone considerably.[84]

The hostages' sympathy with the political aims of their kidnappers explains the carefully constructed nature of Stone's and Tsilka's reports. Their narratives walk the narrow space between the need to give the public a gripping, sensational story reaching a wide readership, and the attempt to show the kidnappers – seen as bandits by the public – in a favourable light. At the same time, as little information as possible was to be disclosed. When questioned by the Ottoman authorities, Stone and Tsilka had given evasive replies. They claimed not to know any names, not to remember any conversations, and not to know which area they had been in. For this reason the Turkish authorities even accused them of being complicit in the whole affair, but could not provide any

---

[81] *Carpenter*, The Miss Stone affair, 151f., 185–189. The reports were published from May to October 1903 in monthly instalments.

[82] New York Times, 4.5.1902.

[83] It is not known what became of Stone's earnings from the talks, but it seems very likely that she used the money to compensate friends and relatives who had contributed to the ransom.

[84] *Sherman*, Fires on the mountain, 89f., 98; *Carpenter*, The Miss Stone affair, 191–197.

evidence of this.[85] The report by Stone and Tsilka gives the impression that they were held in the countryside for the whole period. This enabled them to deflect suspicion from the villages which cooperated with the kidnappers. It is clear from Iane Sandanski's memoirs however that the group quite frequently stayed in settlements, for instance when Tsilka gave birth. The kidnappers' statements also reveal that they crossed the border into Bulgaria.[86]

The women's reports are moreover remarkable for their relatively few uses of clichés concerning the Balkans. It is not clear however to what extent these passages were influenced by the editor of the journal on the basis of public expectations, as evidenced by the publisher of *Everybody's Magazine*: 'It is an extraordinary and intensely interesting story – infinitely removed from Western civilisation in the twentieth century.'[87] During the kidnapping there had been bizarre speculations in the media about the fate of the two women, and now the public wanted to know more. But instead of unscrupulous robbers they were presented with freedom fighters, good Christians driven desperately to their deeds by the cruelty of the Turkish regime.

As a sharp critic of the Ottoman authorities, Ellen Stone could not contemplate returning to Macedonia. She remained in the United States, where she was later known only for her campaign against alcohol and for her writing of her memoirs, which however were destroyed when her house burned down in 1908. She died on December 13, 1927. Katerina Tsilka returned with her family to Albania, where she died in Tirana in 1952.[88] Both Stone and Tsilka outlived their young captors, born in the 1870s, by many years. These died in the struggle against the Ottoman forces or in the First World War.[89]

[85]*Carpenter*, The Miss Stone affair, 183, 188.

[86]*Spomeni*, 209f.; Sonnichsen, Confessions, 264.

[87]The editor of Everybody's Magazine, 6/1 (1902), 44-54, from http://library.ferris.edu/~cochranr/stone/stone2b1.htm (25.1.2008).

[88]Carpenter, The Miss Stone affair, 207.

[89]Krsto Asenov was killed in the early days of the Ilinden uprising (August 1903), Chernopeev 1915 in the First World War; Sava Mihajlov died in 1905 fighting Ottoman troops; Sandanski was murdered in April 1915, probably on the orders of the King of Bulgaria. *Manol Pandevski*, Jane Sandanski i Mis Ston, Skopje 1992, 32-36. There is no reliable information on the use of the gold coins paid in ransom and known in the organisation as 'Miss Stonki'. A large part seems to have been used in Bulgaria in the propaganda battle against the Supreme Committee, and a

The kidnapping of Ellen Stone marks the beginning of a development in which the revolutionary movements emerging in the 19th century, be they nationalist, communist or anarchist, join forces with the mass media potential of the 20th century. It is the rapid international transmission of news which lends meaning to spectacular kidnappings or attacks. For its part, the system of the mass media has need of moving or shocking stories enabling it to simplify complex matters and distinguish between good and evil. The scenes of action tend to be – from the perspective of western industrialised countries – peripheral areas where fragile, comparatively rigid political systems such as that of the Ottoman Empire suppress reform movements and legal opposition, leaving only violence as the way forward.

Often the violent resistance movements are led by young elites oriented towards western political ideas or educated in the west. Time spent in exile contributes to radicalisation and provides knowledge of medial and political mechanisms. Western perception then combines the images of a weak, corrupt and violent state with the oppositional activities of underground movements, forming the overall impression of a primitive, brutal society or culture. This is what happened in the case of the Balkans.

Thanks to the media and communications opportunities of the time, a number of landmark events taking place at the beginning of the 20th century gained great publicity and embedded in western perception the image of a backward, uncivilised region given to violence. Unquestionably, the kidnapping of Ellen Stone was one of these landmarks. The fact that it ended without bloodshed, and that the victims showed understanding for the motives of their kidnappers, was irrelevant. What took effect in the public mind was intensive reporting in a negative context. In an uncivilised country with untamed nature and an exotic population, a Christian American woman who had committed herself for decades to the well-being of the indigenous population had been kidnapped and threatened with death. The Turkish state came off poorly too, since it failed either to guarantee safety or to find the kidnap victims. Bulgaria also received

smaller part paid for weapons and preparations for the rebellion of August 1903. *Pandevski*, Jane Sandanski, 165-169, 172f.; *Randall B. Woods*, Terrorism in the Age of Roosevelt. The Miss Stone Affair, 1901-1902, in: American Quarterly 31 (1979), 478-495, here 493; *Moore*, The Balkan trail, 47.

a bad press for allegedly not behaving cooperatively.[90] It was only the activity of the Protestants that was presented favourably. This produced a dichotomy between positive values associated with the West, and negative attributions to the Balkans. Since the area was little known and rarely travelled, these negative images were not complemented or corrected by other impressions. As a result, the reporting of the kidnapping formed an important part of the discourse consolidating a negative image of the Balkans and assigning the region a certain place on the mental map of the West. Maria Todorova designates this discourse 'Balkanism' within the tradition of Orientalism. Unlike Orientalism however, which constructs 'the fully other', Balkanism – given that geographically the Balkans are clearly part of Europe – designates 'inner difference', an alter ego on to which negative features are projected. Against this background the West appears as the civilised, modern and rational 'Europe proper'.[91] In this process it is not the facts which are decisive but the right of definition and interpretation. The West, superior in terms of power politics, economy and media, judges what is rational and sensible, what is morally right or wrong, which wars are meaningful and which are simply 'Balkan' massacres. It is telling to find that media and public interest in the Miss Stone affair waned in the US as soon as it became apparent that the views of the protagonists, who knew Macedonia better than most, did not agree with the picture of events, the country and its people painted by the press. The suggestive force of the medially constructed image proved more effective than the evidence of those directly affected by events.[92]

---

[90]*Pandevski*, Jane Sandanski, 82, 87, 99.

[91]*Maria Todorova*, Imagining the Balkans, New Yorki 1997. Further proponents of the Balkanism thesis: *Vesna Goldsworthy*, Inventing Ruritania. The imperialism of the imagination, New Haven 1998; *Andrew Hammond*, The debated lands. British and American representations of the Balkans, Cardiff 2007. Critical response to the thesis has come e.g. from *Holm Sundhaussen*, Europa balcanica. Der Balkan als historischer Raum, in: Geschichte und Gesellschaft 25 (1999), 626–653. According to Sundhaussen, the Balkan is not merely constructed as 'Other' – it actually is.

[92]In my opinion, Stefan Troebst overestimates the pro-Macedonian influence of Ellen Stone's series of talks on the English-language public. Cf. *Stefan Troebst*, Von den Fanarioten zur UÇK: Nationalrevolutionäre Bewegungen auf dem Balkan und die 'Ressource Weltöffentlichkeit', in: *Jörg Requate, Martin Schulze Wessel* (eds.), Europäische Öffentlichkeit. Transnationale Kommunikation seit dem 18. Jahrhundert, Frankfurt a.M. 2002, 231–249, here 236.

The kidnapping of Ellen Stone stands at the beginning of mass media transmission of images of the Balkans – earlier information carriers had a far narrower range – and also at the beginning of the symbiosis of revolutionary movements and media. This had not been planned, as the kidnappers aimed simply to gain a large sum of money. They neither foresaw nor were able to make political use of the extensive media interest. The media for their part transmitted mainly the image of an alien and uncivilised Balkans region, though without taking a noticeably hostile attitude at this time.

The next significant episode demonstrates a far greater awareness of public interest among the insurgents, who had evidently learned from the kidnapping of Ellen Stone. On April 27, 1903 Macedonian anarchists set fire to the French steamship *Guadalquivir* in Thessaloniki and blew up the Ottoman Bank (which drew chiefly on French and Italian capital) the following day. Bombs exploded in several cafes in the city. The perpetrators, all of them very young, were influenced by the ideas of Russian revolutionaries some of them had encountered in Geneva. The Macedonians worked on a plan to attack 'European capital' with the aim of drawing world attention to conditions in their homeland. These young men even countenanced the idea that their own deaths would lend greater effect to the action – an early variant of the suicide attack.[93] It turned out to be ill-advised however to attack the very powers on whose sympathy and support the revolutionaries depended. The attacks had disastrous consequences for the image of the Balkans in Europe and badly damaged the Macedonian efforts to gain autonomy.[94] There were further stages in the consolidation of a negative image of the Balkans: the assassination by officers of the Serbian royal couple in the year 1903, which aroused abhorrence throughout Europe; the Balkans Wars of 1912/13, presented as a meaningless, barbaric massacre;[95] and the shots in Sarajevo in 1914 which enabled propaganda in the Central Powers to blame Serbia for the war.

---

[93] *Pavel Šatev*, Solunskiot atentat i zatočenicite vo Fezan, Skopje 1994, 32, 39, 48-50, 61-64.

[94] *Fikret Adanir*, Die makedonische Frage. Ihre Entstehung und Entwicklung bis 1908, Frankfurt a.M. 1979, 173.

[95] Cf. on this e.g. Simplicissimus, 24.2.1913. The powers claim that their own wars however are governed by rational, comprehensible interests.

All this laid the foundations for an image of the Balkans such as we find it in one of Agatha Christie's detective novels, published in 1925. Two Englishmen are talking about a country named 'Herzoslovakia': 'Herzoslovakia?' … 'Yes. Know anything about it?' … 'Only what everyone knows. It's one of the Balkan States, isn't it? Principal rivers, unknown. Principal mountains, also unknown, but fairly numerous. Capital, Ekarest. Population, chiefly brigands. Hobby, assassinating Kings and having Revolutions. Last King, Nicholas IV. Assassinated about seven years ago. Since then it's been a Republic. Altogether a very likely spot.'[96]

Translation from German into English: Rosemary Selle, Heidelberg.
Essay first appeared as 'Die Entführung der Miss Stone: Der Balkan im Blickfeld der westlichen Welt', in: *Historische Anthropologie 16*, 2008, S. 420–442.

---

[96] *Agatha Christie*, The Secret of Chimneys, New York 2001 [1925], 6. Vesna Goldsworthy points to this passage in her book Inventing Ruritania.

A British attempt to organise revolt in Northern Albania during the Greek-Italian conflict in 1940[1]

Basil Kondis

After the outbreak of World War II in September 1939 the British government's first experiment in encouraging guerilla warfare in South-East Europe was made in Albania. In the beginning of the conflict, London, anxious to keep Italy neutral did not seriously consider stimulating Albanian resistance against the Italians. But by April 1940 British Intelligence (D Section) decided to organise a revolt in Albania through organizations run by Albanian exiles in Yugoslavia.[2] With Italy entering the war in June 1940, the British agents in Yugoslavia became more active and started making preparations, including in Greece. The first instructions given to the British Intelligence operatives in Athens were:

A To make contact with and obtain all possible information about the leading exiles in Greece and Turkey.

B To establish dumps of explosive demolition materials in Greece as near the Albanian frontier as possible

C To explore the possibility of recruiting agents on the Albanian side of the frontier who could in turn establish dumps at selected points, from which demolitions might be carried out in a manner designed to hinder any Italian advance into Greece.[3]

At this time a munitions dump was established at Ioannina from which it was hoped that supplies might be sent across to Albania for the formation of munitions depots there. Also, Section D recruited agents who made two exploratory journeys into Albania. The Commander in Chief of the Middle East however warned the Intelligence department that they should not do anything which would stir up trouble on the

---

[1] An earlier draft of this paper was first published in 'Conference Proceedings: The Axis Attack on the Balkans, 1940-1941, Institute of Balkan Studies, Thessaloniki, 1992

[2] Public Record Office papers, London: Foreign Office (FO) 371/29719,S.O.2 memorandum, London, 25 February 1941

[3] FO 371/24866, Section D memorandum, London, 25 August 1940

Albanian border, and thus give Rome the excuse for an Italian invasion of Greece.[4] On August 24th the Middle East High Command approved the Section D programme for work in Albania. The Foreign Office, also, agreed with the plans for subversive activity in Albania.[5]

In discussion between Foreign Office representatives and Section D staff it was decided to set up as rapidly as possible a central coordinating committee for Albanian resistance in London to coordinate the various Albanian political factions living in the Diaspora. Subsidiary committees could be formed at places where Albanian communities were most numerous, such as Constantinople, Cairo and in the USA. The representatives of Section D in those places would be responsible for the necessary organisation. The London committee, which was to be secret and unofficial, was headed by General Sir Jocelyn Percy.[6] The issue was raised of whether or not the exiled King Zog should be asked to provide any assistance, particularly with the coordination of the Albanians in Turkey. In this summer of 1940, the Foreign Office opposed any role for Zog in the resistance plans. The views of P.Dixon, a Foreign Office official, are very revealing about Zog, thus: 'I said that in our view it would be a mistake to put forward King Zog's name in any way as a figurehead for the recovery of Albanian independence. Not only was he largely discredited personally but we did not want to commit ourselves as to the future status of Albania, which we should be bound to do to some extent if the ex-king was so used. At the same time, we should naturally not be averse to letting Albanians abroad know that King Zog among others was behind an independence movement if this would really help'.

It was clear that the Foreign Office opposed any involvement by Zog mainly because they did not want to commit themselves to restoring an independent Albania. In June 1940, when Italy had entered the war, it was stated in the House of Commons that the British government 'hold themselves entitled to reserve full liberty of action in respect of any undertakings given by them in the past to the Italian government concerning the Mediterranean, North or East Africa and the Middle East areas.' With this statement, the British government withdrew their earlier (October 1939) de facto recognition of the Italian Occupation

[4] FO 371/24866/7677, Minutes, Foreign Office, 13 September, 1940
[5] Ibid. Minutes 18 September 1940
[6] Ibid

of Albania.[7] However, it did not imply recognition of an independent Albania as a Foreign Office minute clearly stated.[8]

At this juncture, in Summer 1940, no further action was taken by the British government about an uprising in Albania as neither Yugoslavia or Greece were involved in the war and London was being very careful to avoid giving the Italians any grounds for alleging that the Greeks were concerned in activities in, or against, Albania and thus providing Rome with a pretext to attack Greece. The situation, however, changed fundamentally with the Italian invasion of Greece on 28th October 1940. At the War Office they were convinced that a general uprising against the rear columns of the Italian army would be of great assistance to the Greeks.[9] The Foreign Office – wishing to help Greece at all costs – softened their attitude to Zog, who, on November 8th suggested to the Foreign Office that he considered a revolt could be stirred up among the northern Albanian tribes against the Italians, and that the les warlike tribes of the South could also be induced to at least harry and cause difficulties for the Italians. Moreover, he made the practical suggestion that he should go himself to Constantinople, where there were 14,000 Albanians and organise a force to be landed at Thessaloniki with the consent of the Greek government, and to form a small fighting front.[10]

After Foreign Office- Special Operations Executive discussions in London, it was suggested that Zog should be sent to the vicinity of the front so that his presence there would serve as a signal to the northern tribes.[11] The SOE staff suffered from excessive zeal, in FO eyes, when they suggested Zog should be involved and flown to Greece. Sir Michael Palairet, the British Minister in Athens, thought that 'if Zog goes to enemy occupied Albania in any capacity it is hard to see how he could avoid capture, or raise a force of sufficient military value to influence the course of operations or even prevent it being overwhelmed by Italian

[7]See Barker. Elizabeth,' British Policy in South-East Europe in the Second World War', London, 1976, P.49 ff.

[8]Ibid: FO 371/24868 minute,ForeignOffice,19th June 1940

[9]FO 37124867, note of P.Dixon, Foreign Office, 30th October 1940

[10]FO 371/ Report of Sir A Ryan,London,8th November 1940

[11]The Special Operations Executive (SOE) was a clandestine organization set up by the British government in 1940 to promote sabotage and ant-Axis resistance activity in Occupied Europe. There is an extensive literature on its activity in many countries, particularly France, but as yet much less on SOE Greece

punitive action.'[12] Undoubtedly Zog's presence in Albania would raise political complications with the Greek government about the future of the country, and also concerning his own position. Nevertheless the Foreign Office had the idea that Zog should broadcast a 'rallying speech' from Radio Athens on Albanian National Day (28th November). Athens was asked if the Greek government agreed, provided that the speech did not imply the restoration of Zog or the reconstitution of an independent Albania. Metaxas, however, had the most serious doubts about using Zog; he would not welcome his presence in Greece nor would he support the restoration of an independent Albania.[13]

The attitude of Metaxas was not unexpected in the Foreign Office. It had been anticipated that the Greek government might be averse to allowing Zog to lead a movement against the Italians, with the background reason that the Greeks themselves hoped to occupy and retain Albania and realized that if they supported Zog they would run the risk of committing themselves to the restoration of an independent Albania under his rule.[14]

Metaxas desired to have a free hand in Albanian affairs and in a broadcast on November 22nd 1940, on the occasion of the fall of Koritsa (Korca in south east Albania) into the hands of the Greek army, said that the Greeks were not only fighting for their own existence but for other Balkan peoples as well as the liberation of Albania.[15] It is evident that Metaxas wanted to make clear that by 'liberation' he meant that Greece was fighting to liberate Albania from Italian rule and in no way intended to commit herself to the restoration of an independent Albanian state. The Greek troops did not liberate Koritsa (Korca) from Axis occupation in order to give it back to the Albanians.[16]

Despite the negative attitude of the Greek government, the S.O.E staff at a meeting at the Foreign Office continued to press for a declaration stating that the British government would guarantee Albania's future independence. Against this, F.O official Dixon argued that 'Albania was never likely to be able to stand alone and would always be dependent on

[12]FO 371/24868/8639, Palairet to Foreign Office, Athens, 29th November 1940
[13]FO 371/24867/8483, Palairet to Foreign Office, 23rdh November 1940
[14]FO 371/24867/8483, Dixon minute, 24th November 1940
[15]For a contrary view, see Puto. A,'From the Annals of British Diplomacy, Tirana, 1981, P 57ff.
[16]FO371/24866/8620, Foreign Office to S.O.E, London, 29th November 1940

some other power for support and finance, and that such a declaration would upset the Greeks, and that it might be convenient to allow the Greeks to retain the occupied areas after the War.'[17] At this meeting it was generally agreed that no mention of an independent Albania should be made in the proposed declaration. It was felt, however, that a public official declaration should be made to the effect that the frontiers and future status of Albania were a matter for discussion at the future peace conference, whenever it was held.[18] However this declaration was not actually made, as on further consideration Nichols, the head of the Southern Department of the Foreign Office, and Dixon, the head of the Albanian section had considerable doubts as to the effectiveness of it. The object of making a pronouncement about Albania was purely to rally the Albanians against the Italians. Dixon had doubts whether the suggested pronouncement ' may not have the effect of discouraging rather than encouraging the Albanians since it will be clear to them from the pronouncement that we are not prepared at this moment to commit ourselves to the restoration of an independent Albania. A more encouraging line might be to merely state that we stand for the liberation of Albania from Italian domination.'[19] As the Greek government had already made a statement to that effect, Dixon felt that Athens could not object if the British followed suit. Such a formula would have the advantage of (a) being more encouraging to the Albanians than the one previously proposed, and (b) meeting with Greek approval.[20]

The Foreign Office and the S.O.E agreed with Dixon's views[21] and a text was prepared stating that: 'His Majesty's government wish to see Albania freed from the Italian yoke and will give the Albanians all the support in their power to that end. At the issue of the victorious struggle it will be for the Albanians themselves to decide on their future. At the same time safeguards will have to be devised to prevent the recurrence of such events as those which have of recent years reduced Albania to foreign vassalage and exposed her neighbours to the greatest dangers…'[22]

[17]FO 371/24867/8783,Record of meeting between Foreign Office and S.O.E., 2nd December 1940
[18]Ibid.
[19]FO 371/24867/8783, Dixon minute of 4th December 1940
[20]Ibid
[21]Ibid, Nichols minutes, 5th and 7th December 1940
[22]FO 371/24867 Foreign Office to Palairet, London, 8th December 1940

In spite of the fact that this suggested declaration coincided generally with the views of the Greek government, Metaxas considered it unwise and undesirable.[23] So long as the Greek advance against the Italians continued to be the only action which Athens considered to be practical was guerilla warfare by small bands of men behind Italian lines. Moreover, Metaxas underlined to the British that he neither wished nor intended to occupy Albania permanently but a future settlement must secure certain strategic points for Greece to protect her against the recurrence of the recent attack, and that he had been very careful in his public utterances not to go beyond general statements about the liberation of Albania.[24]

Nevertheless, at this point S.O.E was not discouraged and continued to make plans for a revolt in northern Albania through their representatives in Belgrade. This time, Gani Kryeziu, one of the northern Albanian chieftains, was to be the leader.[25] He was to move into northern Albania from Kosova and occupy Kukes and proclaim an Albanian National Government, with himself at the head. It would make a statement of hostility to Italy and friendship towards Greece. This scheme was dependent on supplies being made available to the rebels by British aircraft operating on the Albanian front, as Yugoslav territory could not be used as a base. The S.O.E estimated that funds of sixty thousand pounds would be needed to maintain the Albanian force for at least a month.[26]

It is indeed strange that the Foreign Office not only accepted this scheme with little reservation but prepared a declaration of support for the provisional government which contained a promise of British aid for the liberation of Albania.[27] It was understood that the whole scheme would have the approval of the Greek government. The scheme, was, therefore, put up to the British Embassy in Athens, which was asked to obtain the consent of Metaxas. The Greek answer was discouraging and showed that Metaxas was in favour of coordinated activities of several small bands and not of any large-scale operations.[28] The British

[23]FO 371/24868/8924, Palairet to Foreign Office, Athens, 14th December 1940
[24]Ibid.
[25]See paper by G.Perolli in this volume on the Massacre at Herec and associated events concerning the Kryeziu family and their followers.
[26]FO 371/24867/8924, S.O.E London to Foreign Office, London, 18th December 1940
[27]FO 371/24867/8992, Foreign Office to Secretary of State, 26th December 1940
[28]Ibid.

ambassador also reported that Athens 'is most averse to the establishment of any provisional government at this stage.'[29]

After the refusal of Metaxas, the proposal was abandoned. It is interesting, however, to refer to Foreign Minister Antony Eden's views about the whole operation: 'S.O.E seem to have rushed ahead without much thought. One thing must be clear. S.O.E do not and must not conduct foreign policy. They are our instrument and not we theirs.'[30] In retrospect, it is clear that the cardinal point of British policy towards Albania was that in the circumstances of the war, no important step could be taken without the consent of the Greek government since they were involved in the successful front-line fighting against the Axis.

[29]Ibid.
[30]FO 371/24867/8992, Eden's minute, 27th December 1940

Reflections upon the massacre of Hereç in 1945

Gani Perolli

At the time of World War II, in the great confrontation between the progressive forces of western democracies and those of Fascism, the great majority of Albanians fought on the side of the freedom-loving people of the western democracies.

Albania became one of the very first victims of fascist aggression in World War II on April 7, 1939, when the country was attacked and invaded by the Italian army. This day also marked the beginning of the armed resistance against the fascist invader. The Italian invaders faced demonstrations and armed resistance everywhere, in Durres, in Shengjin, Has and the northern mountains, the rifles of Albanian nationalists were heard everywhere. The brothers Kryeziu were among the chief leaders of this resistance. Contrary to the account given by the Albanian communist historiography, the resistance and the fight against the invader did *not* begin with the formation of the Communist Party of Albania but in fact *predated* it. It is well known that more than two and one half years had passed from April 7, 1939 until the forming of the Communist Party of Albania on November 8, 1941.

The Communist Party of Albania was formed primarily by two emissaries of Marshal Tito, Miladin Popovic and Dushan Mugosha. They also hand-picked Enver Hoxha as the Albanian most suitable to lead the Party. This was detrimental to the fate of Albania, particularly the fate of Kosova, both in the formation of the Communist Party of Albania by the Yugoslavs and their selection of Enver Hoxha to head it, a man totally without scruples. The Communist Party of Albania accommodated its master, the Communist Party of Yugoslavia in every respect, especially when it came to eliminating and undermining the nationalist oriented movements. Once again the Albanians were shortchanged as a people by the events of history.

The newspaper 'Bytyci' nr. 2, 2005 page 4, states the following: 'Hamit Perolli took up arms against the invader and went into resistance while creating his own *çeta in 1939*. Later on, as the commander of his *çeta* of the region of Has, he joined with the military formation headed by the nationalist leader Gani Beg Kryeziu, and continued to fight the fascist invaders until their defeat in 1944'.[1] Hamit Perolli's 'Kulla' in the village of Perollaj near Kruma and Gjakova in the Albania/Kosova borderland was Gani Kryeziu's base in the region of Has throughout the entire war.

After the conclusion of the war Hamit Perolli harbored Albanian Nationalists leaders who had escaped from Kosova and knew that they dare not surrender to the Albanian Communist Government.[2] They had dug out a large Bunker in the mountain of Oplas, a few thousand meters from the Perolli family house, where they ate, slept, and cooked. The members of this group were well armed and would have been able to put up quite a serious resistance if they were attacked. We used to bring them food articles from time to time. Among the personalities whom he fed and protected in the winter of 1945/1946 were: Ymer Berisha, Mark Perlleshi, Uke Sadiku, Ejup Binaku, Dem Ali Pozhari, Mehmet Age Rashkoci, Qazim Ostrozupi, Shaban Sadiku, Iljaz Peka, Zenel Bobi, Sylejman Haxhiu, Xhem Xhuxha, Avdi Mehmet Halili, Islam Gjini, Isa Gjini, Zaj Gjini, Muse Vuçiterna, Hajredin Vuçiterna, Myhedin Jupa, Halil Lita, Hajdar Keqani, Daman Lita, Skender Uka, Mustafe Ibishi, Mark Duhani, Miftar Dema, Tafe Previzi, Ali Meta, Njazi Alishani, Shahi Llausha, Sulejman Lupoveci, Gani Bokshi, Kadri Çela, Rexhep Alija, Sefë Sadiku, Ahment Halili, Sokol Dini, Sylejman Haska, Zyber Radosta, Asllan Radosta, Latif Radosta, Dan Lashi, Xhavit Stavica, Sylejman Strellci, Halil Sadrija, and Ahmet Krajki.

During the period of World War II in Albania, there were three main military forces: Firstly, that of the Germans, with ample arms, tanks, airplanes, secondly that of the British emissaries with whom Gani Kryeziu was to align his struggle for liberation from the very beginning, and thirdly the Partisan Movement, which was always under the directives of the Yugoslav Communist Party. Those taking part with these forces had the determinant effect on the outcome of the war.

---

[1] Newspaper Bytyçi Nr.2, 2005 Page 4

[2] The Perolli family is one of the seven main families of the Has region of Albania, with branches in Letaj, Prizren, Peje and Shkodra The Perolli family is one of the seven main families of the Has region of Albania, with branches in Letaj, Prizren, Peje and Shkodra

Italy invaded Albania on April 7, 1939. The country remained under the fascist Italy from April 7, 1939 to October, 1943. From October 1943 when Italy capitulated, Albania fell under the occupation of Germany and Italy until November 1944 when the Germans left. I purposely do not use the term 'liberated' because although the country was finally free of foreign forces it fell under a brutal regime which caused much more pain and destruction for many than the fascist occupiers. The very people who had fought the most for the liberation of the country were the most discriminated by the communists after they seized power, and in many instances physically eliminated. The entire country was reduces to a poor satellite of Yugoslavia, then later the Soviet Union, and then still later China. All one has to do is look at the results after almost fifty years of communist rule in order to see that Albania emerged totally bankrupt economically, politically, culturally, and morally from this period. What more damage can one do to a country! This was an evil regime, indeed.

During the Italian/German occupation part of Kosova was united with Albania (55%). This was not the ethnic unification that those who collaborated with the occupiers had portrayed, but nevertheless it was a positive step in the right direction for the Albanians which produced positive results. Being under the Tirana administration it allowed for the opening of Albanian language schools and Albanian administration in Kosova, which made it difficult for the Yugoslavs to reverse it after the war.

During the period of WWII, all political movements were for a democratic and united Albania. Even the people who collaborated and served in the governments created by the Italians and Germans without exception supported an Albania united with Kosova. It was the communists who because of the instructions from their patrons in Belgrade were against the unification believing blindly in the justice of the 'international'. In short they were and remained traitors to the Albanian cause.

Concerning the identity of the national movement led by Kryeziu, a very special characteristic of this movement should be noted: its aim to form a loyal and steadfast alliance with the Anglo-Americans for the sake of the future of the Albanian nation. This was a merit of their correct analysis and their sound judgment in understanding the historical past and the mistakes that had been made, and also their sound judgment of the future, and the needs of Albania. They were sure, and rightly so, that Hitler's Nazi Germany would be defeated, and that the western democracies would prevail.

Gani Kryeziu formed the United Front in 1940 in order to fight the fascist and Nazi occupiers. This was done in concert with the British emissaries Julian Amery and Daryl Oakley Hill. This was not meant to be a government of one color. It was to be a coalition government, with the participation of various political forces. In this movement the center was represented by Gani Kryeziu and the Right by Abas Kupi whom the Kryeziu's brought back from Turkey in order to widen the political participation of this movement.[3] Mustafa Gjinishi as a communist represented the Left. Arben Puto in his book 'From the Annals of British Diplomacy' says this about the movement: 'Gani Kryeziu who was operating in the Prizren-Peja region was to move into northern Albania and occupy Kukës. Here he would announce the creation of Albanian National Government headed by him. The presence of Zog was not indispensable at this stage, but his role was not ruled out. Gani was to create an Albanian Army which would have to be maintained for at least one month. As far as emerges from the Foreign Office documents, this is the only attempt by the British at the creation of an Albanian government throughout the Second World War'.[4]

Ample information about these events with the United Front and the movement headed by the brothers Kryeziu' can be found in the following books: Julian Amery's 'Sons of the Eagle', Peter Kemp's 'No Colours or Crest', Reginald Hibbert's Albania's National Liberation Struggle, The Bitter Victory', Uran Butka's 'Ringjallja', Muhamet Shatri's 'Kosova Ne Luften e Dytë Botnore' and Robert L. Wolff's 'The Balkans in our Time'.

Abas Kupi later on joined the Partisan-controlled 'National Liberation Front' and represented them at the Meeting of Mukje but voted with Balli Kombetar and other nationalists, and against Enver Hoxha. Mustafa Gjinishi was also at Mukje and together with Ymer Deshnica voted with the nationalists. Gjinishi was later assassinated by Bako Dervishi on

---

[3] Abas Kupi(1892-1976) was born in Kruja. He was a controversial figure, originally an opponent of King Zog in resposnse to Zog's murder of his brother, Osman Kupi, but he later became a strong supporter of Zog and remained so throughout the rest of his life. After a period in alliance with the Kryeziu's, he began to move towards the communists, who rejected him and forced him to flee Albania.

[4] Puto, A. 'From the Annals of British Diplomacy'.

orders from Liri Gega who received her directives directly from Enver Hoxha. At first, the communists spread the rumors that the Germans had killed him. This was not believable since a British officer was riding with Gjinishi and he was not harmed.

I had a long discussion about this matter with Sir Reginald Hibbert when we met in Prishtinë in 1999 soon after the Kosova war where I was heading a delegation to Kosova from The Albanian Third League of Prizren.[5] Hibbert was in agreement with me that it was the communists and not the Germans who killed Gjinishi. The British officer riding with Gjinishi was one of Hibbert's colleagues.

The Meeting of Mukje was held on August 1 and 2, 1943. Its aim was to create a committee who would represent all political movements which would make decisions on behalf of the country as how to conduct the war and protect the national interests of the country until the formation of a Provisional Government. This committee was called the National Salvation Committee. Representing NLF were: Y. Dishnica, J. Çaçi, M. Gjinishi, A. Kupi, O. Nishani, M. Peza, Stefan Plumbi, Haki Stermilli, Gogo Nushi, Medar Shtylla, Shefqet Beja, and Sulo Bogdo. Representig Balli Kombetar were: M. Frasheri, Th. Orollagaj, H. Lepenica, H. Dosti, V. Andoni, S. Muço, N. Peshkepia, Jusuf Luzaj, Halil Miniku, I. Petrela, Rauf Fratari dhe Kadri Cakrani. In the Meeting of Mukje agreement was reached between Balli Kombetar and the Nationa Liberation Front, but as indicated above Enver Hoxha opposed this agreement based on the instructions he got from the Yugoslavs. Both Balli Kombëtar and the National Liberation Front were political movements of southern Albania. Neither had a following in northern Albania or Kosova, with very few exceptions like the one with Dali Ndreu and his family, and both movements had a presence in the city of Shkodër. A small communist group existed in Gjakovë, headed by Fadil Hoxha (no relation to Enver Hoxha).[6]

---

[5]The first Albanian League of Prizren was formed in 1878, and campaign for Albanian freedom within the Ottoman Empire. The Second League of Prizren was formed in Prizren under German occupation in 1943, with its first President Bedri Pejani. It was fatally compromised by its collaborationist links. The Third League of Prizren was formed in New York City in 1962.

[6]Fadil Hoxha was later a prominent leader of the Yugoslav League of Communists in Kosova after World War II.

The Kryeziu brothers allied with Anglo-American forces of western democracies, who had demonstrated their fundamental belief and support for the liberty and freedom of all peoples. There were two major reasons why the Kryeziu movement was supported by the allies: Gani Kryeziu agreed to fight the occupation without conditions, and the fact that their political program was based on western democratic principles.

The fight against the Nazi invader was fierce and full of sacrifices. The cooperation, or more precisely, the servility of the Albanian communists toward the Communist Party of Yugoslavia, (aside from the façade of the name '*the national liberation front*'), sabotaged the Albanian national aspirations for democracy and the unification of the territories. Albania's communist brigades participated directly in helping the Yugoslav forces re-occupy Kosova. It was Albania's Communist Party's subservient attitude toward the Communist Party of Yugoslavia that brought about brutal massacres like the Massacre of Hereç, the Massacre of Tivar, and the atrocious crimes in Drenica and the rest of Kosova, during the re-occupation. On this occasion I will dwell only on the events of the Hereç Massacre, to focus on the organizers and perpetrators of this massacre and their accomplices. At the conclusion of the war, the communist forces arrested Said Kryeziu in the village of Dobrej, in the mountains near Gjakova, together with the British Special Operations Executive officer Simcox and the renowned Albanian intellectual Llazar Fundo. Fundo was taken to the village of Kolesjan in Luma, and was then tortured and executed the next day on direct orders from Enver Hoxha. Said Kryeziu and Major Anthony Simcox were taken to Berat, where the First Congress of the Communist Party of Albania was being held (October 1944).

Major Simcox, Llazar Fundo, and Said Kryeziu were arrested on September 20, 1944 by

Ismet Shaqiri (a member of the Communist Group of Kosova), then called the 'Kosmet Group 'by the Serbs in Kosova... Said Kryeziu was told that General Dali Ndreu had requested to meet with him, but it turned out that it was Enver Hoxha who wanted to see him in Berat. From Berat, both Simcox and Kryeziu were evacuated by airplane to the Bari, Italy headquarters of SOE, as ordered by the Allied Mediterranean Command.

Llazar Fundo was a prominent Albanian intellectual from Korça who had participated in the first wave of spread of communism in Europe after World War I, and had risen to an important position in the Comintern in Moscow. Later he became a deviationist and left Moscow. He was pursued by Stalin's agents and sentenced to death in absentia. During the war he was arrested by the Germans who turned him over to the Italians, who in turn, interned him the infamous concentration camp of Ventotene where he met the Kryeziu's. He came back to Kosova with Gani Kryeziu and decided to stay in the capacity of his political adviser. Fundo knew that the Albanian/Kosova border was the most sensitive and the most important area for the future of the Albanian nation. Fundo was a brilliant intellectual having studied law in Paris. After the assassination of Avni Rrustemi he was elected the president of the association 'Bashkimi' and the editor of the newspaper with the same name. 'Llazar Fundo maintained correspondence with Albert Einstein, Ernest Hemingway, Sandro Pertini (President of the Italian 7th Republic) and playwright Luigi Pirandello, amongst others.

The other Kryeziu brothers, Gani and Hasan, together with a small number of their forces, returned to Gjakova, having dispersed most of their men in order to avoid a civil war. Gani Kryeziu continued to hope that the Anglo-Americans would honor their promises which stated that the people who liberate themselves from the occupiers will have the right to self-determination. After their return to Gjakova, they settled in the house of their cousin, Tosum Kryeziu, because the *kullas* of Gani Kryeziu had been destroyed by the Germans. The head of the resistance, Gani Kryeziu, was summoned to the City Hall in Gjakova under the pretense of consultations. As he arrived, the communists unexpectedly arrested him and placed handcuffs on him, and after an improvised court proceeding with trumped up charges, they sentenced him to 5 years imprisonment. When he had finished serving his sentence in Sremska Mitrovica prison, five years later, they eliminated him by poisoning him. After this criminal act, they informed the family of his death and told them to come and collect his belongings. The British Government made extraordinary efforts in order to free Gani Kryeziu from the jail of the Yugoslav government, but it failed.

Against the other brother, Hasan, the secret police of the communist party of Yugoslavia used another even more devious and sinister tactic by visiting him as 'friends' with approximately these words: '

We have reached agreement with Gani Beg, and everything is in order… He will soon arrive and tell you himself. We are appreciative of the fight you have waged against the occupiers, and your place will be guaranteed in the new order. We have come just to conduct the registration of the armament and a medical examination. You may leave your arms here because we will provide you with new and more modern armament'.

They then proceeded to undress all of the brave men under the pretense of a medical examination. One by one, and naked, they moved them from one room to another, tied them up by force and marched them outside. They separated the heroic commander Hasan Kryeziu from his men and, like savages, brutally cut off his tongue so that he would not be able to give any command. Tied up and naked, they loaded the men onto a truck and proceeded toward the village of Hereç in that icy January 10th 1945. In Hereç, upon the arrival of these freedom fighters, the Titoite vultures charged at them, tearing at them with knives, spades, picks and bayonets; they massacred them and threw them in a village water well. These dark forces, Serbs and Montenegrins were afraid to face these brave men while armed, only finding the courage to face them when they were unarmed and bound by rope. Two of them miraculously escaped in the dark of the night, Zenel Ademi and Mal Shyti. Those murdered brutally in Hereç were: Hasan and Xhevat Kryeziu, Selim Mal Dula, Brahim Musli Demaliaj, Shaban Sadik Saraçini, Shpend Zeqir Preng Gjoni, Sali Preng Gjoni, Ukë Arif Preng Gjoni, Halil Preng Gjoni, Metë Rexhë Saraçini, Col Isuf Koka, Sadri Gjon Papaj, Sali Shpend Mujaj, Musë Avdyl Nezaj, Musë Zenel Alimetaj, Ali Miftar Zhuta, Ramë Osmani, Shpend Halili, Mehmet Musa, Smajl Sadik Koka, Rexhë Mehmeti, Ahmet Ali Mehmetaj, Zenel Miftar Zhuta and Shaban Ali Bajrami.[7]

The goal of the Communist Party of Yugoslavia in the perpetration of this and other atrocities, was the elimination of the entire Kyeziu family of Gjakovë, which was the brain and moral force of the movement with its program of liberating the country and uniting the Albanian ethnic

[7]Butka, U. 'Ringjallja' Tetovë, 1996

territories into one free and democratic state, opposing the Titoite plans for the reoccupation of Kosova.

The Kryeziu family trace their participation in politics over a period of 5 centuries.

Professor Uran Butka says that there is mention of a Kryeziu in the Ottoman documents

in the fifthteenth century. The Kryezius pride themselves in having produces eighteen Pashas during the Ottoman Empire. They achieved high positions in the Empire, and at the same time they were always participants in the Albanian national movements after they came into existence.

In the League of Prizren gathering in the city of Prizren in 1878, Adullah Pash Dreni (Kryeziu) was a very prominent personality. Francescan Priest and Poet, Gjergj Fishta, writes thus about Adullah Dreni: ' … For he is, *Zanë,* Adullah Dreni, without whom there is no dialog. He is feared by Prizren, by Prizren and by Gjakova; he is feared by the entire Kosova. He has never reneged on his word. For his guests and his word given, he would set fire to his own house, and start a war with the ruler himself. For he will cast no shame on Albania'. Or in Albanian –

'Aj asht, Zanë, Abdullah Dreni: Njaj, pa t'cillin s' hecë kuvendi E ia dro t'keqen Prizrendi. Dro Prizrendi e dro Gjakova Rreth e cark i a dro Kosova; Pse fjalë peng aj kurr s'ka lanun; Pse per mik e besë të dhanun Vetë i a nep zjarmin shtëpis:

Shi me Mbret pushken e nisë, E as s'i len marre Shqypnis'.[8]

The Ottoman envoy Mehmet Ali Pashë Maxhari traveled to Gjakova on August 31, 1878 and called on Adullah Dreni at his palace. Leaders of the League of Prizeren called on Adullah Dreni to surrender his guest to them or ask him to return to Constantinople. Dreni found himself in a tight spot, as bound by the tradition of the Albanian Kanun he was obligated to protect his guest against the request of the other Prizen League members, including Riza Kryeziu. He chose to perish together with the Sultan's envoy and his entire family in a fierce fight with his colleagues of the League, instead of bringing shame on himself and his family. The Kanun of Lek Dukagjini is very clear on this matter.

---

[8] Fishta, G. 'Lahuta e Malcis'.

Riza Beg Kryeziu, the father of Gani, Said and Hasan Kryeziu was also an important member of The League of Prizren. He is mentioned entering Gjakova together with Sulejman Vokshi and Bajram Curri. Professor Stavro Skendi says that Riza Kryeziu was the main leader of The League of Peja formed in 1899. In the Albanian history books Riza Kryeziu has been overlooked and Mullah Haxhi Zeka is usually credited with the forming of The League of Peja. It is true that Haxhi Zeka played an important role in this movement, but it appears that Riza Kryeziu was the main leader, in the view of historian Stavro Skendi. In time hopefully the Albanian historians will amend their views on this. Professor Skendi says: Riza Beg Gjakova (Kryeziu) was invited to Constantinople in January 1898. According to Skendi, on January 15, 1898, he made the following politically astute statement to the press of the Turkish capital: 'I do not represent here only the Moslems of my country, but also the Christians, since Christians and Moslems are the same. We recognize only race, and religions, consequently, do not divide us'.

The Kryezius had good friendly relations with Great Britain, according to Robert L. Wolff, starting with Riza Beg Kryeziu, which friendship was maintained by his sons before and during World War II.[9] Riza Kryeziu was also one of the important leaders in the liberation of Shkup (Skopje) in 1912. He was designated as Kosova's representative, together with Isa Boletini, to Vlora at the declaration of independence and the raising of the Albanian flag there on November 28, 1912. Albanian history books which do not recognize the important role of Riza Kryeziu in the Albanian national movement are lacking in substance. The same would be true of books that do not give its true importance to the movement led by Gani Beg Kryeziu during the Second World War in Albania and Kosova.

Said Kryeziu participated in the movement led by his brother Gani and together with Llazar Fundo were political advisers to Gani Kryeziu. Later on in exile Said Kryeziu played an important role as the Secretary General of Albanian Committee for Free Albania. He was designated to become Prime Minister of Albania under the program of this Committee. He was the leader of the party which he had declared, named The Albanian National League of Peasants and Farmers (Lidhja Kombetare

---

[9]Wolff, Robert F. 'The Balkans in Our Time'.

Shqiptare e Bujqeve dhe e Katundarve).This Committee was formed in Paris on August 26, 1949 with the following 5 persons: Mithat Frasheri, Abaz Kupi, Said Krueziu, Nuçi Kota, and Zef Pali. Mithat Frashcri was chosen President; Abaz Kupi was Vice-President; Said Kryeziu was chosen General Secretary, and Nuçi Kota and Zef Pali were members of the Executive Council. Later on this body was expanded to include three political parties: Balli Kombetar, Levizja e Legaliteti, and Lidhja Katundare, with an equal number of participants by each of the three parties, all officially recognized inside this body.

After the formation of this committee, as knowledge emerged many years later, ex-King Zog had requested that Said Kryeziu should be excluded from this Committee and he was told by the British that this request would not ever be considered, since Kryeziu was their mos trusted personality in this organization. Apparently Zog was not aware of the power that Kryeziu weilded, and Zog's own position in the eyes of the British diplomacy. Zog had been discredited in the eyes of the most of the official British foreign policy apparatus when he joined Benito Mussolini's camp, hook, line and sinker, in the years prior to WW II. Kryeziu had been the architect of this organization and had good relations with Balli Kombetar, Legaliteti and even Blloku Kombetar Independent, which was not accepted to participate in this Committee as a political Party. But later Blloku members like Ismail Verlaci (its President) and Ndue Gjomarkaj (its Vice-President), and others were accepted in the Committee.

The oldest brother of Gani Kryeziu, Ali Kryeziu, was killed in battle against the Serbs in the village of Zhur, near Prizren. Gani's other brother Cena Kryeziu had been Minister of the Interior under Zog's government in 1924., and then Ambassador to Belgrade and Prague. He was assassinated in Prague in October, 1927 on orders by the Italian government. Although it appears that Zog did not have a direct hand in Cena's assassination, he was not too displeased by the demise of Cena, as it eliminated one of his rivals. Zog had four major rivals, Cena Kryeziu, Shefqet Verlaci, Mustafa Kruja, and Hasan Prishtina. The rumors in Albania at the beginning were that Zog had eliminated Cena. Zog's own sisters believed this. Zog in the meantime spread the word that it had been Shefqet Verlaci's doing, hoping to eliminate a second rival, thinking that the Kryezius would even the score and kill Verlaci. Cena had differed with Zog regarding the country's foreign policy. He advised Zog not to throw himself into fascist Italian camp as he believed this would not serve the interest of Albania. He turned out to be right, but for this he paid with his life.

At the conclusion of the World War, Said Kryeziu was arrested by the Albanian communists and was feared to be in danger. Hasan Kryeziu and Xhevat Kryeziu, together with the bravest sons of the Gjakova mountains had been brutally murdered in Hereç. Dervish Kryeziu was assassinated in a barber shop in Peje by an agent of the Yugoslav secret police (an Albanian emigrant from Mirdita) while he was getting a shave. Myrteza (Xajë) Kryeziu was killed by the communists in Kolgecaj, Albania. His brother, Sefedin Kryeziu, was killed in Gjakove. Ismet Kryeziu was tortured to death in a jail in Albania in 1952. Masar Kryeziu ended up in a concentration camp in Albania. Later on, they eliminated nephews and other relatives of this family who had different family names.

The crimes of the communist regime began from the first days that they took power and lasted for almost half a century. This barbaric regime eliminated the very best sons and daughters of our nation. No other nation has suffered as much as the Albanians from this barbaric system. And Tivar? There several thousand of young Albanian soldiers were executed in order to reduce the fighting ability of the Kosova Albanians and facilitate the reoccupation of Kosova by the Serbs. How about Drenica? There many thousands of men, women and children were brutally massacred, during the reoccupation of Kosova. The exact numbers of the victims is not known, but many writers of these events have quoted figures from 40,000 to 65,000 dead. How about the concentration camp in the swamp of Maliq, in Albania and the jails and other concentration camps throughout Albania, where a large number of the innocent population ended up only because they dared to show a little patriotism by mentioning the name of Kosova, or they had dared to criticize the Yugoslav 'Brothers' or the Soviet 'Brothers'? Many of these families had fought for the liberation of the country from the occupiers. The Communist Party of Albania was nothing less that a subsidiary of the Communist Party of Yugoslavia. In reflecting upon this tragic event, one must conclude:

1: The enemies of our nation, used the Communist Party of Albania as their accomplice in achieving their goals – namely, to eliminate every patriotic idea and person, and undermine and eliminate every patriotic movement aimed at the unification of the Albanian lands, by striking brutally at the leaders and most active voices of the resistance, as they did with the Kryeziu brothers.

2: The communist system did not want to, and could not resolve the basic national question – the unification of the territories – because it had at its base the unfortunate theory of the international proletariat, based on which the national interests had to be subservient to the international interests, i. e. Kosova had to remain under the yoke of Yugoslavia, as Enver Hoxha describes in his book 'The Anglo-American Threat to Albania'.

3: A national monument should be erected in Hereç, in order to honor these martyrs.

The academic conference held in Prishtina in 2006) made a major contribution to the National Liberation Movement by shedding light on this patriotic movement and its personalities in order to fulfill a void in our history, with reliable objective facts. In short: the rewriting of our national history, with honest criteria.

Bibliography

Julian Amery – 'Sons of the Eagle' London, 1948

Uran Butka – 'Ringjallja' Tetovë, 1996

Vladimir Didier – 'Jugosllovensko-Albanski Odnosti' Beograd, 1949

Reginald Hibbert– 'Albania's Liberation Struggle' London, 1991

Enver Hoxha – ' The Anglo-American Threat' Tirana, 1982

Peter Kemp – 'No Colour, Nor Crest' London, 1958

Paul Lendavi – Eagles in Cobwebs' USA, 1969

Arben Puto – 'From the Annals of British Diplomacy' Tirana, 1981

Muhamet Shatri – 'Kosova në Luftën e Dytë Boterorë' Prishtinë, 1997

David Smiley – Albanian Assignment' London, 1984

Robert L. Wolf – 'The Balkans in our Time' Harvard University, 1956

Bytyçi Newspaper – Albania, 2005

Stavro Skendi – 'The Albanian National Awakening' Princeton, 1967

Heu, quid agant in Albania?[1]: Travelers', S.O.E agents', and Catholic Missionaries' Bitter and Meager Victories

Ines Muzarku

Viola: What country, friends, is this?
Captain: This is Illyria Lady,
Viola: And What Should I do in Illyria?[2]

This is how William Shakespeare, in the comical history *Twelfth Night*, introduces Viola, the main protagonist, who has survived a shipwreck. She learns from the captain of their doomed ship and that they are on the coast of Illyria, which is ruled by Orsino, Duke of Illyria. Viola is perplexed as to *Heu, quid ea agat* in Illyria? (Alas, what should she do in Illyria?) In *Metamorphoses* Ovid describes Cadmus and Harmonia being washed onto the Illyrian shore after a shipwreck. So Illyria has become one of the chief literary models for shipwreck in classical literature and a clear inspiration for Shakespeare's account.[3] Although all Shakespearean characters speak English and there are some remarkable resemblances between women heroes like Olivia and Viola, and Queen Elizabeth I, Shakespeare's preference for Illyria as the setting of the *Twelfth Night* is quite remarkable. It is the elusiveness of an unfamiliar place which makes Illyria appealing to the popular imagination. Illyria was probably known to Shakespeare and his contemporaries as an actual region off the coast of the Adriatic Sea in what is today's Albania, Croatia, and Montenegro and the city state of Ragusa.[4] Illyria is both remote and

[1] '*Heu, quid agat? Vario nequiquam fluctuat aestu/diversaeque vocant animum in contraria curae,*' (Alas, what is [Aeneas] to do? He fluctuates on a changeful surge to no purpose, and various anxieties call his mind in different directions) Virgil, Book IV *Aeneid*, Reed, J. D., *Virgil's Gaze: Nation and Poetry in the Aeneid*, Princeton University Press, 2007, p.188.

[2] Shakespeare, William, *Complete Works of William Shakespeare*, Wordsworth Library Collection, London 2007, p.–641.

[3] Wallace, Jennifer, 'A (Hi)story of Illyria,' *Rome and Greece*, Vol. 45, No. 2, October 1998, p.217.

[4] Shakespeare made ten more references to Illyria in the Twelfth Night 1.2.2-3; 1.3.20, 42, 124, 132; 1-5-31; 111.4.294; IV-1-37; IV.2.115. For a detailed study on

an exotic land, unfamiliar to the English, and thus it makes the perfect setting for intrigue, romance, lost and found loves; Illyria is far-flung and unfamiliar enough to seem a natural setting for quite extraordinary experiences.[5] *Heu, quid ea agat* in Illyria? In fact, Lady Viola does much in Illyria and the inhabitants of Illyria emerge not as wild 'riotous and wine bibbing'[6] pirates but as gentle and cultivated companions.[7] Like Lady Viola, Western travelers, scholars, S.O.E-s (Special Operations Executives), diplomats, and Catholic missionaries,[8] who either initiated or revived a long history of contacts with Albania, may have expressed the same sense of marvel and astonishment: *Heu, quid agant* in Albania? Alas, what were they able to do in Albania?

The purpose of this chapter is to explore the religious fractions in Albanian society during the transitory period 1939-1944 which correspond to the Italian and German invasions of Albania respectively. Due to the complexity, the highly charged political situation, and lack of stability, the Byzantine Catholic missions in southern Albania and the Orthodox pro-Rome union movement had meager success. The Catholic missionaries, like the British S.O.E-s, were not adequately prepared as to what to expect in Albania. Although the facts about Albania were to some degree known, they seem to have never been fully understood. Moreover, the divides in Albania's resistance movement were reflected in the divides between and within Albania's religious communities. This made the activity of the Catholic missionaries inefficient.

---

the 'local habitations' of Shakespeare's plays with specific reference to Illyria see Torbarina, Josip, 'The Setting of Shakespeare's Plays,' Studia Romanica et Anglica Zagrabiensia, Vol. 17-18, 1964, pp. 21-59, especially 32-54.

[5] Campbell, O.J., Rothschild A, and Vaughan, S., eds., Twelfth Night, The Bantam Shakespeare, New York 1964, p. 2.

[6] Hotson, Leslie, *The First Night of Twelfth Night*, Macmillan, New York, 1954, pp. 151-152.

[7] Torbarina, Josip, 'The Setting of Shakespeare's Plays,' *Studia Romanica et Anglica Zagrabiensia*, Vol. 17-18, 1964, pp. 46-48.

[8] For more on the Catholic missionaries early nineteenth century encounters with Albania see Murzaku, Ines Angeli, Catholicism, Culture, Conversion: The History of the Jesuits in Albania (1841-1946), Orientalia Christiana Analecta 277, Pontificio Istituto Orientale, Rome, 2006, especially pp. 70-90.

Esoteric Imagology – Western Travelers

Images of Albania were informed in the United Kingdom by a prominent cast of characters including writers, travelers, scholars and linguists, who either made Albania the preferred geographical setting for their literary works or had a first-hand experience in the country and of its people.[9] *Heu, quid agant* in Albania? Derek Hall argued how the images generated by British writers constructed the Balkans' image, from the themes of classical, oriental, and elemental folk culture.[10] The Ottoman legacy as well as isolation added to Albanians' mysteriousness, thus the Westerners' eagerness for fresh re-discovery. Re-discovery is properly the best term to explain the renewed interest in the Balkans and Albania in particular, as the country has never escaped the interest of the West, or the Catholic missionaries like the Benedictines, Dominicans, Franciscans, Basilians and the Jesuits. What these representations had in common was an accentuation of the sense of the other or Albanians' esotericism towards the European or the Western world. This approach, probably unintended and benign, perceived Western civilization as far superior and more sophisticated compared to the conventional structures of a peasant-Balkan culture. Albania, with a Muslim-Oriental majority, made a special case study and added to the wonders of re-discovery of the Orient in Europe. The repository of negative characteristics which constituted and constructed the image of Albania juxtaposed the positive and sophisticated West.

It was the *ars apodemica* (art of travelling) and the travelogues that contributed more images of an enigmatic, remote, enchanting, and wild Albania to the West and especially to the English-speaking world. *I like the Albanians much*[11] wrote Baron George Gordon Byron, the notorious Romantic poet and satirist and author of *Childe Harold's Pilgrimage*, to his mother from Prevesa, on November 12, 1809, after traversing the interior

[9]Hall, Derek, 'Representations of Place: Albania' *The Geographical Journal*, Vol. 165, No. 2, July 1999, pp.161-162

[10]Dingsdale, Alan, *Mapping Modernities: Geographies of Central and Eastern Europe, 1920-2000*, Routledge, 2002, p. 84; Hall, Derek, and Danta, Darrick, eds., *Reconstructing the Balkans : a Geography of the New Southeast Europe*, John Wiley and Sons, New York, 1996, specifically on Albania see pp. 119-148.

[11]Byron, Baron George Gordon, *The works of Lord Byron: in Verse and Prose. Including his Letters, Journals, etc., with a Sketch of his Life*, Silas Andrus & Son, Hartford, 1851, p.17.

of the province of Albania in a visit to Ali Pasha. Byron was marveled at Albanian dresses, 'the most magnificent in the world,' and the Albanian hospitality.[12] Lord Byron followed and built on the Shakespearean unknown and far-away paradigm of Albania. In Albania and among Albanians Byron found conspicuous enchantment, which ignited his inspiration and other Byron-influenced British travelers of the early twentieth century. The prolific critic, biographer, historian Peter Quennell, scholar and soldier Patrick Leigh Fermor, and mountaineer and surveyor Harold W. Tilman, wrote about Albania with a special verve reminiscent of Byron.[13] Other distinguished nineteenth and early twentieth century British travelers-scholars visited and wrote about Albania. Edward Lear, the landscape painter who visited Albania in 1848, in his meticulous journals produced unique insights into the medieval traditional laws or *kanun* which were governing Albania. Indeed, he confirmed what Ackerman in 1938 found: '…a living museum of everything medieval.'[14] Edith Durham, otherwise known as the Queen of the Highlands, was the twentieth century's indispensable interpreter of Albania, and arguably the most important writer on that culture since J. C. Hobhouse journeyed through the Albanian lands with Byron.[15] Moreover, Aubrey Herbert, a linguist, scholar and poet, was a passionate advocate of the Albanian independence after visiting the country several times. Herbert was the original for John Buchan's romantic hero in *Greenmantle*, and was twice offered the Albanian throne, which he refused on the grounds that he was 'too poor to accept.'[16] The fascinating history of Italo-Albanians, or Arbëreshes, did not escape British interest. The prolific Austrian-born British writer Norman Douglas, in his novel Old Calabria, focused his

---

[12]Ibid.

[13]Tilman, W., H., *When Men and Mountains Meet*, Cambridge University Press, 1947, especially pp. 104–153; Bhattacharji, Shobhana, 'I Like the Albanians Much: Byron and Three Twentieth-Century British Travellers to Albania,' *Byron Journal*, Vol. 38, No. 1, 2010, p.39.

[14]Dingsdale, Alan, *Mapping Modernities: Geographies of Central and Eastern Europe, 1920-2000*, Routledge, 2002, p.84

[15]King, Charles, 'Queen of the Highlanders: Edith Durham in the Land of the Living Past,' *Times Literary Supplement*, 4 August 2000, pp.13–14; or on-line at <http://www.kroraina.com/knigi/en/ed/e_durham.html> accessed on September 11, 2010.

[16]Patey, Douglas Lane, *The Life of Evelyn Waugh: A Critical Biography*, Wiley-Blackwell, 2001, p. 112.

attention on less than known colonies of Albanians, who after the death of Scanderbeg settled in Italy's Mezzogiorno, chiefly in Apulia, Calabria, Basilicata, and Sicily.[17] What came out of these first-hand encounters with Albania and Albanians added to the already established perception of esoteric *imagology* of Albania.

Bitter Victory – S.O.E-s

The far-away and extrinsic Albania and its continually changing fortunes did not escape British intelligence and diplomatic attention. *Heu, quid [the British] agant* in Albania? The Albanian scholar Arben Puto summarized British involvement in Albania as follows: instigate and aid subversive activities; and diplomacy.[18] According to Puto, in Albania, the British implemented both, intelligence and diplomacy. What came to be known as the 'Implementation Study-Albania,' outlined the Office of Strategic Services strategy for a full scale intelligence effort in Albania which included carrying out guerrilla warfare and supplying arms to guerrilla groups which were considered friendly towards Allied aims. Furthermore, Albania's strategic position provided sufficient justification for a massive British commitment of men, money and material.[19] It was expected that British diplomacy would apply the findings and intelligence knowledge[20] in its Balkan policy. However, what characterized British policy in Albania during WWII were ambiguity and incongruence, giving the wrong signals to various groups.

The diplomatic attention of Great Britain towards Albania goes back to the 1939 Italian occupation of the country, so five years before the

---

[17]Douglas, Norman, *Old Calabria*, CosimoClassics, New York 2007, p.176. Even Albanians' special musical instruments like *fiscarol* did not escape Douglas's attention. For more King, Hyatt A., 'The Musical Side of Norman Douglas,' *Music and Letters*, Vol. 27, No.4, October 1946, p.219.

[18]Puto, Arben, Nëpër Analet e Diplomacisë Angleze. Mbi Politikën e Britanisë së Madhe ndaj Shqipërisë gjatë Luftes II Botërore, Albin Tiranë, 2001, p. 198.

[19]Brewer, Robert T., 'Albania, New Aspects, Old Documents,' East European Quarterly, XXVI, No. 1, March 1992, pp. 36-37.

[20]Michael Herman considered intelligence and diplomacy to be complementary as they share the same objective: seeking knowledge and understanding of foreign countries. For more on the complementarity of intelligence and diplomacy see two well-argued articles by Herman, Michael, 'Diplomacy and Intelligence,' Diplomacy and Statecraft, Vol. 9, No. 2, July 1998, pp.1-22; and 'Intelligence and Policy: a Comment,' Intelligence and National Security, Vol. 6, No.1, January 1991, pp. 229-239.

arrival of Reginald Alfred Hibbert (to whom this volume is dedicated). One day before the Italian invasion, on April 6 1939, addressing the House of Commons, the Prime Minister Neville Chamberlain said that the UK has 'no direct interests' in Albania. The international community did not react to Mussolini's latest acquisitions, which included Ethiopia and Albania, or, as Count Galeazzo Ciano, the Italian Minister of Foreign Affairs, recorded in his April 7 diary entry: 'the international reaction was almost non-existent.'[21] In fact, the general international compliance with the occupations encouraged Mussolini in his annexationist designs. London, with some reservations, recognized the annexation of Albania from Italy, re-visiting the old paradigm of 'preservation of its special interests' in the region.[22] The British gave de facto recognition of Albania's new status as an Italian occupied territory and part of the Kingdom of Italy, by downgrading the diplomatic mission of the country to the rank of consulate. Lawrence Grafftey Smith was appointed as Consul-General in Durrës on October 31, 1939.[23] However, the British initial de facto recognition of Italian occupation of Albania would change when Italy entered the war. [24] This, however, did not mean that Britain recognized the independence of Albania which happened later.

British policy towards Albania over the two year period 1939-1941 was overriding the Albanian interests and offering them up to the prevailing self-centric considerations.[25] British policy towards Albania from 1941-1944 can be considered highly inconsistent, giving the wrong signals to various factions, which as a consequence ended up in doubt and loss of trust on the part of all parties.[26] *Heu, quid [the British] agant* in Albania? The British did not accomplish much in Albania. In fact Julian Amery in his autobiography explained that the British missions in Albania ended in utter failure.[27] They found a much more complicated

---

[21]Gibson, Hugh, ed., The Ciano Diaries, 1939-1943, Doubleday & Company, Inc., Garden City, New York, 1946, p. 61.

[22]Puto, Arben, Ibid., p. 200.

[23]Ibid., p. 22.

[24]Barker, Elisabeth, British Policy in South-East Europe in the Second World War, The Macmillan Press, London, 1976, pp. 47-49.

[25]Petrov, Bisser, 'Great Britain and Resistance in Albania, 1943-1944,' Balkan Studies, No. 2, 2006, p. 89.

[26]Gjeçovi, Xhelal, 'Shqipëria dhe Aleatët në Vitet e Luftës së Dytë Botërore,' Studime Historike, No. 1-2, 2003, p. 105.

[27]Amery, Julian, *Approach March. A Venture in Autobiography*, Hutchinson of London,

collection of groups and a far more serious fragmentation of opposing parties[28] of the traditional partisan-monarchist split found elsewhere in the Balkans.[29] Furthermore, the British political wavering and indecision as to what faction to support did much damage to the British reputation and contributed to fostering a hostile attitude of Albanians towards the West, especially Western powers.

Meager Victory – Catholic Missionaries

In the fragmented and politically charged WWII Albania, religion was also a cause, although not a leading factor, in society's fragmentation. What happened during this period prepared the ground for the aversion towards religion or religious phenomena in general, and created the framework for the post- World War II religious persecution. *Heu, quid [the Catholic missionaries] agant* in Albania? During the first period of Italian invasion, April 7, 1939 to October 28, 1940 there were high hopes among Albanian Christians that Christianity, especially Catholicism, was going to get special treatment or be the invader's favorite religion. The Italian occupation was expected to open new perspectives on Albanian Catholic missions, including the Basilian monks' missions in southern Albania, as well as to the success of Catholicism in general. However, appearances can be deceiving – *fallitur visus*. The assumption was that the Italians were going to support the pro-Rome union movement of Orthodox Albanians. The average Christian Albanian, both Catholic and Orthodox, thought that the arrival of the Italian troops would boost the Catholic missions in Albania, and the Catholic missionaries would have greater liberty of action and would indeed benefit from the invasion of Catholic Italy.[30] Furthermore, there were high expectations for an *en masse*

1973, p. 405.

[28] Dyrmishi, Demir, 'Problemi i Partive Politike në Shqipëri, 1941-1944,' *Studime Historike*, No. 1-2, 2006, pp. 81-93; and Zelka, Luan, 'Për Organin e Parë të Ballit Kombëtar 'Lufta për Shlirimin Kombëtar,' Nëntor 1942-Gusht 1943,' *Studime Historike*, No.1-2, 2004, pp.83-94.

[29] Fischer, Bernd, 'Resistance in Albania during the Second World War: Partisans, Nationalists and the S.O.E.,' *East European Quarterly*, XXV, No. 1, March 1991, p.21.

[30] Giuria, Demetrio, to Carissimo Padre, Durazzo, 12 Aprile 1939, Cronache delle Missioni in Albania, 1938-1939, (Archive of the Greek Monastery of Grottaferrata-ABGG), p.1; also Gjeçovi, Xhelal, 'Disa Veçori të Organizimit Politik në dy Fazat e Pushtimit të Vendit,' Studime Historike, No.1-2, 2003, pp.64-66.

conversion of the Orthodox believers to Catholicism, a move which had been fomenting since 1895, pioneered by Papas George Germanos and his uncle Bessarione.[31] The pro-Rome movement was initiated by the Orthodox faithful, Orthodox prelates, and the Orthodox elites, especially in the region of Elbasan, middle Albania.

The 'hour of the Lord has arrived,' stated Leone G. B. Nigris, the Apostolic Delegate to Albania, in his correspondence to Rome. By 'the hour of the Lord' Nigris probably meant the regaining of religious freedom by Catholic missions which were until then hindered or persecuted by Zog's government. In fact, Nigris, in his tête-à-tête with Galeazzo Ciano, the very night of the Italian occupation of Albania, was asking Ciano for special guarantees regarding the future of Catholicism in Albania. However, Nigris considered April 7, 1939, Albania's occupation by Fascist Italy, an ill-omened day, not only for the sacrilege of Good Friday, but because the Italian invasion was considered by the Apostolic Delegate as a crime and a tragic error for his homeland, Italy, as well. The only benefit Nigris was anticipating from the Italian invasion which would benefit Albania's Catholicism was a possible concordat between the Holy See and Albania following the 1929 Italian-Vatican concordat pattern, which would eventually guarantee freedom to Catholicism. At least this was Nigris's hope.

Francesco Tommaso Brunetti, a Catholic priest in Korçë (a leading city in southern Albania), in his note to Daniele Barbiellini, a monk from the Monastery of Grottaferrata and missionary in southern Albania, expressed his confidence in the rich missionary field in southern Albania and his unshaken hope that 'with God's help in five months all the region [of southern Albania] was going to be won over to faith/Catholicism!'[32] Furthermore, a considerable number of Muslims in Gjirokastër (a city in southern Albania), did not have any problem publicly stating and taking a lot of pride in their Christian roots. The Muslims were quick to note that due to unfortunate circumstances, they were forced to change

---

[31]For a detailed and documented treatment of Albanians' pro-Rome movement see: Murzaku, Ines Angeli, 'The Road to Church Union for Orthodox Albanians,' *The Journal of Eastern Christian Studies*, Volume 55, No. 3-4, 2003, pp.245-282; and Murzaku, Angeli, Ines, 'Rome's Last Efforts towards the Union of Orthodox Albanians,' *The Journal of Eastern Christian Studies*, Volume 58, No.1-2, 2006, pp.

[32]Brunetti, Francesco-Tommaso, to Barbiellini, Daniele, Missione Cattolica Korça, 16 Settembre 1939, Cronache delle Missioni in Albania, 1938-1939, ABGG, p. 1.

their traditional faith, but now was the right time for them to return to the original faith of their ancestors.[33] The Muslims felt that because of union of Albania with Italy and Catholic Rome, they could not stand at the crossroads anymore. Consequently, they had to choose between the Orthodoxy of Constantinople and the Orthodoxy of Rome.[34]

Given the advantageous political circumstances for a possible union of the Orthodox Albanians with the Catholic Church, Nigris designed a three-step missionary plan, applying an individual proselytizing methodology. The first step in Nigris's three-step union plan was the union of the Orthodox, second, the union of the Bektashi,[35] and third, that of the Sunni Muslims. The conversion of Bektashi to Catholicism was considered an avenue which would undermine the majority Sunni Muslim population and achieve equilibrium between Albania's Muslim and Christian populations. Nigris's personal proselytizing approach focused mainly on the conversion of singular Orthodox individuals to the Catholic Church. To this end, Nigris intended to establish, in traditional Orthodox territory in southern Albania, Byzantine-Catholic missionary stations made up of Greek-Catholic or Byzantine-Catholic missionaries. The stations, if the mission was successful and the response from Orthodox and Muslim communities was sufficient, would evolve into more stable Byzantine or Greek Catholic Churches. The French Cardinal Eugène Tisserant, who at that time was serving as the secretary of the Congregation for Oriental Churches, did not agree with Nigris's missionary approach. He believed that unity achieved in this way would cause additional and unnecessary divisions among Albanians, as the uniates or the Byzantine Catholics were considered as belonging to a fourth religion in Albania.

Instead, Tisserant wanted to make the best of the regained Catholic religious freedom and was hoping for a return in 'great numbers' of the Orthodox to the Catholic Church. For Tisserant it was crucial that the Catholic missionaries encourage and cultivate a collective- conversion- tendency which would be achieved through personal contacts with

---

[33]Ibid.

[34]Ibid.

[35]For a well-argued political history of Albanian Bektashism see Doja, Albert, 'A Political History of Bektashism in Albania,' *Totalitarian Movements and Political Religions*, Vol. 7, No. 1, March 2006, pp. 83–107.

Orthodox clergy and people. The Catholic missionaries were called to communicate and establish contacts, especially with the learned and educated part of the Orthodox clergy and laity. They were particularly asked to work to win the trust, sympathy, benevolence, comprehension and reciprocal esteem of the Orthodox. Obviously, the final goal was conversion, or passing in blocks, as Tisserant put it, to Catholicism of the entire Orthodox population of Albania headed by the Orthodox hierarchy, a unity similar to that of Syro-Malabar Catholics, on which Tisserant was an expert. In the case of Albania, the collective methodology, if applied with sensibility and moderation, could bring forth a good harvest and would save Albania from further religious fragmentation, thus reducing the number of religions from three to only two, Muslim and Christian.

However, the cardinal cautioned the Catholic missionaries that the motives for en masse or group conversions be strictly supernatural, and on this point Nigris and Tisserant were in complete agreement. The Vatican's recommendation specified that if entire Orthodox villages headed by their clergy and leaders demonstrated good intentions toward the Catholic Church, and were willing to unite with the Catholic Church, the missionaries were encouraged to meet the Orthodox's expectations, while displaying extreme prudence.[36]

The harvest for group conversions to Catholicism appeared quite ripe. During the first year of the Italian invasion of Albania 1939-1940, the Orthodox of southern and middle Albania were signaling strong inclinations to unite with Rome. In the meantime, Nigris began to prepare in the event the union project would be successful. The apostolic delegate was planning to have to deal with: 1) an incapacitated or helpless episcopate; 2) an ignorant clergy; 3) an illiterate multitude of Orthodox faithful and 4) two rudimentary seminaries for clergy formation which were in need of immediate assistance. On the Sunni Muslim front, there were indications of good will toward the Catholic Church in both the countryside and the mountains. There were among the Catholics those who believed that Albanian Muslims of the countryside were Muslims only because they were no longer or ceased to be Catholic. The Muslims lived isolated in the countryside or in small villages, where the ruins of former Christian Churches were still discernible, but one could rarely find

---

[36]Tisserant, Cardinal Eugenio, to P. Barbiellini, Daniele, Città del Vaticano, 4 Maggio 1939, Cronache delle Missioni in Albania, 1938-1939, ABGG, p. 1.

a mosque in these villages. According to Dr. Rosolino Petrotta, general secretary of the Italian Catholics of Christian East Association and an Italian-Albanian from Sicily who visited the country during the months of November and December 1940, this part of the Albanian population became Muslim because it was abandoned by Christian missionaries, and once the Churches were destroyed the flock was dispersed.[37] In substance, Petrotta found the Muslim population of the Albanian countryside in 1940 not practicing any type of religion. However, the Muslims still kept the remains of the ancestral Christian traditions, including the special veneration of St. Nicholas, St. George and the Blessed Virgin visible. Moreover, the Bektashi intellectuals spoke openly of conversion. However, what all these potential groups had in common was a lack of religious education. Nigris repeated instruction to the missionaries was that the return should be based exclusively on conviction and the free-will of the individual, and not based on any form of material incentive or other related non-spiritual reason.[38]

The Padua bi-ritual Conventuals joined efforts to help in the Orthodox-Muslim pro-Rome movement. The Conventuals arrived in Berat, Lushnjë, Vlorë and Vuno, where they began to build their missionary stations. The stations of Pogradec and Korçë were under the spiritual care of the Lazarists, otherwise known as Vincentians. While in Tiranë, the Jesuit and Albanian native Fr. Michele Troshani was working to establish cultural contacts with the Orthodox of the capital. In the 1939-1940 missionary enterprise to effectuate the Orthodox pro-Rome movement, the Franciscans of Shkoder were visibly missing. There was an undeniable friction between Nigris and the Franciscans, who, as in the past, were insisting on being part of the Catholic missions in southern Albania.[39] The Franciscans were protesting against Nigris and accused him of not trusting them enough to assign them missions in southern Albania. Probably, it was Franciscans' ambiguity in relation to the invaders, as well as their high visibility in the country's politics, that made Nigris reluctant

---

[37]Petrotta, Rosolino to sua Eminenza il Sig. Cardinale Luigi Lavitrano, Arcivescovo di Palermo, Prelato Ordinario di Piana dei Greci, Palermo 18 Gennaio 1940, *Cronache delle Missioni in Elbasan, 1940*, ABGG, p. 2.

[38]Nigris, G. B. Leone, to M.M. R.R. Missionari dell'Albania Meridionale, Scutari 10 Novembre 1939, *Cronache delle Missioni in Albania, 1938-1939*, ABGG, p. 1.

[39]Morozzo della Rocca, Roberto, *Nazione e Religione in Albania (1920-1944)*, Il Mulino Bologna, 1990, p. 203.

to count on their missionary skills. The Franciscan Fr. Bernardin Palaj became chaplain of the Milizia of Tirana, openly disobeying the orders from his superiors who were insisting on Palaj's dis-involvement in politics. Furthermore, the renowned poet and intellectual, the Albanian Franciscan Fr. Gjergj Fishta, who until the Italian occupation of the country was a proponent of Albania's independence and was expressed vehemently against Italy's annexation design of Albania, underwent a 'conversion.' After the April 7, 1939 invasion, Fishta's initial hostility towards Italy turned into close collaboration, which Italy lavishly recompensed by nominating Fishta for membership to the *Reale Accademia d'Italia* (Royal Italian Academy), which, nonetheless, was a well-deserved honor for the Albanian intellectual. Until his death in 1940, Fishta attempted to accomplish union between the occupiers and the Albanian Catholics.[40]

From Nigris's abundant correspondence with the Congregation for the Oriental Churches in Rome, it was clear that he was successful in obtaining financial assistance for a renewed Albanian Catholic mission and, most important, Nigris had solicited the support of the Lieutenant-General in Albania, Francesco Jacomoni. During the one-year period 1939-1940, Jacomoni seemed favorable to Catholicism and Catholic missions in southern Albania, considering union of the Orthodox with the Roman Church as a logical avenue to pursue in the new political map of Albania. Expressing his support for the union of the Orthodox, Jacomoni commented: 'The [Orthodox] Church authorities understand the new political situation of the country ... and feel the necessity of uniting with Rome, in order to liberate Albanian Orthodox from various Balkan and especially Greek influences.'[41] Moreover, Jacomoni, in his correspondence to Rome, reported on the inconsolable conditions of the Albanian Autocephalous Orthodox Church, both religiously and economically, and on a special meeting he had with Kristofor Kisi, Metropolitan of Tiranë and head of the Albanian Autocephalous Church, regarding the union of Albanian Orthodoxy with the Catholic Church. In the colloquy, Kisi declared that he was fully convinced of the necessity and benefit of uniting with Rome, a unity that, according to Kisi, the Orthodox population would accept without further discussion, if it was

[40]Ibid., p. 198.
[41]Dela Roka, Roberto, *Kombësia dhe Feja në Shqipëri, 1920-1944*, Elena Gjika, Tiranë, 1994, p. 214.

officially decided by the Orthodox Holy Synod. Orthodox expectations for financial incentives from Italy were high. In the eyes of the Orthodox high clergy and lay leaders, now that Italy had occupied Albania, union with the Catholic Church meant that the Italian government would take the responsibility of financially supporting the Orthodox clergy.

The situation was slightly different in other Orthodox-inhabited southern Albanian cities. The inclination of the Orthodox high clergy was confirmed by a detailed report of Monk Flaviano la Piana, who toured some main southern and middle Albanian cities, including Elbasan, Korçë, Përmet, Gjirokastër, Vlorë, and Fier, in August 1939, only a few months after the Italian invasion. However, Flaviano la Piana's observation was that the Orthodox disposition toward union with the Catholic Church in the regions he visited had taken more of a wait-and-see stance. Flaviano la Piana was able to meet and have a colloquy with the bishop of Gjirokastër Panteleimon Kotoko, and Mitrophor Vasil Marko of Korçë. Vasil Marko explicitly affirmed to La Piana that union with the Catholic Church could be effectuated in two to three years.[42] Furthermore, Marko confided to La Piana that the Holy Synod of the Orthodox Church had in fact voted in favor of union with Rome, but because of the complex political circumstances, no concrete steps were taken in that direction. This obviously contradicted the above mentioned statement by Kisi regarding the decision for union with Rome coming from the Orthodox Holy Synod. However, La Piana's report confirmed what Barbiellini reported in his July 1939 report to Nigris. Barbiellini, who was much experienced in Albanian issues, did not think that conversions to Catholicism would happen easily. From his many contacts and colloquia with Orthodox clergy and Orthodox laypeople, Barbiellini had noticed a feeling of hesitation, confusion, and in many instances, individuals who were contemplating a union with Rome were in fear of excommunications by Kristofor Kisi.[43]

Isidore Croce, Abbot of the Greek Monastery of Grottaferrata, whose monks, like Barbiellini, were assigned to missions in southern Albania, was convinced that Rome was nurturing unrealistic expectations to unite

---

[42]La Piana, Flaviano, to Cesarini, G., 22 Agosto 1939, *Cronache delle Missioni in Elbasan, 1938-1939, ABGG*, p. 1.

[43]Barbiellini, Daniele, to Nigris, G.B., Leone, Elbasan, 30 Luglio 1939, *Cronache delle Missioni in Elbasan, 1938-1939, ABGG*, p. 4.

Albanian Christianity. On more than one occasion, the abbot cautioned the Congregation for Oriental Churches about the rush to en masse conversions as well as about lack of good judgment on the part of Rome regarding the entangled Albanian situation and the on-ground religious dynamics. Croce had voiced his concerns and criticism to the Congregation for Oriental Churches, but his observations were not very well received.[44]

In the meantime, Christians' hopes for support on the part of Italy were vanishing as Mussolini was preparing for his attack on Greece. Italy was giving strong signals of a loss of interest in the pro-Rome Albanian movement. Mussolini's policy towards Albanian religious communities, especially Christians, was changing from supportive to indifferent, and during 1941-1943, it turned hostile. After Mussolini's attack on Greece, the Orthodox reaction to the Basilian and other Catholic missions in southern Albania was by no means positive. This was the general attitude that marked the period that followed the April 23, 1941 armistice between the German, Italian, and Greek commands until 1943, which marked Italy's final demise. Barbiellini found the Orthodox of Fier to be more reserved, uncommunicative, and almost impenetrable. The Orthodox behaved as if they were afraid of Catholics[45]. News from Gjirokastër was not encouraging, either. Lorenzo Tardo reported an elevated level of nervousness, insecurity, and ambiguity among the people of Gjirokastër after the bombardments and the losses the population was suffering. There was a sense of distress, bewilderment, or what Tardo called a real abulia.[46]

After the foundation of the Communist Party of Albania and the prominent sense of nationalism among Albanians, the Greekness, or the use of Greek language in the liturgy by the Eastern-rite Catholic missionaries, including the Basilian Monks of Grottaferrata, was causing problems in the city of Gjirokastër, so much as to urge the then prefect of Gjirokastër, Mr. Tahir Kolgjini, to address a formal letter of complaint to monks Teodoro Minisci and Flaviano la Piana. The use of Greek

[44]Croce, Isidore to La Piana, Flaviano, Grottaferrata, 27 Maggio 1940, *Cronache delle Missioni in Elbasan, 1940*, p. 1.

[45]Barbiellini, Daniele, Relazione Trimestrale, Ottobre-Dicembre 1940, *Cronache delle Missioni Fier, 1941, ABGG*, pp. 1-2.

[46]Tardo, Lorenzo, Gjirokastër, 20 Luglio 1941, *Cronache delle Missioni Gjirokastër, 1941, ABGG*, p. 1.

was judged inopportune and was thought to go against the national aspirations. The prefect was arguing that the use of Greek was simply harmful for the Gjirokastër faithful. The letter ended with a harsh note of protest, demanding the immediate suspension of the use of Greek in all monks' and the Basilian sisters' activities. It is interesting to observe the prefect's proposition in replacement of Greek. The prefect was proposing the use of Latin, in the first place, followed by Albanian, or Italian, as second and third choices, respectively.[47] For the prefect, Albania was an integral part of Mussolini's Italian-Roman Empire, so the use of Greek or any expression of Orientalism was out of place and strictly forbidden.

The use of Latin language in the liturgy presented problems for the Basilian Monks of Grottaferrata. The monks were different from other Catholic missionaries operating in Albania. They were monks of the Greek rite, so Greek language in the liturgy was natural to them. In fact, the monks became in Albania – to use the description of Abbot Croce for his monks – what they were in Italy, 'exotic.' The initial language controversy spread in other Albanian southern cities where the Eastern-rite Catholic clergy had established their missionary stations. Progressively, the language controversy assumed clear nationalist, anti-Italian and anti-Fascist undertones, causing upheavals in several Albanian towns. Revolts with specific nationalist and anti-Italian undertones were recorded in the capital, Tiranë. About 600 students of the Girls' Institute in Tiranë demonstrated through the streets of the capital shouting: 'We do not want Italian professors! We do not want the Italian director! Down with Fascism!'[48]

What worried the apostolic delegate the most was the perception diffused among the people that the Catholic missionaries working in southern Albania were instruments and supporters of Italian politics. Italians were not successful in winning the hearts and minds of Albanians and obviously, Nigris did not want his missionaries to share in the same destiny. Some Albanians went so far as to think that Italian authorities made use of the Catholic missionaries to actualize their program of de-nationalization among the Orthodox, while others suspected that

---

[47] Kolgjini, Tahir, to Pater Vlaviani dhe Theodor Milic, Gjirokastër, 7 August 1942, No. 166/1, *Cronache delle Missioni in Gjirokastër, 1942, ABGG*, p. 1.
[48] Kolgjini, Tahir, to Pater Vlaviani dhe Theodor Milic, Gjirokastër, 7 August 1942, No. 166/1, *Cronache delle Missioni in Gjirokastër, 1942, ABGG*, p. 1.

the Italian political and military authorities in Albania acted under the Vatican's and the pope's orders,[49] an exaggeration which can hardly be proved to have been the case.

The allegations against Catholic missionaries, including the Basilians, were triggered by the members of communist groups, which in the greatest secrecy and under the closest security arrangements had founded the new Albanian Communist Party on November 8, 1941.[50] The immediate objectives of the Albanian Communist Party were three: the expulsion of Fascist Italy from Albania; the destruction of all vestiges of the recent monarchist government; and the establishment of a standard communist people's republic.[51] By the end of November 1941, the Albanian Communist Youth Organization was founded in Tiranë. What followed these two important events was the organization of anti-Fascist demonstrations in a number of Albanian towns. The slogans of the demonstrations were 'Down with Fascism,' 'Out with the Invader,' and 'Long Live Liberty.'[52] More anti-Fascist demonstrations were reported from Albania's main cities, including Tiranë, Durrës, Shkodër, Elbasan, Vlorë, Gjirokastër, and Korçë in southern Albania, where the Basilians and other Catholic missionaries had established their missions. In these cities, guerrilla bands, who called themselves partisans like the Yugoslav communists,[53] attacked and blew up arms depots and other military objectives and killed dozens of high-ranking Italian Fascist officials and alleged Albanian traitors and spies.[54] The communists' policy was to cover up their Marxist identity behind an apparently nonaligned policy and instead emphasize their high nationalism and devotion to *patria*. By emphasizing the nationalist rather than the social nature of the movement, the communists were seeking cooperation with other resistance factions on the basis of a common national cause.[55]

[49]Petrotta, Rosolino, 'Appunti sulle Missioni degli Uniti in Albania,' Tirana, 7 Novembre 1942, *Cronache delle Missioni in Albania, 1942, ABGG*, p. 2.

[50]Pearson, Owen, *Albania in Occupation and War, from Fascism to Communism, 1940-1945*, Vol. 2, I.B. Tauris, London, 2005, p. 164.

[51]Jacques, Edwin E., *The Albanians: An Ethnic History from Prehistoric Times to the Present*, McFarland, North Carolina, 1994, p. 417.

[52]Pearson, Owen, *Ibid.*, p. 166.

[53]Jacques, Edwin E., *Ibid.*, p. 417.

[54]Pearson, Owen, *Ibid.*, p. 175.

[55]Crampton, R. J., *The Balkans Since the Second World War*, Longman, 2002, p. 39.

Given the highly charged political circumstances and the fragmented political situation, Rome re-evaluated its approach toward the Albanian Orthodox and their appeals to Rome for union purposes. The missionaries were required to act more prudently and avoid any clamor in serving the faithful. Conversions, if any, should be illuminated solely by *sensus Christi* and should happen under no political pressure as the political situation in Albania was escalating.

On the fourth anniversary of the Italian occupation of Albania, large anti-Italian demonstrations took place in many Albanian towns. Armed clashes were recorded in various Albanian cities. A few months before September 8, 1943, Italy's surrender to the Allies, strong combats were reported in southern Albania. Albanian patriots under the command of Nexhip Vinçani successfully attacked Italian troops near the villages of Shalës and Perat in southern Albania, which resulted in Italians suffering heavy losses.[56] It was reported that most of Albania was under guerrilla control. Following Italy's demise and the advent of the German troops, the possibilities for mission among the Albanian population were suspended. However, the Catholic missionaries, including the Basilians, were ready to respond to other forms of apostolate like ministering to the destitute Italian soldiers who had remained in Albania after Italy's armistice. According to an eyewitness report, the Italian soldiers were disarmed, robbed, stripped of clothes, and very often mistreated and beaten.

From November 15 to December 26, 1943 the city of Gjirokastër was under the control of the guerrillas, who were well-accepted by the majority of the population. Their first measure was the execution of several people for primarily political reasons. At the time, a considerable number of Italian former-military personnel were still living in Gjirokastër. They sought and were offered refuge among the Albanian people and worked as farmers. This particular group continued to frequent the Basilian Church and the sacraments and sought spiritual guidance from the missionaries. From December 27, 1943 until November 1944, the city of Gjirokastër was occupied by the German troops which pushed away the guerrillas, after violent cannon shootings. The Basilians provided the same spiritual

---

[56]Pearson, Owen, *Ibid.*, p. 250.

care to the German prisoners, who numbered around one hundred, after German troops left Albania.

The Basilian mission of Fier was going through the same restrictions and fear during the same time period, 1943-1944. As in Gjirokastër, the Basilian missionaries of Fier concentrated their efforts on private lectures and adult Sunday catechism which was continuing without interruption, although the number of the people who attended was severely reduced. In July 1943, Barbiellini reported twelve Byzantine Catholics, 64 Latin Catholics, and only one conversion to Catholicism in Fier.[57] The Catholic mission and missionaries or freshly converted Orthodox clergy were targeted by the partisan units who were acting in southern Albania. On August 13, 1943, Barbiellini was notifying the Apostolic Delegate Nigris of the brutal killing of Papas Pando Vartopi, the Orthodox priest who had converted to Catholicism in 1939. According to Barbiellini's letter, the priest was killed by unidentified bandits in the village of Bubullimë in the district of Lushnjë.[58] The killers had left a note in pencil near the cadaver indicating that Papas Vartopi was killed because 'he [Vartopi] had become a spy of the colonel of Fier and carabineers of Lushnjë.' The note was signed by partisans of the Legion for the Liberation of Musakje. It was reported to Barbiellini, that several days before the killing, Papas Vartopi was seen conversing with several guerrilla band members, whom, according to an eyewitness account, he (Vartopi) had tried to persuade to fight against communism instead.

As the Apostolic Delegate Nigris, Monk Barbiellini was very critical of clergy involvement in the country's politics. Similarly, Barbiellini did not spare his criticism of the Franciscans, disapproving of a growing trend of clear political alignments and shifting loyalties that he noticed among the Franciscans of Shkodër. According to Barbiellini, several members of the Franciscan order were heading guerrilla attacks, fighting not against the communists but now against the Italians.[59] Barbiellini was anticipating what communism would bring about in impoverished Albania. According to Barbiellini, the rebel bands, which were divided

---

[57]Barbiellini, Daniele, to Nigris, G.B., Leone, Fier, 4 Luglio 1943, *Cronache delle Missioni in Albania, Fier 1943, ABGG*, pp. 1-2.

[58]Barbiellini, Daniele, to Nigris, G.B., Leone, Fier, 13 Agosto 1943, *Cronache delle Missioni in Albania, Fier 1943, ABGG*, p. 2.

[59]Barbiellini, Daniele, to Nigris, G.B., Leone, Fier, 13 Agosto 1943, *Cronache delle Missioni in Albania, Fier 1943, ABGG*, p. 2.

among communists and nationalists, had a common cause that united them, and this was their common fight against Fascist Italy. The second most important focus that united these groups was their fight against the Catholic missionaries and the Catholic Church in general, which was considered an Italian representative or an upholder of Italian policy in Albania. Thus, the path was being paved for the suspension of the Catholic missions in southern Albania.

Following Mussolini's July 1943 overthrow from power by a coup d'état, and Italy's unconditional surrender to the allies, the Italian families who were living in southern Albania began to leave the country in fear of retaliation. After Italy's surrender, the German troops were swiftly pouring into Albania from Greece. Thus a new page began in the history of the Albanian nation and Albanian religious communities. Germany did not anticipate long-term strategic and political designs in Albania. Hitler's immediate goal was to establish a base in the Balkans from which to cut British communications with the eastern Mediterranean and to assure the raw materials so essential to the war effort.[60] Given the nature of the Nazi regime, if Germany was going to win the war, Albania sooner or later was going to be involved in Hitler's design of the Arian-race-priority design over other races.[61] The one-year-long German occupation of Albania was characterized on one hand by a struggle against the national liberation movement and on the other by efforts to organize Albanian forces, which would be able to fight effectively against the partisan-communists and eventually be able to preserve order in the country.[62] German atrocities were reported all over Albania. Germans executed hostages in retaliation for civilian shootings of German soldiers and officers – ten for one, or even one hundred for one.[63] However, the German propaganda machine was doing its best to open the eyes and minds of Albanians to the dangers Bolshevism presented to Albanian families, private property, and Albanian traditional values. 'Albanians unite against Soviet pan-Slavism' and 'Mehmet Shehu has desecrated the flag of Scanderbeg,' were among German political slogans widely circulated

---

[60]Jacques, Edwin E., The Albanians: An Ethnic History from Prehistoric Times to the Present, McFarland, North Carolina, 1994, p. 421.

[61]Morozzo della Rocca, Roberto, Nazione e Religione in Albania (1920-1944), Il Mulino, Bologna, 1990, p. 208.

[62]Ibid., p. 214.

[63]Jacques, Edwin E., Ibid., p. 421.

in Albania.[64] Regarding Albania's religious communities, the Germans were highly indifferent.[65]

In 1944, the German troops abandoned Tiranë and the communist Albanians, led by Enver Hoxha, seized power. On November 29, 1944, one day after Albania's traditional Independence Day, Enver Hoxha marched triumphantly with his troops into the capital Tiranë, assuming control of the entire country.[66] Communism as a totalitarian ideology produced just the same subordination of culture to politics and the same compulsory imposition of an exclusive party ideology on the Albanian society as the previous totalitarian regimes, Fascism and Nazism, that Albania had experienced.[67] The communists treated religion, in both theory and practice, as a reactionary ideology.

In the first years after the war, 1945-1948, the communist state imposed several administrative and economic restrictions against religions, and the Catholic Church and Catholic missions were a special target. Catholic houses and Catholic properties were among the first to be raided and looted by the communists. In May 1945, the Apostolic Delegate Nigris, after his return to Albania from consultations at the Vatican, was arrested and expelled as an undesirable person, while Monsignor Vinçenz Prendushi, Bishop of Durrës and a native Albanian, was appointed as the new Apostolic Delegate, a position which he held for less than a year when he was replaced by Monsignor Gjini. Bishop Prendushi refused Enver Hoxha's proposal to separate the Albanian Catholic Church from Rome and establish a new Independent National Catholic Church whose bishops were going to be appointed by the government. On 20 January 1945, an official from the People's Defense communicated to Monk Teodoro Minisci, superior of the Basilian Mission of Gjirokastër, the order of an immediate expulsion of the Basilians from Gjirokastër. Guarded by armed partisans, the Basilians of Gjirokastër were escorted to an open truck leading them to the People's Defense office of Durrës,

[64]Neuwirth, Hubert, *Qëndresë dhe Bashkëpunim në Shqipëri*, 1939-1944: *Një Analizë His¬torike e Gjedhes Kulturore të Mikut dhe Armikut, Instituti I Dialogut dhe Komunikimit, Tiranë*, 2006, p. 73.

[65]Morozzo della Rocca, Roberto, *Ibid.*, p. 220.

[66]Jacques, Edwin E., *Ibid.*, p. 424.

[67]Russello, Gerard, ed., *Christianity and European Culture. Selections from the Work of Christopher Dawson*, The Catholic University of America Press, Washington D.C., 1998, p. 112.

where they were imprisoned for fifteen days before their departure for Italy. Meanwhile, the superior of the Fier Mission, Monk Daniele Barbiellini, was imprisoned after the monks' residence was raided by the Command of the Third Partisan Division under the suspicion that a radio transmission device was hidden at the Basilian residence. The clergy arrests and killings, the closure of Catholic schools and Catholic Churches, and the prohibition of any Catholic activity by Albanian or foreign Catholics were clear signals of the magnitude of the religious persecution that was going to be executed in Albania. From his prison cell, Barbiellini continued his criticism of the lawlessness and the denial of human rights that was guiding the country, anticipating a distressed future for Albania. With the imprisonment, killings and expulsions of the Catholic missionaries from Albania a new page in Albanian ecclesiastical history began to unfold. Religions' destiny in post-war Albania followed that of the nation. Religion was martyrized as the entire Albanian nation was martyrized.

Then, *Heu, quid [the Catholic missionaries] agant* in Albania? Not much. Rome's pro-union policy was ephemeral and highly inefficient. It appeared that Albania's complicated religious situation was not appropriately understood/evaluated. The initial Congregation for Oriental Churches' expectation for Orthodox *en masse* unions with the Catholic Church was similarly evanescent. The 'investment' in missionary personnel as well as material assistance, which addressed Orthodox requests for Catholic missionaries, and their pleas for union with Rome, bore barren fruit. The Vatican turned away from this policy which was considered to cause more harm than good. In fact, the Vatican, called for any form of Catholic proselytism to be avoided at any cost in Albania.[68] However, on the constructive side, the meager Albanian victory helped Rome in reconsidering its attitude and theology towards the Eastern Churches. The Albanian experience paved the way to a raised consciousness on Christian unity on different terms, as reflected on the Decree on Ecumenism *Unitatis Redintegratio* produced by the Second Vatican Council.

---

[68]Nigris, G. B. Leone, Scutari, Festa di Cristo Re 1940, *Cronache delle Missioni in Albania, 1940*, ABGG, p. 1.

Conclusions

Heu, quid [the travelers, diplomats and Catholic missionaries] agant in Albania?
The travelers, while romanticising Illyria/Albania, this far-away and
mysterious land, created and re-created the Oriental imanology for the
land and the people, a pattern that was followed by Western S.O.E-s and
Catholic missionaries. Both S.O.E-s and missionaries, when on-ground
in Albania, found a suprisingly diferent 'fairyland' with which they were
not cognizant and less adequately prepared to react. Theirs was a meager-
bitter victory. The Albanian elysium remaind exotic and insufficiently
understood by Westerners. It still remains '… as beautiful as fairyland
and as unknown as Africa.'[69]

Bibliography

Archival Primary Sources

Archivio Abbazia Territoriale S. Maria di Grottaferrata (Archive of the
Territorial Monastery of St. Mary of Grottaferrata) – ABGG

- *Cronache delle Missioni in Elbasan, 1938-1939.*
- *Cronache delle Missioni in Elbasan, 1940.*
- *Cronache delle Missioni Fier, 1941.*
- *Cronache delle Missioni in Gjirokastër, 1942.*
- *Cronache delle Missioni in Albania, Fier 1943.*
- *Cronache delle Missioni in Albania, Argirocastro 1943.*

Books and Articles

Amery, Julian, *Approach March, a Venture in Autobiography*, Hutchinson of
    London, 1973.

Amery, Julian, *Sons of the Eagle. A Study in Guerilla War,* Macmillan Press,
    London, 1948.

Bailey, Roderick, 'OSS-SOE Relations, Albania 1943-44,' in Stafford, David,
    and Jeffreys-Jones, Rhodri, *American-British-Canadian Intelligence Relations
    1939-2000*, Frank Cass Publishers, 2000.

Bailey, Ronald, H., *Partisans and Guerrillas,* Time-Life Books, 1978.

Barker, Elisabeth, *British Policy in South-East Europe in the Second World War,* The
    Macmillan Press, London, 1976.

Bethell, Nicholas, *The Great Betrayal. The Untold Story of Kim Philby's Biggest
    Coup*, Hodder and Stoughton, 1984.

---

[69]Dingsdale, Alan, *Mapping Modernities: Geographies of Central and Eastern Europe,
    1920-2000*, Routledge, 2002, p. 84.

Bhattacharji, Shobhana, 'I Like the Albanians Much: Byron and Three Twentieth-Century British Travellers to Albania,' *Byron Journal*, Vol. 38, No. 1, 2010.

Brewer, Robert T., 'Albania, New Aspects, Old Documents,' *East European Quarterly*, XXVI, No. 1, March 1992.

Byron, Baron George Gordon, *The works of Lord Byron: in Verse and Prose. Including his Letters, Journals, etc., with a Sketch of his Life*, Silas Andrus & Son, Hartford, 1851.

Campbell, O.J., Rothschild A, and Vaughan, S., eds., *Twelfth Night*, The Bantam Shakespeare, New York 1964.

Crampton, R. J., *The Balkans Since the Second World War*, Longman, 2002.

Davis, 'Trotsky,' *Illyrian Venture. The Story of the British Military Mission to Enemy-Occupied Albania 1943-44*, The Bodley Head, London, 1952.

Dela Roka, Roberto, *Kombësia dhe Feja në Shqipëri*, 1920-1944, Elena Gjika, Tiranë, 1994.

Destani, D. Bejtullah, ed., *An Englishman in Albania. Memoirs of a British Officer 1929-1955*, The Centre for Albanian Studies, London, 2002.

Dingsdale, Alan, *Mapping Modernities: Geographies of Central and Eastern Europe, 1920-2000*, Routledge, 2002.

Doja, Albert, 'A Political History of Bektashism in Albania,' *Totalitarian Movements and Political Religions*, Vol. 7, No. 1, March 2006.

Dorril, Stephen, *MI6. Inside the Covert World of Her Majesty's Secret Intelligence Service*, The Free Press, 2000.

Douglas, Norman, *Old Calabria*, CosimoClassics, New York 2007.

Fischer, Bernd, 'Resistance in Albania during the Second World War: Partisans, Nationalists and the S.O.E.,' *East European Quarterly*, XXV, No. 1, March 1991.

Fischer, Bernd, J., *Albania at War, 1939-1945*, Purdue University Press, Indiana, 1999.

Gibson, Hugh, ed., *The Ciano Diaries, 1939-1943*, Doubleday & Company, Inc., Garden City, New York, 1946.

Gjeçovi, Xhelal, 'Disa Veçori të Organizimit Politik në dy Fazat e Pushtimit të Vendit,' *Studime Historike*, No. 1-2, 2003.

Gjeçovi, Xhelal, 'Shqipëria dhe Aleatët në Vitet e Luftës së Dytë Botërore,' *Studime Historike*, No. 1-2, 2003.

Hall, Derek, 'Representations of Place: Albania,' *The Geographical Journal*, Vol. 165, No. 2, July 1999.

Hall, Derek, and Danta, Darrick, eds., *Reconstructing the Balkans: A Geography of the New Southeast Europe*, John Wiley and Sons, New York, 1996.

Hibbert, Reginald, 'Dealing with the Dispossessed,' *The World Today*, Vol. 53, No. 5, May 1997.

Hoxha, Enver, *Imperialism and Revolution*, World View Press, Chicago, 1979.

Herman, Michael, 'Diplomacy and Intelligence,' *Diplomacy and Statecraft*, Vol. 9, No. 2, July 1998.

Herman, Michael, 'Intelligence and Policy: a Comment,' *Intelligence and National Security*, Vol. 6, No.1, January 1991.

Hotson, Leslie, *The First Night of Twelfth Night*, Macmillan, New York, 1954.

Jacques, Edwin E., *The Albanians: An Ethnic History from Prehistoric Times to the Present*, McFarland, North Carolina, 1994.

King, Charles, 'Queen of the Highlanders: Edith Durham in the Land of the Living Past,' *Times Literary Supplement*, 4 August 2000.

King, Hyatt A., 'The Musical Side of Norman Douglas,' *Music and Letters*, Vol. 27, No.4, October 1946.

Lucas, Peter, *The OSS in World War II Albania. Covert Operations and Collaboration with Communist Partisans*, McFarland and Company Publishers, North Carolina, 2007.

Morozzo della Rocca, *Roberto, Nazione e Religione in Albania (1920-1944)*, Il Mulino Bologna, 1990.

Murzaku, Ines Angeli, *Returning Home to Rome? The History of the Basilian Monks of Grottaferrata in Albania*, Analekta Kriptoferris 7, Rome, 2009.

Murzaku, Ines Angeli, *Quo Vadis Eastern Europe? Religion and Civil Society after the Fall of Communism*, A Series of Balkan and East-European Studies 30, University of Bologna, Longo Editore, Ravenna, 2009.

Murzaku, Ines Angeli, 'Tutto a Tutti. La Nuova Missione di Evangelizzazione della Chiesa,' in Bianchini, Stefano, *Chiesa Cattolica e Societa Sotterranea ai Tempi del Comunismo. Il Fondo Ricci e le sue Fonti per una Storia delle Religioni in Europa Orientale*, University of Bologna Press, 2009.

Murzaku, Ines Angeli, 'Interne religiöse Spannungen,' in G2W Ökumenisches Forum für Glaube, Religion und Gessellschaft in Ost und West, No. 10, 2008.

Murzaku, Ines Angeli, *Catholicism, Culture, Conversion: The History of the Jesuits in Albania (1841-1946)*, Orientalia Christiana Analecta 277, Pontificio Istituto Orientale, Rome, 2006.

Murzaku, Ines Angeli, 'Rome's Last Efforts towards the Union of Orthodox Albanians,' *The Journal of Eastern Christian Studies*, Volume 58, No. 1-2, 2006.

Murzaku, Ines Angeli, 'The Road to Church Union for Orthodox Albanians,' *The Journal of Eastern Christian Studies*, Volume 55, No. 3-4, 2003.

Neuwirth, Hubert, *Qëndresë dhe Bashkëpunim në Shqipëri, 1939-1944: Një Analizë Historike e Gjedhes Kulturore të Mikut dhe Armikut*, Instituti I Dialogut dhe Komunikimit, Tiranë, 2006.

Patey, Douglas Lane, *The Life of Evelyn Waugh: A Critical Biography*, Wiley-Blackwell, 2001.

Pearson, *Owen, Albania in Occupation and War, from Fascism to Communism*, 1940-1945, Vol. 2, I.B. Tauris, London, 2005.

Petrov, Bisser, 'Great Britain and Resistance in Albania, 1943-1944,' *Balkan Studies*, No. 2, 2006.

Puto, Arben, *Nëpër Analet e Diplomacisë Angleze. Mbi Politikën e Britanisë së Madhe ndaj Shqipërisë gjatë Luftes II Botërore, Albin Tiranë*, 2001, p. 198.

Reed, J. D., *Virgil's Gaze: Nation and Poetry in the Aeneid*, Princeton University Press, 2007.

Shakespeare, William, *Complete Works of William Shakespeare*, Wordsworth Library Collection, London 2007.

Smiley, David, *Albanian Assignment*, Chatto and Windus, The Hogarth Press, London, 1984.

Tilman, W., H., *When Men and Mountains Meet*, Cambridge University Press, 1947.

Torbarina, Josip, 'The Setting of Shakespeare's Plays,' *Studia Romanica et Anglica Zagrabiensia*, Vol. 17-18, 1964.

Wallace, Jennifer, 'A (Hi)story of Illyria,' *Rome and Greece*, Vol. 45, No. 2, October 1998.

Zelka, Luan, 'Për Organin e Parë të Ballit Kombëtar 'Lufta për Shlirimin Kombëtar,' Nëntor 1942-Gusht 1943,' *Studime Historike*, No. 1-2, 2004, pp. 83-94.

A Betrayal Betrayed:
Kim Philby and Albania
Tom Winnifrith

It is difficult to date the beginning of the Cold War. On May 8th 1945, Russian flags were waved in England alongside the Stars and Stripes and Union Jack. Four days later Churchill sent a telegram to Truman referring to an iron curtain stretching from Lubeck to Trieste and Corfu.[1] Before the war had ended there had been confrontations between Communists and Commonwealth forces in Athens and Northern Yugoslavia. In Greece, Yugoslavia and Albania British troops had had a hard task trying to persuade various armed bands from fighting each other rather than the Germans.

Of the three countries in question Albania where there had been no Soviet involvement seemed at first sight the country least likely to cause trouble for the English and Americans. In October 1944 an allied force had landed at Sarande and had cooperated well with the local Partisans. Corfu opposite was freed at the same time. In November British forces marched through the streets of Tirana with the Partisans while Halifax bombers flew overhead. It is true that in this period there had been rather less cooperation with British officers such as Smiley and Amery, trying with difficulty to arrange the escape of non-Communists like Abas Kupi to Italy.

After the war had ended there was a British Military Mission in Albania, and a strong British presence in the United Nations relief organization. But after Hoxha had been elected in December 1945 with a suspiciously overwhelming majority things began to turn sour. Difficulties were put in the way of the Mission and those working with humanitarian aid agencies. A British ambassador was appointed, but did not take up his post. It became clear that many Albanians being arrested

---

[1] This quotation may be found in M. Gilbert *A History of The Twentieth Century* (London, 1998) vol ll, p 665. The more famous Iron Curtain speech at Fulton Missouri in March 1946 makes no mention of Corfu and replaces Lübeck with Stettin. Both changes may be accidental, although the choice of Corfu might suggest that Churchill had become either more optimistic about Albania, or more pessimistic about Greece.

were suspect not because they had been friendly to the Germans but because they had been friendly to the British. Meanwhile, over the border in Greece, pro-Communist forces who had fought the Germans were flexing their muscles, to follow Hoxha's and Tito's example and take over the government. Finally in October a new low was reached when two British ships were blown up by mines in the straits between Corfu and Sarande.

Watching these developments with interest were two groups of people in England. Smiley and Amery could and did say with some justification that the British had backed the wrong side in supporting the Communist Partisans against Abas Kupi, even though the Partisans had been much more active against the Germans. With rather less justification they went on to say that this support was part of a deliberate Communist plot to hand over control of the Balkans to the allies of the Soviet Union. But such a charge was not totally unwarranted, as there was the other group who were concerned with events in Eastern Europe, communist agents planted in the British civil service.

Such a group had been recruited before the Second World War. In the war with Russia and England on the same side they did not have too many conflicts of loyalty. On the whole the Communist resistance was more effective in fighting the Germans than the non-Communist bands, and support for the former was not suspicious. But when the Cold War started matters were different, although the British were slow, perhaps commendably so, in trying to stem this danger. It was not until 1950 that positive vetting was introduced for those with access to secret information. Burgess and Maclean were not unmasked until 1951. Their associate Kim Philby came under suspicion, but his career as a double agent was not finally revealed until 1963.

This background information is necessary for the thesis of this paper that it is wrong to make Philby a scapegoat for the failure of attempts to destabilize the Hoxha regime in the Second World War. Almost every writer on Albania takes this for granted and I plead guilty to making this error. It may seem plausible, and it certainly convenient but there is no certain evidence for it, and indeed much of the evidence for this theory can be interpreted in a different light. In addition those eager to find Philby guilty are, perhaps subconsciously, using him as ammunition for their unfounded thesis of a Communist plot at the heart of the British establishment wrecking any plans for a happy future for the Balkans.

It was in 1984 that Nicholas Bethell in *The Great Betrayal* first put Philby firmly in the dock· although writers like Page had made similar accusations.[2] Philby defected to Russia openly in 1963, and his book *My Silent War* published in 1968 mentions the Albanian operation although not confessing to having betrayed it. Even in a later article in *Izvestzia* Philby, though less coy about his exploits, never gets further than saying that those responsible for sending in the Albanian agents would have been surprised if they had known that a double agent such as he was privy to their plans. He never states what seems now to be assumed as a fact that as the person in charge of the Albanian desk in Washington he was sending off agents with one hand, and informing his masters behind the Iron Curtain with the other of the exact time and place when and where these agents would be dropped. This is how Bethell explains the way in which those arriving in Albania by land, sea or air always seemed to be expected, and were frequently captured or killed. Bethell's theory seemed attractive and plausible. Philby was clearly a traitor to his country, and made a convenient scapegoat for what was clearly an unhappy episode in the history of that country's intelligence service.

Bethell's thesis was the subject of a television documentary again made in 1984. Most subsequent books on Albania and on espionage have accepted it without demur.[3] To their credit the most recent editions of the *Blue Guide* and the Bradt handbook to Albania are less confident.

---

[2] Apart from N. Bethell, *The Great Betrayal*, (London 1982) and B. Page, D. Leitch and P Knightley, Philby: *The Spy who Betrayed a Generation*, (London 1968) the principal books for Philby biography are K. Philby, *My Silent War* (London 1968), A. Boyle, *The Fourth Man* (London, 1979), A.Brown, *Treason in the Blood* (London 1995) and S. Hamnick, *Deceiving the Deceivers* (Newhaven, 2004). Apart from Philby's autobiography these books take Philby's guilt over Albania more or less for granted. The authors often produce later editions damning Philby even more decisively.

[3] David Cornwell for whom Le Carré is the pseudonym was asked to write a book on Philby and indeed wrote the preface to the book by Page, Leitch and Knightley. In September 2009 he wrote an article saying how easy it was to become a double agent, betraying those you were meant to be helping, helping those you were meant to be betraying, quoting Philby and the Albanian spies as an example. There are plenty of such people in his fiction. On August 30th 2010 there was an interview with Cornwell in the Sunday Telegraph by Olga Craig, in which Philby and Albania are again mentioned, although on this occasion it is stated that there was no certain proof of Philby's guilt.

The Wildest Province by R Bailey published in 2008 raises serious doubts, pointing out that there is no concrete evidence to pin the blame on Philby any more than there is any reason to blame left wing influences in the British establishment for their failures to support right wing movements in Albania during the war. But in spite of Bailey the Philby legend persists. In September 2008 the spy writer John le Carré wrote a penetrating account of the secret world of double agents. He mentions Philby and Albania. Obituaries of David Smiley in January 2009 accepted Philby's guilt without reservation. Owen Pearson in his invaluable but not totally reliable account of Albania in the twentieth century is clearly convinced that Philby was responsible for the failure of the operation. He uses several sources for his history, unlike Bethell. Sometimes these sources contradict each other in matters of detail such as the number of agents entering Albania, the dates of their arrival and the degree of their failure. This seems odd in an operation where exact dates and numbers were an essential part of the plan both for those trying to organize it and those trying to defeat it. On the other hand there is a surprising unanimity in our sources about the confusion behind the sending in of agents. Bethell to his credit is scathing about incompetence, and Philby, rather less to his credit, says that the operation was doomed to failure from the start.[4]

This paper holds no brief for Philby. It was said of an earlier Englishman involved in Albania that he was mad, bad and dangerous to know. This was the verdict on Lord Byron given by one of the many ladies who knew him. Philby's wives and mistresses were kinder, but he was undoubtedly bad in betraying his country. He was not, however, mad, and it is not true that it was he who was personally responsible for selecting Albanian agents to embark on a dangerous mission which would lead to imprisonment or death. It is more likely that the whole operation devised by others to help free Albania from Communism was itself mad. This operation involved sending in agents, some of them with a dubious past, into a country geared to ward off a foreign invader. Such a strategy exactly suited the interests of the Hoxha regime, itself guilty of a certain amount of paranoia.

---

[4]Bethell, pp. 180-3, 198–9, Philby, p. 119.

Bethell's book was published in 1984 and describes a campaign that began in 1949. George Orwell whose *1984* was published in 1949 would have been pleased with this neat reversal. Albania in the Hoxha years was very Orwellian. There was the cult of the leader, the slogans embedded on every hillside, the praise of the glorious present as opposed to the miserable past, and the sudden shifts of policy so that Yugoslavia once a gallant friend became like Eurasia a hated foe. There was also squalor, oppression, fear and treachery in both fact and fiction. There were some perpetual heroes like the mythical Comrade Ogilvy and the legendary Scanderbeg, and some perpetual villains like Goldstein and King Zog. But it was easy as Koci Xoxe found to his cost to pass from one category to another. Orwell would have strongly disapproved of any help given to the Hoxha regime and would have had no truck with the likes of Philby who undoubtedly helped the Soviet Union.[5] But in Albania it was not Philby but the Anglo-American authorities who were helping Big Brother Hoxha by providing the gullible Albanian populace with instant traitors as proof of the necessity of his regime.

Orwell's book was largely written in 1948, a year responsible for the title of his novel, and it was in 1948 that the Albanian plot really begins, although in the difficult circumstances of the Greek Civil War some Western agents may have been smuggled across the Greek border in the preceding two years. In 1948 the Cold War became a little colder, although there were triumphs as well as tragedies for the West. The Russians crushed Czechoslovakia, but had to lift the Berlin blockade. In the Balkans they suffered more blows. Tito seceded, and deprived of a safe haven across the Yugoslav border the Communist forces in Greece began to be on the defensive. They were still able to escape encirclement in the North West by retreating to Albania where they could regroup, but Albania was now an isolated part of the Soviet bloc. In Italy the Communists failed to achieve victory in a General Election. Yugoslavia, Greece and Italy were all to provide bases from which anti-Hoxha forces could be launched and to which they could retreat, but all three countries were a little unreliable. Yugoslavia was still a communist state, Italy had a large communist population, and the communist resistance in Greece was though battered not totally broken. All three countries had a substantial

---

[5]One wonders whether Orwell in Spain or in his work at the BBC had any contact with Philby.

Albanian population and all three harboured ambitions on Albanian territory. Attacks launched from them were both dangerous in themselves and a good way of helping Hoxha's propaganda war.[6]

Nor was it the only way. Philby in 1948 was in Istanbul. His work involved covert operations designed to upset the Soviet regime in places like Lithuania, Ukraine and Georgia. Very often this meant working with slightly sinister groups, having a nationalist bias, hostile to Russian control, but with a dubious record in fighting the Nazis. In the Balkans Philby has been linked, albeit with little concrete evidence, with being responsible for the escape from Yugoslavia of an extreme Croatian nationalist, certainly on the German side in the war. The same pattern can be found in the Albanians recruited to fight against the Communists. Obviously their escape to the West showed that they would have been unhappy under Hoxha. Frequently they had sided with the Germans in the war. Again British intelligence was playing into Hoxha's hands.

Some hostile to Communism had made their escape in November 1944 when Hoxha had seized power in Tirana. In the South the Greek border was porous, and escape by this route was made easier if at times more hazardous by the Greek Civil War throwing everything into confusion. Of those who fled not all had collaborated with the Germans, even if their resistance had not been very vigorous. The landowners and Albanian middle class found the new regime distasteful, and their links with the bourgeois class system would be used against them on their return. There was both in the war and after it a division in the ranks of those opposed to Communism. Some were loyal to King Zog forming the Legalitet party, but they were opposed by a republican party called the Balli Kombetar, more nationalist in their outlook, and with a less good record in opposing the Germans who had pandered to this outlook. Those who had managed to escape found refuge in Italy or America. Zog had fled earlier in 1939 and after a variety of homes, including the Ritz Hotel, was in 1948 living in Egypt. The Kryeziu family with their base in Kosova formed a third element in this disparate coalition. They had a good record in fighting the Germans, but were opposed to Zog

---

[6]In October 1951 at the show trial in Tirana of captured Albanian agents, Anglo-American, Italian, Greek and Yugoslav espionage services were expressly linked. See O. Pearson, *Albania as Dictatorship and Democracy* (London, 2006), p. 435.

for family reasons. They also, like the Balli Kombetar, disagreed with his policy of abandoning Kosova.

Members of these three factions were not at ease with each other, and seemed unpromising material to lead a resistance movement. Zog had been out of action for some time. His followers came mainly from the North where escape had been less easy. Even his faithful lieutenant Abas Kupi had had great difficulty crossing the Adriatic. Balli Kombetar members in the South had an exit route via Greece, but had a poor record in the war, and bad relations with the Greeks.

Help was at hand for this motley crew in the shape of a gallant band of ex SOE warriors who had fought with the Albanians against the Germans in the war, and thought that the non-Communist resistance had been badly treated by the British Government. Men like Julian Amery, Peter Kemp and David Smiley had through their energy and forceful personality tried and sometimes succeeded in persuading non-Communist forces to take up arms against the Germans. They now after the war attempted to unite resistance against the Communists. In the war and afterwards the British tended to favour Legalitet, while rather surprisingly the Americans preferred Balli Kombetar leaders like Midhat Frasheri and Hasan Dosti who certainly collaborated with the fascist occupiers.

This preference was odd. We can hardly explain hostility to King Zog by residual hostility to King George III. Amery visited Egypt and was able to persuade Zog and forces loyal to him to join the Movement for Free Albania, although this coalition was to face further trouble.[7]

The Movement for Free Albania was patched together in 1948 and 1949. It is difficult in reading accounts of the manoeuvres of Amery and his friends to avoid a sense of déjà vu. Were they not doing the same things five years earlier? Were there not the same promises of large forces prepared to oust the occupier in both 1944 and 1949? And were not these promises vain? In 1944 it seemed as if the Germans were on the point of defeat, although initially in that year they scored some successes against the Resistance. Similarly in 1948 with trouble in Yugoslavia and its main supporter in Albania, Koci Xoxe, publicly disgraced Communism

---

[7]Pearson, pp. 350-2.

seemed to be doing badly. But in fact Hoxha found it easy to shrug off the efforts of Amery and his friends to overthrow his regime.

As well as involving déjà vu the struggle that began in 1949 and ended rather tamely in 1953 sometimes seems like a Looking Glass War. Britain and America with Philby sometimes at the helm sent in agents, and the Albanians caught some of these agents. Their capture was a victory for Hoxha, and Philby is duly blamed. But the mere dispatch of the agents was a triumph for Hoxha who could claim that brave little Albania was threatened by the Western powers aided by forces of reaction like Balli Kombetar and King Zog emanating from wicked places like Greece, Italy and Yugoslavia. As we shall try to show there is little real evidence for Philby thwarting the Albanian operation, and such an idea relies almost entirely on conjecture. One could as fairly conjecture that Philby in the interests of his Communist masters was at any rate partly responsible for starting the operation.

Amery and Philby had much in common. Eton and Westminster, Oxford and Cambridge, a famous if slightly flawed family. More immediately there was a surprising shared link of service as a journalist in the Spanish Civil War on Franco's side. Amery had served in SOE, many of whose members joined Philby in MI6 after the war. Peter Kemp, who had actually fought for Franco in the Civil War, is a good example. For obvious reasons Amery and Kemp are not anxious in their accounts of their campaigns in Spain, Albania and elsewhere to mention their connection with Philby if there was one. In his book Philby calls Kemp his friend.

Nobody would wish to call the likes of Amery, Kemp and Smiley traitors. Their devotion to their country is obvious, and there is something rather touching both about their romantic patriotism and their loyalty to old friends like Abas Kupi. None of these loyal patriots is exactly modest about their achievements, and Amery in particular is keen to claim the credit for welding together an improbable alliance of right wing figures to fight the Communists in Albania. The dubious past of some of these figures is not stressed. Oddly Philby appears to have been working with similarly suspect agents in other parts of the Soviet bloc.[8]

---

[8]Philby is understandably reticent about support for nationalist movements in the Caucasus and the Baltic whom the Germans had encouraged to fight against the Soviet Union.

Amery and his friends were able to persuade the authorities in Britain and America that it would be good to send in exiles from Albania to stir up revolution in the same way as they had been sent in to cause trouble for Hitler. They were helped by the fact that people working for SOE in the war were now working for MI6. They were inspired by the feeling that justice had not been done in 1944, and that men like Abas Kupi had been wronged in not receiving support which had been instead wasted on the ungrateful Communists. The myth of a left wing conspiracy dictating British policy in the war is like the Philby legend rather hard to prove.[9] Philby is sometimes used to support this myth, but in 1948 he was not helping the Communists openly, and may well have been on the surface aiding Amery.

By March 1949 Amery and the group around him had succeeded in persuading the British Foreign Secretary, Ernest Bevin, that it was worthwhile to start proceeding against Hoxha in Albania. Bevin was no friend of Communism, but he was a man of massive common sense, and would have normally been reluctant to mount the operation. Rumours of internal discontent in Albania following the disgrace of Koci Xoxe may have helped the case for intervention. It was in the interests of Amery to make much of these rumours, and Philby, stationed in Istanbul, could have helped with exaggeration. There had been some cross-border infiltration from Greece before 1949, although this has not been well documented, and appears to have achieved little. A major effort would require American help and would need to be conducted in secret. Britain had little money, and Bevin did not want to start a Third World War. Albania's neighbours, as we have shown, were unreliable, being both full of communists and unpopular with Albanian nationalists.

So sending in Albanian exiles was always going to be a dangerous mission. It was not going to be the same kind of operation as that conducted by SOE during the Second World War. In that war the Germans were not popular anywhere, although through fear of them or of the Communists some of the population, particularly in the North, were partly on their side. There was also an active if divided resistance against the Germans, and the Allies were winning the war. It has to be

---

[9] R. Bailey, *The Wildest Province*, pp. 277-84, 316-19 and R. Hibbert, *Albania's National Liberation Struggle* (London, 1991), pp. 236-8 show up the lack of concrete evidence for this myth.

repeated that it was not like this in 1949. Communism was not on the brink of defeat. The Hoxha regime, sometimes through indoctrination, sometimes through fear, and sometimes through genuine sympathy had considerable support. There does not seem to have been much going for the other side, although exile circles in America, Italy and Egypt made the most of very little.

In the circumstances it would seem to have been a mistake to mount a campaign in 1949 similar to that waged in 1943. And yet this is precisely what the British did. Good soldiers do not make good spies – loyal obedience is of little use in a world where rules are constantly broken, promises are rarely kept, and flexibility is the order of the day. Gallant heroes like David Smiley trained the Albanian exiles in Malta to take the same paths as they had taken in the war, but after the war these paths led only to destruction and defeat. Even without Philby's help the Communists knew the direction of these paths. We can see evidence of this at the landing ground of Bize in central Albania. Remote but yet close to several major routes this spot had proved to be an ideal place to drop British agents in the war. Several bunkers and the presence of a small army barracks show how Hoxha regarded this site.[10]

This pattern of self-destruction can be traced in a variety of sources. As we have shown and will show these sources often contradict each other. Pearson like Herodotus quotes these contradictory sources without comment. He has a right wing bias, being more interested in Zog than in Hoxha even in the years when Hoxha ruled the roost and Zog had vanished from the scene. Convinced of Philby's guilt he says that the spy in his book confessed to the betrayal of the Albanian infiltrators when he did nothing of the kind. He is also anachronistic in introducing sections of Bethell's book and the rather different account of the American journalist Cyrus Sulzberger, *A Row of Candles* under the years 1949 to 1953 when in fact they were written much later.[11] We must dismiss as an exaggeration the statement after Pearson's visit to Albania in 1957 that Hoxha was rumoured to be responsible for the death of half of Albania's population.[12]

---

[10]In 2007 I visited this site in the company of Dr Bailey.

[11]C. Sulzberger, *A Long Row of Candles* (London, 1969) purports to be diaries written between 1930 and 1959. He has no hesitation in blaming Philby for the disaster in Albania, although he does doubt the wisdom of the expeditions.

[12]Pearson, p.528.

In fact, even some of those caught entering Albania as a result of the Anglo-American initiative were punished with imprisonment rather than with death. As in *1984* where Winston Smith suffers torture, betrays Julia, but ends up loving Big Brother live prisoners were more useful to Hoxha than dead martyrs.

With these reservations and with a few additions from sources not quoted by Pearson we can use this author's third volume to give a rough history of the Albanian missions sent out between 1949 and 1953. British and American archives might be able to add a few details, sort out a few contradictory sources, and provide some answers to difficult questions about why individual missions took the dangerous paths that they did. So far they have shown no direct proof of Philby's guilt, and even from Pearson's less neutral account there are several instances where Philby seems an unlikely figure to blame.

In September 1949 two missions were landed on the Adriatic coast. Both missions were divided into two sections, and from the first section of the first mission all four members were either captured or killed. All five members of the other section of this mission escaped to Greece. The second mission had eleven members, and all members of both sections made a similar escape. We are fortunate to have an account of this mission written by Ekrem Bardha whose brother Sami was a member of the second mission.[13] Sami travelled with four companions walking by night and hiding by day from the coast near the mouth of the river Shkumbin to his native village of Radanj near Leskovik and then across the border. We also hear from Bardha some details of the other section of this party which went a little further west and made a similar escape.

The first party landed at the cove, facetiously called Sea View, on the Karabun peninsula. This had become famous as a landing and departure place in the Second World War, where various heroes like Antony Quayle were not able to achieve very much. This lack of success was due to the presence of a strong Balli Kombetar force in the area. Unimaginatively the British thought that the familiarity of Sea View would be a help to the Albanian arrivals. They may have thought that the Balli Kombetar

---

[13]E.Bardha, *Far Yet Near Albania* (Tirana, 2009), pp. 626. This book is quite certain about Philby's guilt, but gives alternative explanations for the betrayal of Sami Bardha. Not surprisingly it is not exactly clear about the objective or even the direction of these expeditions.

would now be more sympathetic. Even without Philby Hoxha, perhaps aware that the British military mind moves in set grooves, may well have decided to guard old landing grounds. The British themselves had done the same thing in the war with the Home Guard.[14] Hoxha would also have been keen to station strong bands of soldiers loyal to him in Balli Kombetar areas. Thus the waiting party of troops under the command of General Beqir Ballaku may have had nothing to do with Philby who did not assume his official position in Washington until October 10th well after the arrival of both landing parties.

This latter fact might seem an obstacle to the Bethell thesis, although not a fatal one. Philby presumably received some kind of briefing in London about the Albanian operation before departing to Washington. The SOE officers now working now working for MI6 were better with daggers than with cloaks. Casual gossip about using well-tried routes could have given Philby a clue to the first landing. The second landing, which was not such a disaster, also took place before Philby arrived in Washington. Indeed by a fine stroke of irony when the eleven Albanians including Sami Bardha were travelling not very comfortably on a boat called *The Stormie Seas* from Corfu to Albania Philby was comfortably esconced on the SS *Carniola* in the company of a crate of champagne and the aristocratic cartoonist Osbert Lancaster.

Bardha takes up the story of the adventures of his brother's party. There are two main routes from the mouth of the Shkumbin to the Greek border. One goes south via Gjirokaster, the other South-East via Korce. It was according to Bethell to these two towns that the two groups headed, being near the homes of members of the group. Oddly Korce and Gjirokaster seem places unsuitable for starting an anti-Communist movement. Enver Hoxha was born in Gjirokaster and taught in Korce. There was the added complication that the Greeks claimed and had briefly occupied the whole area of Northern Epirus including what they called Argyrokastron and Koritsa. Pearson quoting a different source says that the two parties were told to avoid the two towns. Bardha, having arrived at a safe house in Dangelli, poised rather bafflingly in between the

---

[14]The television documentary *The Real Dad's Army* in January 2009 showed how the Home Guard defended invasion routes from the sea and potential landing grounds from the air. Albanian defenders are likely to have been less elderly and more efficient than Corporal Jones and Private Godfrey.

road to Korce and the road to Gjirokaster, was informed of the death of
Midhat Frasheri and told to abort his mission which appears to have been
a muddle from start to finish, both in its execution and in the confused
recollections of its participants.

Dangelli was the place where the Frasheri family originated and we
can understand the Albanian exiles making for it and then abandoning
their enterprise on learning of Midhat's death. This had occurred by an
unlucky coincidence on the same day as Sami's party had landed, October
2nd. Bad news seemed to have travelled slowly, although not as slowly as in
some accounts whereby the Albanian agents did not hear about Frasheri
until they were in Greece. Foul play was suspected by some, although
Philby on the high seas can hardly have been directly responsible. From
Dangelli, Bardha proceeded to his home in Radanj. This is a village near
the Greek border just off the main road linking Korce and Gjirokaster,
although Bardha's group led by Petrit Butka would seem to have belonged
to the Korce party. No doubt the agents would have wanted to see their
families, although such visits had obvious dangers.

Bardha, although he escaped in 1949, was in fact to be betrayed by
members of his family in 1950. Bethell rather unfairly blames Bardha's
mother for gossiping about the arrival of the her son, but Ekren Bardha
puts the blame squarely on the shoulders of his cousin and adopted
brother, although Philby is also accused.[15] Other members of the party
faced different kinds of danger. We have drawn attraction to Petrit Butka
leading Bardha's group. He led it again in 1950, although on that occasion
he turned back to Greece. Butka is the name of a small village between
Radanj and Korce, and this is where Petrit had his home and expected
some support. But the name Butka should have given those organizing
the expeditions some pause for thought.

Albanian surnames are not always a reliable guide to relationships.
Two members of later expeditions were called Hoxha and Shehu, but
had no connection with the Communist leaders of that name. But we
do come across three other Butkas in Albanian history. Pearson tells us
that a Sami Butka was in charge of the Balli Kombetar section of the
camp in Germany preparing for expeditions to Albania. Bardha mentions
Safrat Butka, a famous Balli Kombetar leader in the war, although not

---

[15]Pearson, p. 408, Bardha, pp.68-74.

one with a good reputation. He was a former headmaster who eventually committed suicide. Ruches in his partisan account of the struggles of the Greeks in Northern Epirus gives Safrat a bad name for burning Greek villages. Safrat Butka was the son of Sali Butka who had fought both Turks and Greeks in the First World War, and was again responsible for much bloodshed in Albania, although hailed as an Albanian patriot.[16]

It would seem that Butka was not really a name to conjure with if starting a revolutionary movement in Albania. Nor really was Lepenica, the name of two cousins who had been captured after landing at Sea View, and according to Pearson were later brutally executed at Korce. The public and savage punishment was unusual, but the Lepenica family like the Butkas had an unusual record. The two cousins Hysen and Sami were probably related to Hysni Lepenica a BalliKombetar leader who had fought both the Italians and Communists in the Vlora area during the war and to Hysni Lepenica who was the nephew of the chief of police in Gjirokaster, and was suspected, with him, of complicity in the murder in 1923 of General Tellini, the Italian delegate to the Boundary Commission. The Greeks were blamed for this murder, and Ruches again is not very polite about the Balli Kombetar leadership, including Hysni Lepenica, or about the earlier episode with General Tellini.[17]

These relationships are conjectural, and may turn out to be as fanciful or remote as that between Essad Pasha and King Zog. But it was a mistake on the part of the English and Americans to rely on Balli Kombetar . They did have a bad reputation in Southern Albania not only among the Communists but among the Greek speaking part of the population. Dragging two Lepenicas through the streets of Korce, though horrible, may have been popular in certain quarters. Amery, son of a famous father, had in 1945 stood for Parliament in company with Randolph Churchill for the double seat of Preston. Both lost. In recruiting young Butkas and Lepenicas Amery also lost support in Albania. It is of course possible that the elder Butka and Lepenica members were perfectly honest patriots, doing what they thought was right for Albania, but in sending younger members of these families the British and Americans were playing into the hands of Hoxha.

---

[16]P. Ruches, *Albania's Captives* (Chicago 1965), pp .157, 171 for Safrat Butka and O. Pearson, *Albania and King Zog* (London, 2004) pp. 63, 92, 105 for Sali Butka

[17]Ruches, p. 120.

The complexities of different factions on the Greek Albanian border were probably too much for military minds not geared to the Balkans. In Greece there was the left-wing ELAS movement and the right-wing EDES movement, the latter quite strong in Epirus. The latter partly found a natural ally in Greek bands striving in Albania to unite Northern Epirus with Greece. We do not hear much about these bands, as they fairly rapidly fell a victim to the Balli Kombetar , strongly nationalist and sometimes fighting with the Germans, and the Communist Partisans, naturally friendly to EDES's enemies, ELAS. In sending Balli Kombetar agents from Greece MI6 risked alienating not just their enemies, the Communists, but the Greeks who disliked Balli Kombetar and even the Balli Kombetar who disliked the Greeks. Towards the end of the war EDES had expelled with some brutality the Tsams, Albanian speaking Muslims, from Greece, and these too cannot have been enthusiastic about agents emanating from Greece.

Thus the long and difficult journey made by the Albanian agents in 1949 was fraught with danger, and did not seem to achieve much. A few leaflets were dropped. Perhaps the purpose of this journey was to prepare the ground for expeditions from the Greek border to the coastal plain and land north of the Shkumbin. For by the end of 1949 the Communists in Greece had been defeated, and a friendly Greece seemed the obvious place from which to launch agents. Travel cannot have been easy in either direction. One wonders how the agents managed for food and money. Tired, hungry and grimy they cannot have been much of an advertisement for their cause, but they lived to fight another day, and presumably encouraged other missions.

In 1950 there were more incursions into Albania, and these were even less successful. Philby was ensconced in Washington and events in this year might seem to furnish proof of his guilt, although there are other explanations for these disasters. In April and May there were raids by sea from Corfu and by land from the Greek mainland into South West Albania, but though those taking part often reached their home villages they were then surrounded, and savage reprisals were taken against the villages. But there could, as we shall see later in the sad story of Sami Bardha's capture, have been treachery in the villages or even homes of the agents. The Americans made an air drop at the same time, and those caught were not executed, but imprisoned in return for giving information to the Sigurimi.[18] Here was another source of treachery. In November there was a rather feeble attempt to drop some Albanians from an aeroplane flown by a Pole. Of the sixteen men originally destined for the Vlore and Kruja areas seven got cold feet. Balli Kombetar had been strong near Vlore, and Abas Kupi came from Kruja, but the remaining nine had different zones selected for them in Martanesh and Lume. The pilot missed his cue the first time, but eventually on November 19th one party was dropped near Bulqize and another near Dega. Bize near Bulqize and Dega were two favourite dropping grounds for SOE in the war and therefore automatically suspect.[19]

The false starts involved in this particular operation give an impression of bungling inefficiency, an impression confirmed as in both cases the parachutists did not arrive in quite the right places. This mistake turned out to be a fortunate one, since the parachutists were able to elude the force waiting for them. Two of the first party and all of the second party escaped to Yugoslavia. One of the first group, Adam Gjura, was convinced that Philby was behind his near capture and the reprisals taken against his family. He declared according to Bethell that only Philby could have given exact names, dates and places. As we have shown dates and places were rather vague in this instance. Names were a sore point because of the reprisals. But Gjura and his party had been on the run for a day before they were intercepted, and it would not have been difficult for the authorities to extract his name from villagers or from those of his party who had been captured. In the case of the second party similar accusations were made by Halil Nagjuti after Bethell had published his book. He escaped, his brother was executed, but the captured parachutists were merely imprisoned.[20]

In between these two disasters we have the tragedy of Sami Bardha's second visit, well described by an eyewitness in the shape of his brother. Sami and his party, once again including Petrit Butka, were escorted to the Greek Albanian border by an English officer, about whom Ekrem Bardha is not very polite. Pearson names this officer as Colonel Daryell

---

[18]Pearson, p. 401. The location of the parachute drop is not specified. Possibly like the previous drops it was in South West Albania, thought to be Balli Kombetar territory and a good place for reprisals.

[19]Bailey, pp. 160-4 for Bize and Dega in the war.

[20]Pearson, p. 412 for the expedition and p 436 for the punishment.

Oakley Hill. This episode took place in October 1950, and once again we have an unfortunate muddle in our sources. Oakley Hill's memoirs give the date of his appointment to a mysterious job in Athens as 1951.[21] The good colonel is the soul of discretion about his time in the Greek capital, regaling us with tedious gossip about nothing in particular in an attempt to conceal the real purpose of his visit. His frequent changes of address give the game away. Oakley Hill was in Athens to provide a base from which Albanian agents could start their missions and to which they could if not captured return.

It is not clear whether it was discretion or forgetfulness that led Oakley Hill to change the dates. Possibly Pearson's account is wrong, but Bardha's description of the English officer rigorously sticking to orders even when wrong fits the bill.[22] It is impossible not to feel some sympathy for Oakley Hill, a man with the unhappy knack of being in the wrong place at the wrong time. In 1941 he had marched into northern Albania with some Yugoslav troops just when Yugoslavia was being overthrown by Hitler. In 1945 he had served as United Nations Relief Officer in Albania where his sympathies for the Zog regime had made him unpopular with the Communists.[23] His political views, his double-barrelled name, and even the sad death of his first wife remind us faintly of Brigadier Wynn-Candy, the hero of the 1943 Powell and Pressburger film, *The Making of Colonel Blimp*. Both men found it hard to move with the times and to deal with dishonest opponents.

Bardha describes how the English officer insisted upon his party taking the prescribed route across the border. This proved dangerous and some of Bardha's companions including Petrit Butka fled back to Greece.[24] At first sight this looks like Oakley Hill, clay in the hands of the likes of Philby, sticking to orders which had been conveniently conveyed to Hoxha. For Philby Oakley Hill may have been a square peg in a square hole. But it would not require a great leap of the imagination for the Albanian government to guard the obvious passes from Greece: Colonel Blimp and

---

[21]Pearson, p .408 and D. Oakley-Hill *An Englishman in Albania*, (London, 2002), p .201.

[22]Bardha, pp. 68–9.

[23]Pearson, p. 564. The entry complaining about Oakley-Hill's unsuitability as head of the United Nations Relief Mission comes rather oddly in the account of the death of his successor Peter Floud in 1960.

[24]Bardha, p .70. Bardha's book contains a photograph of Petrit Butka in America.

the Home Guard had guarded obvious entries to Britain in the war. Sami Bardha managed to give the enemy the slip and arrived again at his home in Radanj. There had been another incursion of agents nearer Erseke than Leskovik, and the atmosphere in the villages along the central area of Albania's southern border was tense. The new arrivals had difficulty in making contact with each other, and eventually their efforts to do so betrayed them. Ekrem Bardha blames two of his cousins for this treachery. Oddly unlike in the episodes near Bize and Dega no reprisals were taken against the Bardha family, although life was not exactly comfortable for them in the three years before they fled to Greece. Sami was not executed immediately but imprisoned. His brother's book suggests that efforts were made to win him to the Communist cause, perhaps to act as a double agent in the ranks of the Albanian exiles, following in the footsteps of the traitor Suleyman Cocli who did go to Greece. Nobly Sami Badha resisted such overtures and was executed in October 1953, although cruelly his family did not find out until 1991.[25]

In the autumn of 1950 a large party of exiles had landed by parachute in northern Albania. Twenty nine of these were killed and 14 captured.[26] The North suffered more than the South in the Hoxha years with old scores from the Second World War being settled, more hostility to feudal institutions and the Roman Catholic Church, and even various blood feuds thrown in for good measure. Along the Greek border with memories of assistance to Greek Communists fairly fresh the Hoxha regime was more popular and therefore could afford to be less savage.

And it was to other areas than the South that the anti-Hoxha movement turned in 1951. Other things had changed. Burgess and Maclean defected in May, and Philby left his post in Washington under something of a cloud shortly afterwards. There were the usual rumours of internal dissent in Albania and wild promises of support from the feudal chief Muhareem Bajraktar who said that he would raise five thousand men against Hoxha.[26] Perhaps this optimism encouraged Washington, now deprived of Philby's services, to send three groups by parachute in July to Gjirokaster, Kavaje and Shkoder. All members of these groups were either captured or killed.[27] It seemed odd with

[25]Bardha, pp. 181–7.
[26]Pearson, p. 418.
[27]Pearson, p. 425. For Bajraktar in the Second World war see Bailey, pp. 191–3.

Philby under suspicion that the operation was allowed to continue. Some did not believe in his guilt, and even, mistakenly and inefficiently, may have gone on keeping him in touch with the general progress of the Albanian operation, although hardly with the precise details. Nonetheless the Albanian government continued to show uncanny anticipation in pinpointing the exact location of enemy arrivals.

One rather sinister explanation both of the continuation of the Albanian operation and its continued failure after Philby had left Washington is that the West allowed the parachute drops to take place, knowing that they were going to fail, but hoping that the failure would unmask the traitor, probably Philby but not proved to be so. This is not an explanation that reflects very well on MI6, sending out Albanians to certain capture or death in the hopes of trapping a British spy. Le Carré would find it perfectly feasible. A more plausible explanation, albeit from a rather disreputable source, is provided by Enver Hohxa who briskly dismissed Philby as being responsible for the failure of any Anglo-American operation. Writing after the publication of Bethell's book and shortly before his own death Hoxha gave all the credit to the admirable security arrangements on the ground in Albania.[28] This explanation, although unpalatable to those who maintain that Hoxha was deeply unpopular throughout Albania, is more palatable than one which makes Anglo-American intelligence such a callous body, using the unfortunate Albanian agents as if they were pawns in a deadly game of chess.

Alternatively there may have been traitors in Anglo-American or Albanian ranks who could have betrayed the various operations after, before, or even during Philby's stay in Washington. Greece, Italy and Yugoslavia were not exactly ideal places from which to launch a mission. There were suspicions about the entourage of King Zog whose supporters now began taking more of a part in the campaign with the North rather then the South as the main focus for infiltration. Indiscretion as well as treachery may have lost lives. Zog and his court were famous for the former fault. There was also the possibility of betrayal under torture. The trial of the fourteen agents captured in October 1950 took place a year later amidst great publicity. Only two were sentenced to death. None of these explanations make comfortable reading in Albania or in

[28] E. Hoxha, *The Anglo-American Threat to Albania*, (Tirana, 1982) p. 426.

England. To do them credit neither Bethell nor Bardha put all the blame on Philby, and both authors mention Albanian treachery as contributory causes of the disaster.

In spite of the failures in July 1951 there were further attempts to introduce agents. In October five men were dropped by the Americans near Diber. They were met by machine guns. Two were killed, and three escaped to Yugoslavia.[29] In 1952 the British began to lose interest in the operation. They claimed that potential infiltrators had low morale, understandable in view of previous failures, and were physically unfit. If they were unable to cope with the terrain in Devonshire, they were unlikely to survive long in Albania. King Zog came to the rescue. He sent some of his royal guard to Albania where they worked in conjunction with Hamit Matjani, an independent character who had entered Albania several times and returned safely to Greece.[30] Matjan's native land was like Zog's the district of Mati, and it was to this district that the agents proceeded from Korce. In Mati they left Zemal Shehu and a wireless operator called Tahir Prenci. In the latter half of 1952 these men gave out increasingly optimistic messages. There was something suspicious about Prenci's Morse Code typing, but he gave the excuse that he had injured his right hand. In May 1953 Matjani returned to Albania and was immediately seized. Rather too late Queen Geraldine had become suspicious about the typing. She had asked Shehu a leading question about her jewellery and had not received a satisfactory reply. It soon turned out that Shehu and Prenci had long been in captivity, that the encouraging messages were false, and that gold, supplies and further parachutists had all fallen into the wrong hands.

In April 1954 all the agents involved in this operation were executed. Matjani was hanged.[31] By the time Zog had left Egypt in a rather

---

[29] Pearson, p .436.

[30] Matjani appears in spite of Philby to have led a charmed life returning several times from forays into Albania. Supporters of the Bethell thesis could argue that as an independent agent, acting more like a brigand than a spy, he did not come into the same category as the other agents.

[31] As in life so in death Matjani broke the mould by being hanged rather than shot. This grisly detail is not meant to show that Hoxha was humane or squeamish, merely that he was cunning. Public executions as practised by the Germans who hanged two women in Gjirokaster, Big Brother in *1984*, and the Americans who showed Saddam Hussein's body on television attracted resentment rather than support.

ignominious fashion for America, the anti-Hoxha coalition in the West was fragmenting, and the attempt to destabilize the Albanian regime was an obvious failure. The last episode with its tragic outcome, unlikely heroine and strange mixture of gullible optimism and lamentable incompetence is an important one. It does show that betrayal could be instigated by forces other than Philby. It does show that stories of Albanian resistance to Hoxha could be fabricated, and often were. Philby may before 1951 have fanned such rumours in his own interests, but even as late as 1953 two years after Philby's departure there were still rumours of unrest in Albania. Stalin's death in March and tension between Hoxha and his deputy Mehmet Shehu in August were supposed to be causes of trouble. In fact the population who for ten years had known nothing except life under Hoxha were not ripe for revolt. Of those who manned the defences on the lookout for enemy agents some acted through fear, some for reasons of expediency, but some were filled with a sense of patriotic duty which was reinforced when such agents obligingly crept over a guarded pass or dropped onto a defended airfield.

Files of the Sigurimi or the KGB or even the Foreign Office may yet turn up proving Philby guilty of betraying Albanians. The thesis of this paper is that so far there is no concrete evidence of guilt, and there are some alternative suggestions as to why the Albanian operation failed. Regimes like that of Hoxha and Big Brother needed scapegoats, and obligingly London and Washington provided their own scapegoat in Kim Philby, a traitor in his country, but one whose true history does not need betraying.

Doubt about Philby's involvement in the betrayal of Albanian agents are raised by Stephen Dorril, *MI6: 50 Years of Special Operations* (London, 2001). In 2013 some of the documents relating to the ironically named Operation Valuable were released by the Foreign Office and can be consulted in The National Archives at Kew (FO 1093-452 and 3). They prove neither guilt nor innocence. Some documents have not been released, some names erased. Sadly they only deal with the year 1949 and end inconclusively with no firm decision as to whether to extend infiltration in Southern Albania to more promising areas in the North.

In general they suggest muddle rather than malice as the main cause of the operation's failure.[32]

Most of the correspondence is from officials in the Foreign Office. Heavyweights like Sir William Strang, Sir Frederick Hoyer Millar and Sir Antony Rumbold give at length their finely balanced opinions. There is more incisive comment from junior officials like Nigel Bicknell, C H Bateman and Lord Talbot de Malahide, an improbable name for a civil servant, and, even more improbably, my wife's godfather. It was he who early on in 1949 complains of a swarm of ideas and paper floating around on the subject, and Bateman complains that an American or Greek not liable to blow the gaff must be a very rare species.

A key figure in the operation is W G Hayter, later Sir William Hayter, ambassador to Moscow and Warden of New College, Oxford. It is he who seems to be dealing with what are coyly referred to as his friends, presumably MI6. Philby was one of these friends, but there is nothing to suggest that he was a false friend. Wartime Balkan experts like Amery, Billy Maclean and Alan Hare are mentioned, but seem outsiders. There is a curt scrawl from Ernest Bevin on May 30 1949 asking for news of progress, and an equally laconic question from Clement Attlee on April 6 asking whether Albanians could be bribed, or, as he puts it, 'are for sale'. The replies from the civil service are masterpieces of tactful evasion.

Beneath this veneer of tact we can see an air of confusion. Tito's secession and the Civil War in Greece made Albania a central domino in a pack of three. Information was hard to find towards the end of 1949 and extension of the operation into Northern Albania was in general favoured because the area appeared to be almost unknown. The presence of a large Albanian population in Macedonia and Kosova seemed an almost unexpected and not very relevant detail. In Albania itself it was known that there were different factions, and the Foreign Office was aware of this, although it had difficulty in balancing these factors when for instance forming the Committee for Free Albania. Zog is described as

---

[32]Recently there has been a little more caution about linking Philby to the Albanian operation. The very recent history of MI6 by K. Jeffery is quick to name Philby as a traitor, but not over Albania, although he does mention the Albanian operation. The title of his book *MI6 The History of the Secret Intelligence Service*, 1909-1949 (London, 2010) perhaps shows that he cuts the story short. C. Andrew, *The Defence of the Realm: The Official History of MI5* (London, 2010) is equally reluctant to pin the blame for Albania on Philby, although again there is plenty about his treason.

a thug by one official, and the Balli Kombetar, not much help in the war, was not wholly trusted. The death of Midhat Frasheri was clearly a blow.

Much of the initiative for Operation Valuable came from the Americans, and here Philby may have made his mark. They were more in favour of the Balli Kombetar than the British were. The Kew papers show that intrusions in the South were met by a well prepared resistance, and many of these expeditions failed. This was not thought to be due to treachery, although there was an obsession with secrecy. There were reservations about letting the Americans, the Greeks, the French and the Italians know about the British plans. A great deal of correspondence involved the problem of a suitable launching pad for the operation. South Germany, Trieste, Corfu, even Turkey are mentioned. Libya was much favoured, but the eventual choice of Malta was considered by some to be unsuitable, being a small place and thus like Jane Austen's description of an English village, a neighbourhood of voluntary spies.

If Philby, a rather less innocent spy, had wanted to make Operation Valuable into a triumph for the Communists he could have done so, although the chronology outlined above is an argument against this. On the other hand there are a great many other ways in which the operation could have been known about by the Albanians and yet continued by the West. General muddle wins many victories and suffers many defeats.

In the People's Service:
Self-image of a communist secret police
Michael Schmidt Neke

This essay does not claim to be a history of the Sigurimi, Albania's communist secret police. It is not more than an attempt to reconstruct their self-image which they cultivated in their official publications as far as these were available to a restricted public without being secret material.

Limited access to official publications is highly relevant in a country which prohibited most of its citizens from reading even basic juridical sources. The law gazette 'Gazeta Zyrtare' came out 4-6 times a year during the 70ies and 80ies containing hardly much more than the composition of a new government and a few laws and decrees like on awarding or withdrawing the Albanian citizenship.[1] Many very basic regulations for everyday life were to be found only in a 'General Collection of the Legislation in Force of the People's Socialist Republic of Albania'[2] which bore on its inner title the restriction 'For Internal Use Only' (*Për përdorim të brendshëm*).

The Sigurimi's place within the communist system of power

The Sigurimi had its origins in the information service of the partisan army, founded on 20th March, 1943, which was celebrated as the Sigurimi's anniversary, and also in a special unit called the People's Defence Division (*Divizioni i Mbrojtjes së Popullit, DMP*) which was formed immediately after the war and whose task was the fight against militant anticommunist resistance.[3] Its officers were trained first by Jugoslav, after 1948 by Soviet (and other East European) experts.

---

[1] In 1988, 'Gazeta Zyrtare' came out in four small-sized numbers with altogether 88 pages; in 2008, more than 220 numbers (including extra numbers) of its successor 'Fletorja Zyrtare' were published with more than 12.000 pages.

[2] Përmbledhës i përgjithshëm i legjislacionit në fuqi të Republikës Popullore Socialiste të Shqipërisë 1945-1985. 2 vols. Tirana 1986

[3] Akademia e Shkencave e RPS të Shqipërisë (ed.): Fjalori Enciklopedik Shqiptar (FESH). Tirana 1985, p. 42 and 197

The Sigurimi was always an integral part of the Interior Ministry (*Ministria e Punëve të Brendshme, MPB*) and was led by a deputy minister. It never ranked as an administrative body on ministerial level. This is different from the Soviet Union where at least after 1954 the functions of the interior minister and the Chairman of the KGB were separated, and from East Germany where the interior ministry was in charge of the German People's Police only but was outranked by a Ministry for State Security (*Ministerium für Staatssicherheit, MfS*, commonly known as Stasi).[4] From 1957 until the collapse of the communist system in 1989, Erich Mielke held this office, thus being not only one of the most powerful, but also one of the most public figures of the GDR.

This did not apply to the Sigurimi. Of course, everyone in Albania knew who the interior minister was, as cabinet lists and reshuffles were published. But an Albanian citizen would not have had access to a public directory from which to learn who was the present deputy minister in charge of the Sigurimi. Such sensitive information was spread by word of mouth only.

This dependence from the MPB had serious consequences as this ministry was always in the centre of the many shake-ups in Albania's communist regime.

Interior ministers were:

Haxhi Lleshi (1944-1946)

Koçi Xoxe (1946-1948)

Nesti Kerenxhi (October-November 1948)

Mehmet Shehu (1948-1954)

Kadri Hazbiu (1954-1980)

Feçor Shehu (1980-1982)

Hekuran Isai (1982-1989 and 1990-1991)

Simon Stefani (1989-1990).

In three cases (Kerenxhi, Hazbiu and Feçor Shehu) the minister was a former head of the Sigurimi. Xoxe, Hazbiu and Feçor Shehu were executed, Mehmet Shehu allegedly shot himself in 1981 after having served 27 years as Prime Minister. Kerenxhi was demoted, but not imprisoned; after 1961, he served as director of the Selenica mines; when he unwisely asked to be allowed to return to Tirana in 1982, on the

---

[4]Only between 1953 and 1955, the Stasi was part of the Interior Ministry after its complete failure to prevent the uprising of June, 1953.

peak of the purges after Shehu's death, he was arrested and interrogated, but not sentenced. Isai and Stefani were prosecuted by Albania's post-communist justice and sentenced in 1994 to five respectively eight years (afterwards reduced to four and six years) in prison. So only Lleshi, a high-ranking partisan commander, evaded the many purges which lasted until 1982/83, and was formal head of state between 1953 and 1982.[5]

Within the system of power, the deputy minister was even more vulnerable than his superior. He always risked to be demoted when he ran foul with his minister or to be sacrificed as his scapegoat, but even if he was loyal to him, he would be hit by the minister's downfall. Being demoted would be the least disadvantage, as a demotion was usually only the first step to be followed by expulsion from the Party of Labour of Albania (*Partia e Punës e Shqipërisë, PPSH*), arrest and trial or internment which could be ordered even without a trial by a government committee.[6]

The Sigurimi was one of the main structures which served the political leadership in controlling the country. Even if police, frontier guards and Sigurimi were all authorities within the Interior Ministry, there were frequent rivalries among them on a local as well as on a national level.[7] Most Interior Ministers (except Kerenxhi and Feçor Shehu) rose to candidate and full membership in the Politburo (*Byro Politike*) of the PPSH, Mehmet Shehu and Isai even to membership in the Secretariate of the Central Committee (*Sekretariat i Komitetit Qendror*), headed by Enver Hoxha as First Secretary.[8]

Within the hierarchical structures of communist systems, the communist party is always the dominant authority; it controls the electoral process and the elected state organs as well as the government which formally is chosen or at least approved by the parliament. Thus, the government is not the country's ruling body but an administrative council. The individual power of the members of the Council of Ministers

[5]For biographies see: Hilë Lushaku: Ministrat e Brendshëm 1912-2007. 2 vols. Tirana 2009, Louis Zanga: Biographies of Prominent Public Figures, in: Klaus-Detlev Grothusen (ed.): Südosteuropa-Handbuch. Vol. 7: Albania. Göttingen 1993, p. 769-777, and: Robert Elsie: Historical Dictionary of Albania. Lanham, Oxford 2004
[6]Michael Schmidt-Neke: Politisches System, in: Klaus-Detlev Grothusen (ed.): Südosteuropa-Handbuch. Vol. 7: Albania. Göttingen 1993, p. 204-208
[7]Ismail Kadare: Pesha e kryqit. Paris 1991, p. 142-143
[8]Louis Zanga: Highest Political Institutions, in: Klaus-Detlev Grothusen (ed.): Südosteuropa-Handbuch. Vol. 7: Albania. Göttingen 1993, p. 747-762

(*Këshill i Ministrave*), as the government was usually termed, depended from their ranking within the party or at least from the backing they enjoyed by members of the party's Politburo or CC Secretariate.

Having political control over the repressive organs meant having control over the political power itself. No wonder that Enver Hoxha's wife Nexhmije, always one of the most influential power brokers, rivalled Mehmet Shehu to get hold of the Sigurimi. Many people believed that she was successful.[9]

The Sigurimi as main instrument of 'class struggle'

Communist secret services are omnipresent but not always visible. There were countless offices of the local Branch of Internal Affairs (*Dega e Puneve të Brendshme, DPB*) which was basically a police station. But everybody knew that an inconsiderate word which was overheard by an officer or informer of the Sigurimi might result in imprisonment or internment; the latter fate would be shared by your family if they were not offered to choose divorce respectively other ways of distancing themselves from you. It would have been futile to argue that the measures of police and Sigurimi were contrary to the constitution, as the relevant political document for the MPB was not the formal legal framework but a secret directive of the PPSH Politburo which apparently was set up by the Sigurimi itself.[10]

Communist societies, especially a deeply family and kinship based society such as Albania, were founded on strong concepts of inclusion and exclusion. In Albania, the communist takeover of November 1944 was not the direct result of a Soviet occupation as in most East European countries, but of the victory of the communist-led partisan army in a war which had changed from a liberation struggle against Italian and German occupiers to a civil war between the old social elites allied with Western orientated forces against those who saw the communist model as the only way to overcome Albania's socio-economic backwardness, even if this mainly pre-capitalist society was far from ripe for a socialist revolution.

Political and military involvement during the war defined not only the individuals' position within the new society but that of their families. 'Good families' were those linked with the partisan war and the

[9]Kadare, Pesha, p. 75
[10]Neshat Tozaj: Pse flas … Retrospektivë. Tirana 1993, p. 93

communist party, 'bad families' were those of the old elites (landlords, officials of the Zog era), of collaborationists, but also of anti-communist fighters of monarchist, republican or tribalist background.

Being a member of a 'bad family' was an inherited fate; it would exclude even children two or three generations later from university education and from climbing the career ladder to a higher step. There were rare chances to climb up, if family members had affiliations with both sides.[11]

'Good families', on the other side, could never be too sure about their future as the constant purges might hit them at any time. The way from a villa in the *bllok* (the nomenklatura ghetto in the centre of Tirana) to a shack in an isolated internment village could be very short.

This was deemed necessary by the incessant need to enforce the class struggle (*lufta e klasave*) which was even elevated to a guiding principle in the introduction to the constitution of 1976.[12] Hoxha outpassed the Stalinist model – especially after the breakup with the Soviet bloc – by creating the image of his country and his party as being entrenched in an all-front struggle against the remnants of the toppled old elite who would always try to get hold of the reins of power, even by ideological subversion which infested parts of the party itself, and at the same time as being beleaguered by very many external enemies who also aimed to substitute the 'people's power' by a pro-Western, pro-Jugoslav or pro-Soviet regime. 'Work, Readiness, Vigilance' (*punë, gatishmëri, vigjilencë*) was an omnipresent slogan, especially in factories and other economic units. The metaphorical 'siege' (*rrethim*) made the intensification of the class struggle mandatory, its main instrument being the Sigurimi.

A pseudo-religious perception of Good and Evil served the Party's goal to establish Albania as the first atheistical state in the world. The cult of the martyrs of the Christian churches and of the Muslims were substituted by the cult of the 28,000 martyrs (*dëshmorë*) who had fallen during the partisan war and of the martyrs of socialist reconstruction. This could be a soldier or member of the frontier guards who was killed

[11] e.g. Luan Omari became one of the highest-ranking scientists although his father Bahri had been shot after the war as a member of a collaborationist administration; what saved Luan (but not Bahri) was the fact that his mother was Enver Hoxha's sister.

[12] See Michael Schmidt-Neke (ed.): Die Verfassungen Albaniens. Wiesbaden 2009, S. 199

in a skirmish with the Greeks, a police officer shot on duty, a Sigurimi officer who died while fighting diversants, or even a civilian who accidentally died while protecting other peoples' life or public property. The Sigurimi immortalized the memory of their fallen comrades not only in their review, but especially in the 'Silent Heroes' book series and in an illustrated commemorative book.[13] The most celebrated heroes were those who managed to infiltrate 'diversionist' groups, thus using the enemy's resources against themselves. So, in the early 50ies the Sigurimi annihilated a group of exile Albanians parachuted by the Italians; they then used their wireless set to create the impression that their operations were highly successful and to order more weapons, money and other goods until they finally uncovered themselves.[14]

On the other hand, the merits of their own 'martyrs' sometimes were camouflaged for many years, and even their family members were treated like traitors, like in the famous case of Pal Mëlyshi, who was killed as a double agent in 1950. His family was severely persecuted as kin of an alleged counterrevolutionary; only decades later Mëlyshi was awarded posthumously the title 'People's Hero' and his family rehabilitated.[15]

'A Dear Weapon for the Party and the People'[16]

As the Sigurimi was one of the most important structures to safeguard the stability of the regime and at the same time dependent from the Party leadership's support, they always stressed their strong links with the Party. The MPB had its own Party committee on whose meetings were reports at least once a year.[17]

But the nadir in the relationship between the Party leadership and the Sigurimi came in 1982 when the last bloody purge shook Albania's policy and three former Interior Ministers met a violent death (Mehmet Shehu, Hazbiu, Feçor Shehu). Nearly one year after Shehu's mysterious death, Hoxha rode a scathing attack against the secret police which had no merits in uncovering the conspiration of the group led by Mehmet Shehu; it was due to the vigilance of the Party, not of the Sigurimi which

---

[13]Për popullin, me popullin 1943-1973. Tirana 1973

[14]Për popullin, me popullin 1943-1973. Tirana 1973, p. 75

[15]Tozaj: Pse flas, p. 93-94

[16]Fjalor Enciklopedik Shqiptar. Tirana 1985, p. 755

[17]NSHTP (1977) 3, (1979) 8, (1980) 8, (1981) 8, (1983) 7, (1987) 8, (1989) 8

had been led by traitors since the dark days of Koçi Xoxe.[18] The name of the brutal pro-jugoslav minister and organizational secretary of the Communist Party who was Hoxha's foremost competitor in the struggle for power in the postwar years became eponymous for relentless and uncontrolled terror.[19]

Former Sigurimi superiors now faced persecution (like Kerenxhi) and trial; Mihallaq Ziçishti, head of the Sigurimi in the 50ies and out of office for decades, was now sentenced to 25 years.[20]

Contrary to some expectations, this did not mark the end of the Sigurimi's power. It was curbed only slightly by the rise of the investigation authority (*hetuesi*) which until then had been subservient to the MPB[21] to a third column of the juridical system besides the courts and the prosecution in the only amendment of the 1976 constitution.[22] This added another repressive structure competing with the Sigurimi, but did nothing to protect civil and human rights, as until 1990, there was not even a reestablishment of the lawyers which had been substituted by 'Legal Support Offices' in 1967.

There was neither an open reevaluation of the Sigurimi's past nor a reformed approach towards its future role and duties in the MPB review. The Party committee within the MPB of course kept in line with the anathema towards the Shehus and Hazbiu and accepted the tightening of the Party's control on the MPB.[23] It was notable that Sigurimi-related texts lost their prominence whereas the vast bulk of the articles in the years after the purge dealt with People's Police affairs.

But within the new balance of power after Enver Hoxha's death when his widow Nexhmije became the spokeswoman of the Party conservatives, the Sigurimi, too, reemerged. Zylyftar Ramizi, deputy interior minister and head of the Sigurimi, became a member of the Central Committee

---

[18]in his last electoral speech: Zëri i Popullit 11.11.1982

[19]Tozaj: Pse flas, p. 50, uses the term 'Koçixoxist' for a ruthless deputy minister. The minutes of the Xoxe trial have been edited: Kastriot Dervishi (ed.): E vërteta e fshehur e një procesi. Gjyqi i Koçi Xoxes, lidhjet e tij me Enver Hoxhën. Tirana 2009

[20]Fjalor Enciklopedik Shqiptar. 2nd ed. Tirana 2008-2009, vol. 3, p. 2992

[21]Tozaj: Pse flas, p. 36

[22]Michael Schmidt-Neke (ed.): Die Verfassungen Albaniens. Wiesbaden 2009, p. 51, 216 (§§ 104-105)

[23]NSHTP (1983) 7

of the PPSH on the IX Congress in 1986. In an editorial, Ramizi defined the role of secret police officers as 'Party workers' (*punëtorë partie*), which implied that he denied the necessity of stricter control of his authority by the Party.[24]

The strength of a secret police depends strongly from their ability to set up a network of informers among the public. It is still an object of speculation how many Albanians were informers of the

Sigurimi and how many fulfilled this duty voluntarily. They will certainly have used an official organization of helpers of the People's Police 'Members of the Groups of Voluntary Cooperation' (*Anëtarë të Grupeve të Bashkëpunimit Vullnetar*, AGBV) which frequently held conferences.[25] (In East Germany, about 80.000 police officers were supported by 177.500 'Voluntary Helpers of the People's Police'[26] which perhaps may give an idea about the relation between police forces and informers.)

In practice, Sigurimi officers were not due to keep close personal links outside of their authority to which here loyalty exclusively belonged. They developed a strong esprit de corps, and in Albania this was achieved by the familiar practice to coerce them to take part in violent excesses like torture and executions. Loyalty was a far more important virtue than a high level of education.[27]

The MPB review now and then asked for their readers' feedback via questionnaires[28] and for their cooperation with reports and other texts.[29] Readers' letters were printed which of course did not offer much criticism, but a lot of admiration and support towards the review in particular and the MPB's efforts in general.[30]

Another form of public presence was in sports. One of the most successful football clubs was the MPB's 'Dinamo'. After the Soviet model all sports clubs of the interior or state security ministries in the Soviet bloc were named 'Dynamo', e.g. the 'Sports Union Dynamo' in East Germany which was headed by State Security Minister Mielke himself. Even two members of this umbrella organization, the Dynamo

---

[24]NSHTP (1986) 3

[25]NSHPT (1978) 9, (1981) 7 and 12, (1982) 7

[26]http://de.wikipedia.org/wiki/Deutsche_Volkspolizei

[27]Tozaj: Pse flas, p. 20, 22

[28]distributed e.g. with NSHTP (1967) 12 and (1970) 12

[29]NSHTP (1969) 6

[30]e.g. NSHTP ((1972) 3, (1975) 7 and 10, (1976) 10

football clubs of Berlin and Dresden, were alternately national champions thoughout the 70ies and 80ies.

Albania's 'Dinamo Tirana' was quite successful, too (several other local 'Dinamo' clubs were not), and was 15 times national champion between 1950 and 1990 thus on a par level with the army club 'Partizani Tirana'.[31]

Other sports activities were less popular: when in 1990 demonstrators and people trying to get into the embassies clashed with police and Sigurimi task forces, the excessively brutal infighters were called 'Sampists' (*sampistë*), but no one was able to explain that term. It is slightly inaccurate; it should be *sambistë*, meaning someone who practices Sambo, a Russian form of combat, an acronym for *samosaš ita bez oružija* (self-defence without arms),[32] a remnant from the time when Albania's agents were trained by KGB instructors.

The Sigurimi's publications

The more the class struggle was enforced, the more publicity was given to the secret service which was to become the object of a cult[33] from the late 60ies on. In 1969 the Sigurimi was awarded collectively the highest decoration, the title 'People's Hero' (*Hero i Popullit*). On the occasion of the 30th anniversary of the Central Information Service of the partisan army in 1973 the Interior Ministry published a large-sized illustrated book on the units of this ministry but clearly focussed on the Sigurimi.[34] This anniversary coincided with the beginning of a series of purges among the exponents of culture, defence and economy which shook Albania's society. As introduction and captions were translated into several languages the volume was also meant for distribution abroad, as were many other publications of that kind celebrating socialism in Albania, Enver Hoxha, Stalin, culture, archeology, architecture, arts, economy and the armed forces.[35] In other communist countries publications of this kind eulogizing the secret police were rarely accessible to foreigners.

---

[31] Alexander D.I. Graham: A Statistical History of Football in Albania. Glendale (Isle of Skye) (ca. 2000), p. 2/3, 2/8

[32] NSHTP (1969) 5 and 6, (1971) 5, (1973) 7, (1980) 11

[33] Tozaj: Pse flas, p. 119-123

[34] Për popullin, me popullin 1943-1973. Tirana 1973[34]

[35] 25 vjet Ushtri Popullore. Tirana 1968

In the same year a series of (at least) nine volumes titled 'Silent Heroes'[36] began to appear which was dedicated to the lives of successful Sigurimi officers.

The main source for the image which the Sigurimi wanted to create of itself is a monthly review published by the Interior Ministry since 1963 until the collapse of the regime in 1990, titled 'In the Service of the People' (*Në shërbim të popullit, NSHTP*). Its predecessor had been the review 'People's Police' (*Policia Popullore*), which was published by the Interior Ministry between 1953 and 1962.[37] This review was not on public sale, at least from November 1968, when it was made available by subscription only.[38] It was never accessible to foreigners.[39]

The official encyclopedia of 1985 defined the goals of NSHTP thus: 'It reflects, propagandizes and and explains in detail the directives of the PPSH for the organs and branches of the Ministry of Interior Affairs, makes known the activity of these organs in the struggle against the interior and foreign enemy, the support they receive by the people while defending the socialist fatherland'.[40]

NSHTP was subtitled as 'political literary organ of the MPB', thus it was not a review for professional instruction. So there are only few articles on forensics and criminalistics;[41] the vast bulk of contents corresponds with the aims given by the encyclopedia. There is a lot of articles which are not linked to the Sigurimi but to the People's Police or the Frontier Guards, but many topics are of common importance for all branches of the MPB.

Each edition had 36 pages; their size changed several times between 28:23,5 cm and 34:24,5 cm.

Editors-in-chief[42] were Qazim Kondi (until June 1968), Frrok Pjetër Gega (until early 70ies), Hasan Petrela (from March, 1972 until ?), Gëzim

---

[36]Heronj të heshtur. Tirana 1973-1987

[37]Fjalor Enciklopedik Shqiptar. Tirana 1985, p. 755

[38]NSHTP (1968) 11, p. 2

[39]Christine B. Körner's meticulous bibliography of the Albanian press, Entwicklung und Konzeption der Presse in Albanien und der albanischen Exilpresse. München 1982, does not mention it. – I thank my colleague Prof. Dr. Emil Lafe of the Academy of Sciences of Albania who furnished me with a collection of 137 copies from 1967 to 1990, thus probably preventing their destruction.

[40]Fjalor Enciklopedik Shqiptar. Tirana 1985, p. 755

[41]e.g. NSHTP (1971) 7, (1982) 4, (1989) 2

[42]The composition of the editorial board is sometimes not given for several years, so

Isufi (from October, 1986 to 1990); at least Kondi and Gega rose to the rank of deputy interior minister. Major reshuffles in the composition of the editorial board were at least in 1968, 1972, 1986 and 1989.

Contributors

In 2009, political infighting in Albania got tougher, as the general elections were set for June, 2009. Among the exchange of mutual vitriolic attacks on the personal integrity of the respective adversary, Edi Rama, the Tirana mayor and chairman of the Socialist Party (PS), a painter by profession, was confronted by the newspaper 'Gazeta 55' – an outspoken supporter of Prime Minister Sali Berisha (Democratic Party, PD) – with drawings which were printed in the November, 1983, edition of NSHTP.[43] Rama, who was 19 years old then, contributed a drawing of two border guards titled 'Comrades in struggle' to a short story on the capture of a 'diversant'. This was – according to 'Gazeta 55' – an irrefutable proof that the opposition leader was not only an offspring of the nomenklatura (his father Kristaq was a well-known painter himself and a long-standing member of parliament), but also a zealous collaborator of the secret police.

So it is worthwhile to check who were the contributors of NSHTP, more or less prominent figures of the communist regime as well as those who rose to some celebrity after its fall.

Name	prominent until 1990	prominent after 1990	contribution in NSHTP
Dritëro Agolli	author	author, member of PS leadership	(1981) 10, (1986) 10
Neptun Bajko	trainer of national football team	trainer of national football team	(1981) 7
Skënder Begeja	criminologist	No	(1971) 5, (1974) 5
Mentar Belegu	historian	No	(1982) 11
Dilaver Bengasi	police officer	No	(1987) 5, (1989) 12

this list is not complete.

[43] http://www.gazeta55.net/index.php?artikulli=3041 of 7th January, 2009. – I have not seen the quoted edition of NSHTP, but Rama's drawing was reproduced by Gazeta 55.

Hamit Beqja	psychologist, publicist	psychologist, publicist	(1986) 12, (1989) 10
Kiço Blushi	author	author	(1976) 11, (1982) 7, (1989) 9
Ilir Boçka	diplomat	foreign minister	(1981) 9
Razi Brahimi	literary critic	communist party official	(1970) 4
Dionis Bubani	author, humorist	author, humorist	(1979) 8, 9, 10
Skënder Buçpapaj	no	diplomat, publicist	(1983) 7
Nonda Bulka	author, satirist	no (died in 1972)	(1968) 1
Aleks Çaçi	author	no (died in 1989)	(1985) 11
Muin Çami	historian	historian	(1979) 6
Neritan Ceka	archeologist	archeologist, politician (Democratic Alliance Party, PAD), interior minister	(1989) 6
Mitro Çela	no	publicist	(1987) 2, 5, 9, (1989) 1, 10, 12
Diana Çuli	author	author, politician (Social Democratic Party)	(1989) 1
Frrok Çupi	no	author, politician (PD, PAD)	(1974) 6, (1976) 7, (1981) 10
Petro Dhimitri	no	publicist, first editor-in-chief of Republican Party organ	(1980) 6, (1981) 8, 11
Limos Dizdari	composer	composer, politician (PS)	(1987) 1
Ermir Dobjani	no	Public Ombudsman	(1984) 9
Namik Dokle	no	chairman of PS group in parliament, president of parliament, deputy prime minister	(1968) 9, (1989) 6
Anastas Dushku	author	no	(1969) 1, (1971) 8, (1976) 11, (1980) 8, (1982) 1
Bardhyl Fico	artist, cartoonist	artist, cartoonist	(1975) 10, (1976) 7
Valter File	author, poet	author, poet, politician, chairman of short-lived Liberal Party	(1987) 3, (1989) 3
Kristo Frashëri	historian	historian	(1987) 1
Xhemil Frashëri	historian	no	(1970) 11

Frrok Pjetër Gega	deputy interior minister	no	long-time editor-in-chief
Xhelal Gjeçovi	historian	historian	(1986) 3, (1987) 9
Mark Gurakuqi	author, poet	no (died in 1970)	(1968) 3
Hulusi Hako	atheist theoretician	no	(1969) 4
Zihni Haskaj	diplomat, historian	no	(1982) 2, (1989) 2
Paskal Haxhi	jurist	no	(1980) 2, (1981) 8
Kadri Hazbiu	interior minister	no (executed in 1983)	(1979) 3
Myslim Islami	historian	no	(1987) 3
Kol Jakova	author, playwright	no	(1967) 10, (1971) 11
Nasho Jorgaqi	author, screen writer	author, screen writer	(1979) 3; long-time member of the editorial board
Ismail Kadare	author	author	(1984) 4
Muhamet Kapllani	foreign minister	foreign minister	(1989) 6
Teodor Keko	author, poet	author, poet	(1987) 1, 6, 1989 (8)
Vilson Kilica	painter	no	(1989) 3
Viron Koka	historian	no	(1977) 3, (1978) 2, (1982) 10, (1983) 4
Rexhep Kolli	deputy interior minister	no	(1981) 10
Qazim Kondi	deputy interior minister	no	long-time editor-in-chief
Ahmet Kondo	author	no	(1967) 12
Vath Koreshi	author	author, screen writer, minister	(1971) 11, (1986) 12
Teodor Laço	author	minister, leader of Liberal Democratic Union	(1974) 4
Faik Lama	historian	no	(1984) 9
Qemal Lame	jurist, head of investigation authority	no	(1978) 9
Elmaz Leci	no	publicist	(1982) 5, (1986) 6

Nasi Lera	author	no	(1976) 10, (1978) 6, 10, (1979) 3, (1983) 10, (1987) 2, (1989) 2
Dhimitër Ligori	artist, cartoonist	no	(1969) 7, (1979) 7
Veli Llakaj	army officer, chief of General Staff, deputy defence minister (persecuted)	no	(1978) 7
Xhevat Lloshi	publicist, historian	publicist, historian, politician (PS)	(1987) 3, (1989) 10
Petro Marko	author (persecuted)	no (died in 1991)	(1971) 11
Rudolf Marku	author, poet	author, poet, diplomat	(1987) 4
Ligor Mile	historian	no	(1976) 10, (1979) 8, (1980) 7, (1981) 12
Hysni Milloshi	author, poet	leader of Communist Party of Albania	(1970) 12, (1971) 6, 1973 (3), (1989) 1, 3
Paskal Milo	historian	minister, leader of Social Democracy Party (PDS)	(1972) 9
Zyhdi Morava	author (imprisoned)	spokesman of Tirana mayors, Chairman of Writers' League	(1969) 3
Shefqet Musaraj	author	no (died in 1986)	(1971) 11, (1974) 5
Besnik Mustafaj	author	foreign minister, diplomat, author	(1987) 1, 6
Ruzhdi Pulaha	author, playwright	author, playwright, politician (Social Democratic Party, PSD)	(1987) 5, 9, (1989) 2
Selami Pulaha	historian	no (died in 1991)	(1967) 11
Edi Rama	artist	publicist, Tirana mayor, PS leader	(1983) 11
Zylyftar Ramizi	deputy interior minister, head of Sigurimi	no	(1986) 3, (1987) 1
Napoleon Roshi	no	first editor-in-chief of PD organ	(1975) 6, (1978) 9, (1980) 2, 8, (1986) 10, 12, (1989) 4, 7, 8

Frederik Rreshpja	author, poet	author, poet	(1972) 3
Zihni Sako	author, dramatist, ethnographer	no (died in 1981)	(1968) 6, (1969) 5, (1973) 3
Valdete Sala	youth functionary, director of National Library	director of National Library, Soros Foundation	(1987) 4
Eleni Selenica	member of parliament, High Court deputy chairwoman	no	(1974) 9
Halit Shamata	no	interior minister (PD)	(1971) 6
Agim Shehu	no	deputy interior minister (PD)	(1974) 4, (1986) 10, (1989) 9
Feçor Shehu	interior Minister	no (executed in 1983)	(1968) 3, 1970) 1, (1974) 1, 2, (1981) 11
Dhimitër S. Shuteriqi	author, Chairman of Writers' League	no	(1987) 1
Aredin Shyti	no	interior minister	(1969) 2, (1987) 4
Llazar Siliqi	author, poet	no (Interior Minister, PD)	(1968) 3
Shaban Sinani	no	historian, director of National Archive	(1989) 6
Neshat Tozaj	author	publicist	(1968) 5, 9, 10, 11, (1969) 5, (1970) 1, 6, 8, (1972) 10, (1987) 8, (1988) 12, (1989) 12; long-time member of the editorial board
Përparim Xhixha	no	editor-in-chief of PS daily	(1974) 9
Dhimitër Xhuvani	author	screen writer	(1978) 6, (1982) 1, 2, (1986) 6
Bajram Yzeiri	no	interior minister	(1987) 6, (1989) 8

Bujar Zajmi	painter, screen writer	painter, screen writer	(1974) 1 sqq. (picture editor of NSHTP)
Luan Zelka	media historian	no	(1987) 8
Mojkom Zeqo	author, historian	author, historian, culture minister, director of National Museum	(1984) 9, (1987) 5, (1988) 12, (1989) 4

This list is far from being complete, as the sample of NSHTP editions I have used consists of only 137 out of 304 (?) possible. But it shows very clearly that Albania's cultural elite (at least those with a background relevant for a political and literary review) is well represented. Even authors who were persecuted later (like Marko and Morava) published in NSHTP.

That does not mean that everybody would have feel honoured being invited to write for the MPB organ. But to refuse such an invitation was surely not an option, and not every single article will have been an original contribution. Authors' copyrights were not very strong in Albania, as they were mostly state-employed. Authors who had published with some success could apply to quit their jobs and to become full-time writers, getting their wages plus a minuscule royalty for each published work by the Ministry of Education and Culture.[44]

It is also evident, that very many people who had texts or graphs published in NSHTP were still eligible for a political or academic carreer after the fall of communism. So, suggesting that every author of an article or a picture which was ever published in this review was either an officer or a collaborator of the Sigurimi would be totally misleading, especially as NSHTP was not exclusively the organ of the Sigurimi, but of the Interior Ministry.

Thus, it cannot be surprising that Albania's foremost writer Ismail Kadare contributed at least one short story 'Përçmimi' (The Contempt).[45] This text was apparently written in February, 1984, so almost certainly for publication in NSHTP. In 1986 it was republished with only formal corrections in a volume with several of Kadare's short stories[46] but not added to the 12 volume edition of his literary works.[47] At this time,

---

[44]Përmbledhës i përgjithshëm i legjislacionit në fuqi të Republikës Popullore Socialiste të Shqipërisë 1945-1985. Tirana 1986, vol. 2, p. 1340-1341, 1348-1361
[45]NSHTP (1984) 4, 5 (and 6?)
[46]Ismail Kadare: Koha e shkrimeve. Tregime, novela. Tirana 1986, p. 44-74
[47]Ismail Kadare: Vepra letrare. 12 vols. Tirana 1981; volume 9 which contains the

Kadare was in the good graces of the regime again, after difficulties which he faced in the 70ies.

It is a sad and sarcastic story about Aleko, a partisan who marries a former landlady's daughter for never reveiled reasons. Neither he nor his bride are any good-looking, and there is not much love lost between them. The unavoidable consequence of such a mismarriage is that Aleko is ousted from the party as well as from the army. He is reduced to an accountant's job in a wood factory where he tries to climb up again by petty intrigues as well as by subservience towards his superiors. His hopes are crushed by new polical campaigns for awareness against the remnants of the former ruling classes. At the same time, Aleko's mother-in-law who sees her ambitions failing to return to happier times again with the help of her communist son-in-law, is incessantly throwing her desperation, contempt and hate at him, poisoning his life. She even plans to denounce him at the party authorities, but is prevented by a stroke. 'The Contempt' is a multi-layered short story about a man falling into the deep ditch between the 'ruling classes' from which he himself descends and the former 'exploiting classes' with whom he unwisely links himself by a mismarriage. It allows (as many of Ismail Kadare's works do) several interpretations. It could be read (as most Sigurimi officers will certainly have done) as a warning to mix socially with the declassed strata, thus betraying the duty to stay vigilant. But it could also be taken as a scathing criticism against the policy of eternal exclusion of the declassed and their families and against bribery and intrigues which were strongly denounced, nevertheless omnipresent phenomena in every communist society, Albania included.

The guideline for the choice of authors by the editorial board was not the principle: 'police officers writing for police officers, secret police agents writing for secret police agents'; it was the Sigurimi's self-concept as servants and defenders of the people which entitled them to ask the intellectual elite of their people to support them in their efforts.

Model patterns

Other communist secret agencies clung to the Soviet model, thus evoking the revolutionary tradition of the Cheka, founded in 1917, and their first leader, Felix Edmundovich Dzerzhinsky. Of course, it was rarely

particularly delicate novels 'Pashallëqët e mëdha' and 'Nëpunësi i pallatit të ëndrrave' was added with much delay in 1989.

mentioned that the Cheka which was reorganized and renamed many times was not only Stalin's ruthless tool but also the aim of his incessant purges which hit several of their leaders. Especially East Germany's Erich Mielke loved to refer to the MfS officers as Chekists in Dzerzhinsky's tradition.[48] He promoted a cult around Dzerzhinsky, always quoting his idealized characterisation of a Chekist as 'a person with a cool head, a hot heart and clean hands, clear like a crystal' styling himself as his political heir, especially towards his partners (or superiors) of the KGB.[49] One of the elite units of the MfS was the 'Guard Regiment Feliks E. Dzierzynski'.

The Sigurimi did not follow this pattern; there were only rare articles on Dzerzhinsky or the Cheka.[50] This cannot be explained with Albania's secession from the Soviet bloc, as the epoch of Lenin and Stalin continued to be idolized; Hoxha denounced Stalin's successors as traitors of this glorious tradition. But he also stressed that the new Albania was the fruit of the partisans' victory over the occupiers and their collaborators, not – as in most East European People's Democracies – of the liberation by the Red Army.

Accordingly, the Sigurimi was the fruit of the partisan army, not an imitation of the Cheka. That Jugoslav and Soviet instructors had played a decisive role in organising the secret police, was to be forgotten.

Of course, Lenin and especially Stalin were eulogized, but less frequently than one might expect; Stalin's 100th birthday (21 December, 1979) was celebrated thoughout the country, thus stressing Albania's self-concept as the shining beacon of authentic Marxism-Leninism.[51]

Of much greater importance were the national traditions. Beginning with the commemorative celebrations of the 500th anniversary of Skanderbeg's death, the national hero's cult was spread by the MPB review too, referring to his military exploits against the Ottoman invaders.[52]

---

[48] Erich Mielke: Sozialismus und Frieden – Sinn unseres Kampfes. Ausgewählte Reden und Aufsätze. Berlin (DDR) 1987

[49] Feliks Edmundowitsch Dzierzynski – Ritter der Revolution, in: Mielke, p. 267-272; this article was published on 10th September, 1977, on the occasion of Dzerzhinsky's 100. anniversary in the SED party organ, Neues Deutschland. See also: Mielke, p. 273-283.

[50] NSHTP (1981) 7, a brief extract from the memoirs of Dzerzhinsky's driver

[51] NSHTP (1967) 10 (Lenin), (1979) 6, 9, 12, (1980) 1 (Stalin)

[52] NSHTP (1967) 11, (1968) 1, (1978) 1

The most important model – which was the founding tradition of socialist Albania in general – was of course the Antifascist National Liberation War (LANÇ), as the partisans' struggle against the Italian and German occupiers was called. There is hardly an edition of NSHTP which did not evoke this heritage.

Negative models were the police forces in capitalist countries, including the 'revisionist' (Soviet bloc, Yugoslav and later Chinese systems) and of course the police forces of King Zog's regime which were presented as brutal, oppressive and corrupt as a result of being constantly underpaid.[53]

The Look Outside

With all her isolationism, Albania was never a hermetically sealed-off society comparable to North Korea.[54] At least from the 70ies onward, there was access to foreign radio and TV programmes, the favourite being the Italian. Their image of the West was not always realistic, but it served as a counterbalance against the official propaganda.

Although it was not possible to buy imported literature (to which was only limited access in libraries), there existed a good degree of translations of literary works from the ancient cultures to comtemporary authors even though the choice of translated authors was sometimes erratic.

As a political and literary review, NSHTP frequently published short stories and serialized novels by foreign writers. Some of them belonged to the core of the revered progressive authors, like Mark Twain, Jaroslav Hašek, Guy de Maupassant, Henri Barbusse and Graham Greene,[55] others represented different traditions of police and crime fiction like Georges Simenon, Arthur Conan Doyle and Swedish writers' couple May Sjöwall and Per Wahlöö,[56] and others again are unknown figures.[57]

These crime stories (or stories on poverty and social decay) by foreign authors lent credibility to the dark coloured picture of Western societies

[53]NSHTP (1971) 11

[54]Michael Schmidt-Neke: Kann Albanien Nordkorea erklären? Überlegungen zu Phänomenen peripherer Sozialismus-Modelle, in: Albanische Hefte. (2004) 4, S. 14-24; (2005) 1, S. 10-17

[55]NSHTP (1972) 9, (1972) 10, (1974) 5, (1986 (2), (1987) 1-8

[56]NSHTP (1972) 3, 9, 10, (1990) 2

[57]Due to the usual Albanian practice to fit foreign names to Albanian pronunciation, they are sometimes difficult to reconstruct; e.g. J. Grady (NSHTP (1988) 2), Frank Hard (NSHTP (1986) 12), Stanley Reynolds (NSHTP (1986) 3) etc.

which the Albanian media including NSHTP painted on a daily basis, and at the same time they demonstrated Albania's openness towards progressive or at least critical voices from abroad.

The Foreign Enemy

The self-concept of communist Albania – especially in her isolationist period after the break-up with China – was that of an inexpugnable fortress under encirclement from outside by the two imperialist superpowers, USA and Soviet Union, which are helped by the internal enemy, the remnants of the deposed former ruling classes and people misled by them. Thus the inner adversary of the regime was denounced as being an agent of the foreign enemy who threatened not only the socialist system, but Albania's independence itself.

This perception of the enemy was quite commonplace among communist secret services. The East German MfS[58] had much better reason to identify the survival of the SED regime with that of the GDR itself, as history was to show.

Thus the MPB review sketched vivid portraits of the different categories of the enemy:

- Political Emigrants: Communist Albania never made her peace with her anticommunist emigrants, labelling them as collaborationists and war criminals.[59] Albanians who left the country after the liberation, were not allowed to visit the country nor were his descendants. The groupings and regroupings of the fragmented emigration were under keen observation and sometimes even infiltration. Author Nasho Jorgaqi who during the 70ies and early 80ies was a member of the editorial board of NSHTP derided them in a novel on the adventures of a Sigurimi agent who is sent to Western Europe to spy out and infiltrate the emigrant organizations.[60] The abortive attempts to set up a government-in-exile were ridiculed.[61]

- 'Diversants': Emigrants who clandestinely crossed the border into Albania or were parachuted by foreign agencies to commit acts

---

[58]Christian Bergmann: Zum Feindbild des Ministeriums für Staatssicherheit in der DDR, in: Aus Politik und Zeitgeschichte. (1997) 50, S. 27-34

[59]NSHTP (1973) 1

[60]Nasho Jorgaqi: Mërgata e qyqeve. 2nd ed. 2 vols. Tirana 1982

[61]by well-known satirist Nonda Bulka in NSHTP (1968) 3

of resistance, the so-called diversants, were a favourite topic of the Sigurimi propaganda. As they could not openly publish recent cases, they loved to report again and again how after the war such people were hunted down by the Sigurimi with the full backing of the people. This topic was also treated in countless short stories which even by Albanian standards were rather schematic and blunt.

In a chorus with all Albanian media, the world according to NSHTP was black and white: Albania was the best of all possible societies, whereas the capitalist and 'revisionist' countries were stricken by a sea of troubles. Thus the noble task of the Sigurimi was to defend their country and people against any attempt to bring down the 'people's power'.

Which were the basic attributes of this world outside?

1. They were prone to develop to outright fascism by allowing or even encouraging fascist organizations of all kinds to terrorize the people, e.g. the Ku Klux Klan, Italy's neofascist MSI and Germany's NPD and neo-nazis.[62] In several Western countries fascim was in power again, like in Albania's neighbour Greece (1967-1974) or in Chile after the coup of 1973.[63] Even China came under fire,[64] when Albania refused Mao Zedong's Theory of the Three Worlds according to which the Third World countries should rally with China and Albania fighting the imperialist superpowers; this would have meant alliances with the Shah's Iran, Pinochet's Chile and Suharto's Indonesia as well which Hoxha found unacceptable. An editorial of the PPSH organ 'Zëri i Popullit' of 7th July 1977 thus marked the eclipse of the partnership between Beijing and Tirana.

2. Racism was an everyday phenomenon especially in the USA and also a guiding principle in the US foreign policy towards Africa.[65]

3. The superpowers, later China, too, were aggressive and engaged in an armament race.[66]

4. The Western and Eastern societies were prone to crisis and suppression by the respective superpower.[67]

---

[62]NSHTP (1970) 11, (1971) 11, (1973) 7, (1978) 9, (1982) 8
[63]NSHTP (1967) 9, (1970) 5, (1974) 8
[64]NSHTP (1979) 8
[65]NSHTP (1967) 9, (1969) 4 and 10, (1978) 8
[66]NSHTP (1977) 3, (1978) 2, 6, 8, (1980) 3, 7, (1982) 8
[67]NSHTP (1974) 8, (1976) 7

5. Many people outside of Albania were suffering from poverty and social exclusion, education being a privilege for the wealthier strata.[68]

6. Capitalist and revisionist societies failed to give their youth positive goals to achieve, thus all kinds of decadence were widespread: drug and alcohol abuse, pornography, decadent rock music, violent movies etc.[69] (including references to James Bond).[70] This corresponded with Hoxha's stern attitude towards Western decadent influences[71] and the resulting harsh rules for tourists (men were obliged to cut their hair short, no shorts were tolerated outside of the tourist ghettos, reviews and books with 'indecent' pictures were confiscated etc.). But this campaign faded away in the 80ies.

7. Corruption, especially within the police forces, was common and led to the involvement of policemen in crime.[72]

8. With the police being dysfunctional, crime and even terrorism were rampant and an everyday threat for each citizen.[73] Sometimes completely absurd figures on crime were given.[74]

9. While the police forces did neither serve nor protect innocent citizens, they used brutality and terror against the working masses, especially against demonstrators; innumerous cases from the USA, South America, Italy, Germany, Western and Eastern Europe were reported.[75]

---

[68]NSHTP (1967) 9, (1976) 7 and 11, (1982) 7, (1986) 1

[69]NSHTP (1971) 3, 5 and 8, (1974) 2 and 5, (1975) 7 and 10

[70]in a story about Mata Hari, NSHTP (1967) 9. Although the Bond movies of course never ran in the cinemas of communist Albania, references to James Bond are sometimes to be found in Enver Hoxha's writings, especially when he pretended that his long.time prime minister Shehu had been a 'polyagent' whose British code number was BAB-008, surely an allusion to Bond's code 007; Enver Hoxha: Titistët. Tirana 1982, p. 552.

[71]In his electoral speech of 3rd October, 1974, he said: 'They (the imperialists) advise us to turn our country into an inn, with the doors wide open to pigs and sows in pants or with no pants at all, with hair down to their shoulders, and to hippies to bring in their crazy dances to supplant the beautiful dances of our people.', quoted after: Enver Hoxha: Selected Works. Vol. IV: February 1966 – July 1975. Tirana 1982, p. 875

[72]NSHTP (1969) 9, (1970) 3, (1976) 10, (1986) 2

[73]NSHTP (1968) 9, (1969) 5, (1970) 3 and 8, (1974) 6, (1981) 5, (1982) 2, (1989) 7; reports and cartoons on crime abroad are to be found in nearly every edition.

[74]NSHTP (1980) 11, claiming that 5-10 % of the population in the West were imprisoned

[75]NSHTP (1968) 11, (1969) 3, 4, 6, (1974) 1, 4, 6, (1980) 2, (1981) 9, (1982) 5, 12

10. On the other hand, there was a vast amount of public surveillance by the authorities, especially inner secret services.[76]

It seems strange that a highly oppressive authority like the MPB scandalized oppression in other countries. Seemingly the respective reports (which were very frequent between the late 60ies and the early 80ies, but nearly vanished later) were the result of the close links of the PPSH with Maoist splinter parties which were busy in every Western country, publishing monthly and even weekly newspapers which were full of such reports.[77] After the rupture in Chinese-Albanian relations a minority of those parties stuck with Albania, whereas the majority joined ranks with China. Papers like 'Roter Morgen' (Red Morning) of the Communist Party of Germany/Marxists-Leninists (KPD/ML) continued to be frequently quoted by the Albanian mass media.

Thus, the police was seen as an instrument of class struggle. Clashing with anti-government demonstrators in Western countries meant that the police defended the bourgeoisie in power, whereas persecuting anyone who was doubted to be involved in anti-communist activities was deemed necessary as the Sigurimi thus saved the dictatorship of the proletariat as the highest possible form of democracy.

The Internal Enemy

The Foreign Enemy was closely linked to the Internal Enemy using him as his tool to overthrow the People's Power. Part of this category fell in the responsibility of other branches of the MPB that the Sigurimi. Towards foreigners it was always claimed that the Party had created a New Man and that crime had gone for good as a remnant of former class society.

Of course, the police authorities knew better – otherwise their existence would hardly been justified. So, NSHTP had articles on skipping traffic rules and violation of socialist property[78] as well as on criminology.[79]

---

[76]NSHTP (1968) 2, (1974) 5
[77]Friedrich-Wilhelm Schlomann, Paulette Friedlingstein: Die Maoisten. Pekings Filialen in Westeuropa. Frankfurt/Main 1970; Christophe Bourseiller: Les maoistes. La folle histoire des gardes rouges français. Paris 1996; Andreas Kühn: Stalins Enkel, Maos Söhne. Die Lebenswelt der K-Gruppen in der Bundesrepublik der 70er Jahre. Frankfurt, New York 2005
[78]NSHTP (1981) 9
[79]NSHTP (1981) 7, (1982) 4, (1989) 2

The Sigurimi was not interested in petty thefts (that was police business), as long as they could not be linked with political backgrounds. Sometimes links of that kind were deliberately concocted, as MPB officer Neshat Tozaj told in his novel 'Thikat' (The Knives) in 1989,[80] then a literary sensation. Damaging public property could be interpreted as deliberate sabotage or diversion, thus as a political crime.[81] Theft of socialist property was punishable with 4-7 years in prison; in cases of little value (until 200 Lek) it could be sanctioned by disciplinary measures within the economic unit like wage cuts. But if socialist property was deliberately destroyed or damaged, the culprit would have faced up to 10 years in prison, in severe cases (like arson) not less than 5 years, but even a death sentence.[82]

NSHTP could not report on existing anti-regime activities every month as that would have demolished the image of the unbreakable unity between the people and its leadership – 'The Steel Fist Around the Party' (*Grusht çeliku rreth Partisë*). Thus, these activities were fictionalized or dated back in time to the years of war and after-war. There was hardly an edition without a report or a short story which invoked the relentless fight of the Sigurimi and its predecessors against the collaborators of the fascist occupiers, of militant reactionaries and saboteurs of socialist reconstruction, of agents of Greece or the USA, of diversants (meaning people smuggled into the country to build up resistance cests and to sabotage the economy) or clerics. The nearly unvaried topic of these stories was the clandestine efforts of these evil elements clashing with the unbreakable faith and support of the working people for their socialist state, their Party and the Sigurimi, so the enemy always ends up in the hands of the authorities facing their 'well earned punishment'. This manichaeic outlook was supported by drawings which even iconographically distinguished very clear between good and evil, the wrongdoers invariably desperately looking with distorted and unshaven features.

---

[80]Neshat Tozaj: Thikat. Tirana 1989

[81]NSHTP (1978) 1

[82]Penal Code §§ 61-68; see the official commentary: Ismet Elezi (Hrsg.): E drejta penale e RPS të Shqipërisë (Pjesa e posaçme). Tirana 1983, p. 65-102

Conclusion

The Sigurimi had a self-concept of being the main protector of the Albanian people from all dangers that lured within and without the country. Their legitimation – as well as that of the communist regime itself – rose from the victory in the partisans' war against the occupier which had turned into a victorious social revolution. Dissatisfaction with Albanian socialism as it was could not be tolerated as it would inevitably result in the return of the prewar 'feudal-bourgeois' regime or worse. Thus, the Party had every moral right and even the moral duty to crush any form of dissent in the best interest of the Albanian people, as it did not represent – like a party in a Western democracy – a part of public opinion but was the most progressive part of the workers' class which itself was the revolutionary subject. A contradiction between the best interests of the people and those of the Party were not possible as long as the Party stood faithfully to the teachings of the classics of the revolution – which included Stalin, in Albania's case.

The secret police bore the brunt of this noble task to defend socialism, as even the People's Army had to wait for an eventual aggression, whereas the Sigurimi actually had to fight day by day. This self-sacrificing fulfilment of duty towards the Party as well as towards the people entitled them to ask for their own loyalty returned to them: it was the obligation of the people to help them by denouncing any kind of dissent, be it a casual remark of dissatisfaction over political measures, lacks of supply etc. or be it a substantial attempt of militant resistance, and at the same time they would expect the unconditional backing of the Party whom they defended, without wanting to be bothered by political control or even by restiction of their omnipotence by trivia like laws or the constitution.

They saw themselves not only as a part, but as the vanguard of the Albanian people and its ruling working classes, responsible for the exclusion of their enemies. Within this self-concept, there was no space for any qualms or remorse over the terrible things they had to inflict upon members of the same people they were up to defend at any price.

The world's first atheist state: What happened to religion under Enver Hoxha?

Stephen Nash

Mos shikoni kisha e xhamia
Feja e shqiptarit eshte Shqiptaria
(Vaso Pasha, 1825-1892)

Tirana today bears the stamp of economic dynamism, although atavistic glimpses of the Hoxha period can be seen. Walking down Zhane d'Ark boulevard – as Christian a name as one could ask for – affords a view through the traffic and neon lights[1], of an old wall bearing the faded inscription 'Lavdi PPSh', – 'Glory to the Albanian Party of Labour' ie the Communist Party which Enver Hoxha brought to power in 1944. Ghosts from the past continue to haunt Albania and make their presence felt in the political, cultural and faith spheres. One of those ghosts was the banning of religion.

The aim of this paper is to look again at Enver Hoxha's 1967 declaration of an atheist state in Albania, – what might have contributed to his decision to take this measure, and to gauge the effect it had on Albania then, and the lasting effects which are still evident in some way today.

The extreme measures taken by Hoxha against the adherents of all four main faiths – Sunni Moslem, Bektashi, Orthodox and Catholic – seem to us now to have been fundamental abuses of the Albanian people's human rights. Notwithstanding, I did hear a contrary view volunteered in Tirana in October 2011, by a young Albanian of Moslem origin, from Ulcin in Montenegro: he put forward the view that in some ways the Albanians of Albania were lucky to have experienced the banning of religion, as

---

[1] Now renamed Gjergj Fishta avenue after the celebrated Catholic priest, poet and politician, who supported Fan Noli in his attempts to establish a democratic system in Albania during the 1920s. Tirana is going through a spate of street name-changing.

religion has always been one of the main sources of stress and pain in Balkan history.

Anther positive conclusion to be drawn is that the harsh regime under which the faiths suffered for forty five years may have contributed to the tolerant coexistence between the faiths which we see now. As Nicholas Pano concludes in his 'Religion in Albania: The Legacy of the Communist era': 'The spirit of goodwill and harmony that characterizes the interactions among Albania's traditional religious communities appears to have been reinforced by the common hardships they had endured during the Communist era. This enduring spirit, perhaps, is the only noteworthy positive legacy from this lamentable epoch in Albania's history.'[2]

Considerations from the past

Prior to the Hoxha period, religion had generally been seen as a hindrance to nationalism in Albania. This was true for example during the Albanian 'awakening' of the 1880s and 90s, when nationalist leaders believed that religion might not be conducive to the unity of the nation and that it tended to erode homogeneity. An aim of the leaders of the awakening was therefore to keep religion out of politics and out of the public sphere altogether if possible. At that time, it was also recognized that where the state engaged with religion, it was apposite to include all main faith groups, as at the Congress of Lushnija of 27 January 1920, when all four were represented.

King Zog also saw certain problems inherent in religion, – in particular he believed it could compromise Albanian unity, and made the country more susceptible to possibly mischievous foreign influence (eg from Turkey, Greece or Italy). It could be said that he tried, with limited success, to 'nationalize' religion, for example, taking upon himself the right to appoint the national leaders of the various faiths. Although a Moslem himself, Zog pushed a law through in the early 1930s banning the wearing of headscarfs, and he encouraged his daughters to help in the implementation of this policy. He also closed down several madrassas, leaving one only (in 2010 there were at least five).

---

[2]Nicholas Pano, 'Religion and Civilizations in the New Millenium – the Albanian Case', Albanian Center for Human Rights, 2004, p.162

Stalin's warning

The measures against religion taken in 1967 were among the most extreme taken by a regime which lived by extremes. Hoxha was never one for half measures, but his banning of religion took the regime into uncharted territory. Apart from the temporary banning of religion by Robespierre during the French revolution, this was a measure which even the major revolutions of the 20th century, including the Russian and the Chinese, had not taken. Hoxha's Albania was beholden first to the Yugoslavs, then to the Soviets and then to the Chinese: these patrons might have been expected to try to rein Hoxha in when it came to the religion. Efforts were indeed made by his mentors to warn him to take care. Particularly in his conversations with Stalin, Hoxha himself records Stalin's expression of concern in this area, for example during their first face-to-face meeting in Moscow in early 1949 in the wake of Albania's break with Tito's Yugoslavia. This is set out by Jon Halliday in his 'The Artful Albanian − the Memoirs of Enver Hoxha', where Hoxha revels in giving a detailed account of his meeting with Stalin. This must have impressed the readers of the time.[3] Here was the leader of tiny Albania speaking in confidence with the supreme leader of the Communist world:

'From time to time, while I was speaking, Stalin took out his pipe and filled it with tobacco. I noticed that he did not use any special tobacco, but took 'Kazbeg' cigarettes, tore them open, discarded the paper and filled his pipe with the tobacco. After listening to my answer he said:

'You are separate people, just like the Persians and the Arabs, who have the same religion as the Turks. Religion has nothing to do with nationality and statehood'

And in the course of conversation he asked me:

'Do you eat pork, Comrade Enver?'

'Yes, I do!', I said.

'The Moslem religion prohibits this among its believers', he said, 'this is an old, outdated custom. Nevertheless', he went on, 'the question of religious beliefs must be kept well in mind, must be handled with great care, because the religious feeling of the people must not be offended. These feelings have been cultivated in the people for many centuries, and

---

[3]'The memoirs of Enver Hoxha', edited by Jon Halliday, pp. 129-130

great patience is called for on this question, because the stand towards it is important for the compactness and unity of the people'.

Halliday summarises in his Introduction:

'Hoxha makes a point of recording his conversations with Stalin about religion. Stalin urges a cautious line. Less than twenty years later, Hoxha had accelerated his atheism past any other Communist state, even North Korea. Hoxha continues to keep a beady eye out for religion and the reactions to it by other post-Revolutionary states. He castigates the Vatican's differential attitude towards Albania and China in the 1970s. He also derides China's soft approach to Islam, dictated by foreign policy considerations (or ideological capitulation). And Hoxha also scorns the conciliatory line of the then head of the Spanish Communist Party, Santiago Carrillo. Interestingly, Hoxha does not pull his punches on the role of Islam in 'third world socialist' countries. He condemns the Ben Bella regime for adopting what he calls 'Koranic eclecticism' in Algeria (in 1965), particularly because Ben Bella tried to slip this under the rubric of 'socialism'. Albania's decisive action against Islam, at least as an organised force, is a major achievement which deserves much closer study. Unfortunately, Tirana, and even Hoxha himself, usually so prolix on their successes, pay it little attention and give it little coverage in their propaganda.'[4]

It was perhaps in the character of Hoxha to seek advice from his powerful mentors, and then, after cordial meetings, smiles and hand-shaking, to return to Albania and proceed with his own policies and ideologies, paying little or no attention to the advice which he had received. Hoxha appears to have had a built-in belief in his own intellectual superiority which made him all but impervious to outside influence.

Implementing a policy as draconian as Hoxha's declaration of an atheist state is more likely to be feasible in a small country such as Albania than in a larger, more established nation state. The attitudes of other Marxist-inspired states towards Hoxha's 'atheist state' policy was no doubt tinged with curiosity as well as concern . While the bigger eastern bloc states hesitated before going down the same road as Enver Hoxha, they were curious to see what the result might be and whether they

---

[4] ibid, p.15

might implement similar policies themselves. The Albanians were, in a sense, guinea pigs for a social experiment which had not been undertaken elsewhere. The consequences of this are still felt in Albania and the wounds have not yet healed (Archbishop Rrok Mirdita, interviewed on 31 January 2011).[5]

Albania's Faith Background

We need to look briefly at the historical background. The classical description of the faith landscape of Albania during the 20th century is as follows: 70% Moslem (divided between Sunnis and Bektashis), 20% Orthodox Christian and 10% Catholic. This is the breakdown generally given now in 2011 and the one which pertained in 1944 when Hoxha took over the reins of power. (The last census was taken in 1934, when the population of the whole country was under a million). Within Europe, Albania has had a rather unique place, with a small territory playing host to three or four different faiths. On the positive side, Albania, with its reputation as a country of wild political extremes, can also be seen as a touchstone of religious tolerance.

Tirana, not a large city by European standards, has a central Mosque, a Roman Catholic cathedral and an Orthodox cathedral (recently constructed) all within walking distance of Skanderbeg Square, which is named after their 15th century national hero George Kastriot, who was himself born a Christian, forcibly converted to Islam, and who later in life reverted to Catholicism. The world centre of the Bektashi faith – a liberal interpretation of Islam – is situated on the outskirts of Tirana.

The Jewish community of Albania is small, but there has been much celebration recently of the important contribution which Albanians, Christians and Moslems alike, made in saving Jews under the German occupation. Even the pro-German puppet government in Tirana pleaded with the German authorities on behalf of the Jews. During the early 1990s, at least 500 Jews left Albania for Israel and the US, leaving a population estimated at no more than 250. Foundations were laid recently for a new synagogue in Tirana, which will be presided over by Albania's first ever Chief Rabbi, Yoel Kaplan. The ceremony of appointment was attended by Israel's Chief Rabbi, Shlomo Amar.

---

[5] Rrok Mirdita is the Catholic Archbishop of Durres-Tirana and Primate of Albania. I met with him in his office in Tirana in January 2011.

Albania's faith profile and the relative harmony which has existed between the faiths, these are products of the country's sui generis history, as Ismail Kadare told an international conference in Tirana in 2004:

'Conversion, or changing faith from their primary faith Catholicism to the Orthodox faith, and later on, the conversion of some to Islam, has served Albanians as their first school of tolerance. During this process, it became a common fact among Albanians that a part of a family preserved their original Catholic faith, while the other part was converted to the Orthodox or Islamic faith. There are multiple cases of two brothers living under the same roof, one being of the Catholic and the other of the Muslim faith, and so forth; and that was common for entire tribes and regions alike... To such a man, inter-religious hatred seems something alien, something absurd.[6]

During the first millenium AD, Catholicism was Albania's faith. It was not until the schism between Rome and Constantinople that some Albanian Catholics, particularly in the south, converted to Orthodox Christianity. With the later conquest of the Balkans by the Ottoman Empire, Islam was first introduced. This could have resulted in apartheid between Albanian Moslems and Christians. However, because of the idiosyncracies of Albanian society, links between the two faith communities were in general maintained during the following five centuries of Ottoman rule; and Albanians did not lose their national identity.

Ismail Kadare also refers to the 'tragic-comic farce of the banning of religions by the Communist regime.'[7] This would seem to be a historical aberration, for, according to Kadare, 'The foundation of religious matters in Albania is that all three main faiths are equally important and equally legitimate.' Like other commentators, he tends to stress the historical importance of Catholicism:

'The Catholic community, the smallest in number, represents the first faith of the Albanians. As such, it has a unique vertical descent in Albanian history and culture. As such, it has endowed the Albanian nation with fundamental signs and symbols, from George Kastriot to Mother Teresa. In short, it is the most ancient bridge that has never collapsed, and links

---

[6]Ismail Kadare, 'Religions and Civilizations in the New Millenium – the Albanian case', Albanian Center for Human Rights, 2004, p.13
[7]ibid, p.17

Albania with Europe.'[8] This goes a long way to explain why the Catholic Church was singled out by Hoxha for particularly cruel oppression.

In a conversation in Tirana in October 2011, Professor Aferdita Onuzi (Ethnologist at the Academy of Sciences) made similar points, emphasising that Islam was not the ur-religion of Albania, and that Catholicism had deeper roots than Orthodoxy. Synchretism between the faiths, she told me, still abounds: in villages such as Shpati, Christian icons could be found in homes alongside Moslem faith symbols; and in the villages between Burrelli and Mirdita, Moslem men favour Catholic girls from Rreshen as brides, 'to make good Moslem boys'.

The early years of the regime

It is wrong to think of Hoxha's persecution of religion in Albania as stemming solely from the declaration of the atheist state in 1967. The campaign against the faiths began earlier on in his regime ie from 1944, albeit in a less draconian way than it was to assume later on. Paskal Milo, a former Foreign Minister of Albania, in 'Freedom of Conscience in Albania: Catalogue of Abuses – an Historical Survey' ('Conscience and Liberty' conference, 4th Year, No.2 (8), Winter 1992)[9] describes 1944-1949 as the first phase in the campaign against religion:

'...characterized by efforts to weaken the economic and material support of religion, to bring it into discredit by describing the clergy as collaborators with the occupiers of the country...[the regime] limited itself to atheistical propaganda, mainly within the Communist Party organizations, but not among the masses of the people. Meanwhile, it openly declared its own anti-religious attitude. In 1946, the leadership of the Communist Party sent a circular to all regional party committees, in which it instructed them to do everything within their power to curtail religious ceremonies and holidays, without resorting to administrative measures. This...was conditioned rather by the situation at home (the regime did not feel safe enough) and international circumstances (the Western powers, chiefly the United States and Great Britain during the period 1945-46, brought pressure to bear on Hoxha's government to respect democratic rights), was sanctioned in the first post-war

[8] ibid, p.18
[9] Paskal Milo, 'Freedom of Conscience in Albania: A Catalogue of Abuses – an Historical Survey'

Constitution of 1946 which said: 'Freedom of conscience and belief is guaranteed to all citizens…religious communities are free to exercise and practise their religions.'

During this early period, the regime also began to employ economic measures to squeeze the faiths. Land Reform was undertaken during 1946, in which the state took over three thousand hectares of land and 61,042 olive trees from religious institutions. Demands from leading Moslem, Orthodox and Catholic clergy that Hoxha's government should not touch church lands, fell on deaf ears. Milo provides figures for overall destruction of faith sites by the regime as follows: 740 mosques, 508 Orthodox churches and monasteries, 157 Catholic churches, and 530 tekkes and other Moslem holy places.[10]

The cost to Albania

The cost to Albania of Hoxha's atheist state experiment was immense in all spheres. Firstly, there was the human cost, – the broken lives, not only of priests and their supporting practitioners, but also of the faithful who, for one reason or another were condemned to serve terms in the Hoxha's prisons and labour camps for having breached the diktats of the atheist state. Mosques and churches were systematically destroyed or converted into sports halls, clubs or storage space (it is wrong to think that the Moslem faith was spared because of any family affiliation of Enver Hoxha to Islam). The regime made a point of chronicling the destruction of faith buildings: Albania's national film archive contains evidence on film of this campaign.[11]

Paskal Milo provides evidence (ibid, p. 9) of the financial undermining of the Moslem faith. In the early 1950s the budget of the Moslem community stood at 12 million Leks, whereas by 1965 it had dwindled to 2.8 million Leks. During the early years of the Hoxha regime ie from 1944 to 1959, 95 mosques and 60 tekkes were destroyed; in the 1960s, the rate of destruction was even greater. This was during the period of Albania's alliance with the People's Republic of China, at a time when the Cultural Revolution was at its height. As in China, wall newspapers were used to goad the people into implementing the destruction of

[10](ibid, page 8).
[11]Akademia Filmit & Multimedias, www.afmm.edu.al

religion. Enver Hoxha effectively launched his most extreme policy against religion and religious institutions at the 5th. Congress of the PPSh in November 1966.

Early the following year, on 6 February 1967, Hoxha called for a broad frontal attack on clergy and religious institutions of all denominations; and this was followed by instructions from Hoxha to the PPSh sent out in a circular to all party committees in the districts: this bore the title 'On the Fight against Religion, Religious Prejudices and Customs' and urged the party to 'spearhead our struggle against religion, concentrating on religious dogmas, its philosophical principles, especially its idealistic and mystic contents, as well as against religious rites…' As Milo summarises (ibid. p.10): 'The country had to be rid of all gods, religious beliefs and cult buildings and objects. There could be only one god and one cult, to which everyone should offer his services and prayers, the Albanian Zeus – Enver Hoxha.'

By the autumn of 1967, all churches had been closed. Members of the PPSh youth wing were encouraged to seek out religious objects in people's homes, and the regime's campaign also targeted domestic religious practices. School teachers were given to asking their pupils what they had eaten at home on a particular religious holiday. The regime also entered into the area of the naming of children, encouraging parents to give them 'Communist' names, such as Marenglen – comprising Marx, Engels and Lenin – rather than Christian or Moslem names.

The experience of the Catholics

The regime did not desist however from brutality against the clergy during this early period. This was particularly apparent in the campaign against the Catholics. The Catholic clergy was always perceived by Hoxha to constitute a particular threat. This was because its clergy were generally speaking better educated, maintained close links with the Vatican (ie the West in Hoxha's eyes), and were susceptible to accusations of pro-Axis sympathies during World War II.

According to Milo, during the period 1944-49 in Shkodra alone, 30 Roman Catholic priests were shot (ibid, page 8), died in prison or given long terms of imprisonment: 'Throughout the whole period of the Communist dictatorship, the number of Catholic priests who were sentenced, who died in prison or were shot, exceeds the figure of 110.

The Orthodox clergy did not escape …..either, although the dictatorship was not as harsh on it as on the Roman Catholic clergy…[and] in the period of dictatorial rule, 58 Muslim clergymen and intellectuals perished on account of their religious beliefs.'

The Communist regime also passed laws and issued decrees to try and justify its action against the faiths. On 26 November 1949, the Praesidium of the People's Assembly issued Decree No.763 entitled 'On Religious Communities' (ibid, page 8): 'It was guided by the aim of curbing the rights and competencies of the religious communities and putting them in the service of the Communist regime.' The Decree made it clear that 'The religious communities in their activities should cultivate among the faithful the feeling of loyalty to the people's state power.'

This Decree also laid down strict rules regarding relations with the outside world. It was aimed at totally isolating the Albanian religious communities and keeping their contacts with foreign counterparts to a minimum. Article 25 of the 1949 Decree stipulated that religious communities within Albania should only make contact with religious institutions and individuals outside Albania with the prior authorization of the Council of Ministers and the Ministry of Foreign Affairs. Neither could they accept material assistance from foreign countries without the prior authorization of the Council of Ministers. Foreign religious orders and missions were forbidden from opening branches in Albania, and where such bodies already existed, they were to be closed down within one month of the promulgation of the Decree.

The implementation of this draconian Decree made the plight of the Albanian churches and mosques all the more difficult.

During the period 1950-66, atheistic propaganda assumed new proportions, and appeared to be aimed at the total elimination of the clergy and their churches. Religion now appeared to be one of the prime ideological targets of the regime, and sentences were passed on individual Christian and Moslem priests ranging from terms of imprisonment to the death penalty.

Some individual cases of persecution of priests are particularly harrowing. The Catholics of Shkodra were prime targets. In 1945, there was a total of 180 Catholic priests in the country, and by 1949 more than half of these were dead: fifty had been executed, while others died as a result of prolonged periods of torture.

The story of a young Franciscan priest, Father Zef Pllumi, is particularly poignant. He was first targeted by the regime in 1946, at the beginning of the campaign against the Catholics. At the age of 22, Father Pllumi was arrested and charged with possessing arms and plotting an insurrection, – both fabricated charges, although agents of the regime were able to intimidate some of the faithful into believing their accusations. The Franciscans priests were held in their own seminary and tortured there. Father Pllumi was subjected to more than three years of interrogation and torture.

In Shkodra in particular the parishioners continued to attend mass despite the persecution, and this defiance appears to have been instrumental in persuading Hoxha that shutting down the churches and mosques was the only way to put an end to religious practice. In 1967, Father Pllumi was arrested again along with other priests, and was sentenced to 25 years of imprisonment with hard labour. He experienced the barbaric living conditions, mistreatment and torture meted out in seven prisons and labour camps, culminating in a heart attack which he suffered in 1984. He survived this and eventually was released in 1990, to be appointed parish priest of St Anthony's church in Tirana. He wrote a 700-page account of his experiences as a prisoner of Hoxha's regime entitled 'Rrno vetem per me tregue' ('I only live on to tell'),[12] one of the most moving such accounts to come out of this chapter in Albania's history. Father Pllumi died in Rome on 25 September 2007.

The experience of the Moslems

Despite Enver Hoxha's family links to the Moslem faith, he showed no inclination to cushion the country's Moslem practioners from the implementation of the 1967 banning of religion. According to Miranda Vickers, '…the majority of Albania's 1,200 mosques…were either destroyed or turned into warehouses, sports halls or cinemas. Only those religious buildings of great historical or architectural interest, such as the beautiful Ethem Bey mosque, with its graceful minaret in the very centre of the capital, Tirana, were preserved as part of the country's heritage.'[13] Because of their more liberal approach to the tenets of Islam,

---

[12]'Rrno vetem per me tregue', Tirana: Shtepia Botuese 55, 2006
[13]Miranda Vickers, 'Islam in Albania', Advanced Research and Assessment Group, Defence Academy of the United Kingdom, 2008, p.2

the Bektashi Moslems suffered less under Hoxha than did the Sunni Moslems. Their tekkes were less likely to be targetted by the Hoxha regime than the main Sunni mosques, 'due to their small size, often remote rural locations and lack of obvious Ottoman symbolic meaning'.[14] It is generally true now that the Bektashi tend to be represented in the countryside, while the Sunni are stronger in the cities. Since the fall of Communism, the rich Arab countries of the Middle East, Saudi Arabia in particular, have pumped money into the building of new mosques in Albania, although whether these have been a good investment in fostering Albanian Moslem piety is an open question. Moslem missionary work in Albania has grown during the past 15 years. As Miranda Vickers posits: 'Fundamentalist missionaries are making inroads amongst Albania's Muslims mainly in two areas: training of imams and the distribution of religious material.' (ibid, p.3)

Divisions among the Albanian Moslems are also making themselves apparent and causing the sort of 'stress and pain' which my informant from Ulcin referred to (see page 1 above). The Sunni community, formed in 1924, is divided into two distinct factions, whose differences have become accentuated in the laissez-faire religious environment of post-Communism. Miranda Vickers describes the fundamental division thus: 'The Selefi faction is an anti-modernist puritanical school, which promotes a strict traditional interpretation of Islamic doctrine, whilst the Hanefi school advocates a more traditional liberal interpretation of Islam.' (ibid, p. 3). But further divisions have emerged in recent years, particularly in the wake of the tumultuous events of 1997, when Albania imploded after the collapse of the pyramid schemes. These events resulted in the return of the Socialist Party to power, under Fatos Nano (of Tosk, Orthodox Christian background), to replace the government of Sali Berisha (of northern, Gheg, Moslem origin).

According to Miranda Vickers, young Albanian Moslems who were paid to go and study abroad in Moslem countries have been returning to Albania with a 'distorted view of their country's recent past, namely that following Enver Hoxha's persecution of Muslims in 1967, the Socialists unleashed a second crusade against Islam in Albania with their 'coup d'etat' in 1997', (ibid, p4). This bizarre interpretation of the events of

---

[14]ibid, p.3

1997, when Albania all but fell apart as a result of the pyramid scheme collapse, seems only to have emerged with hindsight, and is not, in this author's view sustainable.

Young Albanian Moslems, returning from countries such as Yemen, were only too ready to interpret events in a tendentious manner. According to them, the Socialist Party leaders – the 'former Communists' who had been brought to power with the help of Greece – had launched a crusade against Islam in Albania, which 'closed most of the Arab-Islamic organizations operating in the country…[and this slowed] the process of re-Islamisation of Albanians'. Post 9/11 2001, the climate became even more hostile to zealous Sunni Moslem organizations, and a number of Islamic organizations have now abandoned their work in Albania, (ibid, p.4). The post 9/11 'war on terror', coupled with the antipathy of Albanians towards extremist ideologies, were more probable drivers in the fall-off in support for imported radical Islam.

Miranda Vickers (ibid, p.4) also cites the discovery in 1998 of a cell of Egyptian Islamic Jihad with bases in Tirana and Elbasan, as a trigger for stricter monitoring – doubtless with strong western encouragement – of Islamic associations and foundations. This monitoring will have become more intense in the wake of 9/11, and will have persuaded some of the radical Islamic organizations to leave Albania.

It will be interesting to see what effect, if any, the Arab Spring has on Islam in Albania. The relative success of the Islamists in the elections in Tunisia and Egypt (not only the Moslem Brotherhood, but now also the Salafists in recent polls) is one of the most interesting effects of the Spring.

The atheist state declared

It is important to keep track of the developments in Albania's alliances during the period of Hoxha's rule. The first change in allegiance came in 1948 – only four years after Hoxha had taken power – when Hoxha broke with Tito, after Cominform had denounced Yugoslavia: this led to a purge of pro-Yugoslav Albanians. During the period of Soviet ascendancy, Albania became almost totally dependent on Soviet economic support. But this period was to last only 12 years, and in 1960, the year when the Sino-Soviet dispute began, Hoxha denounced Khrushchev. By 1961, the Soviet Union had broken off diplomatic relations with Albania. Then began the alliance with China which lasted until 1977, ie during the period in which the Cultural Revolution was in full swing. The break with China left Albania almost totally isolated internationally and more than ever a victim of Enver Hoxha's paranoid state of mind.

Hoxha's ideological experimentation went further than any other Communist regime had gone and resulted in a total negation of the basic freedoms enshrined in the Universal Declaration of Human Rights. Fatos Tarifa, in 'Freedom of Conscience in Albania – The End to an Experiment' identified three main areas in which freedom of conscience among Albanians was violated:

1. the abolition of religion and other non-Marxist philosophical world views;
2. the closing off of foreign sources of political, cultural and scientific information;
3. the violation of the right to freedom of opinion and expression.

Tarifa continues: 'The mass movement of 1967, which led to the near total collapse of religion and its institutions in Albania, marked the beginning of a unique experiment in the history of civilization, which even the great Utopians and the Illuminists of the 18th century would not have imagined.'[15]

Mindful of possible opprobrium from other Communist powers, Hoxha's regime was keen to present the campaign to ban religion as a grass-roots movement, not one imposed by Hoxha himself or the regime's hierarchy. In a conversation on 28 January 2011 with Hunusi Hako, who taught Marxism-Leninism and atheism at the Institute of Marxism-Leninism in Tirana, and who advised Hoxha's Politburo on religious matters, I was given this same explication for the policy. Hako told me that the banning of religion did not 'bear Hoxha's stamp' and that there was no text attributable to Hoxha which postulated the measure. The move to ban religion stemmed, he said, from an event which occurred at the Naim Frasheri school in Durres on 6 February 1967. There, an anti-faith movement spontaneously broke out, according to Hako, in which the pupils at the school effectively declared war on religion, calling for the uprooting of faith from people's minds and the destruction of all religious institutions in the country.

---

[15]'Freedom of Conscience in Albania – The End to an Experiment', Fatos Tarifa, Faculty of Philosophy and Sociology, University of Tirana

Tarifa comments on the Naim Frasheri school incident: 'An entire myth was set up concerning this unprecedented movement. The demographic propaganda of the dictatorship presented it as a legitimate movement based on the people's will, and as an initiative of the youth.'[16]

My view coincides more with that of Tarifa, as it seems improbable in the extreme that a policy as radical as the banning of religion could have been delegated by Hoxha to a band of schoolchildren. It was very much in Hoxha's interest though to be able to present his campaign against religion as emanating from the grass roots (Mao pursued a similar tactic in China's Cultural Revolution).

In 1976, Hoxha was to go one step further in enshrining atheism in the constitution of Albania. This appears to have been a controversial step because Hunusi Hako told me on 28 January 2011 that the year before ie in 1975 he had received a draft of Albania's new constitution, which included an article on Albania as an atheist state. Hako objected to this and went to the Secretary of the Politburo, Foto Cami, to register his view that the constitution should speak of freedom of conscience as a goal of the state, but should not insist on Albania's being an atheist state. It appears that Hako's demarche fell on deaf years, because the new constitution contained the following articles:

'The state recognizes no religion whatever and supports atheist propaganda for the purpose of inculcating the scientific materialist world outlook in people' (Article 37).

'The creation of any type of organization of a fascist, anti-democratic, religious, and anti-socialist character is prohibited. Fascist, anti-democratic, religious, warmongering, and anti-socialist activities and propaganda… are prohibited.' (Article 55).

Hunusi Hako told me that he had had a major role in setting up Shkodra's museum of atheism, which was demolished in the early 1990s. A more important building – the Pyramid in Tirana – has been listed for demolition, despite its heritage value in the eyes of many Albanians who had no sympathy with Hoxha. My hope is that the destruction of the Pyramid can be averted.

Tarifa comments on the enshrining of atheism in the constitution as follows:

---

[16]ibid, p.52

'The Party of Labour, which through the Constitution had banned the creation of other political parties in the country, hoped that in the near future this ideology would become the only one existing in Albania. Atheism and Marxism became <u>legal obligations</u> for all Albanian citizens… In the name of the struggle against religion as the opium of the people, Albanian Marxism was itself served to the people as opium. In the name of combating the 'spiritual dictatorship of religion ', another spiritual dictatorship was established in Albania.'[17]

There was, it has to be said, something of a Messianic cult surrounding Hoxha. Having demolished organized religion, it was tempting for him to try and step into the shoes of a Prophet or a Christ figure, and himself become the object of adulation and devotion. His copious works were generally bound within soft leather covers such as you would find on a mosque or church book. A personality cult projected him as a sort of Albanian Messiah promoting the one true religion of Albania, – Albanianism (as defined by Vaso Pasha, the former Ottoman ruler of Lebanon, and as quoted by Enver Hoxha, and referred to by subsequent Prime Ministers and Presidents until the present day: see text reproduced above on page 1 above, in the subtitle to this paper). Having assumed this quasi-theocratic role, Hoxha was not going to brook competition from Albania's established religions.

Following the Chinese model

The consolidation of Albania's relations with China during the 1960s came after Enver Hoxha's 1961 break with the Soviet Union and its East European allies, whom he saw as 'revisionists'. Hoxha claimed that Albania and China comprised an 800-million strong alliance.

The notion of this 'alliance' also gave Hoxha confidence to embark on Albania's 'Ideological and Cultural Revolution', whose aim was to dismantle Albania's faith organizations and eradicate religious influence.

This 'Ideological and Cultural Revolution' constituted the final phase of Hoxha's campaign against the faiths. Its foundations were laid at the PPSh's Fourth Congress in February 1961. This, according to Hoxha, was part of the 'two-front war' which the 'true Marxist-Leninists' ie Albania and China were to wage against the twin dangers of imperialism

---

[17]ibid, pages 52,53

and revisionism. Hoxha claimed that Albania had finished building the 'economic base' of socialism and was now ready to embark on 'complete socialist construction', which would involve an ideological campaign of Communist education.

Hoxha described this campaign thus:

'The complete construction of a socialist society cannot be realized without creating at the same time a new person with new ideas and thoughts, with lofty virtues and morals. The bourgeois and petit bourgeois remnants in the consciousness of the people pose a serious obstacle to the complete victory of socialism in our country. The contradiction between the new socialist base and the capitalist remnants in the consciousness of the people is one of the most important contradictions in the life of our nation. A great effort must be made to overcome this.'

Ideologically beholden to China, Hoxha was both fascinated by and wary of the Cultural Revolution. He claimed that the Cultural Revolution in China did not start in a 'serious' way, but was instigated by the People's Liberation Army and later Peking University. Hoxha expressed disapproval of the fact that China's Cultural Revolution appears not to have been initiated by the Central Committee of the Party. In Albania he did not allow any other institutions to usurp the power of the PPSh's Central Committee when the Ideological and Cultural Revolution and the campaign against religion were launched.

There were aspects of Albania's Ideological and Cultural Revolution which mirrored the tactics employed by the Red Guards in China. The wall newspaper became a tool of propaganda as in China, and was used in various campaigns, including the campaign against religion. Also, in Albania, as in China, bands of students and schoolchildren were used in the movement which began in the spring of 1967. Organized gangs of children were deployed to strip homes of religious symbols, and were also used as informers against practising believers.

The long-term effect of Hoxha's anti-religion policy/ religious pluralism restored

The 1976 constitution in which the Albanian State's opposition to all manifestations of religion was enshrined, remained in force until April 1991, when a constitutional ordinance restored freedom of religion.

Despite the institutional ban on religion, during the period between Hoxha's death in 1985 and the collapse of the Communist regime in 1990, there were increasing calls for the restoration of religious freedoms within Albania. The Albanian Government in May 1990 agreed to the restoration of the right to practise religion in private or in public and to give back other freedoms which the faiths needed in order to function properly. Also in 1990, Mother Teresa came to Tirana and symbolically unlocked the door of the Zemra e Krishtit Catholic Church in Rruga Kavajes which had been closed for worship since 1967.

Since the reopening of Albania to religion, there has been a mushrooming of missionary activity, not only in support of the already existing faiths and churches, but including new persuasions such as Protestants and Evangelicals. (At the end of the Second World War there were barely a thousand Protestants in the country). There has been controversy too, particularly in the influx of funds from abroad to support the construction of new mosques, new Orthodox and new Catholic churches. Because of a lack of seminaries, there has been a continuing dependence on foreign rather than Albanian priests. The unity of the state has not however been in real doubt (this was always the atavistic fear of previous rulers including King Zog and Enver Hoxha), except in 1997, in the aftermath of the pyramid scheme collapse, when religion was not an issue at all in the near break-up of the state.

One example of the new pluralism in religion is the entry into Albania of the (Mormon) Church of Latter Day Saints (LDS). This is chronicled by Nathan Pali in a thesis on the history of the Mormons in Albania.[18] The 1991 Albanian Constitution, he points out, declares that 'The state observes the freedom of religious belief and creates conditions to exercise it.' Since then, Albania has gone from being the first officially atheistic country in the world, to being the East European country with the highest ratio of evangelical Christian missionaries per capita. By 1992, the first LDS missionaries had joined the throng of evangelical proselytizers which were already flooding into Albania. According to Pali, 'Years of religious repression in Albania did not crush religious yearning rather it fostered longing for divine peace and spiritual hope.' Currently the

---

[18]Nathan Pali, Brigham Young University thesis submitted 2008, entitled: 'The Church of Jesus Christ of Latter-Day Saints enters Albania, 1992-1999'

LDS is trying to buy a major site in central Tirana and is also trying to open up in Kosovo.

Especially among the generation of Albanians who lived through the Hoxha regime, there is still a certain apathy towards religion which could be put down to the official abolishing of religion. But, it has to borne in mind that the period of outright abolition lasted for little more than twenty years ie from 1967 until the late 1980s, when under Ramiz Alia's period of office, the atheist state's future was already beginning to look uncertain. That Albania has had its religious freedoms restored is to be celebrated, and it does not seem that religious pluralism will, for the moment, get out of hand or be a cause for concern. There remains a strong secular strain in Albanian life, reflected also in the educational sphere, and this seems healthy. At a time when, in western Europe, societies are having to learn to live with a multitude of faiths including Islam, Albania offers something of a lesson to others in religious pluralism and tolerance.

Albania's National Liberation Struggle: According to another British author

Xhervat Lloshi

Albania's National Liberation Struggle: The Bitter Victory by Reginald Hibbert was published in Albanian in 1993, after being translated by the author of this paper into Albanian less than two years after the English edition was published. For the Albanian historiography of the Second World War, and also for general Albanian public opinion this book by Reginald. Hibbert represents an event that forcibly attracted our attention even in the much overburdened and troubled circumstances in our post-communist but still pre-democratic society. These circumstances focus attention to a book which presents from a new point of view facts and evaluations of a period in which everything that would determinate the destinies of Albania for half a century originated. This is a book that turns to the roots of our historical development, and that difficult task it carries on with seriousness and responsibility demanded by the importance of the World War Two epoch under examination, and by the responsibility of the scholar working with documents concerning the life of whole nation and families down to specific names of still living persons. There is also the inner voice of the consciousness of a man who once lived through this war with all the insights of the experience accumulated of almost five decades.

In the *Preface* the author says: 'My interpretation of all the material is of course my own, and I alone am responsible for it.' But it is exactly this insistence on a whole personal point of view that, in this particular case, represents an index of higher degree of objectivity. The translation and presentation of this work was not an easy task. The main sources were from the 3 volumes of a personal diary of the author, from the British Public Record Office, documents from the memoirs of other British officers who were in Albania in 1943-44, and also from other publications in Albania and elsewhere, including Enver Hoxha's writings, and the book *Struggle for the Balkans* (London, 1990) by Svetozar Vukmanovic-Tempo. The historical writing of Hibbert is very concentrated. Its style also is concentrated, yet restrained, in profound English. Its pages will for a long time continue to be analyzed in various papers and writings by scholars and journalists, and without any doubt it has become a part of the permanent fund of the sources of our historiography. With this concentrated richness of material I would like to attempt with these notes to give some impressions based on the most striking problems, without any pretensions of making a complete or deep analysis.

Two aspects determine the special nature of Reginald Hibbert's work. First, it is published after a series of books by other British officers from one side, and by Enver. Hoxha with his *The Anglo-American Threat to Albania*, on the other. In these circumstances there where there is direct information, we also have if not a virtual polemic, at least a third voice which is very familiar with the other two voices. The pages of this book many a time have parallels with the books by other authors, and their essence can be caught in a real parallel reading of already mentioned various books. Second, this is an edition after the deep upheaval in Albania entering the road to democracy and pluralism. The previous authors had no possibility to profit from such a perspective. Hibbert was fully aware that his book was directly involved in the present day stream of events in Albania.

As already has been pointed by A. Mulita in 'Luftëtari' newspaper (October 10, 1991, with some errors in translated excerpts) in the important British newspaper *The Times* of March 4, 1991, Hibbert opposed a *Times* editorial of February 22 under the title 'Post-scriptum for 1989', and demanded that if Western Powers really desire to help Albania, they must first of all have a better and fuller understanding for the road which brought Albania to this particular situation, and isolated it from the rest of Europe for half a century.

The first sentence of the book reads: 'The Albanian are one of Europe's oldest peoples.' The last sentence is: 'But the fact remains that it was and is the Albanians themselves who determined the fate of their country under the harsh pressures imposed on them not by Britain but by the German war. And eventually it will be the Albanians who will have to deliver a verdict on the outcome.' Between these parameters is the whole content of the book, and in the middle of it is the author himself with this assertion: 'In worldly matters, Albania was to be my university.' One cannot help having a profound respect for an author which writes about Albania within such parameters.

Hibbert's name does not appear at all in Hoxha's book. The head of the mission, Richard Riddell never published a book, and the other British authors neither speak in detail about this mission, nor are so widely based on archive documents. Consequently the whole information contained in of Hibbert's book sounds fresh and unknown. I shall pick up superficially only something that is surprisingly impressive.

Until recently we had the information that Yugoslav communist and co-founder of the Albanian communist party Miladin Popovic was detained by Italian fascists in Peqin. In autumn 1941 he was freed from detention and participated in setting up the Communist Party of Albania. Through Hibbert we learn that Miladin Popovic was already sent to Albania in summer 1939 to contact the Shkodra communist group for the purpose of forming a communist party. The author goes on: 'The 5th Congress of the Communist Party of Yugoslavia was held in the summer of 1940 and Miladin Popovic delivered a report on the situation in Albania. The Congress reaffirmed a resolution which has been adopted in 1928 to the effect that Kossova should properly belong to Albania, in line with the COM intern's injunction that Balkan frontiers should be readjusted in accordance with the principle of self-determination.' (p. 16)

This information is from a Yugoslav author, V. Dedijer (1948), so we have access to other sources which were unavailable in Albania , and later also were buried by Yugoslavs. According to Hibbert, 'The history of the Albanian Communist Party does not mention it: from Enver Hoxha's Korçë-based point of view it went to the wrong address in going to Shkodër.' The Kosova question and the relations with CPY are present through all the work and merit a separate treatment. I would mention only one or two things.

By December 1943, as Hibbert mentions it, Vukmanovic Tempo was reined in by Tito himself. He was told to drop both the idea of a Balkan General Staff, and the suggestion that, if the Albanians of Kosova joined in the national-liberation struggle, they might be able to choose to secede from Yugoslavia. This latter thesis Tempo was told, would have played into the hands of the enemies of the national-liberation struggle in Yugoslavia. (p. 26) It is worthwhile to mention here that precisely at the end of that December took place the Bujani Conference, and in its resolutions was included the right solution of Kosova question after the War. And in that same month in Cairo was prepared a large report, perhaps the most elaborated report on Albania of that time, by Bill Mclean, David Smiley – both of them having been in Albania – and Julian Amery who happened to be also there, and had a keen interest in Albanian affairs during his work in Belgrade in 1940-1941.

Because of its importance, to this Report is dedicated the whole 8th Chapter. In Cairo also was Col. Velebit, Tito's delegate. I am quoting the third point from the Summary and conclusions of the Report: 'In Northern Albania many of the leagues of Bajraktars and tribes could be encouraged to be less pro-German by a declaration on the part of Tito that the future of Kosovo will be left to the Kosovars themselves to decide after the war, and that elections would be held in which the Kosovars would choose their own form of Government and the country in which they wished to live. Col. Velebit has also said that this declaration had already been made and that he could arrange to have it given the widest possible publicity from the Yugoslav side.' (pp. 130-1)

In the authors opinion not only Kosova issue was complicated, but it was not duly estimated before and during the war, because Albania, the Albanian nation and their problems had almost no impact on the consciousness of the governments of the principal Powers. Meanwhile it was the strong national sentiment and the importance of the Kosova issue itself that shaped the Albanian politics. In Përmeti Congress an American liaison officer of Albanian origin, Thomas Stefan, was present as an observer. 'The acts of the Congress of Përmet were authentic Albanian acts, masterminded by the CPA in fulfillment of the Central Committee decisions of mid-May at Helmës, and not masterminded by the CPY.' (p. 147)

I believe I am not going beyond the limits quoting Hibbert's opinion on V. Stojnic and N. Dizdarevic: 'The two officers wore strikingly smart uniforms and made it clear that they belonged to a superior culture. They were very much on their dignity but pleasant and friendly to us. We were struck by their apparent ignorance about events in Albania.' (p. 229)

Paradoxically the new facts in history do not necessarily clarify definitely the truth. They have a great power to re-awake the curiosity of the mass of people, and stimulate scholars to further research, and to write the history in all its complexity. According to Enver Hoxha, it was the AFHQ that proposed to send a military delegation headed by him. An Albanian delegation was sent to Bari in July-August 1944. According to Hibbert, it was Hoxha himself that in March 1944 expressed the desire to send representatives to AFHQ in Cairo and not to Bari. Palmer sent a recommendation to Bari that Enver Hoxha should be invited to Italy, but on May 5 the proposal had been turned down for fear that others would see political implications in such a visit. In connection with these talks is the threat by Enver Hoxha that if BLO would be captured together with the men of Abas Kupi, they would be considered war criminals. According to Hoxha the incident was resolved in the following day: AFHQ didn't dare to continue the action, Palmer was sent to talk over the problem and this time his attitude was more moderate. According to Hibbert, Alan Palmer saw Enver Hoxha again on September 4: 'On this occasion Hoxha withdrew his allegation and threat, saying that they had been made in a moment of passion following the recent deaths of Mustafa Gjinishi and other colleagues at the hands of Quislings and Germans.' (p. 200) It is interesting that in this meeting were also present the American LO and a new addition to the HQ entourage, a Soviet Liaison officer, Major Ivanov. About the liquidation of Mustafa Gjinishi the British author gives an absolutely different hypothesis.

The new data and polemic comments in the Reginald Hibbert's book could be very interesting, but the main stream in it is represented by the National-Liberation Struggle of the Albanian people, the facts and judgments on it. Everything is given by the author on the base of documents with data, names, events, figures, following the best model of a military history. I would give only one example. Enver Hoxha in *Titoites* says: 'In this period was with us also Dushan Mugosha.'. Hibbert speaks concretely: 'Dushan Mugosha had been in Albania since late October 1941.' This is the reason why it is impossible to make another summary of this concentrate, so I am obliged, with great omissions, to quote only something with the aim to give an idea of its fundamental orientation.

In German-occupied Europe, Albania was the only country which did not have any of the Allied armies march into it or through it. Its fate therefore rested in the hands of those who managed to constitute a mass resistance movement within the country. (p. 49) Albania and the Albanians would have to pass through blood and fire if they were to qualify for a good position when peace came. (p. 107) During 1943 the military actions of partisans were still weak, but they hold out against fierce battles prolonged through the winter of 1943-4 and later. Hibbert gives us his opinion that the Partisans were, after all, Albanians standing up to foreigners, and resisting alien rule, and there were individuals why sympathized with them to a greater or lesser degree throughout the North. Sons and daughters of Gheg villagers were to be found in the ranks of the chetas. Even at their worst moments, the Partisans still had filaments of roots among the people and in this way they could draw a thin sustenance. (p. 89)

After the Winter Operation in 1943-1944 the Partisans recovered, their forces were growing up very quickly, and they had the initiative in the battlefield. Even Mclean's report admitted that LNÇ was the only military force of any value in the country. In another report dated May 30 which reached the FO on June 30, one of the conclusions is that LNÇ is the only party in Albania with the same war aims as British ones, which are willing to make sacrifices for them. They were not an agglomeration of feudal or tribal chieftains with personal followers, but an organized party, representing both religions, local divisions and at least 75 per cent of the population in Southern and Middle Albania. 'The primary aim of LNÇ is to rid the country of the Germans. It has been suggested that this is a ruse on their part to obtain further aid from the Allies. The Nation that will go barefoot in the snow, have it homes burned and pillaged, and starve in the mountains as means of deception deserves to succeed. Partisan military successes in Albania have not and cannot, by virtue of the nature of the Country, be as spectacular as elsewhere, but there can be no doubt that the Partisans are waging active war against the Germans.' (p. 140) The expansion of the partisans of ANLA forces in the spring of 1944 was an extraordinary phenomenon, astonishing to the British officers: 'As the National Liberation Army gathered strength in the spring it enjoyed a wave of popular support by virtue of appearing successful, of being Albanian, of advocating the cause of the underdog (that is, of the vast majority of Albanian peasants), and of standing for change, liberty, independence and other values little known in Albania. Many who joined the ANLA must have become disillusioned once the war was over, but there could be no doubt about the vogue for being Partisan which swept through Albania in the middle months of 1944.' (p. 146).

Living and fighting together with the Albanians, the British officers were compelled to live Albanian – to eat, drink, sleep, breathe and think Albanian. Through hard difficulties and conflict situations, knowing that in the registers of Enver Hoxha there was a question about them, all the same Hibbert kept alive the sympathy of the young officer towards the true fighters, and he writes on the page 187: 'We managed to camp near units of the Brigade in the evenings and enjoyed the poignant singing of the Partisans round their camp fires in the warm summer nights.' For him only Partisans were offering something constructive, they were disciplined, condemned crimes, and had high morale. The Albanian partisan resistance was so important that Tito's army indirectly benefited from their operations.

The 11th Chapter is entitled 'The Battle of Dibra'. This is Hibbert's most important historical writing. Here are closely interwoven all the threads of the war and politics, and it posed clearly the basic attitudes and valuations of the author. The battle continued for two months. It was without any doubt a battle against the Germans. They retreated from the area on August 30, having lost some 400 dead and large quantities of war material. The Partisans were fighting half hungry, in ragged clothes and improvised footwear, but their endurance was extraordinary and admirable.

In every war, apart from the two adversary parts, there is also another division. On the one hand, there are people that enter the battlefield and shed their blood. On the other hand, there are people that lead or manipulate it, that gain their profits in the achieving of battle aims or instrument it. This division is evident in Hibbert's book. For the first aspect, he follows closely the documents, and as direct testimony asserts openly that the Albanian people fought a National Liberation struggle. This is also the title of the book. For the second aspect, different from all the other authors involved in writing about this issue, he insists that the picture was much more complex, with endless complications and zigzags, a part of which continued without having a final solution for half a century, not to say that didn't fade away even in the recent years. This explains the sub-title of the book: 'The Bitter Victory'. It is precisely this complex and versatile treatment – with a serious and painful search to go deeper into the truth, as much as can be truth in this aspect – that distinguishes his text.

In the Hoxhaist perspective, it is decidedly opposed that in the National-Liberation Struggle were present elements of civil war. On the other hand, it is called people's revolution, which even resolved at the same time the strategic task of national liberation and the establishment of the new power, representing not simply a dictatorship of revolutionary forces, but also a power containing in itself the seed in quick development of the proletarian dictatorship. According to Western authors, all this is expressed by the words 'establishment of the Communism'. The words 'civil war' sometimes are used in inverted commas by Reginald Hibbert, and towards it as well as towards the establishment of the Communism he has once more a distinguishable position. We read in the book:' It is an over-simplification to say that the LNÇ forces were being built up only to seize power and not to fight the Italians and Germans. For the CPA and the Partisan/LNÇ in general, the two things were inseparable.' (p. 58) When the outcome of the various discussions was reported to Force 133 at GHQ Middle East, a reply was sent confirming that there could be no support for either side in a civil war, but the mission was to do its best to support efforts against the Germans from either side. On September 17 General Davis sent a telegram to Cairo, a telegram that is already known from the documents brought in 1972 from London to the Archives of Albanian Institute of History. According to Hibbert, unfortunately for the LNÇ, for Britain's relations with Albania, and perhaps too for Albania itself, the Brigadier's mission in Albania virtually ended with this telegram. But in the telegram Davis put his finger on the essence of the this situation – the civil war had already begun and, from the point of view of the Albanian 'nationalists', the Germans were acting in it as the nationalists' instrument for the destruction of the LNÇ. 'In fact, the first part of the civil war was fought in the Germans' winter offensive, and once it had been fought and the LNÇ partisans had survived it, there was no way in which the second part could be prevented in 1944.' (p. 78). And in the middle of 1944, once more according to the author, the truth was that the partisans, who had been the victims of civil strife during the winter, were now turning the tables on those who had collaborated directly or indirectly with the Germans to destroy them. (p. 173)

The thrust northwards by the 1st Partisan Division before long made it impossible for the British authorities to hold the line that the Partisans had plunged Albania into civil war, and had therefore forfeited a claim to British help. (p. 179)

In one place the author frontally puts the question: could the situation be described simply as a civil war? If so, where did the responsibility for it lie? In describing the battle of Dibra as a culmination point, he doesn't hesitate to say that it was not a civil war episode, but a war against the Germans and their collaborators. His main conclusion, I would say expressed with a decisive and angry polemic tone, is the following: The foreign country which most contributed to the communisation of Albania was not Britain but Germany. It was Hitler, not Winston Churchill, who brought Communism into Eastern Europe. It was the Albanian nationalist leaders who threw away their chance of playing a part in post-war Albania by hesitating to play a part in fighting the German occupier. (p. 240).

The Stables Mission Hibbert belonged to as a junior officer, was at first working with Muharrem Bajraktari group and with other chieftains like him. Afterwards the Mission was working with the Partisans. So the author became acquainted with both parties. Through all the book he cannot find positive words for the forces under the common denomination 'nationalists'. He saw that the Northern chieftains would make long-term promises but never organized a serious action of resistance. The British officers failed with all nationalist chiefs in launching them against the Germans.

'The nationalist Albanian reluctance to fight was, in historical terms, unforgivable, and as the war drew to a close it was not forgiven, and they reaped a terrible requital.' (p. 107) In a very interesting telegram sent from Cairo in late February by Ch. Steel to Douglas Howard, the head of FO's Southern Department. Steel reported that there was no doubt that considerable numbers of BK supporters were closely co-operating with the Germans against the LNÇ in South Albania, and the information implicating the BK in the capture of Brig. Davies had been authenticated. (p. 138) In a sense, the Germans and the Balli Kombëtar with their reprisals became the architects of the Partisan upsurge. The author gives the full names of the collaborators of the Italians and Germans. The 'nationalists' had missed completely their chance by failing to lift a hand against the Germans even at the eleventh hour, reserving it exclusively for action against the Partisans. One last quotation from the chapter 'The Battle of Dibra': 'Civil war occupied only a corner of the scene for BLO's with the Partisans and seemed to them to deserve less and less to be so labeled, because the 'Nationalists' who were not taking the field against the Germans were becoming increasingly indistinguishable from those who were actively taking the field with and for them. (p. 185)

I would say that in one sense Hibbert wrote this book to defend his struggle. He was sent to Albania as a military man. For this young soldier the only purpose in sending British officers to Albania was to step up the fight against Germany. He could not imagine in what a mighty vortex of world conflagration he was to fall into. Being a military man in him gradually grew the anxiety about countless threads entangled around an issue, that he thought would have simply been resolved in the field of the battle. Even later this entanglement was nor undone, not dissolved, and remained part of his life. In the famous phrase, You can take the Man out of Albania, but You cannot Take Albania out of the Man.

This is the reason why after almost half a century later he decided to fight once more for his struggle through a written work. This book also is a return to the personal roots, to the dreams and the enthusiasm of the youth. It was not very difficult to win the historical arguments against the simplified and extremely ideologized position of Enver. Hoxha, for whom there was only the Anglo-American threat, diabolic aims, espionage, interference, intrigues, an England that temporarily changed the skin but remained the same imperialistic, reactionary England, with the same precise and unshakable goals. More difficult was for Reginald Hibbert to defend his struggle in face of his own countrymen, people of influence in political and military structures, beginning with his colleagues in Albania, and up to the top representatives of British Government and Allied HQ.

For a better understanding of this aspect of the book, we have to distinguish two layers. The first one is connected with the whole military and political line adopted towards Albania.

When the first British missions arrived in Albania, neither they nor the SOE staffs in Cairo, nor even the Foreign Office had any real information about the situation in Albania. The SOE thinking about Albania tended to be more adventurous than that of FO. The British policy was not coinciding with the Albanian pretensions for their boundaries and this was the reason of many misunderstandings and failures of British efforts in Albania during the war. Even Brigadier Davies mission was based on several misconceptions. Hibbert's diary shows what a gulf existed between his experience on the ground and their thinking about Albania at higher military and political levels. At every stage Britain's successive attempts to evolve an effective policy in relation to Albania were overtaken by events. London, Cairo and Bari were not in harmony in their opinions and actions, therefore whenever at the end a resolution was adopted, it was too late. I shall not go further in details about this. There is one thing more to point out. A telegram was sent on July 18, 1944 from Bari to Algiers reporting the imminence of a German counter-attack, and explaining that the Partisan forces were short of ammunition. The situation in northern Albania was no longer a straight issue of civil war, and the Partisans were now facing a definite German threat. The next day when the Prime Minister, W. Churchill saw a copy of this telegram, he minuted on it: 'Let me have a note on this, showing which side we are on.' (!)

Based on documents the author gives exact figures of British supplies, the number of flights and dates. But the question is the same: how they are judged? Once more the position was complex. For the British there was an obligatory condition – the supplies were to be used against the occupiers. The level of a supply was proportionate to the level of activity, the quantities involved were modest and the course of events in Albania could not be determined by them.

Enver Hoxhas's complaints about the inadequacy of the quantities of supplies are nearer the mark, but he ought to have shown more gratitude for the help his army received from Allies in July and August 1944.

Before I pass to the next layer, I have to remind readers that N. Plasari published on 27 September 1991 in 'Zëri i Popullit' an article under the title: 'Light upon the truth about British missions in Albania.' The title is pretentious but the content is superficial. There is a leap there from the unrestrained offences of E. Hoxha to unrestrained praise, ignoring just the complexity of the phenomena. As an argument I would give a paragraph from a review by James Pettifer, published in one of the central British newspapers, *The Independent*,-:

'So far our knowledge of these days has been totally dominated by books written by other SOE officers whose politics are of the right, particularly Julian Amery MP, who in 'Sons of the Eagle' and other writings, has made the case that the British HQ of SOE in Cairo was Communist-dominated, and that Albania was handed over to Enver Hoxha by a leftist conspiracy that denied arms drops to the non-Communist leaders. His views have been reinforced

in books written by David Smiley and Lord Bethell. In the latter's
'Great Betrayal', Sir Reginald is described as being on 'the political
left' in terms that can only be described as MacCarthyite.'

On my opinion, when we are to speak about complex political and social
events and circumstances, it is as naïve to speak about 'the Albanian' in
general as is ridiculous and mystified to speak about 'the Foreigner' in
general, in this case about the British particularly. Everywhere there are
different strata and interests, distinguishable political, military, economical,
social orientations, bureaucrats and incapable as well as capable and
talented people, hypocrites and honest men.

Billy Maclean and David Smiley arrived first in Albania at the end of
April 1943, and stayed with the partisans; they left Albania at the end of
October, after Brigadier Davies and Nichols were dropped at Biza on
the night 15-16 October. In December the Brigadier was swept out of
the scene. Stables Mission was dropped on December 1943 and joined
'the nationalists' in North, but to the end of May 1944 they resulted with
the partisans. On April 19, 1944 entered in Albania once more Mclean,
Smiley and Julian Amery, but this time they joined the Zogist forces.
Therefore in the most decisive moments of the struggle in Albania there
happened to be two groups that had relations with the partisans as well
with 'the nationalists'.

One group was the Concensus II Mission (McLean, Smiley, Amery)
whose books dominated so far – with the nationalists.

The other group was Stables Mission (Riddell and Hibbert) with
the partisans.

On August 1944 the partisans liberated the Mati valley. Very closely,
divided by only some hills, were face to face the two adversaries, and at
the same time the two groups of British missions. It is almost unbelievable,
but as it is put by the author: The two groups, or sides as they can fairly be
called in view of the strong feelings engendered by their work, remained
clearly divided until the end of the campaign and, as will be seen, into
peace and even into old age.' (p. 123)

The pages of this book are a testimony of this bitter truth, which
was also bitter outside the pages of the book. Hibbert afterwards, as a
result of his high diplomatic career was given the title 'Sir'. It was not
given to Julian Amery, it seems because his brother was executed as a
Nazi collaborator. On September 8 Captain J.F.P. Oliver was dropped

in Albania, and on September 19 Lieutenant Rowland Winn. Reginald Hibbert met them on September 23. They insisted that the prime task of BLO's should be to check the advance of Communism, therefore Hibbert and Riddell were wrong to be supporting the partisans, and they claimed to know that the Foreign Office shared the same view. 'The hot debates which we had at Biza on 23 and 24 September – writes the author – were completely beside the point, but they were my first taste of the excessively polarized arguments about Communism and how to deal with it which continued unabated in Britain for all the forty five years between them and 1989 when the communist regimes in eastern Europe began to fall.' (p. 228)

It is really shocking to read on the last pages of the book that in 1951 Hibbert was told by then the head of the Security Department at the Foreign Office that information had been laid against him by someone who had known him in Albania to the effect that Hibbert has been a communist at that time, and had acknowledged that this was so. Hibbert was duly interrogated. He told to the interrogator that the informant must have been Rowland Winn and the interrogator tacitly confirmed it. The case was dropped. Many years later, at the beginning of 1980 when Hibbert was Ambassador at Paris, he was warned by the Foreign and Commonwealth Office that Rowland. Winn (by now Lord St. Oswald) had once more been laying information against him, this time to influential acquaintances in France including Count Michel Poniatowski, a very close collaborator of the President of the Republic, M. Giscard d'Estaign. The FCO took steps to persuade him to desist from giving them further currency. 'Those who took part in the events of those days – concludes the author – still feel strongly about them, and those who believed in conspiracy theories seem still to believe in them today. Most would not push their passion or fanaticism to the extreme of dilation or of trying to discredit their own country's ambassador, but many trace whatever they regard as evil in the modern world to an origin in their own Albanian experience.' (p. 243) I believe it is sufficient to have an idea about all this question and it is necessary to read the last chapter of it, for understanding how deep and hard the things go in this way, and preventing hasty judgment with naiveties or fanatic obsessions about the Albanian people and their history.

Among the opinions of Hibbert on Enver Hoxha I would point out to two things for their original flavor. Firstly, in those hard days at the end December 1943 Brigadier Davies suggested to Hoxha that he and an Albanian should slip off southernwoods alone, so that he could find his way to Cairo to report and would exercise his influence on Cairo and London for policy decisions in favor of the partisans. Enver Hoxha opposed this and it is particularly ironic that he wrote with pride of having vetoed this initiative. Hoxha had thrown in this way his chance to get recognized as a fighting ally, whereas Tito had had the stature and skill for such a recognition. Secondly, Hibbert asserts that Hoxha possessed a particular capacity in precipitating the crisis, to bring the situation to the edge of the catastrophe, and then to escape it. At the end of the war, in the time of Berati Plenum he had to find ways of continuing the fight in order to survive. 'It so happened that this was where his genius lay. He had a mastery in accumulating power and confounding rivals by perpetuating struggle, and he enjoined the sort of luck which attends brinkmanship of the highest class. These are the qualities which have caused him to be called a Stalinist. He was not formed by Stalin, and he turned to Stalin for help only when it was convenient. But he eliminated his opponents and rivals with a regularity and precision which make him seem to be Stalin's best disciple.' (p. 221)

The topicality of this book is more than evident. It is addressed to British opinion and to a wider audience, transmitting the message that today's Albania can be understood following her inner processes very complicated. But from the first page it attracts the attention to the fact that: 'Those outside have consistently underestimated the strength, persistence and importance of Albanian national feeling.' It is a very precious message also for us, the Albanians, involved in the present day vortex.

The Political Economy of Albania's Transition from Planning to the Market

Michael Kaser[1]

When Albania won its freedom at the concluding stages of the Second World War it was one of the poorest nations in Europe. After four centuries of Ottoman rule (1478-1912), Albania had enjoyed a mere three years of relatively democratic government (1921-24) before the succession of a brigand-king (1924-39), occupying armies (1939-45), and repression under a paranoid communist dictator (1945-85), Albania's transition to a market economy from 1991 was shackled by opaque governance with endemic corruption and misconceived, even if well meaning, policy-making by its international partners. Two decades after the start of its transition from a repressive political economy it remains one of Europe's poorest countries, with an income per person of $ 7950.[2]

Albania was bypassed by the political and industrial revolutions of Europe of the nineteenth and first half of the twentieth centuries. For thirty years after independence (1912), economic activity remained dominated by subsistence farming and handicrafts, and the country as a whole was left further from the beaten track than any European nation. Railway projects to link Albania with the European network came to naught (but under a 1979 agreement with Yugoslavia a line was finally completed in 1986 linking Vlorë via Shkodër to Podgorica).

In the economy, as in politics, the Second World War was the turning-point. Mussolini's Italy, which invaded Albania in 1939, needed oil, copper and chrome, but it was the War which forced ahead the opening up of Albania's natural resources. A start was made on modern transport

---

[1]A revision of this chapter appeared in Dirk Bezemer (ed.), *On Eagle's Wings: The Albanian Economy in Transition*, Nova Science, New York, 2006, pp. 1-15, with additional material incorporated by Greg Kaser.

[2]Measured in terms of national income (GDP) per person at purchasing power parity for 2008; see World Bank data at <http://siteresources.worldbank.org/DATASTATISTICS/Resources/GNIPC.pdf> accessed on 14 March 2010. This level of income is about one-third higher than that of China ($6020 per person) and only 22 per cent of that enjoyed in the UK. Only Azerbaijan, Ukraine and Moldova have a lower level of income.

links. The first bitumen roads (200km of them), an international airport and numerous local airstrips were laid. The first railway was begun, but was not operational until after the War, and took thirty years, until the 1970s, of youth-brigade labour to reach the nickel mines at Pogradec it was intended to serve. The War, of course, brought still more profound changes: the Albanian Communist Party was founded in 1941 and its partisans proved victorious not only over the Italian and German occupiers, but also over all domestic opposition. For the entire history of its wartime struggle and the subsequent socialist regime one man, Enver Hoxha, dominated Albania's political scene.

The group around Hoxha in the mountains of Peza in 1942 (when the National Liberation Front was formed) included two who went on to act as his key aides for the next forty years – Hysni Kapo, No 2 in the Party until his death in 1979, and Mehmet Shehu, the prime minister until his suicide in 1981 (following his death he was denounced as 'an enemy of the people' and an agent not only for the 'revisionists' in Yugoslavia, but also of the USA and the USSR). They had sided with Hoxha as each change of international alliance brought purges in the Party and government – from Yugoslavia to the USSR in 1948, from the USSR to China in 1961, and in the prolonged deterioration of relations with the latter between 1972 and 1978. The triumvirate's guiding principle was self-help, often entailing isolation. But Albania's situation meant that isolation from its wider region entailed stunted development.

The early years: between Stalin and Tito

Albania is rich in non-ferrous metals and in energy resources (oil and hydroelectricity) and has a scenic coastline of fishing villages and small towns. But the very hills and mountains that offer the potential for energy, mining and tourism restrict the area of arable land. Albania's development is heavily dependant upon trade based on its natural resources and external aid, which initially came from the USSR. The predominantly agrarian Albanians[3] were promised rapid economic development within

[3]Fishta (2001) gives the following distribution of land in 1939 in thousand ha: landlord (*çiftlik*) ownership 127, state and religious ownership 41, peasants 494 (among whom 51,888 families had land and 18,063 were landless). Post-war land redistribution to peasants was soon overtaken by collectivisation, but Albania remained more rural than any Soviet-type economy, with 65 per cent of the population living in rural areas in the 1980s (Lerman et al., 2004, Table A2.1).

their several states when Communist partisans gained power in the closing year of the Second World War. Those in Kosovo, Macedonia and Montenegro were furnished with a Five-year Plan on the Soviet model by Tito's federal Yugoslavia, and shorter-term plans for industrialisation were set up by Enver Hoxha for Albania itself. Outside the communist fiefs, most of the Albanian minority in Greek Epirus migrated under duress to Albania (Vickers and Pettifer, 1997, pp 207-8).

The economic integration of Albania with Yugoslavia began with an agreement to remove customs barriers between the two countries in 1946. The post-communist release of Party documents shows that this was not fully implemented (Malcolm, 1998, p. 319), but both Hoxha and Tito were headed for political federation. Such would have reduced the barriers between Kosovo and Albania, re-erected after the partisan victories in both Albania and Yugoslavia: During the second world war, following the German invasion of Yugoslavia in 1941, most of Kosovo had been united with the Italian puppet regime of Albania (Malcolm, 1998, ch. 15) and Kosovars had expected a partisan victory to maintain the union (Vickers, 1998, ch. 7). Stalin's advice to Tito's close aide, Milovan Djilas, 'You ought to swallow Albania – the sooner the better' (Djilas, 1963), was a decisive factor in the sundering of the two countries' mutual relations in 1948. The break between Belgrade and Tirana forced each government to seek development assistance elsewhere – the one hesitantly from the West and the other with alacrity from the USSR. As Hoxha's relations with Khrushchev deteriorated (a key issue was whether the Albanian economy should pursue import-demanding industrialisation or export-enhancing agricultural development), the government tentatively approached the one apolitical source of funding, the United Nations. The writer was a member of the first UN mission to the country in 1960, which had to explain in Tirana that only the Expanded Programme of Technical Assistance (EPTA, established 1949, later UNDP) was available and was limited both in its funding and in type of assistance. Money through the IMF and the World Bank would not have been available to a communist regime in those years of the Cold War, but Albania might not have turned to China had the UN then had its own soft-loan development finance. As Emmerij, Jolly and Weiss (2001, p. 43) observe, that facility of SUNFED (Special UN Fund for Economic Development) 'the [World] Bank, in line with strong US resistance had opposed root and branch'. A biography of Sir Hans Singer, SUNFED's main proponent in the UN Secretariat, documents the McCarthyite attacks on him for a 'socialist UN plan to disarm and bankrupt the United States' (Shaw, 2002, p.90). As it was, when Soviet support finally ended with the severance of diplomatic relations in 1961, Hoxha relied on China from then until 1978; when he forfeited further aid by declaring his country's support for Viet Nam in the latter's conflict with China. From that year until his death in 1985 Albania was confined within political, economic and intellectual isolation.[4]

Muscular socialism

Following the momentous split in the world communist movement between the USSR and China of 1960, in which the Albanian leadership sided with Beijing, Albania was rewarded with substantial Chinese aid, although of lower value than that from the USSR. The author has calculated that aid from the Soviet-led Council for Mutual Economic Assistance (CMEA), which ended in 1961, financed imports triple the value of Albanian exports to them. (Several thousand technical advisers, mainly from the USSR and Poland, were also withdrawn.) Chinese aid, which ended in 1978, seems to have enabled imports to have been 1 ½ times exports (the figures are estimates from official indications of bilateral trade). Nevertheless Chinese assistance permitted the development of the Berat textile mill and the Elbasan metallurgical complex (eventually completed without assistance). Since the break with China, Albania was reliant upon its own resources.

With donors both at great distances and ideologically, though variantly, communist-ruled, Albania's economy was almost totally sealed off from the world's market economies (Schnytzer, 1982). Symbolised by the change of name in 1948 from Albanian Communist Party to Party of Labour of Albania (PLA) as part of the break with Tito, and in petty terms by such prohibitions as private ownership of motor cars and the

---

[4]Limited tourist groups were allowed: 6,000 annually during 1981-85 (Pier, 1993, p. 418). The writer participated in a group, mainly of staff and students of Oxford University, in 1983, which was given access to the Institute of Economics, though a later, unsolicited letter to the author of an article in the Institute's journal, *Probleme ekonomike*, resulted in the recipient's imprisonment for unauthorised contact with a foreigner.

sale of produce from private plots,[5] the economy reverted to its Ottoman-period reliance on human and animal motive-power in what could be termed 'muscular socialism' (Kaser, 1983). The Party of Labour was correspondingly pro-natalist: during its dominance, the population rose from 1.2 million to 3.3 million between 1950 and 1990 and in the 1980s was the fastest growing in Europe, at 2.1 per cent annually. It was thus at that rate GDP would have had to grow to keep per capita output constant. The index numbers of GDP published in the communist period greatly exceeded that rate, but a recalculation by the UN Economic Commission for Europe shows real GDP growth at only 1.5 per cent from 1980 to 1990 (ECE, 2001, p. 115), demonstrating a per-capita decline during that decade. The economy was indubitably transformed – the employed labour force sextupled and the industrial capital stock in 1989 was 27 times that of 1955[6] – and Albania improved its per-capita GDP ratio from 11 to 13 per cent of the EU level between 1950 and 1989 (Kaser, 2001, p. 630). Paranoiac defence of the realm brought wastage of resources on fortifications[7] and on autarky. National self-sufficiency was no guide to international comparative costs and most industrial enterprises proved uncompetitive when the economy was opened to imports and subsidies for exports were withdrawn as domestic prices were liberalised.

During the 1960s and 1970s, Hoxha selected four courses from the Maoist menu. The first was a pseudo-system of 'workers' control' (exercised by mass meetings in enterprises) to restrain managerial or technician independence from Party supervision, since severe penalties in the prison camps awaited those who failed to vote the way expected. The second was to limit the spread of salaries and the abolition of personal income tax was abolished in 1967, since its redistributive function was no longer relevant. The size of the personal plot was limited to 0.1 hectares and surplus produce could only be sold to the collective farm. Urban

---

[5]Nexhijme Hoxha, the dictator's wife, was especially vindictive against peasant women whom from her car she spotted hawking a few vegetables at the roadside.
[6]Schnytzer (1993), p. 341; he shows (p. 342), however, that 1989 industrial capital productivity was little more than 70 per cent of that of 1955.
[7]Sealing the frontier in mountainous terrain and peppering the lowlands with 180,000 concrete bunkers absorbed much labour and building material. Hashi and Xhillari (1999, p. 119) report 180,000, but *Financial Times* (2004) puts the number at 700,000. The work and funds needed to demolish them has deterred local authorities and landowners from greatly diminishing their number.

markets were closed. A third policy was that of 'self-help', which set villagers to work on labour-intensive projects such as contour terracing, draining marshlands and earth dams on rivers for irrigation. Whereas the total area sown in 1960 was 370,000 hectares, by 1978 a further 30,000 hectares had been gained. The final element, decreed in 1971, was the introduction of 'cooperative farms of the higher type' (KTL) to improve agricultural productivity. By 1978 the 41 such farms comprised 22 per cent of the cultivated land but produced 26 per cent of the grain, 59 per cent of the rice, 49 per cent of the cotton and of the sugar-beet, 37 per cent of the milk and 25 per cent of the meat produced in the cooperative sector.[8]

The author was able to assess first hand the extent, and, in fact, the lack, of development that had occurred from his two visits in 1960 and 1983. During the latter visit he was surprised that the range and qualities of retail goods in Tirana shops were as poor as those on sale in 1960. There was still only a small 'bundle of goods' on offer, and even though there were many more consumers able to make the purchase their incomes had barely risen. Under a campaign for 'workers' control' launched in 1966, which was intended to eliminate the difference between shop-floor and management, along with moves to reduce salary inequality (decrees were issued in 1967 and 1976), the highest salaried official earned no more than twice the wage of the average worker, whether in factory or farm. As Schnytzer, 1982, pointed out, an egalitarian income distribution solved the problem of microeconomic monetary equilibrium. Egalitarian income meant that consumer demand was more or less the same for all households and was not driving economic growth. Self-reliance had not facilitated Albania's development; rather, it had simply meant that its resources were shared more equally but still left its population poorer than their neighbours.

Albania's one-year *perestroika*

In retrospect, the loss of political power was inevitable when Communists surrendered economic control. That, of course, had not been the Party's intention. The economic reforms initiated during the 1980s in the USSR and China were aimed at increasing economic efficiency and

---

[8]See Kaser (1982), p. 125.

consolidating the legitimacy of the ruling Communist Party. Initially these reforms did not envisage any convergence with capitalism or towards a regulated market that had characterised the earlier breakaway regimes in Hungary and Yugoslavia. The Soviet-type economy had relied upon 'taut planning' to impel enterprise managers to produce at the limit of their capacity (of equipment, materials and staffing) regardless of the saleability of their output. Enterprise managers in turn 'struggled for an easy plan' by concealing reserves, by informal exchanges of supplies with others and by over-employment. The reforms aimed to relax the 'tautness' by setting each enterprise a production quota which was less than its estimated capacity; these new quotas thus permitted key allocations to be made from within the enterprises own reserves for investment or for consumption (i.e. by paying higher wages). The state would no longer be the prime source of capital and production above the quota would be, by definition, profitable – as enterprises would not seek to sell more unless they could see a return. A dual track was initiated, whereby part of production was controlled by the state plan, and was consumed by the defence sector and social programmes (housing, transport, health and social care, and such like), while a smaller fraction was offered to consumers on the market. However, the success of the reforms ultimately depended upon the existence of sufficient effective demand and flexibility in pricing. This in turn required the state to adopt a Keynesian approach to general economic management. But it also meant that attention had to be given to market regulation and to the entry of new producers into the market (or to importers), to ensure that competition was effectively controlling prices.[9] Negotiating these issues while retaining popular support proved elusive in the USSR, leading to the downfall of Gorbachev, although it was achieved more successfully in China, where the latter was buttressed by a more repressive state apparatus.

The death on Enver Hoxha in 1985 and the ascendancy of Mikhail Gorbachev to the Soviet leadership a month beforehand signalled that change was in the wings. Hoxha's widow Nexhmije and other cronies managed however stall the transformation for some four years (she was arrested on corruption charges in 1991). Indeed, for a few months after

[9] See Kaser (1987) for a discussion of the macroeconomic and microeconomic issues and the domestic policy contexts.

the installation in Poland of a non-communist government (September 1989), Albania seemed immune from the serial collapse affecting Central and Eastern Europe. With the execution of Nicolae Ceau escu of Romania in December 1989 the region's revolution was complete, save for Albania. Ramiz Alia, the President who had succeeded Hoxha in 1985, bowed to the inevitability of change, but took as his model not the neighbouring Balkans, but the then USSR under Gorbachev's *perestroika*. The first measure, which he announced in January 1990, was typical of the year's limited devolution – it copied a Soviet requirement of 1997 to directors of state enterprises to be elected by its staff and to allow them wider devolved powers on wages. Similarly, detailed production planning was restricted to a narrow range of goods (like the Soviet *goszakazy*), enterprises were to be self-financing under a modified subsidy regime, some retail prices were decontrolled and the produce of private plots could be freely sold.[10] The Soviet provision was also copied that state enterprises were responsible for finding redundant workers another job, but where, as in the vast majority of cases, this was impossible, the state undertook to pay each 80 per cent of the previous wage; neither system then provided unemployment benefit, which Albania introduced in mid-1992.

Gorbachev's *perestroika* lasted as long as he ran the USSR as leader of the Communist Party – just over six years; Alia's *perestroika* was correspondingly politically coterminous. The Democratic Party of Albania (DPA), led by Sali Berisha, was formed in December 1990 and took part in the first multi-party elections of March 1991. Although the DPA did not gain a parliamentary majority until fresh elections were held in March 1992, a 'Government of National Unity' with 12 non-PLA ministers was formed in June 1992, with Ylli Bufi as Prime Minister. At the same time the PLA changed its name to Socialist Party of Albania (SPA), electing Fatos Nano as its leader. Berisha withdrew his party's participation in the government in November 1991 and triumphed in the new elections. The intense rivalry between him and Nano dates from this period, launching a political duopsony simultaneously with Albania's systemic transition to the market.

---

[10] The Albanian and Soviet measures are concisely summarised in Jeffries, 2002a, pp. 100-101, and Hanson, 1990, pp. 49-61, respectively.

Attaining macroeconomic stability with international help

Albania joined the International Monetary Fund (IMF) in October 1991[11] and adopted a stabilisation programme with effect from the following July. Help in closing the 'two gaps' – the fiscal and the external – was immediately forthcoming. The government began to draw on the Fund's General Resources Account as a stand-by facility and was in July 1993 accorded a Structural Adjustment Facility (SAF1) for 1993-95. As elsewhere, an IMF-agreed programme signalled other international and bilateral support: overall, Albania received $959 million in official transfers between 1992 and 1995 and $234 million in official medium and long-term loans. Berisha's defiance of IMF tutelage resulted in there being no IMF programme when the first SAF ended in 1995. Other official transfers tapered off to a total of $154 million in the two years 1996 and 1997, and longer official loans to $99 million. When in 1997 Nano, fraudulently imprisoned by Berisha's government in 1994, was freed by the rioters from jail and overwhelmingly returned to the premiership in free elections, the IMF provided a Post-Conflict Emergency Facility and then an Enhanced Structural Adjustment Facility for 1998 to 2001; the latter was re-designated a Poverty Reduction and Growth Facility (PGRF) in November 1999. These and other official aid cumulated to $632 million in 1998-2000, with longer official loans at $195 million. When PGRF1 ended in mid-2001, the IMF took its time to agree a PGRF2, citing Albania's political crises as reason for its hesitancy. When in June 2002 the Fund approved PGRF2 covering 2002-2005, at $37 million, somewhat smaller than its predecessors, but support by the World Bank expanded: in December 2004 the Bank had 20 projects under implementation, with an aggregate credit of $289 million.

Albania joined the World Bank in 1991 and since then has drawn upon $1.1 billion of concessional finance and grants, becoming full credit-worthy in 2008.[12] Projects backed by the World Bank involved energy,

---

[11]By then all major international agencies, of the UN and the EC, already had representation in Tirana, providing advice to appropriate ministries; the writer participated in a UNICEF/WHO mission in August 1991, which included study of the most poverty-stricken region of the north.

[12]See <http://www.worldbank.org.al/WBSITE/EXTERNAL/COUNTRIES/ECAEXT/ALBANIAEXTN/0,,menuPK:301421~pagePK:141132~piPK:141107~theSitePK:301412,00.html> accessed on 14 March 2010.

water supply and sanitation, flood protection, irrigation and drainage, agriculture, roads and highways, education, health and social services, improving the business environment and land administration. Albania also joined the European Bank for Reconstruction and Development in 1991, from which it had borrowed €330 million by the end of 2009 mainly for projects in infrastructure, energy, manufacturing, including small business finance, agribusiness and tourism.[13] From 1992 the European Union (EU) provided support, mainly in the form of technical assistance, through its Phare Programme. This was focussed on supporting the transition to an open market economy through privatisation and industrial restructuring in its earlier phases, but from 1994 also supported potential candidates for EU membership by providing help in harmonising legislation and policies to comply with the EU's body of regulation, the *acquis communautaire*, and in institution building. With respect to Albania, the first Phare Country Strategy, adopted in 1995, was oriented towards supporting the development of the productive sector but was later judged to be 'over ambitious and unfocused' (according to an evaluation in 2001). From 1999 the EC prioritised the support for EU integration and the establishment of a regional free trade zone. Altogether between 1991 and 2000 the EC provided grants and technical assistance of €635 million under the Phare Programme.[14]

Another important area of EU-Albanian cooperation was in trade and the liberalisation of foreign direct investment (FDI). The EU granted duty-free access to Albanian exports in 2000 and by 2006 the stock of FDI from EU members in Albania amounted to €845 million.[15] In the following year the programme of Country Assistance for Reconstruction, Development and Stabilisation (CARDS) was launched. In January 2003, Albania started negotiations with the European Union for a Stabilisation and Association Agreement. An agreement was signed in June 2006, and entered into force on 1 April 2009, following ratification by all EU

[13] EBRD, April 2009, <http://www.ebrd.com/pubs/factsh/country/albania.pdf> accessed on 14 March 2010.

[14] See report by Investment Development Consultancy and Development Strategies, 2001, *Evaluation of EC Country Strategy: Albania 1996-2001*, pp ii-iii on <http://ec.europa.eu/europeaid/how/evaluation/evaluation_reports/reports/cards/951607_en.pdf> accessed on 14 March 2010.

[15] See < http://ec.europa.eu/enlargement/potential-candidates/albania/relation/index_en.htm> accessed on 14 March 2010.

member states. In the same month Albania formally applied for EU membership. Since January 2007, pre-accession financial assistance to Albania has been provided under the EU's Instrument for Pre-Accession Assistance, which has a much wider remit than either the Phare or CARDS programmes. In 2009 Albania became a new member of the US-led North Atlantic Treaty Organisation (NATO).

Albania's accession to the World Trade Organisation (WTO) in September 2000 marked the point at which it gained market economy status and had effectively completed its transformation. However, the transition period had been socially and economically traumatic. Even with international assistance, the Albanian economy underwent a severe crisis during the 1990s, experiencing the largest decline in Central and Eastern Europe, with the exception of war-torn former Yugoslavia. National income had fallen to 60 per cent of its 1989 level by 1992 and only recovered its position in 2000.[16] The liberalisation of most prices and of the foreign-exchange system in 1992 followed the collapse of domestic production as industry lost both domestic recipients guaranteed under a planning regime and foreign markets in other previously-planned economies. Agricultural output fell under the combined effect of a severe drought and the chaotic break-up of collective farms: peasants even tore up signalling wire and sleepers from the railway to fence off their claims. As an insensate protest against 45 years of bondage to the state, looters stripped factories and public buildings – some thousand schools, health centres and the like were rendered unusable. Transport and other state services were disrupted as civil order crumbled – the Italian Army helped to restore control and to provision remoter areas. Antipathies remained profound in the rural areas. Lemel, 1998, describes those of long-established families towards immigrants of the communist period, numerous in the coastal plains and around Tirana. Surveys (Lemel, 2000) showed that of the seizures of 1991-92 over half of those parcels on which the homestead stood had been in the same patrilineal group or clan (*fis*) before 1946, but virtually no investment (other than in the family dwelling) had been made where it had not been so owned.[17]

---

[16]EBRD, 2009, p. 133.

[17]Lemel's analysis is of household samples in five of the country's 36 districts (selected by terrain and climate). Such non-investment was for fear of later forfeiture, but by mid-2002 agrarian ownership had been regularised by the almost

Inflation was inevitable given economic imbalances present, but at 36 per cent in 1992 and 193 per cent in 1993, it was then among the lowest of the transition economies. As in all such economies, the disappearance of the revenue streams characteristic of a planned economy (such as profit deductions from state enterprises and turnover tax levied on price-controlled goods and services) coincided with the irreducibility of most heads of public expenditure – some, such as unemployment benefit and other constituents of a 'social safety net', increased. With no market in government stock to allow normal public borrowing, recourse was either to inflationary finance or to foreign funding (Clunies-Ross and Sudar, 1998). The Albanian government policy, under IMF aegis, made macroeconomic stabilisation its priority, showing average consumer-price index (CPI) rises of 23 per cent in 1994, a mere 8 per cent in 1995 (the second-lowest among 26 transition economies) and 13 per cent in 1996. McNeilly and Schiesser-Gachnang, 1998, find that this relatively low inflation may be attributed to a rapid realignment of relative consumer prices and to a 106 per cent appreciation of the lek against the dollar between August 1992 and December 1995. As they foresaw, further convergence towards international price relativities has since been accompanied by more real exchange rate appreciation. By end-2004 the nominal rate, after a period of depreciation (it had averaged 150 in 1998), had, partly of course due to the depreciation of the dollar, returned to that of end-1995 – 94 lek to the US dollar at both dates. Taking account of US inflation of 23 per cent and of Albanian of 107 per cent, reversion to the nominal rate of nine years previously constitutes a real appreciation of 68 per cent.

Renewed civil disturbance

Repressing inflation was one of Berisha's objectives, but repressing the population was another. The insurgency of 1997 was sparked by investors frustrated at lack of redress against the politically well-connected fraudsters of pyramid schemes. Similar scandals had erupted in Russia and Romania, facilitated, as in Albania, by lack of a financial regulator and by citizens' innocence of financial products. Three years of rapid recovery – measured GDP rose by 8, 13 and 9 per cent successively and the informal ('shadow')

---

complete registration and certification of land nationwide.

economy flourished – had made many households flush with cash, to which was added remittances from emigrant workers (15 per cent of the 1989 population had subsequently gone abroad), and income from arms and fuel smuggling into Yugoslavia (Serbia-Montenegro) in defiance of UN sanctions, and into Macedonia to break the Greek blockade. Berisha's corrupt administration tolerated these, as well as drug-trafficking and money-laundering, which brought in yet more money.

Unlike the other transition states, the Albanian economy had begun to be monetised only when communism fell. Barter had been the main means of exchange until the end of the Second World War and under Enver Hoxha's communism, private trade was forbidden and transactions between state enterprises were conducted by altering their balances at the State Bank of Albania. Thus the euphoria engendered by marketisation was accompanied by ignorance of its financial parameters.

Political awareness was, by contrast, spreading and Berisha became increasingly authoritarian and reliant on corruption in his administration. To counter growing opposition in the run-up to the parliamentary election of May 1996, the government-controlled media attacked the SPA as a party of unreconstructed communists. Media that refused to back the DPA were censured or even shut. Without the 'even playing field', the main opposition parties boycotted what proved to be a fraudulent ballot, allowing the government 122 out of 144 seats in the People's Assembly. The Organisation for Security and Co-operation in Europe (OSCE) saw the irregularities, but did not declare the election invalid. Western governments, notably the US, also withheld criticism as they wanted to avoid further Balkan unrest following the Dayton Agreement of 1995 which had ended the war in Bosnia and Herzegovina.

By late 1996 and early 1997 the Ponzi deposit-taking schemes were collapsing: their offer of 15-100 per cent interest on three-month deposits could only be sustained by payment to early investors from funds collected from later depositors. It became a social crisis because many households invested all their savings and sold their homes to raise further cash, losing an estimated $2 billion. Although the IMF warned the government about the danger of the pyramids, the schemes' founders had been generous in funding the DPA and ministers were reluctant to act. As Clunies-Ross and Sudar (1998, p. 30) put it in analysing the pyramid schemes, the opposition saw 'anarchy as a way out of enforced impotence and the risk or actuality of imprisonment'.

A socialist government regains power

The collapse of order prompted the deployment of another Italian-led international intervention force and the formation of an interim coalition government, including opposition parties. Because the 1996 election had been fraudulent, it called new elections for June 1997, which were won by an SPA-led coalition under Nano. Berisha resigned the Presidency (to which a compliant parliament had appointed him the previous year), to be replaced by Rexhep Mejdani, the SPA Secretary-General, who embraced an apolitical role. Political peace did not ensue, for Berisha claimed that the election had been flawed and demanded, with rallies of increasing ferocity, a new ballot. DPA deputies boycotted the assembly virtually continuously until July 1999, given fresh impetus in September 1997 by the wounding of a prominent DPA deputy, Azem Hajdari, within the parliament building by an SPA deputy, and still more in September 1998 by Hajdari's assassination with the complicity of renegade policemen. Stirred by Berisha's rhetoric, rioters invaded government buildings in Tirana, forcing Nano to flee, albeit briefly, to Albanian allies in Macedonia and then to resign. He nevertheless retained considerable support among the SPA rank and file and was soon elected party chairman, whence, as described below, he vied with the successor Premiers for control of government and of his party. Pandeli Majko, with a reshuffled coalition in October 1998, regained control in the south, but was less secure in the north, where the DPA's strength is concentrated. The government's writ in the north of the country weakened further when Belgrade's repression of neighbouring Kosovo turned into active combat by the Kosovo Liberation Army (KLA), supported by volunteers and weapons from Albania.

The turning point was reached in mid-March 1999, when the Rambouillet/Kleber multilateral negotiations failed to resolve the status of Kosovo. Between 24 March and 8 June the North Atlantic Treaty Organisation (NATO) launched air-strikes over 78 days on Yugoslavia, until the government of Slobodan Milošević accepted a UN (from 2004, an EU) administration of Kosovo, albeit under continued, but formal, Yugoslav sovereignty. The operations placed the Albanian economy under considerable strain. An estimated 418,600 refugees from Kosovo entered Albania during that period, either directly (234,400 passed through the Morine border-point alone) or indirectly via Macedonia. Including Kosovar Albanians who had fled earlier, Albania accommodated 445,000 persons, coincidentally about the same number as its own emigrants at the time.[18] All Albanian political parties backed both the NATO attack and the subsequent entry into Kosovo of the Kosovo Force (KFOR) and UN civilian administrators. The return of Kosovar Albanians was prompt and NATO contributed to the renewal of highways from the Albanian port of Durrës to the frontier with Kosovo. But disorder remains a serious threat, for the looting of army arsenals has left – despite government and UNDP recovery incentives – by mid-2002 nearly half-a-million of these weapons still in unlawful hands in Albania, Kosovo and Macedonia.

Division within the main parties

In a country where, as in many states of the Commonwealth of Independent States and in Yugoslavia, 'there is practically no consensus on the fundamental norms of political activity' (Adam and Tomšić, 2002, p. 439), the principal threat to consistency in economic policy and in closer relations with the European Union is the apparently implacable division within the governing and the opposition parties. Within the SPA, Nano's resignation of the party chairmanship in January 1999, after losing his premiership, proved temporary, for he was re-elected by a party congress in October 1999. From that position until his defeat for the presidential succession in June 2002 Nano undermined his successors as prime minister. He secured the resignation of Majko, accusing him of being too friendly to the DPA and to the Greek minority. The next premier, Ilir Meta, was also soon confronted by Nano, who sought the dismissal of the minister of public economy and privatisation, Zef Preci, and several other officials. Although Meta retained parliamentary backing, he was pressurised into further cabinet reshuffles in July and November 2000 and was in further conflict with Nano after the SPA victory in the parliamentary elections of June/October 2001. Meta was re-appointed premier against Nano's candidate, Arben Malaj, but Nano,

---

[18]On population movements in and out of Kosovo and the contemporary issues, see Kaser, 2000, and for an almost day-by-day account of the Kosovo conflict, see Jeffries, 2002b, ch. 6.

after a countrywide tour to rally popular support, forced Meta to resign in January 2002, under allegations that no fewer than six ministers were corrupt. Majko returned to the premiership in February 2002, but had to include in the key post of finance minister Kastriot Islami, a Nano supporter, as replacement for Anastas Angjeli (whose dismissal Nano had particularly targeted) and in July 2002 Meta as Deputy Premier. The latter survived just a year, resigning in July 2003, and in September 2004 leaving the SPA to establish a new party, the Socialist Movement for Integration (SMI), into which he attracted ten SPA deputies. Their departure was to be expected: the SPA Congress in December 2003 had, as well as re-electing Nano as leader, pushed through changes in the party statute which compelled deputies to follow instructions of the leadership. SPA representation in the 140-member Assembly thus sank from the 73 elected in the 2001 election to 62. Even with the seven deputies from two smaller parties, which Nano had brought into coalition in December 2003, the government lost its majority.

Divisions within the DPA also culminated in a break-away. Although Berisha had been re-elected as chairman at its congress in September 1999, his main rival, Genc Pollo, rallied moderates against his populist demagogy.[19] He brought them together in the Democratic Alternative (later the Reform Movement) and tried to convene an extraordinary party congress with the aim of removing Berisha. His group failed and in February 2000 Berisha secured the expulsion of the reformist deputies from the parliamentary party. Although the reformists did not oppose official DPA candidates in the local elections of October 2000, won by the SPA, they blamed the defeat on Berisha and formed the New Democratic Party (DPA). They gained six seats in the 2001 parliamentary elections, and were the sole opposition to the SPA-led coalition while the official DPA boycotted the assembly for the remainder of that year, returning in January 2002. Seeking to exert extra-parliamentary pressure to bring the government down, Berisha convened in Tirana during February 2004 two large rallies, the first riotous, the second peaceful.

---

[19]See particularly Tarifa and Spoor, 2000, p. 109 (chapter by Remzi Lani).

Political objectives of the SPA

Following the electoral victory of 2001, Meta declared the SPA-led coalition's policy to 'successfully and seriously face the challenge of European modernisation and integration', but that 'corruption, trafficking and bureaucracy' still had to be controlled. A Regional Centre for Combat against Trafficking (with Germany, Italy and Greece) has gone some way towards reducing such activities, which saw fast motor launches being used to smuggle drugs and people across the Adriatic into Italy, and the two rounds of the EU-sponsored Stability Pact for South East Europe, with associated funding, have supported another of the government's international priorities, regional integration in the wake of a reformed Yugoslavia, now to be an equal union of Serbia and Montenegro. But its negotiation with the EU for a Stabilisation and Association Agreement (SAA) had been stalled by political instability. The stability with which the European Commission is concerned was somewhat advanced during 2002, most significantly by the election of a President by consensus when Mejdani's term lapsed in June. A three-fifths vote of the assembly was required, with new elections having to be called if such is not achieved after five rounds of voting. Nano's supporters could have blocked a sufficiency of votes for a decision, but could not muster enough for his appointment. The DPA argued that the President should come from the opposition to 'compensate' for what it continued to allege had been a 'stolen' parliamentary election. Alfred Moisu, a former DPA deputy minister, was elected President by 97 votes to 20. (In 2007, the DPA's candidate for President, Bamir Topi, won on the back of five opposition votes.) Other developments of 2002 which offered a better perspective for political calm were the establishment of a bipartisan commission to investigate the deficiencies of the parliamentary elections of 2001, the end of the boycott of parliament by Berisha and his party, and the peaceful return, at parliament's invitation, of the royal pretender, Leka Zogu.

The Parliamentary elections of June 2009 saw Sali Berisha's DPA retain power with 47 per cent of the vote, against the SPA's 45 per cent. Ilir Meta, whose Socialist Alliance for Integration coalition held the balance of power in the new parliament with 5.5 per cent, was rewarded with becoming Deputy Premier and Foreign Minister in the new government formed by Berisha.

Growth and the external gap

Under PRGF2 for 2002-05 the government agreed a Poverty Reduction Strategy with the IMF and the World Bank focused on economic growth combined with macroeconomic stability and the reduction of domestic poverty. With the exception of 2002, GDP growth averaged at 5.9 per cent a year until 2008 and CPI inflation held within a 2 to 3 per cent band showing achievement of the first two objectives.[20] Significant progress remains to be made towards the third aim for poverty reduction. To implement one of the highest steady rates of growth in Europe (only the Baltic States are ahead of it), Albania has been relying on proportionately the largest double deficits of the continent – external and fiscal. The past heavy external imbalance on current account must continue to be funded partly by private remittances from Albanians working abroad and partly by international concessional lending. The current account deficit on external trade remained at 6-9 per cent of GDP in 2000s, and was forecast to be as large as 14 per cent in 2010. The government's programme for foreign trade inevitably focuses on export promotion. EU partners constitute the largest group on both imports and exports; within the latter, outward processing trade (OPT)[21] makes up most of the exchanges with the EU, and the Ministry of Economic Cooperation and Trade has long-run expectations under the preferential tariff for sales in the EU that have been operative since 2000. Within imports other than for OPT the share of machinery and equipment is expected to rise in line with dynamic domestic investment. Closing the gap is rendered the harder by a rising trend of imports, mostly generated by growing domestic demand, but also in response to lower customs duty and the appreciating currency.

The good growth record depends on a number of inter-related variables. Albania has significantly raised the share of gross capital formation in GDP – which was 16.5 per cent in 1999 and 22.7 per cent in 2002 – partly supplied by foreign direct investment (FDI) – a net $51 million in 1999, $324 million in 2004 and $844 million on an EBRD estimate for 2008 (EBRD, 2009). Nevertheless shown per capita and cumulated since 1989, Albania has received less than half the average

---

[20]See EBRD, 2009, p. 135.

[21]Fabricating products, mainly footwear and clothing from suppliers' materials and re-exporting to those suppliers.

for South-east European transition countries – $1,101 over 1989-2008 against $2,669. FDI brings more productive technology and contributes to closing the external gap, to which remittances from emigrants is an important contributor. When in 1996 money was flowing in to invest in the Ponzi pyramid frauds, such private transfers equalled 65 per cent of total imports, fell off, but were back to 58 per cent of the value of imports by 2000.[22] Public transfers of international and bilateral aid have also helped close both the savings and the external gaps. Most remittances contribute to household consumption, but where they complement domestic savings, some are invested in the 'shadow' and the illegal economy. The addition which the overall shadow (i.e. excluding the illegal) economy generated to officially-measured GDP is large, but uncertain. A study of 109 countries at the Institute of Labour (University of Bonn) estimates that it added 33.4 per cent to the measured economy (Schneider and Klinglmair, 2004, Appendix Table 2) in 2000, but two successive issues of a special report on Albania by the *Financial Times* (2002, 2004) put the added amount at as much as half of GDP. Schneider and Klinglmair show, however, on their estimates that among all transition countries the Albanian share of 'shadow economy' was the lowest, save for those countries that were to join the EU in 2004 and which had hence been introducing laws and regulations of the *acquis communautaire*.

Inequality and the internal gap

In recent years international financial institutions have been covering about half the general government deficit and have contributed significantly to the investment requirement of the savings equation (mostly in public infrastructure projects intended to attract private sector capital to other branches[23]). Reform of financial institutions, notably of the largest commercial bank in 2004, has enhanced the banking system's intermediation for corporate and household savings, and in addition to FDI some portfolio investment has been attracted by the privatisation programme and the gradual improvement of the business environment.

---

[22]Remittances grew from $150 million in 1992 to over $1 billion by 2004, equal to 14 per cent of GDP, according to de Zwager et al, 2005. Between 600,000 and 800,000 Albanians are believed to have migrated since 1991, mainly to work in Greece and Italy. Nearly 70 per cent of migrants send money to their families in Albania according to a survey by the International Organisation for Migration.

[23]Especially to small and medium enterprises (Hashi, 2001).

On the EBRD's nine 'transition indicators' – measurements of progress to a market economy on which 1 is 'no progress' and 4+ 'the standards of an industrialised market economy' – Albania had achieved 4- by 2009.[24] Albania needs to generate tax revenue at least proportionately in line with its regional neighbours.[25] Privatisation was effectively completed by 2009, with the result that revenues from asset sales disappeared. The improvement of tax-collection rates, especially of customs duties, goes hand-in-hand with the staunching of corruption: the international agencies and other governments alike have pressed, and are helping, in that campaign. A reform of income taxation in 2008 that introduced a flat 10 per cent tax led to an increase in revenues. Overall, the primary deficit (revenue less expenditure other than debt service) should, according to the Letter of Intent to the IMF of June 2002, have been slimmed to 2.2 per cent of GDP in 2005. But the government has nevertheless continued to operate with a consistently higher deficit, of between 3 to 6 per cent over recent years.

While deficits persist of such magnitude, a policy of macroeconomic stability precludes significant increases in government expenditure on poverty reduction. Until 2002 that expenditure absorbed over 30 per cent of GDP and it is falling rather than increasing. Subsidisation of workplaces and other job-creation schemes on any substantial scale are not an option to reduce unemployment, which since 2001 has been a steady 13-15 per cent of the resident labour force; of the total labour force 27 per cent were in emigration, in principle available for return to Albania if work were available.

The first full assessment of poverty in Albania was undertaken in 2002 by the World Bank. It found that about 25 per cent of population (around 780,000 people) had consumption levels below the poverty line, even after receiving income support. That said, only 5 per cent of people were

---

[24] The EBRD turned its attention towards strengthening the business environment in 1999, compared to its previous focus on supporting structural change. 'Transition economies' are evolving towards a 'well-functioning market economy', in which the state and private institutions are working 'well together': 'transition is not just about the size of the state's 'footprint' in the economy but also where and how the state treads'. There is thus a renewed emphasis on creating an enabling business environment, focusing on competition, market structures, management practices and performance; see EBRD, 2009, pp. 96–97.

[25] Treichel, 2002, p. 17 points out that in 2000 Albanian tax revenue was 16 per cent of GDP while states of former Yugoslavia were between 24 and 39 per cent.

without adequate nutrition. The rural population, comprising 55 per cent of the total, was significantly poorer than urban inhabitants, with nearly 30 per cent living below the poverty line. In the Mountain Region of the North and Northeast, almost half the population was poor and 20 per cent could not meet basic food needs. Among the poor only 20 per cent of children enrolled in secondary education. In terms of basic services, less than 50 per cent of the rural population had access to running water and toilets.[26] Certainly, poverty persists as a serious social problem. That a more equal distribution of income and wealth will take time is evident from the government's acceptance under the IMF's PRGF2 that 'it aims at balancing increased spending to reduce poverty against the need to ensure macroeconomic stability' (IMF, 2002a). What is clear is that Albania is not able to eradicate poverty and develop sustainably without the support of the international community.

Concluding remarks

At the turn of the millennium it seemed as though Karl Marx had been proved correct. In *Das Kapital*, Marx had argued that any system of property rights ('productive relations') and their political superstructure which fails optimally to exploit the available economic resources and technology ('productive forces') must give way to a system which can do better. Such an expression of dialectical materialism, he asserted, need not be by violent revolution, but it was historically ineluctable. Slave-owning societies had faded before feudalism, which in turn lost out to capitalism because of their inadequacy for economic management as new opportunities emerged for growth. In 1989/91 the countries of Central and Eastern Europe, the republics constituting the Soviet Union and then China turned again towards capitalism because the form of socialism they had adopted had proved to be a poorer mechanism for generating welfare from the land, labour and capital at their disposition.

However the subsequent period of 'decontrol' saw the formerly socialist countries move along different trajectories. The outcome of what was termed 'the transition' has proved to be sub-optimal in several cases, of which Albania is, so far, clearly one. A number of problems emerged or were left unresolved. At the microeconomic level, systemic transformation

[26]See the Living Standard Measurement Survey reported in World Bank (2006), pp. 6-7.

required not only the abrogation of the Communist Party's monopoly of power but the free flow of information (full and open reporting of enterprise performance and market prices, timely publication of accurate statistics, including data for the national accounts, registration of property titles, transparency within the state administration, and so on).[27] Decontrol without good information means that the signals upon which a market economy relies for self-regulation are distorted or confused. The Albanian political economy tried to operate with corrupted systems and it is not surprising that the outcomes were sub-optimal. Additionally, at the macroeconomic level, Albania's transition was hampered by the legacy of major imbalances and structural features (large-scale absolute poverty, clan networks and lawlessness, relative isolation from the rest of Europe, etc.) that were never addressed in a fundamental way, and, perhaps, simply could not be addressed, by the international community – not to mention the impact of the Yugoslav tragedy on its doorstep. The international community, as represented by the IMF, the World Bank, the EBRD and the EU, expected the microeconomic reforms to promote macroeconomic and structural adjustment. Whether this over-ambitious reliance on 'the market' should be considered part and parcel of the 'Washington Consensus' is beyond the scope of this chapter, but the Albanian experience suggests that economists should preserve a modicum of humility whenever they are asked for advice in future. As a result, the macroeconomic adjustment in Albania occurred through the shake-out of labour from enterprises and the dissolution of collective farms into unsustainably small holdings, which in turn depressed effective demand and investment for a prolonged period. Marx might well have been disappointed, and possibly outraged, at what was constructed in his name. Nonetheless, his critique would surely have been trenchant in the op-ed columns of the *New York Daily Tribune* and *Die Presse* of Vienna (or their modern successors[28]) at the subsequent travails of transition.

---

[27]See Kaser (1990).

[28]The *New York Herald Tribune* (formerly the *New York Tribune*) closed in 1967 but its international edition kept going as the *International Herald Tribune* and is now owned by the *New York Times*. *Die Presse* foundered in 1896 but was re-launched in 1946.

References

Adam, Frane and Mateuž Tomšić, 2002, 'Elite (Re)configuration and Politico-economic Performance in Post-socialist Countries', *Europe-Asia Studies*, vol. 54, pp. 435-45

Barro, Robert and Jong-wha Lee (2002), 'IMF Programs: Who is Chosen and What Are the Effects', NBER Working Paper no. W8951 (May)

Clunies-Ross, Anthony and Petar Sudari (eds), 1998, *Albania's Economy in Transition and Turmoil, 1991-97* (Ashgate, Aldershot)

ECE, 2001, *Trends in Europe and North America 2001* (United Nations Economic Commission for Europe, Geneva)

Djilas, Milovan, 1963, *Conversations with Stalin* (Penguin, Harmondsworth)

Emmerij, Louis, Richard Jolly and Thomas G. Weiss, 2002, *Ahead of the Curve? UN Ideas and Global Challenges* (Indiana University Press, Bloomington and Indianapolis)

EBRD, 2002, *Albania Strategy Overview* (European Bank for Reconstruction and Development, London)

EBRD, 2004, *Transition Report 2004* (European Bank for Reconstruction and Development, London)

EBRD, 2009, *Transition Report 2009* (European Bank for Reconstruction and Development, London)

Financial Times, 2002, 'Special Report: Albania', 18 December

Financial Times, 2004, 'Special Report: Albania', 18 May

Fishta, Iliaz, 2001, 'Agrarproblem und Agrarreform im Albanien der Zwischenkriegzeit', *Südost-Forschungen*, vol. 59/60, pp. 387-422

Grothusen, Klaus-Detlev (ed.), 1993, *Sudosteuropa Handbuch VII: Albanien* (Göttingen, Vandenhoeck and Ruprecht)

Hanson, Philip, 1990, 'Industry' in Martin McCauley (ed.), *Gorbachev and Perestroika* (Macmillan, London), pp. 49-69

Hashi, Iraj, 2001, 'Financial and Institutional Barriers to SME Growth in Albania: Results of an Enterprise Survey', *Moct-Most*, vol. 11(3), pp. 221-38

Hashi, Iraj and Lindita Xhillari, 1999, 'Privatisation and Transition in Albania', *Post-Communist Economics*, vol. 11, pp. 99-126

IMF, 2001, Albania: Article IV Consultation and Review under the Poverty Reduction and Growth Facility, IMF Country Report no. 01/117 (International Monetary Fund, Washington DC)

IMF, 2002a, Memorandum on Economic and Financial Policies of the Government of the Republic of Albania for 200203 under a Three-year

Arrangement under the Poverty Reduction and Growth Facility (PRGF) (International Monetary Fund, Washington DC).

IMF, 2002b, Poverty Reduction and Growth Facility: Albania, Country Report no. 02/135 (International Monetary Fund, Washington DC)

IMF, 2004, Albania: Joint Staff Assessment of the Poverty Reduction Strategy Paper Annual Progress Report, IMF Country Report no. 04/205 (International Monetary Fund, Washington DC)

Jeffries, Ian, 2002a, *Eastern Europe at the Turn of the Twenty-first Century* (London and New York, Routledge)

Jeffries, Ian, 2002b, *The Former Yugoslavia at the Turn of the Twenty-first Century* (London and New York, Routledge)

Kaser, Michael, 1982, A new Statistical Abstract from Albania, *Soviet Studies*, vol XXXIV, no 1, January, pp. 123-125

Kaser, Michael, 1983, 'Albania's Muscular Socialism', *Contemporary Review*, vol. 243 (1411), pp. 89-94

Kaser, Michael, 1987, 'One economy, two systems': parallels between Soviet and Chinese reform, *International Affairs*, vol. 63, no. 3, Summer, pp. 395-412

Kaser, Michael, 1990, 'The technology of decontrol: Some macroeconomic issues', *The Economic Journal*, 100, June, pp. 596-615

Kaser, Michael, 2000, 'Albanian Political and Economic Stability in the Wake of the Kosovo Conflict', in Roland Schönfeld (ed.), *Structural Changes in Transforming South-eastern Europe* (Südosteuropa-Gesellschaft, Munich), vol. 67, pp. 87-102

Kaser, Michael, 2001, 'Economic Continuities in Albania's Turbulent History', *Europe-Asia Studies*, vol. 53, pp. 627-37

Lemel, Harold, 1998, 'Rural Land Privatisation in Albania: Evidence from the Field', *Europe-Asia Studies*, vol. 50, pp. 121-40

Lemel, Harold (ed.), 2000, *Rural Property and Economy in Post-Communist Albania* (Berghahn, New York and Oxford)

Lerman, Zvi, Csaba Csaki and Gerschon Feder, *Agriculture in Transition* (Lexington, New York and Oxford).

McNeilly, Caryl and Doris Schiesser-Gachnang, 1998, Reducing Inflation: Lessons from Albania's Early Success, IMF Working Paper no. 98/78 (International Monetary Fund, Washington DC)

Malcolm, Noel, 1998, *Kosovo: A Short History* (Macmillan, London)

Pier, R. 1983, 'Tourismus', in Grothusen, 1993, pp. 417-26

Schnytzer, Adi, 1982, *Stalinist Economic Strategy in Practice: The Case of Albania* (Oxford University Press, Oxford)

Schnytzer, Adi, 1993, 'Industry', in Grothusen, 1993, pp. 312-42

Shaw, D. John, 2002, *Sir Hans Singer: The Life and Work of a Development Economist* (Palgrave, London)

Tarifa, Fatos and Max Spoor (eds), 2000, *The First Decade and After: Albania's Democratic Transition and Consolidation in the Context of Southeast Europe* (Institute of Social Studies, The Hague)

Treichel, Volker, 2002, Stabilization Policies and Structural Reforms in Albania since 1997 – Achievements and Remaining Challenges, IMF Policy Discussion Paper PDP/02/2 (International Monetary Fund, Washington DC)

Vickers, Miranda, 1998, *Between Serb and Albanian: A History of Kosovo* (Hurst, London)

Vickers, Miranda and James Pettifer, 1997, *Albania: From Anarchy to a Balkan Identity* (Hurst, London)

World Bank, 1997, Albania: Growing Out of Poverty, Report of the Human Resources Operations Division, no 15698-ALB (World Bank, Washington DC)

World Bank, 2004, *Albania Data Profile* (World Bank, Washington DC)

Zwager, N, de; Gedeshi, I; Germenji, E; and Nikas C, 2005, *Competing for Remittances*, (International Organisation for Migration, Tirana)

World Bank, *2006, Country Assistance Strategy for Albania for FY 2006 to FY 2009*, Report No. 34329-AL (World Bank: Washington)

Elite dissent and its role in the collapse of communism in Albania

Bernd Fischer

Introduction

In 1974 my friend Fatos Labonja, the son of a disgraced member of the central committee of the Albanian Party of Labor, was arrested after the Albanian Secret Police (the Albanian Directorate of State Security or Sigurimi) found his diaries in his uncle's attic. The diaries indicated that the twenty-three year old student had been reading proscribed foreign literature. Following a hasty trial he was originally sentenced to seven years in a labor camp. But because he was serving his sentence in a camp from which a protest letter was sent to the dictator Enver Hoxha, two years prior to his scheduled release he was sentenced to an additional twenty years. Mr. Labonja, who today is one of Albania's most important writers and a political commentator, has said 'In Albania dissidents did not exist. There is a difference between a dissident and a victim of the regime. A dissident is someone who has the possibility to enlighten other people, to express his opinions, maybe go to prison but to inspire others and make a choice. While in Albania, we were just victims which means we did not inspire others but were instead people whose experience instilled fear in others.'[1] Mr. Labonja is uniquely positioned to make such a judgment and so the questions remain, was there effective dissent prior to the 1970s and why was intellectual opposition to the Hoxha regime in its later decades so limited and ineffective? What role did elite dissent play in the collapse of the communist system in Albania in 1991-1992 and what is the legacy of the lack of effective dissent in Albania?

Internal Party Opposition to Enver Hoxha

Enver Hoxha, who ruled Albania from 1944 until his death in 1985, certainly experienced considerable early opposition and dissent from within his own movement and there were more than a few occasions

---

[1]Misha Glenny, *The Balkans 1804-1999, Nationalism, War and the Great Powers* (London: Granta, 1999), p. 568. See also Fatos Lubonja, *Second Sentence* (London: I.B. Tauris, 2009

when his political and physical survival was very much in doubt. The strength of early opposition to his regime and to him personally does much to explain the brutal repression which even a vague hint of divergence from his prescribed line would later engender. When the Albanian Communist Party was founded in November 1941 it was divided and tiny, boasting no more than 130 members who had been dispersed throughout a number of squabbling cells. Hoxha used the war years to fight and destroy the plethora of non-communist resistance groups, attempt to expand support for his party among the Albanian population, and often only as an afterthought, fight the fascist invaders. He also was quite active in uniting the communists in part by purging deviants from with the movement. He found it necessary, for example, to dissolve the entire Gjirokastra district committee to destroy what he termed 'liquidatory elements.'[2] Closely following the advice of his Yugoslav advisers in terms of the creation of an army and a state, Hoxha was able to prevail and by 1946 most organized opposition was eliminated – with the exception of small groups which held out in the rugged mountains of the north until the late 1940s.[3]

But Hoxha's troubles had really just begun. Following the war Albania became a virtual satellite of Yugoslavia which had played an important role in the success of the communist resistance during the war. This status created various challenges for Hoxha from both the Yugoslavs and from within his own party. With the signing of the Treaty of Friendship, Cooperation and Mutual Aid with Yugoslavia in 1946, Albania fell further under Yugoslav control. The treaty included coordination of economic plans, standardization of monetary systems, a customs union, unification of prices, and the introduction of Yugoslav experts into every Albanian government department as well as the army. While Hoxha recognized Tito's designs on Albanian independence, he did not initially feel strong enough to resist them. As a result he was challenged by nationalist elements within the party who were anti-Yugoslav. At the same time the much more powerful staunchly pro-Yugoslav elements, led by the brutal and ambitious minister of the interior Koci Xoxe, accused him of

[2]Institute of Marxist-Leninist Studies at the Central Committee of the Party of Labor of Albania, *History of the Party of Labor of Albania* (Tirana: Naim Frasheri, 1971), p. 99.
[3]Elez Biberaj, *Albania in Transition*, (Boulder CO: Westview Press, 1999), p. 21.

lack of diligence in tying Tirana closer to Belgrade. Tito much preferred Xoxe over Hoxha, in part because Xoxe was actually the only worker in the Albanian leadership, but principally because Xoxe approved of Tito's plan to establish some form of con-federal link between Albania and Yugoslavia. In early 1948 Hoxha's position weakened to the extent that he was forced to admit errors in policy. He would certainly have ended up in front of one of Xoxe's firing squads had it not been for the Yugoslav-Soviet break. Hoxha staunchly supported Stalin in this dispute, renouncing all economic arrangements with Yugoslavia and initiating violent anti-Yugoslav polemics. He also took the opportunity to arrest and shoot Xoxe and many of his followers, in the process purging fully a quarter of the members of the renamed Albanian Party of Labor.[4]

Hoxha had survived what was likely the most serious threat to his leadership and Albania moved from being a sub-satellite of the Yugoslavs and became a full satellite of the Soviets.[5] By the mid-1950s, Hoxha's regime was considered the most Stalinist regime in Eastern Europe and Hoxha himself was therefore again seriously jeopardized by the process of de-Stalinization which the communist bloc endured. The death of Stalin in 1953 resulted in a certain liberalization in both foreign and domestic policy throughout much of the socialist world, accompanied by a denunciation of the excesses of Stalin. The Soviet Union under Nikita Khrushchev initiated a reapproachment with Yugoslavia, and both the Soviets and the Yugoslavs encouraged Hoxha to rehabilitate Xoxe. However, Hoxha refused and immediately began moving towards his third protector, China, while at the same time himself moving further towards the extreme left. Hoxha clearly saw the danger – he, like Stalin – had by this point instituted a personality cult based upon a reign of terror. In defending Stalin and his policies, he was defending himself.[6] And he did so with increasing brutality.

But Hoxha again survived what was the last important attempt by internal forces to remove him. As in 1948, Hoxha was again saved by events beyond his control. In this case the invasion of Hungary by Soviet and Warsaw Pact forces in order to crush a move towards liberalization

[4]Glenny, *The Balkans*, p. 560.
[5]Nicholas Pano, *The People's Republic of Albania* (Baltimore: Johns Hopkins University Press, 1968), p89.
[6]Elez Biberaj, *Albania: A Socialist Maverick* (Boulder, CO: Westview Press, 1990), p. 23.

allowed him to move against those in the party who hoped to follow Khrushchev's de-Stalinization example. Hoxha used what became his usual tactics. He admitted that some mistakes had been made but blamed imperialist agents who just happened to be all of those in the party whom he suspected of disloyalty. These people were quickly removed, many of them liquidated, and replaced by more reliable communists, usually the relatives of his closest supporters. As a result of repeated purges and increasing paranoia on Hoxha's part, by the mid 1950s more than half of the fifty- three members of the central committee of the party were related to one another. The party leadership, which was increasingly bound together by common complicity in murderous purges, had become Hoxha's clan – he had essentially adapted local conditions to Stalinism.[7] As opposition and dissent became less effective, Hoxha seems to have become more intolerant, more brutal and more paranoid.

In 1960, in the midst of the Albanian-Soviet break, he again felt threatened by the pro-Soviet cadres within the party who objected to his turn towards China. The economic hardship caused by the loss of Soviet credits encouraged Hoxha to increase his repression through the institution of the so-called Ideological and Cultural Revolution. The principal aim of this wrenching shakeup was again to eliminate potential alternative centers of power to the party and to Hoxha himself. Unlike the Chinese version, the Albanian Cultural Revolution was meant to further centralize power.[8] The small intelligentsia was particularly targeted. Ramiz Alia, Hoxha's chief ideologue and his eventual successor, laid down the line that the chief function of literature and art was to provide young people with the necessary immunity against the poisons of both bourgeois and revisionist ideologies.[9] This was accompanied by an attack on religion, bureaucracy, and the traditional structure of the army. Some resisted these changes and Hoxha felt threatened by conservative members of the military and the economic establishment.

The Cultural Revolution, with its main phase between 1966 and 1969, exhausted the party and the country as a whole. While Hoxha's

[7]Miranda Vickers, *The Albanians: A Modern History*, (London: I.B. Tauris, 1995), p. 176.

[8]R.J. Crampton, *The Balkans Since the Second World War*, (London: Longman, 2002), p. 160.

[9]Anton Logoreci, *The Albanians: Europe's Forgotten Survivors*, Boulder CO: Westview Press, 1977), p.159-160.

excesses did not, and could not, result in a widespread, organized dissident movement, they did result in increasing restlessness among young people and intellectuals. For the youth, who had no wartime experience and for whom the slogans about the partisan struggle were becoming increasingly irrelevant, the issues included hair length, popular music and access to western literature. The intellectuals craved at least a slight shift away from the straitjacket of socialist-realism. Similar to Stalin's second five year plan following the horrors of collectivization, and meant as something of a correction, from 1969 to 1972 Hoxha flirted with limited cultural and economic reform. Again he was challenged, this time by conservatives within the party who feared the effect of even limited relaxation. While the actual changes were certainly imperceptible to all but the most careful observers, Hoxha eventually saw them as another threat and quickly reversed course. Hoxha struck again and buried the first signs of an independent post-war culture in Albania. Officials of the writer's union and Albania's radio and television services were sacked and the official youth movement was overhauled to enhance party control. Literature returned to the only acceptable theme which was the anti-fascist struggle during World War II. The arts returned to socialist-realism and the press, radio and television returned to their original purpose of political indoctrination and ideological education, with central control strengthened in each field. The Albanian press became one of the dullest and least informative in Europe, haranguing its readers with preachy, exhortative, patronizing, self- righteous pronouncements.[10] Hoxha's developing cult of the personality was strengthened. The shadow of Hoxha was soon everywhere from high billboards and endless slogans painted on the sides of buildings, to young pioneers defacing the sides of mountains with white stones in thirty feet letters spelling out 'ENVER.'

As the Chinese connection began to fade due to what Hoxha termed a Chinese slide into revisionism, Albania receded into a state of siege mentality fearing 'coordinated aggressive activity by Greek monarcho-fascists, Italian neo-fascists, Yugoslav and Soviet revisionists, all supported by U.S. and British imperialists.'[11]

---

[10]Logoreci, *The Albanians*, p. 177.
[11]Institute of Marxist-Leninist Studies, *History of the Party of Labor*, p. 350.

Albania began to resemble what an analyst has described as a 'collage of fantasies.'[12] The masses were mobilized for the most fantastic projects, two of which perhaps best demonstrate the level of Hoxha's extremism. The most evident was the construction of tens of thousands of concrete and steel bunkers (a project headed by Alfred Moisiu who served as president of Albania from 2002-2007) to accommodate Hoxha's emphasis on a 'people's army' which could be carefully controlled by the party. The bunker system was augmented by a sort of do-it-yourself air defense system that saw young pioneers fix long spikes to the tops of trees to impale enemy parachutists attempting to evade the bunkers. While the bunkers are slowly disappearing, Albania still remains scarred by these physical monuments to Hoxha's paranoia.

Instruments of Repression

So as we have seen, there was a good deal of sporadic party opposition to Hoxha and his policies, at least until the 1960s, but little dissent beyond that period. The next task is to attempt to determine why Albania is different from the rest of the communist bloc in this regard. Certainly at least part of the answer can be found in the nature of Hoxha, the security apparatus which underpinned his regime, and the way Hoxha used it. Hoxha was the strongest of the communist strongmen who built an inflexible totalitarian structure. While some Balkan dictatorships seemed to mellow with age, Hoxha became more radical, building a regime based on labor camps, prison camps, arbitrary arrests, beatings and government sanctioned murder. The regime rested in large part on the extensive security apparatus which – including the military – was eventually made up of about 3.5% of the population at the cost of 10-11% of GNP.[13] With an accompanying army of informants, Hoxha and his police were allowed into virtually every living room in the country.

Hoxha's security service was one of the most comprehensive in Eastern Europe. All reporting to the minister of interior, there were four main branches including the Sigurimi (the secret police), the frontier guards, the people's police and the auxiliary police. The Sigurimi, the most feared component of the system, was divided into a number of departments including political affairs, censorship, prisons and labor

[12]Glenny, *The Balkans*, p. 559.
[13]Ramadan Marmulluku, *Albania and the Albanians* (London: Hurst, 1975), p. 70.

camps, counter-intelligence, and visiting and resident aliens.[14] The prison and work camp system run by the Sigurimi included six institutions for political prisoners, nine for inmates convicted of non-political crimes, and fourteen labor camps where political and non-political prisoners suffered together. Conditions inside these institutions were of course appalling. Inmates were routinely tortured and starved of decent food and medical care. Further, the state ran an internal exile system where tens of thousands convicted of lesser political offenses were forced to relocate to remote villages where they were treated as pariah by the local peasantry. In some cases the exiles were even required to build their own villages. A person was rarely condemned to exile alone; like under Stalin in the Soviet Union his or her entire family – and often friends and supporters – would also be sent away. The former politburo member Liri Belishova stands as an example. Purged in 1960 for her support of some aspects of de-Stalinization, she was exiled to a remote village where she lived for thirty years. Her husband was imprisoned and her relatives and supports suffered imprisonment or exile along with her.[15]

While figures are still disputed, its is estimated that on Hoxha's death in 1985, Albania's prison population totaled some 32,000[16], many of whom were condemned with the help of their own children who were considered a primary means of government surveillance. At school children were encouraged to spy on family members and report all anti-government activity to authorities. Children were rewarded for such activity with better grades. This system seemed to be quite effective, at least until about the fourth grade, at which point competing family loyalties became stronger. Albanians, unable to trust their own children, were cowed into a fearful state of submission, conformism and apathy, with their thoughts kept secret, paranoid and suspicious of all around them.[17]

For the elite, party members and their children, dissent was further discouraged by what can be described as a continuous purge which Hoxha instituted. During the bloody reign of the Ottoman Sultan Selim

[14]See James O'Donnell, 'Albania's Sigurimi: The Ultimate Agents of Social Control' *Problems of Post- Communism* Vol. 42 Issue 6, (1995).

[15]In conversation with Liri Belishova, Tirana, July 2010.

[16]'Human Rights in the People's Republic of Albania,' Minnesota Lawyers International Human Rights Committee, Minneapolis, 1990.

[17]Vickers, *The Albanians*, p. 209.

I, a common curse was 'may you become Selim's GrandVizier' due to the many he dispatched. Under Hoxha, who one biographer called the 'Red Sultan,' the curse could have been 'may you become Hoxha's minister of the interior,' all seven of whom were purged as foreign agents. The Albanian party was by far the most purge-effected of all of the East European parties.

The first of many purges took place in 1942, only months after the founding of the party, and the purges continued until the death of Hoxha. A number of major purges stand out, including the arrest and execution of minister of the interior Koxi Xoxe and his followers following the Yugoslav-Soviet break. The next major purge was equally as extensive and involved. As we have seen, following the death of Stalin Hoxha refused to contemplate de-Stalinization, since this path would likely have resulted in his own removal. Instead, Hoxha shot or exiled his remaining potential rivals in the politburo. The end of the Soviet period allowed Hoxha to purge again, arresting ten senior party officials, followed by a wide ranging purge of those party members with Soviet leanings. By 1962, of the thirty-one members of the central committee elected at the first party congress in 1948 only nine remained. Fourteen had been liquidated and eight forced to retire. The sixty-one members of the central committee included five married couples and in all no fewer than twenty persons were related to one another as sons-in-law or cousins.[18]

But even those within this tight inner circle were not always safe. Between 1971 and 1976, forty-one percent of the politburo was replaced by fiercely loyal younger people will little experience.[19] One of Hoxha's last major purges was perhaps his most bizarre and remains something of a mystery to this day. Mehmet Shehu, the prime minister and head of the Sigurimi, had been Hoxha's trusted right-hand since the war. Shehu was the assumed successor but Hoxha seems to have decided sometime in 1981 that he was not the one to carry on his work. Among other considerations, their wives had fallen out and Hoxha feared for his wife's safety in the event of his death. Publicly Hoxha chastised Shehu for agreeing to marry his son into a 'war criminal' family supposedly in an attempt to undermine the regime. But this was only the beginning.

[18]Ibid., p. 189.
[19]Nicholas Pano, 'Albania.' in Joseph Held (ed.) *The Columbia History of Eastern Europe in the Twentieth Century*, (New York: Columbia University Press, 1992), p. 41.

In December 1981 Albanians were astonished to learn that Shehu had committed suicide in a fit of depression. In 1982 they were perhaps even more astonished to learn that Shehu had all along been a multiple agent in the pay of British, Yugoslav, American and Soviet intelligence services. Shehu's death was followed by yet another bloody purge this time falling principally on the military and the Sigurimi, the institutions with which Shehu was most closely associated. Shehu's wife, also a member of the inner power circle, was sentenced to twenty-five years in prison. There are indications that more purges would have come, had Hoxha not died in 1985. His personal physician Ylli Popa maintains that just before his death Hoxha was afraid that his doctors had hatched a plot to do him in. While waiting in Hoxha's library, before being granted access to the dictator, Popa came across a book which dealt with the so-called doctor's plot in the last days of Stalin. Hoxha had recently and emphatically underlined a number of critical passages.[20] On this occasion, Hoxha died before he was able to act.

Clearly, no one was safe. Given the nature of Hoxha and his regime, then, there was simply no opportunity for an organized dissident movement to materialize after the early 1960s. Tolerated dissident groups, like those that ultimately helped to overthrow the regimes in Poland, Hungary and other East European states simply did not exist in Albania.

The Collapse of the Regime

Without the dissent found in the other communist bloc states, dissent which clearly contributed to the collapse of those regimes, what explains the demise of the Albanian regime following Hoxha's death? Certainly a minor role was played by Albania's rather anemic intelligentsia – but not until the early 1990s, just prior to the collapse. The Albanian intelligentsia was considerably weaker than those found elsewhere in the communist bloc, in part because of Albania's level of development. The intelligentsia was almost entirely located in Tirana and had only started to become a force in society with the opening of Albania's first university in 1957. When compared to those in other Eastern European countries, it must be considered immature and certainly closely aligned with the party. Its style tended to be paternalistic and authoritarian, frequently combining

---

[20] Ylli Popa, personal physician to Enver Hoxha, recounted this story to the Albanian press in 2009.

intellectual mediocrity with a blind loyalty to even the most extremist elements of the Hoxhaist dogma.[21] Although Hoxha, who was clearly more intelligent than some of the other crushingly boring Eastern European dictators, could be counted among their number, he remained suspicious of them. As we have seen, the intelligentsia became a particular target during the Cultural Revolution. For the subsequent two decades, writers and intellectuals faithfully carried out the party's policies of socialist-realism, serving as little more than propaganda tools with which the party could control the people. The Albanian intelligentsia never fully recovered from the onslaught it experienced during the Cultural Revolution and subsequent purges.

The most important member of this small group was, and still is, Ismail Kadare, possibly the best known of the living novelists from the former communist bloc. His relationship with the regime was certainly unclear. He himself, to this author and others, takes pains to demonstrate that everything he did under communism was part of a perpetual dynamic of persecution and resistance. Some analysts, including Noel Malcolm and Fatos Labonja, argue conversely that much of his writing during the Hoxha regime nourished the principal points of Albanian national-communist mythology.[22] Malcolm suggests that while his work was utterly different in spirit from the socialist-realist novels of the time, with their bright sunshine, cheery peasants and hydroelectric dams, Kadare himself had complex loyalties to an inner mythic world, while remaining clearly an employee of the state.[23] It can be argued that this is at least one of the reasons his writing largely escaped the traditional censorship and suppression, although his international reputation likely played a role as well. In any case, his works certainly can be considered an aberration when compared to the virtual propaganda being produced by most of his contemporaries.

It is not surprising that with the slight easing of the internal conditions under Ramiz Alia, who succeeded to the position of first secretary of

---

[21]Miranda Vickers and James Pettifer, *Albania: From Anarchy to a Balkan Identity*, (New York: New York University Press, 2000), p. 16.

[22]See Fatos Labonja, 'Between the Glory of the Virtual World and the Misery of the Real World,' in Stephanie Schwandner-Sievers and Bernd J. Fischer, *Albanian Identities: Myth and History*, (London: Hurst, 2002).

[23]See Noel Malcolm, 'In the Palace of Nightmares,' *New York Review of Books*, November 6, 1997.

the party on the death of Hoxha in 1985, some attention was focused on Kadare and he did, perhaps a bit late, find his voice. In August 1989 Neshat Tozaj, a party member and former Sigurimi official, published a novel called *Thikat* (Knives). The story line involves police agents falsifying evidence to convict innocent people. The novel itself cannot be considered a dissident work, particularly since there is not even a hint of criticism of the party; indeed the party emerges as hero for unmasking the corrupted officials. Kadare, however, skillfully used its publication and wrote a very positive review of the book in October 1989.[24]

In this important review, Kadare called for a more just society based on the rule of law, for greater respect for the rights of the individual, and for increased freedom of expression for writers and artists. At a literary conference held in November 1989, he went further and publicly criticized the government's interference in literature, arguing that no government had the power to grant or deny the writer his freedom to create. But Kadare was careful not to criticize Alia, even leaving the impression that he was a strong supporter of Alia's piecemeal reforms.[25] The fear that even Kadare harbored for the regime even as late as July 1990 – months after spontaneous demonstrations had erupted – is clear from the account of an open meeting Alia called with intellectuals in July 1990. Alia demanded that the assembled intellectuals support the government. While there was a discussion of human rights violations, excesses of the Sigurimi, the issue of Stalin – whose statutes and busts still stood in every Albanian town of any size – only Sali Berisha (Albania's leading cardiologist and a minor communist functionary) who would succeed Alia as president two years later, called for changing the system with multi-party elections. Kadare maintains that he had planned to demand political pluralism, but changed his mind. He was afraid that the meeting was called to provoke the intellectuals as a pretext to further repression. Some of Kadare's colleagues expressed the fear that they might not leave the meeting alive.[26] A few months later, Kadare asked for and received asylum in France.

Kadare's statements and actions certainly helped to encourage a greater independence of thought among some intellectuals and those

---

[24]Biberaj, *Albania in Transition*, p. 33.
[25]Ibid.
[26]Ibid., p. 54.

so influenced eventually began pushed the party leadership to do the same. While their writing did not directly challenge the regime, they did help to corrode political authority and foster social attitudes that ultimately undermined communist legitimacy and interfered with the party's capacity to govern the country. After having been in the forefront of the government propaganda campaign, there were signs of collective defection, creeping though the pace might have been. Still, intellectuals had failed to effectively articulate and publicly present alternative political programs to communism.

So, the intellectuals contributed, but the regime would likely have collapsed without this contribution. Hoxha's policies had led to little more than grinding poverty and geopolitical isolation. And in the midst of this disaster, Albania entered the television age, which presented Albanians with a glimpse of the outside world from which the regime was protecting them. The first experimental television sets became available to the selected few in 1960 and full operation was implemented in 1971. The number of sets increased dramatically from 35,000 sets in 1974 to over 200,000 by 1985.[27] Albanian programming naturally operated under strict controls and was used for the usual purposes of political indoctrination and education. But Albanians could also watch Yugoslav, Greek and Italian channels. This activity was discouraged but particularly after Hoxha's death, the lure was simply too strong. Cracks in the state of siege began to appear. By the late 1980s students were listening to rock music and growing their hair. This was accompanied by the first signs of criticism in the media of the dogmatism of the party. All of this was further accompanied by increasing dissatisfaction among the workers, who suffered from an economy plagued by over-centralization, persistent –often inept– interference from the center, a tremendous waste of resources, distorted prices, inefficient enterprises, widespread corruption, and constant shortages of basic goods. Alia's response to the growing crisis was woefully inadequate. He tinkered with the economy, loosened the party's grip in the cultural sector, and gradually expanded Albania's relations with other countries. His measures clearly were aimed at improving the functioning of the communist system rather than

---

[27]Pano, 'Albania,' p. 48.

changing it. Even had this been possible, which is certainly doubtful, Alia responded far too late with far too little.

Rising discontent soon spilled over into spontaneous popular demonstrations, encouraged by the fall of the wall and the execution of Nicolae Ceausescu in Romania in December 1989. Trouble began in January 1990 in Shkodra, the traditional northern center of opposition to communism. The issues included a combination of food shortages, fuel shortages in the midst of winter, with an ill-defined call for democratic reform. The government reacted by dispatching the Sigurimi and troops but Alia clearly decided against the extensive military repression used in Romania and China, which shocked the world. Reporters at the official newspaper Bashkim took advantage of the developing crisis to demand independent editorial control. This event helped to serve as a catalyst for a wave of open discussion, particularly among students at the University of Tirana. Alia, in what would become his usual response, reacted defensively with piecemeal reform, which resulted in rising expectations. Every minor reform encouraged the population to demand more. Alia's response actually made him reasonably popular for a time with many Albanians seeing him as a progressive reformer.

But by July 1990 he had lost that support as a result of another seemingly spontaneous event, the storming of the Western embassies in Tirana. On 2 July 400 climbed fences into western embassies, following the example of a family of six who had climbed the fence into the Italian embassy in February. The 400 soon became 4,500.[28]

Alia let them go, and it seems clear that neither his party, nor his regime, ever recovered from the episode which did much to demolish the conventional wisdom concerning the invincibility of the regime. The next months saw the development of an increasingly anarchic, violent street culture which appeared in almost all of Albania's towns and cities. An attack on a public building at night by a few people was more typical than the large scale organized meetings and street demonstrations like those that occurred in other Eastern European countries, but the effect was similar.[29]

The final push towards political pluralism, and with it the eventual end of the regime, came from the students at the University of Tirana.

[28]Ibid., p. 25
[29]Ibid., p. 34.

Students began serious protests on 8 December 1990, complaining about poor conditions and the slow pace of reform. Alia first tried to negotiate through his discredited government, then resorted to the arrest of some of the leaders. The student protests actually attracted little support from the population or from the intellectuals and seemed to be on the verge of collapse until student leader Azem Hajdari regrouped the demoralized protestors. Alia responded by sending Sali Berisha, a northerner like Hajdari, and Berisha put himself at the head of a movement which seemed to be forming by itself. On 11 December 1990 as yet another part of his piecemeal reform, Alia decided again against the use of force and took the momentous step and accepted political pluralism. The Democratic Party, with Berisha at the helm, was formed the next day and would, following a difficult two elections, take control and attempt to steer Albania onto a new course.

The Legacy of the lack of Dissent in Albania

When Enver Hoxha was buried with honor under the socialist-realist statue of Mother Albania in the martyrs' cemetery in Tirana, the date of his death – 11 April 1985 – was omitted from his tombstone. Ramiz Alia was responsible for the omission; he argued (in a spirit that would find an echo today in Pyongyang) that such a man could never die. It is arguably Albania's misfortune that a plausible case can be made that Ramiz Alia was right. In many ways Hoxha still haunts Albania. The lack of dissent on the part of the intelligentsia is an important part of that legacy. The weakness of Albania's intelligentsia can be explained in part as a result of the level of social development, the nature of Hoxha, his state, and his powerful security forces. Unlike in most other communist bloc states, they were – like Kadare – closely tied to the regime; too closely to play the role of dissidents when the need for dissent arose. The lack of a well-developed liberal, intellectual elite was certainly one of the most significant political legacies of the communist period in Albania. Because of the lack of a dissident community, there was no real leadership or direction during the collapse, which helps to explain its anarchic, random and violent nature. With no one to project an image of a peaceful democratic future, the reaction on the part of the people to Alia's regime in the last months of its existence seemed to alternate between resignation, apathy, and rage. Popular rage would result in extensive wanton destruction of public property which ultimately put Albania even further behind its neighbors. Leadership from a well-defined, well organized dissent group would certainly have acted as a strong mitigating factor and helped to construct a civil society in the process.[30]

The weakness of dissent was also one of the greatest obstacles to the creation of basic democratic institutions when communism did collapse. It helps to explain why Albania remains mired in what is still euphemistically called 'the transition' with the current government under Prime Minister Berisha taking two steps forward and one step back. When communism collapsed, with few exceptions, the leaders of the new parties came from the former Albanian Party of Labor and as a result tended to have only the vaguest notion of democracy. Sali Berisha, who as we have seen was one of the first to call for pluralism, is perhaps the best example of this unfortunate trend. As the first post- communist president and leader of the new Albania, he left much to be desired. As an enthusiastic member of the party until months before the collapse, he was certainly no dissident. Some western analysts have even suggested that by sending Berisha to talk with the students in December 1990, Alia effectively chose the leadership of the opposition.[31] Once in power, Berisha quickly drifted towards something with which he was seemingly more comfortable, a form of authoritarianism from which Albania has yet to extract itself. The lack of effective dissent in the 1970s and 1980s, then, continues to weigh heavily on Albania today

---

[30]Biberaj, *Albania in Transition*, p. 81.

[31]Vickers and Pettifer, *Albania*, p. 36.

The Kosovo Diplomatic Observer Missions

Shaun Byrnes

Discussion of the dramatic events in Kosovo (Kosova in Albanian) over the past two decades has overlooked a small but important part of the story of the Atlantic community's engagement with Kosovo: the role of the diplomatic observer missions established in the summer of 1998 as part of an international effort to prevent the deepening crisis there from turning into another Balkan war.

The Kosovo Diplomatic Observer missions (KDOM) succeeded in producing a short-lived armed peace in October 1998. Even though that peace broke down within months, KDOM did delay the onset of Serbian strongman Slobodan Milosevic's full scale onslaught against his Albanian subjects, and his attempt to rid Kosovo of most of its Albanian population. KDOM thus saved Serb and Albanian lives. On the policy front, the monitors' timely and objective documentation of Milosevic's brutal suppression of Albanian resistance to the loss of Kosovo's autonomy and the re-imposition of harsh Serbian rule removed ambiguity about what was occurring inside Kosovo, made choices clearer for western policymakers, and played an important role in shaping and refining the West's Kosovo policy. In particular, the monitors' reports made clear that restoring autonomy was not a viable option; the Albanian elites and the street shared a common goal: independence. The monitors also confirmed that the Kosovo Liberation Army (UCK) was a genuinely popular political force that had to be brought into negotiations if they were to produce a viable settlement. The observer missions helped make inevitable NATO's intervention and ultimately, Kosovo's independence.

For the Albanian population, the observer missions provided a psychological lift. The monitors were the first concrete manifestation of genuine and serious international interest and engagement after a decade of Serbian repression. The monitors' evenhandedness and humanity earned the deep gratitude of Albanians and the respect of Kosovo's Serbs and laid the foundation for Kosovo's warm post-war relationship with the EU and the US. The time has come to shine more light on these missions, why and how they were established, their operations, and their political and social significance.

Background

The conflict between Serbia and the ethnic Albanian population of Kosovo had deep roots. While Milosevic sharpened the conflict after his rise to power in 1988, his oppressive rule was not its source. Tension between Kosovars[1] and Serbs had existed for at least a century. The crux of their differences lay in Serbia's claim to Kosovo as its national heritage, the spiritual and historical cradle of Serbia, and the seat of Tsar Dusan's fourteenth century Serbian Empire.[2] From at least the late nineteenth century, Serbian nationalists argued that Serbs had ruled Kosovo since the Nemanja dynasty (1160s-1355) spread Serbian power throughout the western Balkans. They therefore saw Kosovo as an inalienable part of Serbia's patrimony.

There is historical validity to this argument. At one point the Serbian Empire included much of the Adriatic coast and extended south to the Aegean and Ionian seas. However, in the late fourteenth and fifteenth centuries, as the Ottomans expanded into the Balkans, they destroyed the Serbian kingdom, which had been weakened by a dynastic succession crisis. The turning point occurred in 1389, when the Turks defeated the Serbs at Kosovo Polje (The Field of the Blackbirds) near Prishtina. After this defeat, Serbia was not present in Kosovo for over five centuries. Furthermore, during the ensuing five centuries of Ottoman rule, many Serbs left, gradually reducing the Serbian ethnic footprint in Kosovo. Meanwhile, Kosovo's ethnic Albanian population, which appears to have been present in Kosovo before Slavic tribes arrived in the seventh century, grew even though some Albanian Christians also fled north to escape Ottoman rule.[3] By the eighteenth century, the population balance had shifted in favor of the Albanians. Demographically, the Albanians had a greater claim to Kosovo.[4]

---

[1] I use the term 'Kosovar' interchangeably throughout the text with 'Albanian' to refer to ethnic Albanians from Kosovo. The term of course can be applied to Serbs and members of other nationalities in Kosovo.

[2] Malcolm, Kosovo. A Short History, pp. 46-9.

[3] Malcolm, Kosovo. A Short History, pp. 28-40.

[4] For a thorough and objective discussion of this period, see Malcolm, *Ibid.,* Kosovo. A Short History, chapters 3 through 11.

In the nineteenth century the re-emergence of an independent Serbian state and the decline of the Ottomans accompanied the rise of nationalism in Europe. These currents revived Serb ambitions of regaining Kosovo. Serbian nationalists stoked them, calling for avenging Serbia's defeat at Kosovo Polje and the restoration of the burial place of the Nemanja kings – Kosovo – to Serbian rule. In 1912, Serbia achieved that, allying with Bulgaria and Montenegro to defeat the Ottomans. Serbian rule did not last long, however. German, Austrian and Bulgarian troops conquered Kosovo in 1915 and Serbia did not regain control until 1918.

What happened after the return of Serbian power to Kosovo set the tone for the remainder of the twentieth century. Belgrade treated the Kosovars as foes rather than as liberated former citizens, governing Kosovo with a heavy hand between WWI and WWII and immediately thereafter. Serbia sought to restore the demographic balance in its favor. To achieve this, Belgrade sent tens of thousands of Serb 'colonists', confiscated land from Albanians, suppressed the Albanian language and closed Albanian schools, and harassed the Albanians in an effort to force them to emigrate. Many did, primarily to Turkey.[5]

Kosovo in Tito's Yugoslavia

After World War II, Tito's communist regime brought little change. Many Albanians had welcomed their Italian, and later, German occupiers, not because the Kosovars preferred fascism or nazism, but because of the harshness of Serbian rule between the wars. Furthermore, Kosovars welcomed the Axis decision to reunite Kosovo with Albania.[6] Few Kosovars joined Tito's partisans. Indeed, their arrival – most of Tito's partisans were Serbs – following the German retreat, provoked serious armed resistance that Tito's forces did not succeed in suppressing until the early 1950s.

Until 1966, one of Tito's closest allies, the Serb Aleksandar Rankovic, ruled Kosovo with an iron fist. Rankovic treated Albanians as second-class citizens and pressed them to emigrate.[7] Kosovar anger and frustration grew,

---

[5]Malcolm, *Ibid.*, pp. 267-9, 279-85.
[6]The brief period of Kosovo's unification with Albania left a powerful and lasting impression on the Kosovar population, inspiring many to seek reunification with Albania after Tito reintegrated Kosovo into Serbia after WWII.
[7]Malcolm, *Ibid.*, p. 323.

boiling over in the form of massive and violent protest demonstrations in 1968 and 1981. Some demonstrators called for unification with Albania. Growing unrest in Kosovo prompted Tito to make some concessions. He sacked Rankovic, opened an Albanian-language university and, in 1974, adopted a new constitution that gave Kosovo virtually the same status as the constituent republics of Yugoslavia and a substantial measure of home rule.[8]

The Rise of Milosevic and Kosovo

Milosevic's rise to power in the late 1980s changed the equation, reversing Tito's efforts to give Kosovo greater autonomy. To promote his political career, Milosevic stoked Serbian nationalism.[9] He stripped away the autonomy provided by the 1974 Constitution, took over Kosovo's governing institutions, closed its schools, fired Albanian teachers, and stepped up repression against the Albanian population by what had become an exclusively Serbian police force.[10]

The Kosovars responded first politically, and later with armed resistance. Led by the literary scholar Ibrahim Rugova, Kosovars choose to oppose the new Serbian-imposed order with passive resistance. Rugova established a parallel government, including a network of schools, a university, and clinics. On 19 October, 1991, Kosovo's underground parliament proclaimed independence.[11]

Despite the danger these developments posed to stability in the southwest Balkans, Kosovo received little international attention. The EU and the US were heavily focused on the outbreak of conflict in Bosnia. Rugova's commitment to passive resistance served EU and US interests by preventing the outbreak of another conflict in the Balkans, enabling them to concentrate their attention on Bosnia. In their contacts with Rugova, Western officials urged him to sustain non-violent resistance, pledging that the West would take up the Kosovo question. Lacking

---

[8] Bosnia, Croatia, Macedonia, Montenegro, Serbia, and Slovenia.
[9] For a thorough discussion of the Milosevic period, see Sell, Slobodan Milosevic and the Destruction of Yugoslavia. For an objective summary of Milosevic's treatment of Kosovo, see the chapter by Serbian and Albanian historians Dusan Janjic, Anna Lalaj, and Besnik Pula, *Kosovo under the Milosevic Regime* in Ingrao and Emmert (eds), Confronting the Yugoslav Controversies, pp. 272-301.
[10] Janjic *et al*, pp. 282-3.
[11] Judah, Kosovo. War and Revenge, pp. 61-98.

arms and an assurance of EU and US military support, Rugova had no alternative, even though Milosevic continued to step up repression. By 1995, more and more Kosovars, particularly youth, concluded that Rugova's policy was a failure. For many, the final proof came in late 1995 when Richard Holbrooke failed to put Kosovo on the Dayton Conference's agenda, despite an apparent pledge to Rugova to do so.[12] For many angry, frustrated, and fearful Kosovars, violence had finally become the only option.[13]

And that option existed. In 1993, a small group of Albanians from Kosovo and Macedonia founded the Kosovo Liberation Army (UCK, *Ushtria Clirimtare e Kosoves* in Albanian). For the first several years of its existence, it carried out occasional attacks on Serbian police patrols and posts. After Dayton, small UCK bands became more active and by the end of 1996 attacks on Serbian security forces became more frequent.

In October 1997, the UCK made its first public appearance, sending three of its senior leaders, masked and in uniform, to the funeral of an Albanian school teacher killed by the Serbian police. They declared the UCK had formed to 'fight for the liberation and national unity of Kosovo!'[14] Their appearance sent shock waves through Kosovo, by signaling that armed resistance against Milosevic's repression had become a real alternative.

By 1998, the growth of the Albanian insurgency, the sharpening of the conflict with Milosevic's security forces, and increasing civilian casualties and claims of human rights abuses attracted greater attention from the West. Widely reported massacres of Kosovars by the Serbian police in February and March provoked demonstrations throughout the province

---

[12]Holbrooke's decision not to put Kosovo on the Dayton agenda has become a source of contention, with the late Holbrooke arguing that he had no choice but to renege on his pledge to Rugova because Milosevic had made clear that he would walk out of Dayton if Kosovo became an agenda item. A senior US diplomat close to one of Holbrooke's key aides at Dayton claims, however, that the aide privately characterized Holbrooke's pledge as nothing more than an effort to buy time with Rugova, adding that Holbrooke never had any intention of raising Kosovo at Dayton. (Conversation with the author, 31 October 2011.) See also Sell, Slobodan Milosević and the Destruction of Yugoslavia, pp. 271-2, 277.

[13]Judah, *Ibid.*, pg. 124-5, Sell, *Ibid.*, 274.

[14]For good accounts of the Kosovo Liberation Army, its genesis and operations, see Perritt, Kosovo Liberation Army. The Inside Story of an Insurgency, and Judah, *Ibid.*, pp. 99-163.

and prompted the convening of the Contact Group, consisting of the US, UK, Germany, France, Italy and Russia. Their officials descended on Belgrade and Prishtina in an effort to calm down the situation to no avail. Buoyed by growing popular support, the insurgency intensified and by May the UCK succeeded in gaining control of large swathes of territory in central Kosovo. However, a Serbian counteroffensive in June drove the UCK into the hills, destroyed numerous villages, and led to the deaths of civilians and the displacement of tens of thousands of Kosovars.[15]

In an effort to halt the bloodshed, the Contact Group increased pressure on Milosevic, applying limited sanctions. Nevertheless, the number of deaths and displaced civilians grew. By then, Kosovo was page one news and international journalists were feeding disturbing clips of burning villages to western TV news programs. This increased the pressure on the US and EU governments to act. The crisis spawned the Kosovo Diplomatic Observer missions.

KDOM's Genesis

The missions grew out of a 16 June meeting in Moscow between Milosevic and Russian President Yeltsin. Alarmed by increasingly angry Western statements, the Russian leader invited Milosevic to Moscow in an apparent effort to urge restraint. In early July, Richard Holbrooke, the US mediator, seized on a passage in the Milosevic-Yeltsin meeting *communique* that permitted freedom of movement throughout Kosovo for diplomats accredited in Belgrade. Eager to halt the growing conflict before it turned into a full scale war that would threaten the Dayton regime in Bosnia, and frustrated by the spiraling propaganda claims of both sides in Kosovo, Holbrooke proposed the establishment of diplomatic observer missions. With Russian and Serbian agreement, three unarmed diplomatic observer missions formed by mid-July, one by the EU, another by the US, and a third by Russia.[16]

The missions' primary purpose was to provide clear and objective information from the ground. Both the Albanian insurgents and the

---

[15]For a grass roots perspective on the conflict, see the following books by Western journalists who were on the ground in Kosovo: Pettifer, Kosova Express. A Journey in Wartime, pp. 188-255, and Sullivan, Be Not Afraid, for You Have Sons in America. How a Brooklyn Roofer Helped Lure the U.S. into the Kosovo War.
[16]Judah, *Ibid.,* p. 177, and Sell, *Ibid.,* pp. 286-87.

Serbian security forces were manipulating news about what was happening, arousing public opinion in the EU and US and muddying the policy perspectives of Western leaders. The insurgents' claims of the casualties and destruction wrought by the Serbian security forces were often exaggerated, and Serbian denials were often erroneous.

Western leaders also hoped the presence of the missions would put both sides on their best behavior and thus contribute to calming down the situation. With better information and monitors on the ground prepared to call out irresponsible behavior, Holbrooke and other western officials hoped to improve the prospects of reaching an agreement that would end the Kosovo crisis.

The three missions reported directly to their capitals by means of unclassified daily reports.[17] The missions also provided a weekly summary to the Contact Group through its ambassadors in Belgrade.[18] The three mission heads negotiated this report. To the surprise of the EU and US KDOM chiefs, the Russians cooperated in good faith and rarely contested their western colleagues' observations. The EU and US missions drafted the reports because of the far wider scope of their missions' operations, with little quibbling from the Russians.[19]

KDOM Operations

Brussels and Washington laid down firm guidelines for their missions' operations. The first requirement was absolute objectivity: nothing but the facts. The missions were strictly enjoined not to make judgments; they were only to report what they observed in the field. Likewise, the EU and

---

[17]Slight redacted versions of the US KDOM's daily reports may be found at www. State.gov/www/regions/eur/rpt_current_kdom.html.

[18]To emphasize Washington's commitment to transparency and objectivity, the US *Charge* in Belgrade, Ambassador Richard Miles, regularly provided the US KDOM daily report to the Foreign Ministry and to senior Serbian officials dealing with Kosovo.

[19]The Russians played a quiet but constructive role. In perhaps the best example, the chief of Russian KDOM played a significant part in arranging and implementing the successful departure from Kosovo of Selmon Morina, a Kosovar who had miraculously survived the execution of fourteen alleged UCK fighters by the Serbian police in September. Holbrooke negotiated Morina's departure with Milosevic; the three monitoring missions carried out this agreement on October 7, with the Russian KDOM chief personally leading the convoy carrying Morina through Kosovo and Serbian border posts into Macedonia.

US directed their missions to treat officials and members of every ethnic group in Kosovo with respect, and to be evenhanded in their dealings with all parties and in their reporting.

In an effort to demonstrate its good faith, Washington placed its monitoring mission in Kosovo Polje, a town six kilometers west of Prishtina with a large Serb population. Washington rented the Serb-owned 'Motel Herzegovina' in a predominantly Serb neighborhood and transformed it into US KDOM's main operating base.[20] The EU mission's headquarters was located in Prishtina itself, in the predominantly Albanian quarter of Germia.

Washington also insisted that US KDOM not engage in anything resembling intelligence collection against Serbian security forces. This was not entirely altruistic; Secretary of State Albright and Holbrooke did not want to give Milosevic any excuse to discredit the mission and thereby destroy its usefulness. A US military officer assigned to US KDOM violated this directive shortly after the establishment of the US mission and was immediately sent home.

However, because little was known about the insurgents, Brussels and Washington developed an appetite for information relating to the UCK's leadership, organization and political aims. In addition, they had a keen interest in finding out the source of the UCK's weaponry, and whether it possessed modern shoulder-fired anti-aircraft and anti-tank missiles. During their eight months of existence, the EU and US missions developed a relatively deep understanding of the UCK's structure and leadership without apparently damaging their relationship with the insurgents.

Brussels and Washington placed top priority on their missions' safety and security. The capitals directed that mission personnel leave any area where actual fighting was underway and observe it from a safe distance. The monitors also had strict orders not to intervene directly to halt ongoing fighting or to prevent the destruction of property and not to assist wounded combatants from either side.[21] While concern for the

---

[20]Velko Odalovic, an ethnic Montenegrin born and raised in Kosovo Polje and who was Belgrade's senior civilian official in Kosovo for most of KDOM's existence, resided but a block away from the 'Herzegovina' and was a regular visitor.

[21]However, EU and US personnel did not hesitate to advise the International Red Cross or other medical elements operating in Kosovo when they came upon wounded or injured, regardless of their nationality. For an observer's perspective

safety of their monitors was their paramount consideration, Western leaders also feared that observer casualties could prompt the closing of the missions and end their usefulness. For security reasons, capitals forbade their missions to operate after dark. As the insurgency wore on, this rule was increasingly honored only in the breach.

The EU mission was the first to be established. The European Commission (EC) had earlier set up missions (ECMM) in Bosnia and Albania to monitor the turmoil in those states and drew on them, and their experience, in setting up the EU operation in Kosovo. In July 1998, the EC moved elements of its Albanian monitoring mission across the border into Kosovo, rechristening it EU KDOM. Nicholas Turnbull, a former British Army officer, headed EU KDOM. His deputy, Andrew Greene, was also a former British Army officer who had served in Bosnia during the conflict there. Led by British officers, EU KDOM included staff from other EU member-states, particularly Germany, France, Italy and Spain. EU KDOM at the outset numbered about fifteen officers but doubled in size by November. The American mission was set up later in July and the Russian mission only in late August.

The Russian mission, headed at first by Sergey Lavrov, was small, and reached a complement of about six officers. Lack of numbers, the absence of Albanian-language speakers and armored all-terrain vehicles, and the hostility of the Albanian population, and particularly the UCK, limited the Russians' ability to operate. The Russians legitimately feared operating in UCK-controlled or contested areas. Responding to this problem, the EU and US mission chiefs regularly included Russian diplomats on their respective monitoring patrols. The inclusion of the Russians on such missions was successful. They gained a clearer view of what was happening in the countryside, particularly with regard to Serbian destruction of Albanian villages and the plight of Albanian civilians displaced by the Serbian offensive operations. Russian inclusion on EU and US patrols enhanced Russian KDOM's cooperation with its western partners in reporting to the Contact Group. Russian participation in monitoring patrols was not without costs, however. The presence of Russian diplomats in US KDOM vehicles complicated passing through

---

on the humanitarian crisis in the field, see Capps, R., *Yellow*, in the online journal *JMWW*, 13 September, 2011.

UCK checkpoints; on several occasions, the Russian diplomats were threatened by hostile, armed UCK soldiers.

American diplomats and military officers staffed the US mission in roughly equal numbers. They generally served six to eight weeks before being replaced by other volunteers. (EU mission members served longer, some for the entire period leading up to NATO's intervention in March 1999.) Initially, the US Embassy in Belgrade and the US European Command provided officers but by late August volunteers began arriving from embassies and military units around the world. A senior US diplomat headed the mission; his deputy was a senior military officer. US KDOM was subordinated to the US Embassy in Belgrade, and through it to the Department of State. By late November, the US mission's complement had swelled to about 70 officers. Albanian and Serb interpreters, mechanics, drivers and administrative staff formed a key component of the western missions. Since only a handful of the US officials knew Albanian or Serbian, the Albanian and Serbian interpreters were critical to the functioning and success of US mission. By late November, it employed over 100 Albanians and Serbs.

The EU mission brought their Land Rovers from Albania and over time added more. The US mission began operations with several armored but unarmed Chevrolet 'Suburban' SUVs and Land Rovers; by October the US military began providing armored but unarmed 'Humvee' jeeps. By the end of the year, the US monitors' motor pool contained over thirty unarmed armored vehicles. The Russian mission drove several old Russian 'Neva' jeeps that lacked armor. Initially, the EU and US KDOM vehicles were painted white, a color favored by the UN agencies operating in Kosovo. However, after it became apparent that the Serbian police, which also had a fleet of Land Rovers, had painted some of theirs white and used them for reconnaissance into UCK-controlled areas, the EU and US KDOMs repainted their vehicles a fluorescent orange, a color that could be distinguished easily at great distances and in poor light. This color was unique to KDOM and prevented confusion and Serb exploitation, while reducing the risk of drawing fire from nervous UCK soldiers.

The two missions' early operations were run on a shoestring. The EU mission enjoyed an early advantage in area knowledge because it had been operating in neighboring Albania and its personnel had some familiarity with Albanian culture as well as rudimentary knowledge of the language and the Kosovo insurgency. The US filled out its mission quickly, however. By mid-September it had more than twice the personnel of its EU counterpart and a core group of officers with Balkan expertise.

Working in Kosovo was a challenge for the missions from the start. Neither the EU nor the US KDOMs had the resources needed to monitor the widening conflict everywhere. To work as effectively as possible, the missions divided up responsibility for covering hot spots on a daily basis. EU KDOM generally concentrated its patrols in western Kosovo where they had small operating bases in Pec/Peja and Prizren. Washington ruled out the establishment of bases outside of Prishtina. US KDOM generally ran missions in central Kosovo, concentrating particularly on Drenica, a hotbed of the insurgency; Malisevo (the so-called UCK capital) in the Pagarusha valley; and, around Podujevo, a town northeast of Prishtina astride the strategic road linking the Kosovo capital to Serbia. Patrols maintained regular contact with their base station by means of radio. Every evening the EU and US mission chiefs and their deputies, sometimes joined by the Russians, met to review the results of that day's missions, share information, and coordinate the deployment of the next day's patrols. Following this meeting, both missions faxed their daily reports, including information provided by the other mission's patrols, to their respective authorities. Thanks to a rigorous commitment to provide only information the missions could confirm themselves, Contact Group capitals quickly came to depend on these real time reports as their primary source of information about the crisis zone and the basis for formulating policy initiatives. In Washington, the US KDOM report was one of the first messages Secretary of State Albright read every morning.

In deciding where to deploy their limited resources, the KDOM chiefs relied on known concentrations of Serb security forces and reports of their movements, usually from Albanian or international sources in the field, e.g., the International Red Cross, UNDP, journalists, etc. EU and US KDOM dispatched patrols early in the morning to potential trouble spots. If on arrival patrols found Serb police, paramilitaries, or on occasion, army units present, the patrol would linger. KDOM learned quickly that Serb security forces would not carry out operations against Albanian targets, civilian or military, if a KDOM patrol was nearby.

If a potential trouble spot was found to be quiet, KDOM vehicles patrolled the surrounding area, showing the flag in an effort to reassure the local population that the international community was engaged, and collecting information from them about the local situation. Over time KDOM acquired deep knowledge of the geography and political, economic and social character of Kosovo.

Milosevic and KDOM

Serbian authorities facilitated the establishment of the missions, quickly accrediting them. Belgrade did not obstruct the monitors' work, providing them with considerable access to senior Serbian officials in Belgrade and in Kosovo, affording them access to scarce fuel, and permitting them to roam freely in the province. Only military and police facilities were off- limits.

The introduction of the EU and US missions compelled Belgrade to alter its operating tactics but not its goals. Milosevic strove to find a balance between giving full scope to the international monitoring missions while continuing to press the fight against the Albanian insurgents, between allaying western concerns about human rights abuses and destroying the insurgents and their base of support. While Belgrade did not directly obstruct the monitors, the observer missions quickly found themselves in a cat-and-mouse game with the Serbian security forces. Both adapted their operations to each other. It became apparent that Belgrade's forces were under instructions to avoid scorched earth tactics and harsh treatment of civilians when KDOM patrols were nearby. Since KDOM did not patrol after dark, the Serbs often waited to carry out operations until dusk when observers departed. And because KDOM initially stood down patrols on the weekends for crew rest and vehicle maintenance, the Serbs shifted important offensive operations to weekends. EU and US KDOM responded by adopting rolling stand downs for rest and maintenance so that there were KDOM patrols in 'hot' areas every day of the week.

The monitoring missions did compel Milosevic to be more restrained in the use of violence in Kosovo even if they were unable to halt it. Milosevic modified his tactics not to suit the observers, but to permit him in altered circumstances to pursue his strategic goals: the destruction or severe weakening of the insurgency and the base that supported it before sitting down at the negotiating table with Rugova and Holbrooke. Milosevic hoped to restore Serbia's control of the entire province under the watching eyes of the international monitors, and to rebuild his ties with key international actors, in particular the US, before negotiating. He appeared to believe that by seeming to scale back Serbian violence and welcoming the monitors, he could manipulate their presence to advance his own agenda in Kosovo and enter negotiations from a position of strength. Milosevic put his best foot forward in his reception of the missions, and he sought, but failed, to exploit the monitors to calm the international community and persuade it that the insurgents were 'terrorists' while all the time sustaining harsh anti-insurgency operations at little or no diplomatic cost.

Despite the modification of Serbian tactics, it soon became clear that Milosevic had no intention of halting offensive operations against the UCK, and villages where the UCK was active, even in the presence of monitors. Milosevic sought to avoid giving the US and the EU reason to step up pressure by imposing tougher sanctions or even intervening militarily. Hard as Milosevic and his security chiefs tried, however, they failed to mask Serbia's ruthless destruction in the Kosovo countryside and often inhumane treatment of defenseless Albanian women, children, and the elderly. Though lacking regional expertise, and isolated from western capitals, KDOM maintained its independence and never permitted itself to become an instrument of either the Serbs or the UCK.

KDOM Achievements

Though the monitoring missions failed to halt the bloodshed and wanton destruction, they did delay the onset of full-scale war, thereby saving lives and averting the destruction of property. At the strategic level, KDOM bought time for the US and EU to assess their interests, deepen their understanding of Kosovo's political, humanitarian, and security dynamics and of Milosevic's intentions, and develop an appropriate policy response. At the grassroots level, KDOMs' presence delayed or even prevented Serb attacks on villages; on several occasions the arrival of KDOM vehicles appeared to have prevented possible massacres of civilians by Serbian paramilitaries. Furthermore, the monitors negotiated ceasefires and arranged for the exit of hundreds of women and children from villages encircled by Serbian security forces. Finally, KDOM arranged for the exchange, or release, of prisoners. For example, thanks to US KDOM's intervention, on November 27, 1998, UCK General Staff officers turned over to OSCE Mission chief Ambassador William Walker two Belgrade journalists seized by the UCK in September. A more dramatic example occurred on January 13, 1999, when EU KDOM and US KDOM officers brokered the sequenced exchange of eight Serbian army soldiers and three elderly Serb peasants seized the week before for nine UCK soldiers captured in December while trying to enter Kosovo across the Albanian border.

KDOM and Kosovo Policy

Over time the EU and US missions' contributed to the shaping of Western policy. Neither Brussels nor Washington intended their missions to participate in policy formulation; that was not their role. However, because of the quality of the monitors' reporting, which provided EU and US leaders with reliable, clear, objective, and timely, if not all inclusive, information about developments in Kosovo, they influenced policy. For example, US KDOM's confirmation of the slaughter of 21 people near a small village in Drenica on September 26 prompted Secretary of State Albright and Holbrooke to press NATO successfully to approve a plan for air operations against Serbia, a major step toward actual military engagement -- and the beginning of a new phase in the international community's engagement in Kosovo. Authorized by NATO to threaten the bombing of Serbia, Holbrooke went to Belgrade to press Milosevic successfully for a cease-fire and negotiations with the Albanians.[22]

On October 12, Milosevic agreed to draw down his security forces to pre-war levels, to begin negotiations with Rugova, and accept a new, larger and somewhat more intrusive monitoring mission. The Kosovo Verification Mission (KVM) was formed under the rubric of the Organization for Security and Cooperation in Europe (OSCE). Ambassador William Walker, a career US diplomat, headed the new mission.

KDOM did not disappear with the Holbrooke Agreement. KVM elements first arrived in early November and only then did the KVM begin to take over KDOM functions, which now included verifying

---

[22]Judah, *Ibid.*, pp. 179-88.

the withdrawal of Serbian police and military forces to Serbia and the deployment of the remaining army units to agreed operating bases at key points on strategic roads in the province in accordance with the October 12 agreement. In the absence of KVM, Albright and Holbrooke directed US KDOM to explain to the UCK leadership the terms of the Agreement, in which Belgrade agreed to a cease fire, and to persuade the UCK to abide by it. Albright and Holbrooke were particularly interested in ensuring that the UCK would not provoke the Serbs into violating the ceasefire in two key strategic locations: at Podujevo, a town adjacent to Kosovo's border with Serbia astride the strategic Prishtina-Nis highway. This was Serbia's main communications link with Kosovo and the lifeline for the Serbian security forces there.[23] One of the UCK's best trained and most aggressive military formations, the Llap Zone, operated there and posed a serious threat to the Serbian logistics lifeline.

Holbrooke's second point of concern was central Kosovo, the locus of the bloodiest fighting. UCK headquarters were located there, and enjoyed strong popular support, while Serbian security forces patrolled aggressively there in order to keep supply lines open to their bases in western Kosovo.

The US and EU KDOM chiefs took up this task in Podujevo and central Kosovo, respectively, and after intensive and difficult discussions with the regional commanders, as well as representatives from the UCK General Staff, succeeded in obtaining verbal agreement to respect the ceasefire. Holbrooke was not satisfied, however. He had wanted a document signed by the UCK commanders, particularly in the Malisevo region. Nevertheless, this agreement held in central Kosovo, apart from several small exceptions until NATO's intervention in March 1999. As a result, displaced civilians returned to their villages, underground schools began to function again, and limited trade and agricultural activity resumed.

The agreement reached with the Llap Zone did not last as long. There were regular incidents, prompted in part by the heavy Serb military and police traffic on the key strategic road at night, when Milosevic returned police and army units under cover of darkness to Kosovo -- in violation of the Holbrooke Agreement; in part by nervous Serb policemen tasked

---

[23]The main supply base for military units deployed in Kosovo was in Nis.

with protecting the strategic highway; and, in part by the aggressiveness of 'Commander Remi',[24] the Llap commander, who like his fellow UCK zone commanders, assumed that Milosevic would use the cease fire to regroup for what both sides expected would be renewed fighting in the spring. Remi did not wish to be caught off guard so he prepared by moving his troops closer to the strategic road, reinforcing Serb concerns that the UCK intended to cut that strategic communications link. The cease fire in this area effectively ended in mid-December when Belgrade, in violation of the Holbrooke Agreement, moved a combined military and police battle group from Prishtina to Podujevo to protect that highway.

By early mid-December, KVM had put in place its operational structure and was functioning effectively from a network of bases spread across central and western Kosovo. However, even as it shifted from its previous monitoring role to a more traditional diplomatic function, KDOM contributed to KVM's mission. US KDOM continued to patrol troubled areas; a US KDOM patrol tipped off KVM monitors to a brewing conflict at Racak, for example. Moreover, US KDOM remained the main channel for high level communications between senior KVM and Contact Group officials, and the insurgents' leadership because of its access to senior elements of the UCK. For the UCK leadership, US KDOM was its partner of choice. In part, this was self-serving since the insurgents' first priority was to draw the US into the conflict.

The transition from KDOM to KVM occurred relatively smoothly even though the KVM advance party that arrived within a week of the Agreement showed little interest in taking advantage of the political, military and area knowledge gained by EU and US KDOM officers. The KVM lead elements sought only contact information and KDOMs' personnel and vehicles. (The EU and US had agreed to transfer the bulk of their personnel and equipment to the new KVM but not to close down their observer missions. Ambassador Walker fought to have the two KDOM missions subordinated to him but his efforts failed.)[25]

---

[24]'Commander Remi' was the *nome de guerre* of Rrustem Mustafa. Mustafa is now a prominent political figure in Kosova.

[25]While this was a matter of some debate in Washington, both Brussels and Washington decided to maintain independent missions and gave them a new mandate. They were to support KVM whenever necessary, collect information independently, report on political and social developments in the province, and

The continuing ability of the two KDOMs to provide real-time information in concise summary form to capitals confirmed the soundness of the decision to maintain them. Because of KVM's cumbersome bureaucracy, it generally failed to provide fact-based reporting on a real-time basis. Rarely did its 'daily report' arrive on the same day at OSCE headquarters in Vienna for retransmission to OSCE member-states; in general, it took several days for the draft report to wend its way through KVM's multinational, and sometimes fractious, bureaucracy. The lack of timeliness of KVM's otherwise excellent daily reports led EU and US policymakers to continue to rely on the reports routinely filed the same day by EU and US KDOMs.

Contacts with the UCK

EU and US KDOM contacts built with the UCK also confirmed the wisdom of maintaining them as entities independent of the OSCE's KVM operation. Thanks to the monitors' reporting, EU and US officials gained a deeper and more precise appreciation of the guerrillas' capabilities, structure, leadership, and objectives. Furthermore, US KDOM developed such excellent access to the UCK General Staff that it could set up meetings for visiting western policymakers on short notice and convey important messages to the UCK leadership very quickly. Finally, US KDOM's reporting and operations contributed importantly to the shaping of US policy on Kosovo.

EU and US KDOM were the first official western entities to have direct, regular contacts with the UCK's regional ('zone') commanders and its top political and military leadership. According to the UCK's leader (and current Kosova prime minister) Hashim Thaqi, the first US diplomats he met and had extensive discussions with were US KDOM officials. Over time, EU and US KDOM officers met regularly with a troika from the UCK General Staff, press spokesman (and current president of the Kosova Assembly) Jakup Krasniqi; deputy chief of the General Staff (and current mayor of the town of Klina in western Kosova)

---

support the EU and US special envoys for Kosovo, Austrian Ambassador to Belgrade Wolfgang Petritsch and US Ambassador to Macedonia Christopher Hill, respectively. Support of Pertritsch and Walker by the multilateral OSCE mission would have been inappropriate. In effect, EU and US KDOM became operating units of their respective embassies.

Sokol Bashota; and, Political Directorate member (and current Kosova Minister of Education) Rame Buha.

In the early autumn of 1998, the observers' main focus in meeting UCK leaders was to explain the KDOM mission, seek UCK cooperation in stemming violence and protecting the civilian population, and assess the UCK and its support among the population. Later, and in particular after the Holbrooke Agreement, KDOMs' top priority was to obtain UCK cooperation in respecting the cease fire, and, subsequently, to persuade the UCK General Staff to participate in the Rambouillet Conference in February 1999. KDOM officers devoted countless hours to pressing UCK officers to respect the Holbrooke cease fire and did not hesitate to chastise the UCK for provocative behavior and cease fire violations. KDOMs also used their contacts with senior UCK officers to secure the release of Albanian political prisoners, Serbian civilians and journalists, and captured Serbian policemen and soldiers. On the diplomatic front, the monitoring missions arranged for senior UCK political leaders to meet with the EU and US special envoys who sought their acceptance of the draft document that Ambassador Hill was negotiating with Milosevic in an effort to end the Kosovo conflict, and which served as the basis of the document put forward at the Rambouillet Conference.

The EU and US missions' reporting also contributed to the shaping of EU and US understanding of the political dynamics in Kosovo, and in particular of the role of the UCK in the negotiations process. While US KDOM was not a party in the debate among US policymakers over how to resolve of the Kosovo Question and the UCK's role in that process, it influenced it. As policy discussions in Washington, and between Washington and Brussels, intensified as autumn turned into winter, US KDOM's reporting pitted it increasingly against Holbrooke and especially the special envoy for Kosovo, Ambassador Hill. Hill did not trust the UCK leadership and believed it was pointless to include the UCK in the negotiations between Milosevic and Rugova that Hill was mediating.

Hill resisted the UCK's inclusion in negotiations primarily because of its unconditional demand for independence. He rejected independence, primarily because he believed that putting it on the table only three years after the Dayton Agreement would provoke Milosevic to walk away from the latter and thus cause Bosnia to collapse. Hill (and his mentor

Holbrooke) saw Milosevic as a 'guarantor' of peace not only in Bosnia but also throughout the Balkans. Alienating him would put the entire region at risk, in their view. Meanwhile, Hill believed the passive Rugova – whose aim likewise was independence -- could be persuaded to accept a return to home rule similar to that provided by the 1974 Constitution. Such an agreement would preserve Kosovo within Milosevic's 'former Yugoslavia' of Serbia and Montenegro, gain Milosevic's signature and remove the threat to Bosnian stability.

However, opinion about Milosevic had shifted in the three years that had passed since Dayton, in part because of his repressive policies in Kosovo and the bloodshed there, in part because of his increasingly obvious authoritarian rule at home. His stubborn unwillingness to accept the results of the municipal elections in Serbia in November 1996 and his attempt to suppress the democratic opposition exposed the hollowness of his professed commitment to democratic norms. Despite the role Milosevic had played in securing the Dayton Agreement, some Western officials who had seen him as a potential democratic reformer in the mid-1980s now began to doubt his reliability and to regard him as nothing more than another petty Balkan dictator. Senior officials, like President Clinton's second Secretary of State, Madeleine Albright, had not been at Dayton and never had the personal relationship with Milosevic that Holbrooke and Hill did. Instead they watched newscasts that reminded them daily of what had happened in Bosnia, and their tolerance for Milosevic was diminishing.

Hill in particular was wedded to the Dayton Agreement and looked at his Kosovo challenge through that prism. Preserving the Dayton order in still fragile Bosnia was his overarching priority. From Hill's point of view, Serbia was key. Like many of his diplomatic colleagues, Hill subscribed to the argument that stability and order in the Balkans ultimately depended on Serbia. In this view, the path to change, to the building of a democratic order in the Balkans, lay through Belgrade. While he recognized the brutality of Milosevic's policies in Kosovo and sought to end them, Hill still gave primacy to working with Belgrade and thus maintaining the status quo. That meant that the West had to deal with Milosevic, like it or not. Unlike some fellow diplomats, Hill felt some confidence that Milosevic at heart was a responsible statesman and could be persuaded to compromise, as he had done in Bosnia. In hindsight, it appears that

Hill may have failed to grasp that the nationalist tiger Milosevic had mounted made compromise over Kosovo impossible. Every subsequent Serbian leader certainly has come to understand that.

As autumn turned into winter in 1998, Hill apparently became aware of skepticism in some quarters in Washington about Milosevic's willingness to reach a compromise acceptable both to the Kosovars and the US and the EU. Of course, there were also the normal bureaucratic rivalries between bureaus and offices that were involved in crafting and implementing US policy in the Balkans. Hill felt some concern that his policy, and his control of it, was threatened.

In this connection, Hill apparently believed that US KDOM had begun not only to favor independence but also to sympathize with the UCK. Hill apparently feared that the spread of such sentiment to policymakers in Washington would endanger his efforts to broker an agreement that would provide Kosovo with more self-governance but keep it within Milosevic's Serbia, thereby preserving the Dayton settlement. Willingness by policymakers in Washington to consider a more radical solution would also endanger Hill's grip on policy. As a consequence, he sought to limit Department of State officials' access to Kosovo, and in particular to the UCK leadership. But the Kosovo crisis was by then generating too many headlines to keep officials away. A parade of officials, including influential Republican senators Robert Dole and John Warner, visited Kosovo in the autumn and saw with their own eyes the destruction Serbian arms had wrought on the countryside and its population.

Perhaps more important was the success of the directors of the Balkans Office and the Balkan Task Force at the Department of State in evading Hill's gatekeepers and visiting Kosovo in person in late December. They met Ibrahim Rugova and, with US KDOM's help, they also met members of the UCK General Staff. They returned to Washington with the clear understanding that Rugova and the UCK leadership were on the same page and that nothing short of independence was an acceptable option for the Kosovars. Furthermore, key officials at the policy working level at the Department of State were no longer solely dependent on Hill's assessment of the senior leadership of the UCK, its objectives and its willingness to cooperate with Washington. The working level was relying increasingly on US KDOM's reports, which were sent by the US Embassy in Belgrade, where there was more skepticism of Milosevic, his intentions, and the possibility of cutting a deal with him than there was in Hill's mission in Skopje.

There were other factors that influenced Hill's thinking about Kosovo's prospects and future. He was deeply skeptical of the capacity of the Albanians to govern themselves, in large part because of his experience as deputy chief of the US Embassy in Tirana in the early 1990s. The corruption of the Albanian political elite, its pettiness, incompetence and extreme partisanship had left a powerful negative impression on him. Hill likewise had little respect for the UCK leadership, which he argued smuggled narcotics, cigarettes, oil and trafficked in women to pay for weapons, in the process enriching themselves. Hill worried that an independent Kosovo would become a haven for criminals and a destabilizing factor in the region. There may also have been a personal dimension. According to officials close to Hill, he was fascinated by the Serbian strongman and privately had great respect for Milosevic; Hill once remarked during the Kosovo crisis that if the West treated Milosevic as a statesman, he would respond as a statesman.[26]

US KDOM's reporting and informal contact with senior officials in Washington helped tilt the debate in favor of advocates of UCK participation and opening a path toward independence. As US KDOM's contacts with Kosovo society expanded during the autumn of 1998, the US observers advised that the Albanian political class and population would accept nothing less than independence. Return to the *status quo ante*, even genuine home rule, was not an option. Milosevic's ruthless effort to suppress Albanian resistance to the loss of Kosovo's autonomy under the 1974 Constitution and the re-imposition of Belgrade's authority had destroyed whatever willingness there might have been among the Kosovars to return to the 1974 order. Milosevic's brutal repression had radicalized the population, including even moderates around Rugova. For all intents and purposes, Milosevic's policies had cost Serbia whatever chance it might have had to keep Kosovo. It was Milosevic who lost Kosovo. US KDOM officers saw that Western imposition of Hill's package would not end the insurgency and would risk losing all the good will the US and the EU enjoyed among Kosovo's population.

---

[26]October 31, 2011 conversation with the author.

US KDOM also pointed out repeatedly the UCK's large and growing popular support. UCK exploits were the talk of the cafes in Prishtina and other towns, and young men and women were flocking to the countryside to volunteer. While Rugova remained respected, it was to the UCK, with its call to resist, its insistence on independence, and its sacrifices that the Albanian public looked for leadership.

From these observations two conclusions flowed naturally. First, no agreement with Milosevic would be worth the paper it was written on if the UCK did not participate in its negotiation and accept it. The West was not prepared to fight the UCK in defense of an agreement with Serbia that the UCK rejected. Like the UCK or not, it was now the primary Kosovo Albanian political force and had to be part of the negotiating process. Second, the EU and US needed to rethink their policy and find a path that would at least open up the possibility of eventual independence. Hill resisted including the UCK in the negotiating process and apparently ruled out independence as an eventual option. He of course had good reason to do so as it was a subject Milosevic would never agree to discuss.

Nevertheless, the force of US KDOM's reporting, and meetings it arranged for visiting officials from Washington with UCK General Staff officers helped shift thinking away from Holbrooke's and Hill's views toward those of Secretary Albright, who was increasingly angry with what she considered Milosevic's brutal repression, and his duplicity and intransigence. By the late fall, Albright was more willing to consider direct military intervention on behalf of the Kosovars.[27]

Albright directed Hill to meet with the UCK leadership, brief them on the status of his discussions with Milosevic and Rugova, outline his proposed agreement, and seek their participation in this process. Hill thus began a long and painful process that culminated in March 1999 in Paris where the Albanians – Rugova and the UCK -- grudgingly signed on to an agreement that removed Belgrade's authorities from Kosovo and transformed it into an international protectorate but avoided discussion of independence. Milosevic rejected the draft, thus triggering NATO's aerial assault on Serbia and its forces in Kosovo, as well as Milosevic's decision to use force to drive much of the Albanian population into Macedonia, Albania and Montenegro.

---

[27] Albright, *Madam Secretary. A Memoir*, p. 518.

Following the failure of the Rambouillet and Paris conferences and the NATO decision to bomb Serbia, the OSCE, EU and US monitoring missions withdrew to Macedonia. They helped NATO, UN humanitarian agencies and other international organizations deal with the torrent of refugees that Milosevic's security forces drove over the border. Once refugee camps were established and NATO, UN agencies and the International Red Cross had put in place the infrastructure necessary to cope with the steady flow of refugees, Washington directed US KDOM to collect reports of alleged war crimes from refugees sheltering in camps and among the local population in Macedonia and Albania. Meanwhile, US KDOM also maintained daily contact via satellite telephone with the UCK General Staff and some zone commanders inside Kosovo in order to learn about Milosevic's efforts to carry out 'ethnic cleansing' of Albanians in Kosovo and the plight of civilians displaced by the fighting. Finally, Washington also dispatched senior US KDOM officers to Tirana to liaise with members of the UCK General Staff there as well as with senior members of Ibrahim Rugova's League of Democrats of Kosovo (LDK) who had set up an office in the Albanian capital to maintain communications with key international actors.

Brussels terminated what remained of EU KDOM at the conclusion of the conflict but Washington moved its monitors back to Prishtina after the entry into Kosovo of NATO's forces. (Moscow had tucked its small observer mission into KVM after the latter's establishment.) US KDOM evolved into the initial official US diplomatic mission in Kosovo. The former US monitors worked closely with NATO and the new UN mission, in particular sharing information and facilitating their introduction to key local political and media contacts (including Serbs) as well as to the UCK political and military leadership. The new US Office in Prishtina maintained regular contacts with the provisional government established by the UCK and led by Hashim Thaqi. The US Office provided assessments of the political, economic, humanitarian and security situation; assisted NATO in promoting efforts to disarm the UCK; cooperated closely with the acting UN representative, Sergio Di Mello; and, supported a wave of visits by senior US government officials, including members of Congress.

Conclusions

The Kosovo diplomatic observer missions are now forgotten but their small role was important in the Kosovo conflict. They provided the first concrete manifestation of genuine EU and US engagement, revived the Kosovars' faith in Europe and the US, and became an important stage in the process that led to NATO's military intervention, the expulsion of Serbian security forces from Kosovo, and its eventual independence. Though the missions' presence did not halt the conflict, it slowed its momentum and paved the way for the Holbrooke Agreement and its short-lived ceasefire. Furthermore, the observer missions bought time for Western policymakers who were wrestling with the challenge of resolving the Kosovo crisis while preserving peace in Bosnia, promoting democracy and reform in Serbia, and respecting international law. The monitors' objective and real time reporting brought into sharp relief what was occurring on the ground, making it clear that Belgrade bore primary responsibility for the deepening crisis because of its brutal scorched earth policies and systematic repression of the Albanian population. KDOM reports also undermined Milosevic's effort to portray resistance to his repression of Kosovo's Albanian population as simple 'terrorism'. Meanwhile, the observers did not ignore Kosovo Liberation Army excesses and provocations. KDOM gave Western policymakers a solid basis on which to make critical decisions and brought NATO's intervention closer.

KDOMs' presence ultimately failed, though, to modify either side's behavior. Unarmed, and subordinated to an EU and US that sought to avoid confrontation with Milosevic, KDOM lacked the tools necessary to halt the conflict between Serbian security forces and the growing Kosovar insurgency. KDOM's confirmation of a massacre in Drenica at the end of September did trigger a firm NATO response that led to an uneasy peace. But the OSCE's follow on Kosovo Verification Mission was unable to keep the peace. The lesson that emerges from this is that no international monitoring mission can be an effective peacemaker or peacekeeper without being backed by the clear and credible commitment to use force. The experience of the Arab League monitors in Syria at time of writing underscores this.

At the policy level, US KDOM reporting helped modify Washington's views of the Kosovars' agenda as well as the political importance of the UCK. US KDOM contributed to Washington's recognition that its decade long support for the restoration of Kosovo's previous autonomy within Milosevic's 'Former Yugoslavia' was no longer a viable option. Likewise, the US monitors' reporting helped persuade Washington that the UCK was a significant force in Kosovo's political landscape and had to participate in any negotiations with Belgrade if such talks were to have a chance of success. The US KDOM's contribution in reshaping Washington's policy view was no small success. It was the US that drove the policy process inside NATO.

Nor should it be overlooked that the strong relationship the US KDOM built with the UCK General Staff contributed considerably to bringing the UCK into the negotiating process, participating at Rambouillet, and disarming after the conflict. Furthermore, the strong US KDOM-UCK relationship became the cornerstone of the deep bond that exists today between the Kosovars and the US, and accords Washington preeminent political influence in Prishtina.

Finally, and most important, the monitoring missions saved countless lives. Had Richard Holbrooke not conceived the idea of the missions, Milosevic would have continued military action against the growing insurgency and his brutal repression of the Albanian population, producing more victims and suffering while the West dithered. Because of Bosnia, NATO probably would have intervened at some point, but only after Milosevic's policies had claimed more Albanian and Serbian lives and wrought more destruction.

Bibliography

Albright, M., Madam Secretary. A Memoir (NY: Miramax Books, 2003)

Capps, R., *Yellow*. In the online journal, *JMWW*, October 2011.

Gow, J., *The War in Kosovo, 1998-99*. In Confronting the Yugoslav Controversies. A Scholars' Initiative, pp. 302-44. Edited by Charles Ingrao and Thomas A. Emmert. West Lafayette, Indiana: Purdue University Press, 2009.

Ingrao, C. and Emmert, T.A. (eds), Confronting the Yugoslav Controversies. A Scholars' Initiative (Purdue University Press, 2009)

International Crisis Group. Reality Demands Documenting Violations of International Law in Kosovo (International Crisis Group, 1999)

Janjic, D., Lalaj, A., and Pula, B., 'Kosovo under the Milosevic Regime.' In Confronting the Yugoslav Controversies. A Scholars' Initiative, pp. 272-301. Edited by Charles Ingrao and Thomas A. Emmert. West Lafayette, Indiana: Purdue University Press, 2009)

Judah, T,. Kosovo. War and Revenge (Yale University Press, New Haven and London, 2000)

Malcolm, N., Kosovo. A Short History (NYU Press, NY, 1998)

Pavlovich, M., 'Kosovo under Autonomy, 1974-1990.' In Confronting the Yugoslav Controversies. A Scholars' Initiative, pp.49-80. Edited by Charles Ingrao and Thomas A. Emmert. (West Lafayette, Indiana: Purdue University Press, 2009).

Perritt, H.H., Jr., Kosovo Liberation Army. The Inside Story of an Insurgency (Urbana and Chicago: University of Illinois Press, 2008)

Pettifer, J., Kosova Express. A Journey in Wartime. (Hurst: London, 2005)

Sell, L., Slobodan Milosevic and the Destruction of Yugoslavia (Duke University Press, Durham, NC and London, 2002)

Sullivan, S., Be Not Afraid, For You have Sons in America. How a Brooklyn Roofer Helped Lure the U.S. into the Kosovo War. (St. Martin's Press: NY, 2004)

The Preshevo Valley Crisis 1999–2002[1]
Bob Churcher

Following the peace agreement in Kosovo in June 1999 NATO ordered the creation of an exclusion strip (known as the Demilitarised Zone, DMZ, or the Ground Security Zone, GSZ) around the Kosovo border, on the Serb side, where Serbian forces were not to enter. This strip in south-east Serbia was utilised between 2000 and 2002 by albanian[2] speaking groups from Preshevo to form a successor organisation to the Kosova Liberation Army (KLA) called UCPMB – The Liberation Army of Preshevo, Medjeve and Bujanovac, a small armed group of local people who intended to try and stop the Serbs from returning to the Preshevo Valley after the war, and who hoped to negotiate a peace settlement reuniting Preshevo with Kosovo. The albanian rebel leaders had close connections both to the KLA leadership in Kosovo and to albanian speaking rebel movements in Republic of Macedonia, known amongst internationals officials as FYROM.

The conflict of 1999-2001 by albanians against the Serbian Government in the Presevo area (the Preshevo valley, which is also known as PMB– Preshevo, Medjeve and Bujanovac – the three main towns) was ended, successfully in the view of most of the International Community (IC), by a NATO sponsored negotiation. This paper examines the background to conflict and the question of what connection it had to the slightly later albanian insurgency in FYROM.

There are three main background points:

- The cause, which in the author's view should be seen as the present borders, and not a question of human rights – goes back to the Serbian seizure of albanian inhabited territory to the south of what was then Serbia, from the Ottoman Empire in both 1878-9 and 1912. There were already basic slav/albanian ethnic differences, and there grew up

---

[1] I am grateful to International Crisis Group who first commissioned the start of this research in 2001, although it was never published by ICG, the Conflict Studies Research Centre at the Royal Military Academy Sandhurst who published an earlier draft of this paper, and to James Pettifer for editorial assistance.

[2] In this paper Albanian is used to indicate the country, and albanian is used to indicate ethnicity, an albanian speaking person resident in another state.

an albanian dislike of being ruled by Slavs in what they see as their land.

- This in turn connects back to Serbian expansionist ambitions of the late 18th and 19th century, matching those of Bulgaria and Greece, versus the albanian ideas of remaining within a reformed Turkish Empire for reasons of religion (the majority being Moslem) and the protection of their lands.

- NATO Negotiation – The 'peace agreement' in Preshevo was widely portrayed as the result of a NATO 'negotiation process', and not merely as a result of NATO ending the demilitarised zone safe area so necessary to any guerrilla war in such a small area (the Valley comprises only around 1200 sq km). There is also the question of the withdrawal of US support for albanian nationalist causes after Milosevic's fall, and the outbreak of the Macedonia conflict, when NATO fears precipitately ended the DMZ, where the rebellion had concentrated. The 'negotiation' was for the Preshevo albanians to simply accept what was known as the Covic plan and return to the status quo and Serbian rule, or face total destruction, by the Serbian Army. The Covic Plan included some very reasonable provisions on 'multi-ethnic policing', and municipal reforms but crucially did not include any real element of international or outside supervision or verification. Despite facilitating four meetings inexperienced NATO 'negotiators' allowed three meetings to degenerate into stating Serb demands for the return of Serb prisoners. The fourth briefly touched on the Covic plan for police reforms, and was then followed by NATO announcing the end of the DMZ, and that any ex-fighters could cross the administrative border into Kosova, if they surrendered their weapons. In reality the only negotiation was by NATO, in arranging that OSCE would have some oversight role in the re-constituted 'multi-ethnic' police force.

The NATO led negotiation was at first carried out by Sean Sullivan, a US political adviser in KFOR. Later it was lead by Peter Feith, who was styled as a 'special representative of the NATO Sec Gen'. By then the negotiation, or rather ending the Preshevo rebellion had become very urgent, as the Macedonian albanian rebellion had broken out, and at that early stage Robertson was describing albanian rebels as 'terrorists' in talks with the Macedonian government.

There was little or no negotiating skill on the Preshevo albanian side at the negotiation. The albanian rebels in Preshevo were not a unified movement – in contrast both the Kosova and Macedonian rebellions by albanians against Slav rule, (or misrule as they saw it) were reasonably unified, both had only one large and one small organisation involved in commanding parts of the armed rebellion. In Preshevo it was hard to distinguish how many organisations were involved in armed revolt, but there were at least 6 or 7 local village defence forces, each working back to a supporting organisation elsewhere. Admittedly this did have precedents in the early Kosovo conflict, but in Preshevo it was greatly exacerbated by the lack of any educated (intellectual) leadership in the villages. What passed for an 'educated middle-class' opposition in Preshevo supported Riza Halimi and his PDA (Party of Democratic Action) party, akin to the pre-war LDK in Kosova.

Many conspiracy theories allege the Preshevo conflict to have been started by the US, (which was highly unlikely in the author's view) or at least encouraged and supported as part of the plan to destabilise Milosevic. The conflict can also be seen as part of wider Pan-Albanian aims, or at least part of aims of a small element of radical nationalists who saw success in Kosova as only part of regaining control of all their lands which had fallen under Serb control successively in 1876/9 and 1911/12.

The conflict also has an unusual geo-strategic significance: the hills around Preshevo were always seen as potentially controlling Serbia's route to Greece, although in reality the development of modern artillery has probably ended this consideration. However, this possible threat to the main route south from Serbia to Salonica still has great significance in Serb minds.

The real interest in the Preshevo problem is that it continues, albeit at a markedly lower level, to the present day. Occasional violence against the police, including the so-called multi-ethnic police (Serbian press now refers to any police in Preshevo as 'multi-ethnic', although in reality most are Serbian Gendarmerie, an overwhelmingly ethnically Serbian paramilitary force). Serbian Army military expenditure on bases and road building remains very high, and the Serbian press continues to carry alarmist articles on how Serbs are being forced out of the area. The Serb's new base near Vranje was the largest new construction in mainland Europe for an army in the early post-2000 period. In Belgrade the ongoing problems remained one of the main causes of dispute between the old unreformed VJ-generation soldiers and reformers (albeit very limited reformers) such as Covic. Serbian arrests of former albanian activists, on apparently trumped up charges of weapons possession, also continue. Shefket Musliu (ex commander of the UCPMB) had stated to Zeri in Pristina (Dec 26th 2001) that there could be no lasting peace until the Covic agreement was fully implemented. In essence, there is much to be said to support this view, as the unsatisfactory developments in Preshevo, depopulation, and the stagnation of the reform process in recent years have shown.

The Background to the Conflict and the Connection with the Northern Macedonian (FYRoM) Villages

The conflict broke out around the borders of Serbia, Kosovo and FYROM, but this was no geographic accident. These particular (formerly internal Yugoslav administrative) borders have never been gazetted[3], or, until very recently even delineated in any way that western Europeans would understand, and were created for the first time in 1946-47[4]. At that time serious violence between the victorious communists and local resistance groups, predominantly the albanian nationalist Balli Kombetar militia of Mullah Idris Gjilane was in progress. Prior to that the international and regional administrative borders in the Kosova Lindore/ Preshevo region had changed radically several times in various ways over the previous 70 years, revised village by village at various times subsequently, by different Belgrade ministries, and were recently changed again by 'FRY' and FYROM[5] without reference to the UN mandated administration of Kosovo, or their inhabitants, (much to the irritation

---

[3]Meaning formally and legally established, perhaps because Tito was against the creation of Internal Borders.

[4]Since there seems to be no official gazetting of the new border, or at least it is not accessible, evidence on the local claims is hard to come by. However, useful sources are the village lists of the Conference of Berlin, and more importantly the records of which districts sent Deputies to the Skupstina (Parliament) in Belgrade. {Record of the Proceedings of the National Assembly, Book One, Belgrade 1947, printed 1955] Also useful are the 1947 Acts governing where pre-war Serb settlers expelled from Kosovo could return to.

[5]Border agreement of February 2001.

of the local albanian inhabitants, who once again found their land in someone else's jurisdiction).

The changes all had one thing in common. They cut across contiguous districts inhabited by people of albanian ethnicity and language, who have not been consulted in the process. To take the village of Tanushec (on the Kosova/FYROM border), where the FYROM conflict started in February 2001 as one example – this village was previously the summer grazing village of Vitinje, in Kosovo, and the two were part of the same administrative division (the Vardar Banovina) until 1947. The separation of Yugoslavia has torn these villages apart, but for strong economic and social reasons they wish to remain together.

Most international observers of the Balkans problems over the last 10 years have resolutely set themselves against any mention of history, citing as their justification its alleged irrelevance to the problems of today. Whilst it is true that most of the wars of the Yugoslav succession were largely caused by the Serbian desire to keep all Serbs in one state, as distinct from the desire of states such as Croatia to separate, the roots of the current troubles in the southern Balkans lie not in the Serb treatment of their albanian citizens, (whilst it is true that they would like to expel them, or get them to leave) but in the delineation of borders by the 1912 Ambassadors Conference of London. This conference apportioned Albanian majority territory between the neighbouring states, leaving many more outside the new Albanian state than inside, (not to mention making northern Macedonia part of Serbia, rather than Bulgaria, which is what most local Slav–speakers thought at the time thought of as their closest language).

The years of 1912/13 (the years of the First and Second Balkan Wars) were accompanied by the still normal 'Balkan style' ethnic cleansing of villages which resisted Serbian conquest (with all the usual atrocities), as the Serbian Army occupied what is now Kosovo and northern Macedonia. In particular the Serbian ethnic cleansing after the Battle of Kumanovo remained notorious for many years afterwards. In the Preshevo and Bujanovac villages, these memories remained very strong, since their neighbours in Medveja had been subject to the same process in 1878, following the Conference of Berlin, and such oral histories of expulsion and atrocity can easily be found in households in the area on both sides of the 1947 administrative border today. Many Preshevo village families are descended from impoverished ex-middle class families who were expelled from Kumanovo by the victorious Serbs, an important factor in creating the traditional radicalism of the region. A district of Prishtina in Kosovo is still inhabited by Preshevo valley refugees from that time, joined by those of the post 1945 expulsions.

The result of the Great Powers (principally Russian[6]) backing of the Serbs expansionist aims was serious fighting and instability in the southern Balkans for most of the last century, with the exception of the communist period, which saw its own horrors. The fears and uncertainties of the Serb dominated government consequent on Yugoslavia containing large numbers of albanians who did not regard it as their state are with us till today. Whilst present events may, as noted above, result directly from Macedonian (FYRoM) and Serb repression of their albanian, ultimate stability is unlikely to come only from addressing issues of human rights, (or changing the borders). Belgrade governments, Royalist or communist or post-communist never showed any intention of implementing the numerous agreements made in the past.

Lastly here, international speculation is that the Preshevo conflict was fuelled by militants from the former KLA (Kosova Liberation Army). This was almost certainly true, but largely irrelevant. In terms of intra-state war it is not, unfortunately, the wishes of any majority that brings a state to radical measures, or terrorism, but the aims and intentions of a militant but violent minority The key problem in the Preshevo communes is the rule of a highly centralised Serbian Belgrade government over a territory, which remains contiguous with its albanian speaking neighbours in Kosovo. International Community and Serbian opposition to any form of autonomy is based on borders which were created in two of the communes only decades ago, and which have little validity in local minds today.

Southern Serbia or Eastern Kosova?

The towns of Bujanovac and Preshevo lie in the upper part of the southern Morava river valley along the route of the main north-south land corridor for the entire Balkans. This road connects Belgrade with the Macedonian (FYRoM) capital of Skopje and the Greek port of

---

[6]Although Britain and France became the principle creators and backers of the Kingdom of Yugoslavia post World War I.

Thessaloniki (Salonica). Comprising the Morava and Vardar river valleys, this main corridor is the route of the main road and rail routes between central Europe and the Aegean Sea. Loss of Bujanovac and Preshevo is seen by the Serbs as effectively cutting Serbia off from FYROM and Greece and give albanian forces a wedge to use in any demands against the Serb and FYROM governments. In this context Greece has played an important background role in the conflict, as the breaking of this link is seen in Athens as a Turkish objective in the region.

Slightly further north, Medvedje[7] lies in the mountains to the south-west of the city of Leskovac in the Jablanica river valley, which feeds into the southern Morava. Although in a strategic sense of lesser importance than Bujanovac and Preshevo, albanian control of Medveje could drive a wedge towards Leskovac, cutting off this route at yet another point.

Over late winter 2001 fighting between the approximately 700 or 800 albanian guerrillas and Yugoslav security forces was been confined largely to skirmishes with infantry weapons, (including 82mm and later in Macedonia 120mm mortars).[8] Extremists on both sides in the early stage of the conflict appeared intent on creating provocations, the albanians in the hope of NATO intervention, and the Serbs in the hope of lining up international public opinion in favour of dissolving the buffer zone (the DMZ).[9] In the first stage of the conflict, the Serbs won the battle for international opinion, producing what Serb Prime Minister Zoran Djinjic later described as 'our first victory for ten years' when Serb troops re-entered the demilitarised Ground Security Zone. Ironically, it appears that the guerrillas purchased at least a portion of their weapons directly from the Serbs and the VJ.[10] Much of the remainder appears to have been coming through FYROM, where the police are alleged by FYROM

---

[7] Note that Medveje was retained by Serbia after 1879, whereas Preshevo was taken in 1913 as part of what is now Kosovo.

[8] If Serbian claims are to be believed, the guerrillas number 3,000. 'Ado do anti-teroristicke akcije dode, pacace se samo na naoruzane ljude,' *Nedeljni Telegraf*, 21 February 2001. [This claim would appear to be implausible, with UCPMB admitting to only 200 fighters, with reality being perhaps around 600-700, according to KFOR sources.]

[9] *VIP*, 7 February 2001.

[10] 'Kosovo–Unsafe Zone,' *AP*, 18 February 2001.

press sources to have been assisting the arms smuggling operation in return for bribes.[11]

In the view of many in the NATO KFOR force in Kosovo, the UCPMB guerrillas were at least unwittingly aided in their efforts by the US Army[12], which should have been patrolling most of the Kosovo side of the administrative boundary with southern Serbia. One explanation was that operating under a policy of 'Force Protection' which placed the safety of US soldiers ahead of actually accomplishing any given mission, it was suggested in early 2001 that the US forces were reluctant to risk incurring casualties and leave their bases to engage in the heavy patrolling necessary to prevent cross-border infiltration by the guerrillas. Defenders of US KFOR have claimed that the heavily wooded and remote border is impossible to police effectively, and that KFOR views were based on experience in the much easier territory in MNB Central Zone where BRITFOR had been the lead force. The dispute may be as revealing of the dominant pro-Serb ideologies within French and British KFOR as anything connected with ground level military realities. But as a result, there was a relatively unhindered flow of volunteers across the boundary from Kosovo into Kosovo Lindore/Preshevo.

The limiting factor in the early stages of the Preshevo conflict was to be Yugoslav/Serb unwillingness to provoke a KFOR or international community response should the Serbian Army (VJ) enter into the five kilometre-wide buffer zone created by the July 1999 Kumanovo military-technical agreement between KFOR and the VJ (the peace agreement over Kosovo). This agreement, which regulated the terms and conditions of KFOR's entry into Kosovo and the VJ's withdrawal, permitted only police with small arms inside the buffer zone, while forbidding all VJ forces. Heavy weapons were specifically excluded. Given the unwillingness of the VJ to provoke a NATO response and international condemnation, as well as the reluctance of the police to incur losses in frontal infantry assaults without artillery support, the UCPMB guerrillas

---

[11] Widely alleged in Macedonian Press reports of the shooting of the local chief of Police in Sept 2000. Quoted in Start magazine, published Skopje dated Oct 6 2000.

[12] As stated above, based on their behaviour and tactics, it would appear that the UCPMB may have benefited from US style training or trainers, (though not necessarily funded by the US of course). This training could have occurred after NATO entered Kosovo and before Milosevic was overthrown, and it has been suggested that it was part of a plan for destabilising the Milosevic regime.

in the region successfully seized large parts of the 5 kilometre wide buffer zone along the Preshevo border with Kosovo. This process began as early as November-December 1999, when the various groups that became part of the UCPMB began to form and develop their local military activity.

Based on their behaviour and tactics, it would appear that the UCPMB may have benefited from US style training or trainers, (though not necessarily funded by the US of course).[13] This training could have occurred after NATO entered Kosovo and before Milosevic was overthrown, and it has been suggested that it was part of a plan for destabilising the Milosevic regime.

In the 1998-1999 wartime period, the Serb forces had ravaged the Preshevo valley completely destroying 3 Islamic buildings and causing serious damage to 11 of the other 23 mosques in the valley. Serbia had already excluded albanians from the education and health care systems, subjected them to dismissal from jobs in state-owned companies, the police, and other public sector jobs, while limiting severely access to Albanian language media and political office. As in Kosovo, the wholesale disenfranchisement of an entire sector of the population caused the homogenisation of the local population against the Serbs. Coupled with the successes in removing Serbian (FRY) power across the administrative border in Kosovo, it was only a matter of time before the situation boiled over.

It suited Milosevic to both create and then to ensure the continuation of the rebellion in Preshevo, since it kept the 'threat' to Serbia alive. Interestingly it seems also to have suited his immediate successors. Kostunica and Djindic both used 'the Albanian threat' as a talking point, and both, and especially Djindic, exploited the conflict in the international arena, as each time they refrained from military action it could be presented as a public relations coup. The Belgrade regime employed substantial foreign expert help in presenting its case. It enabled Belgrade to publicly demonstrate the new 'moderate democratic' government at work, and was initially successful. The problem is, that creating this media 'situation' has been very easy, but finding a real solution in the three South Serbia/Preshevo communes has been much harder.

---

[13]Personal interviews with NATO officers in Kosovo. Supported by various articles in UK and other international newspapers.

The Serbian media presented the UCPMB as part of an irredentist movement intent on carving out sections of Serbia to form a Kosovo-centred Greater Albania or Greater Kosovo. As was common during the Milosevic era, the Albanian speaking forces in the region were and still are portrayed in the Belgrade massmedia as potential or actual 'terrorists,' local Albanians are referred to by the derogatory term *Siptar* (something about the equivalent of 'nigger' in American English), KFOR is depicted as incompetent, and Kosovo and other Albanian areas are havens for drug trafficking, white slavery, and other crimes.[14] The Serbian press whipped up hysteria with sensationalist headlines and stories, including the threat of Albanian artillery attacks on the city of Vranje.[15] No mention was made as to what the albanian demands were, or whether these demands may or may not be legitimate. International community and diplomatic figures in Belgrade, anxious to assist the new Serbian (then DoS) government, were prepared to overlook the lack of change in the Serbian Army and various Serb police forces.

The then Yugoslav President Vojislav Kostunica took a hard line in the press in regard to southern Serbia, refusing to negotiate with 'terrorists,' and encouraging the army and police to stamp out the rebellion.[16] In retrospect, this illustrates the central dependence of the then so-called 'democratic' Serb regime on army support. Kostunica refused to acknowledge the background of Serb policies that led to the albanian insurgency.[17] He also publicly encouraged calls for reducing or eliminating the buffer zone, so as to permit the VJ to bring artillery and tanks to bear on the insurgents and – if Kosovo was any guide – the civilian population. By February 2001 he seemed confident that this would happen, only to find that whilst NATO was prepared to reduce the zone, the offer was hedged about by restrictions on Serb withdrawals of controversial units such as the army's Pristina Corps. But NATO gave way fully to Serb demands later in the summer of 2001, (probably or largely due to the new conflict in Macedonia) and the Ground Security Zone was fully opened on August 17th 2001, a major political victory

---

[14]See 'KFOR pustio, KFOR da vrati,'; 'Rasadnik droge I prostitutke,'; *Glas,* 20 February 2001.

[15]'Pred Srbijom na pomolu novi rat: teroristi haubicama od 122 milimetra I lakim raketnim sistemima spremaju napad na Vranje,' *Nedeljni Telegraf,* 21 February 2001.

[16]*VIP,* 15 February 2001.

[17]'Dogovoren niz mera za zastitu od terorizma,' *Danas,*20 February 2001.

over NATO for the unreformed army then under Milosevic henchman (and subsequently Kostunica's Chief of Staff) General Nebojsa Pavkovic[18].

In contrast to Kostunica, the then Serbian Premier Zoran Djindjic did not rule out talking with anyone, provided that the party be willing to enter into constructive dialogue. With foreign help, Serbian vice-president Nebojsa Covic came up with an innovative three-part plan, (the Programme for the Solution of the Crisis in the Pcinja District) to solve the problem by promising to emancipate the Preshevo Albanians and reintegrate them into Serbian civil life, political, social and economic life. This plan combined a series of confidence-building measures, which include reintroducing Albanians into the local police force, combined with a gradual phased disarmament plan, with economic aid for job creation, and various social reforms. By contrast, the Albanian did not have the same International Community expert help, and thus allowed the Serbs to set the political agenda, which NATO then quickly forced through by agreeing to end the safe haven of the ground security zone.

Set against the good efforts from the DOS government in Belgrade, Milosevic's SPS extremists in early 2001 still maintained control over most of southern Serbia's media, and their efforts appear aimed at stirring rather than calming tensions. The SPS used the issue in an effort to destabilise the DOS government. The police and army favoured a forceful resolution of the problem, and engaged in deliberate provocations, hoping to provoke an UCPMB response that would permit them to enter the buffer zone and settle the matter once and for all through ethnic cleansing. For their part, the UCPMB guerrillas appeared all too willing to deliberately provoke the military and police and to respond in kind to provocation, hoping to draw a Serbian response that would draw in KFOR and NATO. Despite the partial implementation of the Covic plan, Kosova Lindore/southern Serbia is still capable of providing a rallying point for nationalist passions on both sides of the ethnic divide, where nationalist extremists see regional problems as an ideal way to advance their wider agendas. Serb weapons sales to the albanian guerrillas were one manifestation of this in the wartime period. It is also clear that the

---

[18]The grip that hardline unreformed officers such as Pavkovic retained on the VJ was demonstrated by the controversial retirement list of December 2001, whereby some 20 moderate generals were forcibly retired from the VJ, and long planned reforms once again put off.

lingering remains of the Preshevo crisis are a hindrance to army reform plans. The high expense of keeping forces in the Preshevo theatre has led Belgrade army leaders to request NATO help in finance matters, arguing that it is an asset in the war on terrorism.

Although the FRY, NATO, and much of the international community supported the Covic initiative for resolving the crisis in the Preshevo-Bujanovac-Medvedja region of southern Serbia, strong nationalist forces within the Serb Police and Army were pressing for a military solution, if the negotiations failed. There clearly was and is a lack of goodwill amongst many sections of the Serbian security forces even now. Looking back, an 18th February 2001 joint closed-door meeting between the then Serbian and FRY governments decided on unspecified 'measures for protection against terrorism.' Following the meeting Serbian Minister of Justice Vladan Batic's said 'the boundaries of patience have disappeared,'[19] while Federal Minister of Defence Slobodan Krapovic added that if negotiations failed, 'our forces will be forced to undertake anti-terrorist actions.'[20]

Already signs were appearing that Serbian and FRY security forces in southern Serbia would adopt new tactics against potential renewed insurgency.[21] The army started a very large construction operation in the area, building large new bases and roads to access the new Kosovo administrative border, many of which were not competed until as late as 2008/9.

Official VJ statements that the UCPMB was planning a spring offensive in 2002 gave credibility to the likelihood that they themselves wish to act, and everyone saw the spring as a likely time for a provocation from either side.[22] In the event nothing much happened, and for the last twelve years the Preshevo Albanian side has continued with political efforts, whilst the Serbs have used the courts and arrests for 'terrorism' to continue a policy of silent ethnic cleansing. The unsatisfactory political situation from the Albanian point of view has led to a lack of inward Albanian Diaspora investment, unlike Kosova, with its positive economic role.

---

[19]'Leks specijalis protiv korupcije,' *Danas,* 20 February 2001.

[20]'Ako do anti-teroristicke akcije dode, pacace se samo na naoruzane ljude,' *Nedeljni Telegraf,* 21 February 2001.

[21]'Protiv ofanzivnih oruzanih akcija,' *Blic,* 20 February 2001.

[22]*VIP,* 8 February 2001.

On the question of Preshevo/southern Serbia, Serb diplomacy has successfully lined up international opinion on its side, and appears to have won significant backing from NATO, the US and the EU to implement the 'negotiated' solution. There was increasing western acceptance towards Belgrade's proposal for shrinking or eliminating the buffer zone. Technically this was been agreed to in phases, but not starting with the Preshevo area. In practice, it was completed along the whole Kosova border by September 2001 (see below).

The problems in southern Serbia are presenting a political headache to the Serbian government as well as creating a litmus test on nationalist issues, reform and co-operation with the west. Preshevo/Southern Serbia is also still diverting sorely needed resources away from the country's dire social needs towards not only the army and police, but also towards repair of civilian infrastructure. All told, the southern Serbia question has exposed significant weaknesses in the army, Serbia's police, Serbian civilian government and Serbia's policies towards its minorities. It will continue to create instability until such time as Serbian authorities and the local albanian population can come to agreement on the proper role of an Albanian minority in a Serbian state, if this is still a possible, practical scenario.

The events of 2001 – the relation to the Macedonia conflict.

The Preshevo valley continued to be in the news after the spread of the conflict to FYROM in February 2001. However it was overshadowed by events on the adjacent FYROM border, and then in Macedonia itself in early 2001. Macedonia remained a central part of the new crisis in the southern Balkans, with the United Nations, OSCE, NATO, the Council of Europe and France all strongly condemning violence there, but unclear as to what to do.

Whilst superficially the two problems were separate, in fact both related to ethnically Albanian populations in the borderlands of Slav (Serbian and Macedonian) states, and there were wide connections between the Albanian speaking populations of the border areas.

Today large numbers of Albanian inhabited villages and areas in Preshevo are still depopulated – of a population of perhaps 7,000 in Medvedje only around 600-700 are alleged to remain, the remainder having fled from the alleged depredations of the Serbian forces in 1998/9 (the Kosovo war years). In March 2001 the violence spread to neighbouring FYROM, in the shape of an Albanian armed takeover of part of the village of Tanushec, high on a ridge forming the newly defined FYROM-Serbian border, where the inhabitants have also fled into Kosovo.[23]

Despite the wishes of the International Community to pretend otherwise, Serbs and Albanians have had a cordial dislike for each other since time immemorial[24], or at least since 1876, when the Serbian army first drove large numbers of Albanians out of what is now south Serbia[25], giving rise to a cycle of violence and expulsion that haunts the southern Balkans until this day.

By the end of January 2001, the Serbian army was again shelling villages, this time in what is now Serbia, and the first Serb soldier has been killed by the UCPMB, the clumsy acronym for the local albanian defence and/or resistance force. KFOR, rather than the UN, became involved in talks with Serbia, and was running political negotiations to try and prevent the situation escalating.

The most fiercely contested area, Preshevo, was part of the same Banovina (Royalist Yugoslavia administrative unit) as Kosovo until after WWII (1947), and closely connected to Gjilane in Kosovo; however the area is important both as being part of Serbia in Serb eyes (most Serbs are unaware of the former Kosovar connection) and as being very close to the strategic Nis - Skopje highway. Up until 2001 the new Yugoslav government seemed to be benefiting from the clash, winning considerable sympathy for their restrained views on not 'going in hard'. However, 'going in hard' was clearly the view of the Yugoslav army, which had continually exerted pressure locally with its ex Pristina Corps,

---

[23]It may be worth noting that the whole problem of all these areas lies within a 30km radius or less.

[24]Following the events of the last 50 years (of Macedonian speakers controlling the Republic of Macedonia, rather than Serbs ruling both communities) albanians living there (who form an overwhelming majority along the west of Macedonia) have become the object of extreme dislike by most middle-class Macedonians, who (perhaps with some justification) see them as wishing to break away from Macedonia.

[25]With the usual accompanying events of massacre, rape, violence and theft of property, which has transmitted itself through oral history in the districts to which the refugees fled ever since, and is known as the movement of the 'mohajir'.

and the notorious SAJ units (plus the JSO 'Frenkie's boys' – extreme nationalist paramilitaries) squeezing up against the edge of the zone, (GSZ) and whose original behaviour, taking revenge for their defeat in Kosovo on the largely albanian speaking inhabitants in 1999 is alleged to have resulted in the local albanian taking action to defend themselves and forming the UCPMB.

Another cause of ill feeling was the occupation of socially-owned buildings. When the Pristina Corps moved in from Kosovo they took over the only working factory in Vranje as a base, putting 400 (mainly albanian speaking) workers out of work.[26] It was hardly the way to start winning hearts and minds, but the security forces intentions back in 1999 seemed to be more to get rid of their remaining Albanian citizens after losing Kosovo, rather than to win the battle for International Community opinion.

In Belgrade the original Covic peace plan was said to be endorsed by the Albanian mayor of Preshevo, Riza Halimi, although what he is quoted as saying locally was that he favoured 'complete demilitarisation',[27] and a locally recruited police force, reflecting the local population ratios, which would produce a very different force.

He favoured a multi-ethnic police force based on the local population percentages. Despite the difficulties it would probably have been wise to incorporate ex UCPMB fighters into this, or risk continued violence , (which would of course have been very difficult for the Serb Government). Halimi's main demand however has always been that the basis of negotiations should be the unofficial local referendum of 1992,

---

[26]One of the main albanian objections to the Serb Army presence, at least in the towns, was that the army was based in former working factories, schools, community halls and other public buildings. Military plan for new roads and barracks – northern Ireland style watchtowers and bases are quoted in the JNA news as having cost 100 billion Dinar in 2001, budgeted for 200 billion Dinar in 2002 (exchange rate quoted 30 Dinar to 1 Dm). Of this around 400million Dinar seems to have been spent on 22 new container bases in PMB. Krstic defended this on the grounds that living outside of inhabited areas would be safer for the army, an interesting reflection on the Serb feelings about security in PMB post the Covic plan. This money was said to represent just the JNA spending, and does not reflect the separate Serbian Government spending on policing, and especially new police posts.

[27]Meaning the removal of Serb forces from the whole of the communes as well as UCPMB from the GSZ.

which voted overwhelmingly for autonomy for the region (but not independence).

The Albanian side was always complicated by the existence of numerous groups – there are two political parties, and were probably six armed groups, under the umbrella title (but not command) of the UCPMB, which was in turn represented by the joint Political Council of PMB. All the Albanians were however united in stating the UCPMB should have the lead role in negotiations with Belgrade, as the 'protectors of the inhabitants of PMB'. NATO was also ostensibly keen that all the groups are represented in any talks, in order that they should be fully committed to any possible settlement or plan.

Perhaps more interesting is what Covic said when introducing the plan early in 2001. He would not rule out using the Yugoslav army for 'anti-terrorist' action, but was able to rule out changing borders, or any form of special status or autonomy for the area. He also suggested that if this formula worked for Preshevo it could also work for Kosovo, which may provide an indication towards the direction the Serbian government would have liked to move in. Kostunica then (Feb 2001) added to this by stating that there would be no negotiation with terrorists under any circumstances, and by suggesting the ground safety zone be ended, and policed by joint Serbian and KFOR patrols on both sides of the administrative border (the Kosovo – Serbia border).

No negotiations with 'terrorists' caused a predictable problem with the albanians, who insisted on the UCPMB taking the lead,[28] and who anyway referred to their fighters as defenders, armed protectors, or freedom fighters. The albanian side also complained about the detail of the plan, its length and seeming lack of room for flexibility. They claimed that in essence the Serbs were saying you can accept the plan, disarm, and live as you always did, which from the plan seems to mean that about 50 albanians could re-enter the police,[29] and for Albanian speaking children to re-enter the schools, learn Serbian and live in a Serbian society. The Covic plan, if genuinely implemented, might have

---

[28]See above paragraph.

[29]Around '100 Serbs and albanians' (the proportions were not specified) are quoted as completing the one month OSCE supervised course by end of 2001, and some 62 albanians are said to have completed the three month course. The next intake was to include 10 women.

been acceptable, and succeeded, a generation ago, but in its 2001 form seemed unlikely to enjoy any success, except perhaps as a basis for talks. The result was atrophy, in that little or no progress was actually achieved, except in forming a local, and 'multi-ethnic' police force. This was set up and worked, but was entirely overridden by the national, and nationalist, Serbian Gendarmerie, who more or less arrogated all policing powers over the local albanian community to themselves.

Unbiased information as to how well the plan has succeeded is still difficult to come by, since the two sides are still so polarised, and even personal visits do not produce clear results. Economically there does not seem to have been much progress, except for (military) road building up towards the border. Following the start of the implementation of the Covic plan the Serbian press has almost invariably referred to the police in PMB as 'the new multi-ethnic police', although to what extent this has really changed as yet is open to question. Surprisingly recently there does seem to have been an effort to put some sort of discipline into the local police.

In December 2002 22 Preshevo Police Dept Chiefs, LtCol Srdjan Ilic and Presevo Town Police Chief Stole Filopovic were dismissed for taking part in the kidnapping for ransom of a leading albanian businessman. The head of the Economic Crime Unit in Vranje was also arrested for unspecified offences.

In addition 44 other police personnel were reported suspended for various offences in or around Vranje (source Dec 2002 VJ news). The army seem to have taken a delight in reporting this, although they have been less forthcoming on their own problems.

Around '100 Serbs and albanians' (the proportions were not specified) are quoted as completing the one month OSCE supervised course, and some 62 albanians are said to have completed the three month course. The next intake will include 10 women.

Despite the Covic plan being for a civilian style of reintegrating the population the Serb Army seems to have retained much of the lead in the area. There were previously differing attitudes in the Serbian Army. Whilst the Serb three fingered V sign (a deeply offensive gesture to albanians) was given by senior generals leading reoccupation of the GSZ, there was constant conflict within VJ over LtCol-Gen Krstic – head of the army in PMB during the re-occupation, and deputy head of Covic's team, who was finally dismissed by the VJ (Kostunica in effect) after various failed efforts to get rid of him in summer 2002. His dismissal or rather retirement was announced in the Belgrade Press on Sept 26th 2002. This clearly represented a triumph of the hardliners in the VJ over Preshevo in that year, although Krstic was given a task by Covic.

Lt Col Gen Lazarevic, Commander of the Third Army, of which the Pristina Corps was part, issued a number of provocative statements (Dec 2001, quoted in Politika) He warned that albanian extremists were grouping in northern Macedonia and Kosovo ready to attack southern Serbia, and claimed that two Brigades of terrorist forces had been transferred from Kosovo to Kumanovo. He also said that reliable sources indicated new groups forming in the Gjillane area of eastern Kosovo.

Both he and the Third Army made frequent statements about Serbs being forced to leave southern Serbia, or feeling so insecure that they were leaving. Politika quoted a 3rd Army spokesman on a story that 1500 Serbs in PMB had signed a petition asking for the army to stay on and protect them, whilst 20 albanian demonstrated daily asking for the army to leave public buildings in Preshevo.

Although the Covic plan appeared to be an innovative step forward, it is remarkabley similar to much earlier ideas in Kosovo, which in the end proved to be too little and too late. It does not meet international minority rights standards on minority education rights, or even those of pre-1990 Yugoslavia. It does not incorporate any ideas of international supervision, nor any guarantees of citizens or human rights, especially policing, other than incorporation into Serb institutions.

Tanjug, the official Serbian Press Agency, stated that the 'concessions' would not start until demilitarisation (by which Covic seems to mean the withdrawal of the UCPMB, not Serb forces) was in progress. Demilitarisation, in this case, seems to mean withdrawal or disarming of the UCPMB, and did not seem to incorporate any reciprocal offer other than to reduce VJ levels to those pre-conflict, which could mean anything. Whatever it did mean, (unless complete withdrawal by both sides) it was unlikely to be acceptable to local albanian, especially the several thousand displaced by fear of the Serb forces.

As with previous peace proposals in Kosovo the International Community had, in diplomatic terms, enthusiastically endorsed the plan, thus backing the Serb interpretation of the history of the Preshevo dispute. This has resulted in the usual trap – the International Community endorsing one side's position, which is not one of negotiation, but of a fully formed plan, published in Cyrillic in Belgrade papers, but not presented to the albanians in Preshevo at all, being tabled on a 'take it or leave it' basis, to be followed by 'robust anti-terrorist' actions.

Following widespread hints by Kostunica and the 28th February 2001 talks in Brussels it seemed that NATO had agreed to Belgrade's demands for a phased reduction of the GSZ (demilitarised zone). Two things need to be borne in mind – as always in negotiations over the last few years with the FRY there were two stories. Belgrade announced a phased reduction of the GSZ, whilst NATO, in a press comment by General Secretary George Robertson, suggested that this would depend on Serbia withdrawing the more provocative elements of its forces, (possibly this means the Pristina Corps, and perhaps part of the SAJ), and that the phased reduction would be linear, (i.e it will not start adjacent to Preshevo, but further north).

The spring 2001 initiative by the EU, (based on Carl Bildt's report to the Security Council) with monitors setting up offices in Bujanoc, Preshevo, was undoubtedly a sensible step forward. EU monitors were to rise to 30, but in practice did not achieve this, and of course had absolutely no power locally. The original plan, which in the end did not happen, was that they would report directly to Carl Bildt, (sidelining in this case OSCE and the UN). This, combined with more effective policing of the border by KFOR, (resulting in several dozen arrests in 2001/2), slowly stabilised the situation, although resolution will be a different matter.

As always in these negotiations there was a snag. Once again there was a demand for an International Military Rescue force (to rescue the EU) to be standby somewhere close. The obvious answer would have seemed to be KFOR, but press reports[30] indicated that there were differences in the International Community over who would supply and command the force, with France advocating a non-NATO purely European force, and some suggesting that as a result this would have to be located inside Preshevo and or Bujanoc. Paradoxically no one seems to have noticed that this would have achieved the guerrillas main aim, of internationalising

---

[30]London Times, 5th March 2001.

their conflict and obtaining an international peacekeeping force, so if implemented this could bring peace, at least in the short term.

But in reality, by April 2001 the current situation and the dramatic outbreak of a new international-scale crisis in FYROM made a settlement imperative for both sides. It was suggested that the only way to get the UCPMB out was for KFOR, or some other international military force, to go in, supervise the disarming of the UCPMB, and then for Serbia to implement Covic's plan. This was originally anathema to NATO, and outside the KFOR mandate, but some peoples views changed under the pressure of events. The American AFSOUTH commander in Naples, Admiral Ellis, expressed his desire to get NATO out of the political mediation started by their local spokesperson, Sean Sullivan, and for another organisation, more suited to political negotiation, to step in[31]. The US in February 2001 was currently holding in Camp Bondsteel around 80 – 100 alleged members of UCPMB who were arrested by KFOR at various times, and there was no clear or effective way to try them(they were eventually mostly quietly released). This alone would seem to be a good reason for seeking a political solution, since even in the dictatorial legal climate KFOR enjoys in Kosovo, there was a limit to how long any western nation can hold people without trial on suspicion of intending to commit political violence in another country.

Once again the International Community was left with the choice of condoning continued nationalist violence, this time finally in (southern) Serbia, or sending in International Monitors or Observers, risking assuming some degree of responsibility for the area. The alternative to this was likely to be a rerun of KDOM's and OSCE's experience in Kosovo in 1998 and 1999, of simply bearing witness to more Serb atrocities. The problem is that whilst the Serbian government may have changed (though many doubt the reality of this where their albanian citizens are concerned), it is very unlikely that the Serb army and police have. They will certainly revert to type when attacked by albanians, whether local people acting in self defence, or politically motivated extremists intent on provoking a violent reaction.

---

[31]In the event he was replaced by Peter Feith, a personal representative of the NATO Secretary General. This transferred responsibility from KFOR to NATO in Brussels.

Carl Bildt, in a report to the UN presented on January 15th 2001, advocated doing just this, (sending in Monitors). He suggested the withdrawal of some Serb forces, followed by the creation of a multi ethnic police force, but admitted this would take time. He also suggested that the Serb side agree to share power – 'divide government' – with the albanian community. He suggested that Belgrade start with confidence building measures outside the security zone, and suggested completing this programme in 'the presence of international forces'.

His report went on to describe the enormous difficulties in doing this, but nevertheless stressed it as essential. In addition to his report the UN has appointed an inter-agency task force, headed by UNDP and OCHA to look in the humanitarian problems of Preshevo. Only the first part of his plan, the EUMM monitor force, was partially implemented, with the International Community as a whole seeming to favour the Covic plan.

In addition to this NATO, in the form of Secretary-General George Robertson, also stepped in at a higher level. Robertson ostensibly welcomed the Covic plan, as a basis for negotiation, but publicly stated it should not become an ultimatum, nor be used as an excuse for violence or 'so called anti-terrorist action' by Serb forces. In fact his spokesman went as far as suggesting that the withdrawal of the notorious Pristina Corps and the paramilitary SAJ 'anti-terrorist' unit would be helpful. Despite these statements the Covic plan did of course become an ultimatum (in many ways it already was), and the elements of the VJ previously in Kosovo also remained in situ.

Violent incidents in early February 2001 intensified the conflict. On February 13th and 16th Serb buses in Kosovo were attacked by Kosovar albanian extremists, with 10 dead in the latter incident. Belgrade immediately suggested a connection with Preshevo (although there was no geographical connection, and the albanian Kosovar arrested had no connection with Presevo), and accused 'albanian terrorists' of attempting to de-stabilise the peace talks (although these had not yet started). Interestingly the UCPMB joined in the general albanian condemnation of this attack. These incidents were then followed by the deaths of three Serbian police who drove over a mine well inside their lines – perhaps predictably the albanians suggested they had driven unknowingly over a Serbian army mine. This in turn was followed by the killing of a senior UCPMB commander by Serbs less than a couple of hours later.

The political Council of the UCPMB did not seem to be very strong, and the real power may well have been with the Preshevo Mayor, Riza Halimi. He was probably perfectly correct in insisting that all military groups within UCPMB should be included in any negotiating team, suggesting that otherwise they would not be fully on board, and that any peace agreement might not hold. In the end only one or two groups were actually represented in what passed for talks, and in effect it was NATO's agreement to ending the DMZ which forced the groups to give up. In conversations at the time it was very clear that it was the perceived change in US support, and clear opposition by NATO which demoralised the mainly poorly educated villager leadership of the UCPMB groups.

Despite all these different problems, progress, of a sort, was made. The albanian community in Preshevo appointed a nine person negotiating team (in itself quite a step forwards, since as noted UCPMB had several separate components), but insisted on international mediation in any talks. In practice this did not really happen. NATO provided the tents for the talks, and attended the meetings, but there was not mediation. As previously noted of the four brief meetings three were allowed to degenerate in arguments over Serbs alleged to be held by the UCPMB.

A Military Note

In this case the changing nature of the situation both affected by the weaponry being used, and prospects for peace or war may be indicated by changes in this. A key event, as often in Balkan history, was a funereal. The military conflict started when ethnic Albanian men in uniform appeared at the funeral of two brothers, Isa Saqipi (36) and Shaip Saqipi, (32), who were allegedly killed by Serbian police forces whilst driving a tractor in January 2000.

This brought the formation of the UCPMB into the open, when uniformed men came to the funeral in events which seem indistinguishable from those at the start of the main Kosovo ground war. The UCPMB (Ushtria Climitare Presheve, Medveje edhe Bojanoc) then started a campaign of using small arms (mostly AK47s) and the occasional anti-tank mine to drive the by now entirely Serbian Police (MUP) out of the GSW (ground security zone). They were assisted in this, since for reasons of force protection (and avoiding getting lost), US troops, who should control the adjacent Kosovo border, not only do not come into the GSZ, but do not come within one and a half kilometres of it either (see above).

Later (as previously noted) they also seem to have received training assistance from someone or some organisation training[32] in an American military style. This became apparent both from the style of marching, complete with US type marching songs, and the infantry tactics used. The effectiveness of this was seen in November 2000, when a series of well coordinated infantry attacks demonstrated the UCPMBs ability to use of 82mm mortars, and to effectively 're-organise on the objective' – the latter something that the Armija (the Bosnian army) never learnt in three years.

Since then UCPMB had acquired a number of 120mm mortars, and 79mm recoilless anti-tank weapons, (which to the uninitiated look like small artillery pieces, but can only fire directly, not over hills). Publicly the Serb forces claimed never to fire back, but in fact this is pure nonsense, since they always engaged the 79mm pieces with tank fire, and also occasionally used artillery and mortar fire, in what might be very loosely described as counter-battery fire. Serbian statements claimed that the insurgents had at least two genuine artillery pieces, with both D30s and 122mm (relatively large, long range artillery) being alleged as in UCPMB possession.

The Preshevo link with FYROM

It was widely alleged by both the International Community and the Serbs and Macedonians that the initial border conflicts in Macedonia were a spill over from the Preshevo conflict. From personal experience and understanding this was not the case, although later in the year ex-fighters from Preshevo went to join their countrymen in Macedonia.

It is probably that some form of insurrection in Macedonia was in the planning stages in early 2001, (and had been since before the Kosovar war). Albanian political thinkers, members of the two smaller left wing parties (LPK and LKCK) were hoping to follow up on the Kosovo war by armed action in Macedonia. There were of course close connections between all albanian armed groups, but the UCPMB seems to have

---

[32]It is of course well established that a US firm MPRI (Military Professional Resources inc) trained the Croatian army prior to their re-conquest of the Krajina in 1994.

been largely spontaneous armed village defence groups, with no clear intellectual leadership.

Despite this planning for an insurrection it would seem (and seemed to informed observers at the time) that the start of the Macedonian insurrection in Tanusec or Tanusevci in February 2001 was precipitated by the Macedonian government. FYRoM Prime Minister Georgievski confirmed this indirectly in December 2001 when he stated that the Skopje government had been warned by Belgrade about the start of an Albanian uprising a week or so before both the Tanusec incident and the start of the Balkan PMs summit. The following description details the development of the incident.

The Role of the Macedonian 'Wolves'[33]

Diplomats reported that government circles in Belgrade, and especially those of Kostunica, were apparently becoming obsessed by the problem of albanian irredentism in the Balkans. The obsession served two purposes. Firstly it kept attention away from Serbia's own problems, and secondly pandered to what the Serbs evidently see as the West's obsession – again the problem of Albanians in the southern Balkans, and enabled the Serbs to set the International Community agenda.

The Macedonian Ministry of Interior sending the Macedonian Special Forces Unit, the Wolves, (a unit not frankly known for their community policing skills) into Tanushec/ Tanusevci[34] only days before the Balkan summit produced a predictable public relations coup for Kostunica, who was able to keep the issue at the top of the agenda. Only Ilir Meta, the Albanian Prime Minister, was able to offer a suitable rejoinder, when he observed that 'how a representative of Serbia was able to complain about human rights, given the events over the last two years', was beyond him.[35]

---

[33] The 'Wolves' is the name of the FYROM special forces unit deployed in Tanushec. Exclusively recruited from ethnic Slav-Macedonian speakers with some Serbs from Kumanovo, it had a self publicising reputation for tough action.

[34] Language Policy in this paper: Almost all places have two names in this area, a local albanian one, in use by the inhabitants, and a Slavic one in use by the government. This paper tries to use both where appropriate, or where relevant that word appropriate to the context or ethnicity being discussed.

[35] Ilir Meta, Albanian Prime Minister, in a brief rejoinder to Kostunica's speech to the Balkan Summit, Skopje, February 2001.

Predictably 'crying wolf' had its own more genuine results a few days later. The 'Wolves', a special forces unit composed solely of Slav Macedonians, plus a number of Serbs from Kumanovo and elsewhere, duly shot a Macedonian-albanian boy, claiming to have been engaged in a major gun battle. Furthermore, they claimed that 200 black uniformed invaders[36] were lurking in Kosovo and Preshevo waiting to invade the homeland. At the time this seems to have been untrue, since KFOR could find no evidence of anyone in any uniform, and the villagers denied the boy was armed or involved. Interestingly the Skopje government hastily issued strong denials of any problem in Tanushec, but the damage was done. The villagers evacuated into Kosovo, (Tanushec, though now in FYROM, is the summer grazing village of Vitinje in Kosovo). A few days later, following the boys funeral, albanian guerrillas in camouflage uniforms were visibly occupying half of Tanusevci, US units had pulled back a further kilometre and a half, and yet another small war was well on the way to starting, with three FYROM soldiers dead, Macedonian and Kosovar albanian refugees streaming down from the hill villages, and the border with Kosovo closed.

Tanusevci/Tanushec, Geography, and History

What seems to have been intended to be a small 'incident to order', (for the Macedonian government) in advance of the Balkan Summit[37], or to divert attention from the then current telephone tapping scandal in FYROM resulted in the death of one Macedonian-Albanian villager, and due to its proximity to Preshevo the local violence spiralled out of all control. The subsequent reprisals by FYROM special forces in Albanian villages left yet another legacy of bitterness and violence in the southern Balkans.

There were minor violent incidents along the Macedonian Kosovo border throughout 2000/2001, and indeed isolated incidents of terrorism or violence since 1992. The difficulty was distinguishing between Albanian para-militarism and ordinary armed smuggling, in which all

---

[36]Black uniforms are or were the uniform of UCK Field Security Units in the Kosovo war, whereas both in that war and later in Macedonia almost all albanians fought either in camouflage uniforms, (if they had them) or their own clothes. Black uniforms were however a great 'bogeyman' of the Serb and Macedonian press.

[37]Note PM Georgievski's remarks on this in Dec 2001

three ethnicities (Serb, Macedonian and albanian) participated, keeping Serbia in consumer goods and food throughout the time of sanctions. This, whilst successful for Belgrade, and financially successful for Skopje, has left a legacy of violence and police corruption which has been hard to eliminate in the area. However, the events of early 2001 were clearly politically inspired, albeit by both sides. The February 2001 problem seems to have started with an independent and hitherto unknown Macedonian TV crew (though working for a well known station, TV Al) managing or alleging[38] to have been kidnapped on Feb 16th for a few hours in Tanusevci.

Following their release there was supposedly a one hour gun-battle as a Macedonian unit, apparently initially from the border forces, attempted to enter the village. According to villagers, and the Deputy Minister of the Interior, there was no one firing back at them, but an Albanian village boy, or young man, Muzafer Xhaferi, was shot in the back of the neck, and later died. A series of minor, but ever escalating incidents in the area then followed, culminating on Feb 26th in a two hour gun battle.

It is alleged, by both Macedonian press sources, and informed international observers, that the first shooting was not a gun battle at all, but a single shot which resulted in the death of Xhaferi. It is further alleged, on credible analysis, that the intention was purely for international public relations, to provide a talking point on the dangers of Albanian irredentism in the Balkans for the Balkans Leaders Summit in Skopje on Feb 22/23rd. It is certainty a fact the FYROM Ministry of Interior is still widely regarded as containing many pro Serbian officials.

Tanushec/ Tanusevci lies on that part of the Macedonian-Kosovar order adjoining the Presheve Valley area and the GSZ. Located high (1050m) on what is now a border ridge, as stated above, it was in origin the summer grazing village of Vitina, now in Kosovo. The population remains very mobile, since the terrain, and the primary occupation of sheep raising does not provide much of a living for most families. They certainly resent the new border, as being 'an unnatural imposition upon their traditional regional habits and rights'.[39]

---

[38]Conveniently or inconveniently they said they had their film confiscated. The cameras and mobile phones were later recovered by Macedonian Security forces.

[39]UNHCR Skopje internal report dated 26th Feb 2001. Two separate reports from the Macedonian government categorically denied that there had been a gun

Following the reported gun battle Macedonian army units then moved into or closer to the border villages, and the local inhabitants, who are 100% Albanian speaking, mostly fled, alleging security force and police intimidation and violence. UNHCR reported that families, or at least women, children and old men had moved out of the area from both sides of the border. In February-March 2001 informed sources among the International Community in Macedonia believed that 'ethnic armed Albanian groups' – EAAG – would continue to try to extended their hold over the area[40]. The tri-border point, where the FRY ground security zone, (GSZ), Kosovo and FYROM meet lies less than 15km east of Tanushec, and UNHCR reported that all the inhabitants they have spoken to expressed a wish to be Kosovar, rather than FYROM citizens.

On Tuesday 6th 2001 March US Forces shot two albanians apparently pointing weapons at the patrol, which is the first time presumed members of UCPMB or EAAG had been hit by KFOR troops. By March 8th US Forces had occupied quite a large part of Tanushec, seemingly convinced that their GPS's (locating devices) showed it to be in Kosovo.[41]

Behind the scenes the Skopje government was looking for a military solution, and avoiding talks with its own albanian governing coalition partner, the DPA. Both Belgrade and Skopje advocated the creation of five kilometre strip,(free-fire zone?) running parallel to the Kosovo border inside Kosovo, and starting by crossing the old GSZ. The implications for instability, if not all out war between Albanian fighters and Serb or FYROM special forces, were obvious. In the end the conflict was ended by the Ochrid agreement, though, like the Preshevo agreement

---

battle. It was the time of the Balkan leaders summit, and no much more can be said. UNHCR Skopje internal report dated 26th Feb 2001 GPS Ground Position Satellite system used to find the position of a patrol. GPSs are almost invariable very accurate but unfortunately the maps on which the results are plotted are not always so accurate. In this case the answer is rather more amusing – the American maps which show the administrative borders were based on old Yugoslav maps, which showed the border prior to the Belgrade-Skopje changes announced in Feb 2000.

[40] In fact they (the albanian groups) showed considerable strategic ability, and shifted the fighting firstly to the hills above Tetovo, and later to villages closer to Skopje.

[41] In February 2002 both KFOR and UN spokespersons seemed to be arguing strongly (if belatedly) for the integrity of the Macedonian border with Kosovo, and by implication seemed to be placing in doubt the revisions of the Belgrade –Skopje agreements of 1999.

this seemed more likely to be a temporary solution, based on human rights and equality of employment, rather than who controlled what land. Armed problems in the Macedonian/Kosovo border region have continued until the time of writing (2010)

Overall View in the Balkan Context

Implications for Serbia

The security situation in Preshevo since 2002 remains tense. One of the key preconditions for Balkan stability is that Serbia finds its natural borders, (whatever these may be). Until such time as this occurs, Serbia will continue to stir up trouble among its neighbours and citizens. Until its borders are set, Serbia will have trouble attracting reputable foreign investment, and may also find itself unable to carry out the necessary internal reforms necessary to adhere to modern European standards of good governance. The underlying problem remains that what Serbs see as their natural borders is not what a lot of people actually living in those areas see as Serbian lands.

Implications for FYROM

The main fear of the International Community in relation to Preshevo is that any renewal of conflict there will not only be destabilising for the newly democratic (albeit still very nationalist) government in Belgrade, but also for Macedonia as a whole. There are good reasons for this fear. Although the International Community is endlessly pleased that FYROM broke away from the FRY peacefully, in doing so it created a great deal of ethnic tension. It cut off its own albanians from their relations in Kosovo, and from their university education, (few of the younger generation in Preshevo speak anything apart from albanian). More importantly the new Macedonian constitution declared FYROM to be 'the state of the Macedonian nation,.. using the Macedonian language... in its Cyrillic form'. This made it perfectly clear that there was little room other nationalities, of which the albanians are the largest, concentrated in a relatively compact geographical arc around the north-west and west. Theoretical the Albanians comprised 22.9% of the overall population, but in reality most observers feel this figure should have been higher. The first (SDSM) Skopje government then did its best to minimise the numbers of albanians in FYROM, by various methods of legalistic gerrymandering, such as provisions on citizenship (1994) and the census (1995). This would not necessarily be relevant to any briefing on Preshevo were it not necessary to show that there is also considerable potential instability in adjoining FYROM, and the remainder of this paper attempts to put this into context.

The situation is further complicated, in the eyes of the local inhabitants at least, by the FRY government in Belgrade having signed an agreement[42] delineating the new Macedonian-Kosovo border (with large amounts of land passed unilaterally to Macedonia) without any reference to either the UN, who control the area by virtue of a UN resolution, or with any Kosovo political parties, or the local inhabitants. Whilst possibly legalistically correct this was a move calculated to inflame passions among albanians (and at the same time establish a precedent in international terms, and to flout UNMIK).

Despite the allegations in the International Press, and in Belgrade, Kosovo is not a hot-bed of arms smuggling, but FYROM has a large legitimate and smaller 'grey' small arms market, and has had since 1991 or '92. The presence of KFOR forces in Kosovo and frequent arms searches has meant that UCPMB (although basically Kosovo based) has found it much easier either to buy arms from the Serbs, (as they, UCPMB, allege) or to smuggle them in via FYROM, where it seems (at any rate according to the Skopje press) to be very easy to buy off the police. The year 2000 saw complex incidents involving shot local FYROM police chiefs with albanian mistresses, jailed Kosovars and kidnapped FYROM border guards are all alleged, in the Skopje press, to be connected to arms smuggling and bribes. These and similar incidents have continued to the present .

Tanusevci (Tanushec to its albanian speaking inhabitants) lies directly on this route, though why the Macedonian government should have chosen to send one of their Special Forces (the Wolves) into the village just before the Balkan summit, if it was not for political reasons, to highlight albanian issues, remains a mystery. Tanusevci is largely devoted to herding sheep, the men mostly stayed as it was the lambing season, whereas the women and children fled from the FYROM forces.

---

[42]Border agreement between FRY and Macedonia announced Feb 2001

This area largely supported then the old (formerly socialist/communist oriented) albanian PDP (Party of Democratic Prosperity), whereas the then VMRO government was in coalition with the newer (and then much stronger) offshoot of the PDP, the DPA – Party of Democratic Albanians, led by Arben Xhaferi, which originally broke away as a more nationalist offshoot of the PDP. The DPA's electoral party support is stronger in Western FYROM, rather than in this border region. This split has relevance, in that all the time the conflict was confined to this narrow group of villages adjoining Preshevo there was less risk for destabilising FYROM as a whole.

However, the Wolves, and other FYROM units fully intended to 'go in hard', and this was undoubtedly going to leave a legacy of bitterness in the albanian community in FYROM, as the future course of the war in summer 2001 showed. Up until now the programme of albanians in FYROM has been one of seeking equal rights, and the use of language in local government, a university and similar civil rights issues. Ultimately they might have gone as far as wanting federalisation, or a form of cantonisation on the Swiss model, but they did not do publicly, either at that time or later.

It is quite clear that the entry of Skopje special forces units into Tanushec prompted albanians to take military action, in what they saw as defence of the villages. The situation rapidly escalated to violence, if not virtual war, or low intensity conflict. However, the NATO (KFOR) initial ideas of letting the FYROM and Serbian governments use force to solve the problem this would only have been a temporary fix, as NATO and the EU and US rapidly realised. It would have both helped to turn Kosovars against KFOR, and store up a legacy of bitterness amongst the albanian community in FYROM which would bring much greater problems later.

Implications for Balkan Stability

The implications of a second series of wars on the territory of the former Yugoslavia seems obvious, and are largely dealt with above. The break up of the Ottoman and Austro-Hungarian empires, followed by that of Yugoslavia, has resulted in what Albanians in the southern Balkans (and perhaps the Russians) see as a proliferation of Slavic states. The Albanians, whilst carefully avoiding the phrase 'greater Albania', or 'Greater Kosovo' have started talking about a proliferation of Albanian states, (the United States of Albania perhaps?).

The ultimate comment must be that there is clearly more trouble ahead on the territory of the former Yugoslavia – unless radical action is taken by the International Community to solve the problems of the albanian majority-inhabitant borderlands of Southern Serbia/Presevo and western Macedonia. The wars of the Yugoslav succession have possibly not yet ended. The present international policy of tinkering with seemingly attractive partial solutions for minority rights or human rights is likely to be destined to fail when dealing with people who do not see themselves as minorities.

Kosovo: Reflections on a failed UN Mission[1]

C. Dennison Lane

The violent events in Kosovo of 17 and 18 March 2004 appear to have taken the United Nations mission(UNMiK) in Pristina, the capital of Kosovo, by surprise[1]. Although I left Vushtrri for Peje(Pec) in December 2002 to take up a new post as Municipal Administrator (MA) there and Peje for Iraq in August 2003, as far as we were concerned in Vushtrri, it was only a matter of time before something along the lines of the events of March 2004 occurred. The rioting and destruction and ethnic conflict of that spring served to underscore the omissions of UNMiK. In its aftermath many of us were angry, contrite and bewildered. Had the international community (IC), most notably UNMiK demonstrated a greater degree of leadership and flexibility, coupled with moral and intellectual vision and the courage the think beyond what was familiar, the events of March would probably not have occurred. I am not alone in my disappointment. A former well-respected colleague from the Organization for Security and Cooperation in Europe (OSCE) shares my views. The former OSCE officer wrote to me:

> 'With the anger is a burning need to deal with those traitors, those who would sell their land and their future, and the lives of other human beings, for the price of a bullet, or a litre of gasoline. But we have to go beyond that and ask what role we have all played in getting to this point. This is a question that cannot be ignored; the responsibility and the accountability required of the international community since 1999 in Kosovo have been considerable. How could such events have occurred on our watch?'[2]

For its part, during the course of summer 2004, the Secretary-General of the United Nations, Mr. Kofi Annan, dispatched the Norwegian Representative to the United Nations General Assembly in New York, Ambassador Kai Eide, to Kosovo. Ambassador Eide's 18 page report on the

[1]An earlier draft of this paper was published in 'Mediterranean Quarterly', Washington DC, Summer 2005 edition.

[2]A note from a former OSCE colleague.

March events to the Secretary General is, for the UN, uncharacteristically direct. In part the Report noted that:

> 'The international community in Kosovo is today seen by Kosovo Albanians as having gone from opening the way to now standing in the way. It is seen by Kosovo Serbs as having gone from securing the return of so many to being unable to ensure the return of so few.'

The report further offers that the International Community (IC) in Kosovo had been 'caught by surprise' and had been unprepared to react in an intelligent and timely manner. It also presupposed that there had been 'intelligence failures' as they pertained to the identity and the activities of the extremists[3] and that IC failed to read 'the mood of the majority population'. The report further suggests that the efforts of the IC were likened to a 'static, inward-looking, fragmented and routine operation'.

The level of violence that occurred in that March could only have occurred in a vacuum created by the failure of the International Community (IC) as a whole to do or to address something fundamental. Ultimately it was our collective failure to develop and implement a meaningful plan for the future of Kosovo that led inextricably to the events of 17 and 18 March 2004. We never undertook the genuine empowerment of the leaders of the local ethnic communities, most notably the Albanians and the Serbs. There was never a realistic plan to provide Kosovo with a meaningful economic base, nor was there a workable plan that called for the systematic re-integration of Serbs and other minorities back into the social fold, and now in the aftermath of March 2003, UNMiK, and the IC as a whole, must accept its part of the blame for what occurred.

Shortly after leaving Kosovo, someone recommended that I read Michael Ignatieff's recent book, 'Empire Lite', a book that directly

---

[3] The suggestion that UN field officers did not know the identity of the extremists, at least in Vushtrri/Vucitrn Municipality and no doubt in other Municipalities, is untrue. This information had been routinely made available to both the UN Regional HQ and to Pristina. In the same context UNMiK's unwillingness to create a meaningful information system that was available to Administrators and that could provide background information as it pertained to prominent figures and events, assured that UNMiK, from an informational point of view remained, to borrow from Norman Dixon, 'wrapped in a cocoon of catastrophic ignorance'. (see Dixon, Norman: *On the Psychology of Military Incompetence*, Futura Publications, Aylesbury, England 1979) p. 293.

addresses Kosovo. This is a book that should be required reading for everyone associated with the Kosovo or any Kosovo-like Mission. Mr. Ignatieff writes:

> '…the strategy must be to force responsibility on to local elites, rather than trying to hold onto it itself. Power should be used to keep Kosovo free of external interference and aggression as well as internal civil war. But it must be the local political authorities who rule in fact as well as name. At the moment we have neither. Everything is done on the cheap, from day to day without any long-term security guarantees and short-term financial assistance that would genuinely create the conditions for true national independence. To exercise power in this way is to risk losing authority, and to risk everything eventually, since peoples disillusioned with our promises will have enduring reasons never to trust us again.'[4]

As it happened when Kosovo re-erupted in March of 2005 I was in Iraq back at the grass-roots level, where my functions were again, in theory at least, essentially those of a Municipal Administrator. I mention service in Iraq for a series of reasons paramount among them being that while I remain critical of the performance of the United Nations in Kosovo and elsewhere, I believe strongly in the UN as an institution, particularly in the wake of having spent seven intellectually and emotionally devastating months associated with Ambassador Paul Bremmer III's Coalition Provisional Authority (CPA) in Iraq. CPA was widely perceived to be internally incoherent and politically divided and CPA's interaction with Iraqi society was at best intermittent. CPA, with few Arabic specialists appeared to believe that Iraqi exiles would provide their eyes and ears. Instead they elicited hostility and anger on the part of many Iraqis. The experience afforded me an opportunity to compare grass-roots service with the UNMiK to service under CPA in Iraq. Suffice it to say that in the course of 30 plus years spent largely in the field, never have I encountered any organization as ill-led, irresponsible, arrogant, and callous as was the Coalition Provisional Authority.[5] It gives one cause to wonder what my generation learned from the Indochina conflicts.

---

[4]Ignatieff, Michael. *Empire Lite*, Vintage/Random House, London (2003) pp. 126-127

[5]I draw an important distinction between being 'callous' and simply being 'insensitive'. It is possible to be inadvertently 'insensitive'. One may, for example, be

What, however, immediately becomes clear, is that despite its shortcomings, in a world that is becoming increasingly complex and inter-related, the UN is all that we have. It is accordingly my most sincere hope that the UN will, in the very near term start, to re-invent itself. Hopefully, at the end of the process of introspection, what will emerge is a revitalized and meaningful entity capable of playing its role on the world stage.

The four years that I spent with UNMiK was my second mission with the United Nations. In 1989/90 I was seconded to the United Nations Border Relief Organization (UNBRO) from the US Army and posted to the Thai border town of Aranyaprathet. I was the de facto leader of the Special Liaison Team that had been specifically created to write a legal code and to raise, train, and equip three Cambodian Police Services, one for each Cambodian refugee faction[6] that was then arrayed along the Thai/Cambodian border. And while UNBRO's mission did not have the expanse of responsibilities that were associated with UNMiK, when I returned to the main-stream US Army in mid-1990, I was convinced that UNBRO's leadership in Bangkok evidenced at best only the most marginal grasp of the realities and problems encountered in the field. The Centre had for all intents and purposes decided what they wanted to hear and the reality of what existed in the field was of only passing importance. UNMiK, some ten years later, was not so very different.

My only disagreement with the views advanced in 'Empire Lite', relates to Mr. Ignatieff's suggestion that the first Special Representative of the Secretary General (SRSG), Dr. Bernard Kouchner, was too politically correct and consultative in lieu of simply 'laying down the law in a classic imperial fashion'.[7] I served with three SRSGs. From the perspective of a Municipal Administrator in Mitrovica Region under SRSG Kouchner, political correctness and a penchant for consultative deliberations were not the order of the day. It was the departure of Dr. Kouchner and the subsequent departures of Messrs Jack Covey (Principle Deputy to the SRSG), and Tom Koenigs (Director of Local Administration),

---

inadvertently ignorant of local customs . 'Callousness' suggests that one is aware of the customs and simply doesn't care.
[6]Armee Nationale Sihanoukienne (ANS), Khmer People's National Liberation Force (KPNLF), and the Khmer Rouge (KR).
[7]Ibid. pp 72-73

that signalled the end of what might best be described as UNMiK's dynamic period. The leadership and personal involvement and interest demonstrated by the senior-most members of Dr. Kouchner's team was replaced by a general lack of 'assertiveness' and a penchant for 'political correctness' at the Centre that became a way of life that ultimately came to permeate the entire mission. Personal charisma and leadership were replaced largely by unimaginative, pedantic, and self-serving-bureaucratic management that was more often than not divorced from the realities of Kosovo. It was the Centre's failure to systematically visit or to listen to voices in the field, or to support and/or defend beleaguered UNMiK staff members that personified everything that took place in the 'deluge' that followed the departure of Messrs. Kouchner, Covey, and Koenigs. There exists in French the term 'deresponsibilization'. It was 'deresponsibilization' on the part of Pristina as a whole that became synonymous with everything that came to pass. And the fact that there would ultimately be the implosion that occurred in March 2004 was, for many field officers, a foregone conclusion. The only question was when it would take place.

The central problem with Ambassador Eide's report to the Secretary General is not what it addresses, but rather what it lamentably fails to address. It simply does not go far enough. There is no mention of any of the endemic problems related to decision making and the phenomenon referred to by some UN officers as 'UN culture'. This is important because it was the failure of the bureaucracy in Pristina and in some Regions to lead and assert themselves in times of need that more than anything else that led to the events of 17 and 18 March 2004.

Sadly, the overwhelming number of Kosovo-Albanians and Kosovo-Serbs perceive UNMiK as an organization whose members are primarily interested in their respective pay checks and subsequent UN assignments. By and large the overwhelming number of Kosovo-Albanians and Serbs are correct. Even disregarding the March riots UNMiK's record of accomplishments is far from sterling. After five years of UNMiK administration, the power stations at Obelic were still only marginally functional, job opportunities scarce, 'privatisation' remains a bitter joke, law and order[8] and local administration in many municipalities continue

---

[8]Just prior to leaving the mission, as Vushtrri MA I was asked to provide answers to certain very basic questions related to the Judicial system. In compiling our

to be dysfunctional, and the issue of 'returns', despite considerable fanfare, remains in reality a charade.

I came away from my almost four years with the UNMiK, on the one hand, elated with what we were able to accomplish in Vushtrri/Vucitrn, but on the other distressed at our ability to accomplish very much in Peje/Pec, and generally saddened by the fact that no matter how good we might have been at the Municipal level across the board, without there being the same degree of vision and understanding at the Centre, whatever it was that we might have accomplished in the Municipalities, was at best fleeting.

When I arrived in Mitrovica Region in mid-August 1999, the then Regional Administrator[9] (RA) required that each Municipal Administrator (MA) write a Daily Report. For the most part, MAs, as soon as they could get away with it, stopped the writing of daily reports. I opted to continue the practice, because I found that writing a synopsis of the day's events at day's provided a sort of philosophical catharsis apropos where we had been and where we needed to go. Ultimately, there were 743 reports written while I was in Vushtrri/Vucitrn. A further 128 reports were written in Peje/Pec. The combined reports, I am informed, represent the only detailed day-to-day account of the activities of an UNMiK administrator. Taken altogether, the reports consisted of some 4,000 pages. Remembering that Dame Rebecca West's 'Gray Lamb and Black Falcon',[10] written following a six-week trip to the Balkans immediately prior to WWII, contains some 1,000 pages; 4,000 pages in four years is by comparison a mere trifle.[11]

response from Peje/Pec, we only scratched the surface, but what we started to uncover was horrendous. It became rapidly apparent that the questions we were being asked to respond to were at best self-serving and in no manner addressed the corruption and influence-buying that were, in the summer of 2003, endemic in the judicial system throughout Kosovo. We were essentially asking the wrong questions.
[9] In the 39 months that I was a Municipal Administrator in Mitrovica Region there were no less than eight Regional Administrators.
[10] *Black Lamb and Gray Falcon* by Dame Rebecca West first published in 1942 by Macmillan London.
[11] Shortly before he left the mission, Tom Koenigs, one of the few individuals in Pristina who actually read the Vushtrri reports, suggested that at some point I should compile the reports because they might be of interest to the United Nation's archives. This I did, at not inconsiderable personal expense when I left Vushtrri, only to have them confiscated by Mr. Koenigs successor. I assume that they continue to occupy space in some obscure office in Pristina unread. It is

It is important to note that the problems that I found to be related to mission accomplishment within the UN are not necessarily peculiar to the UN. In the interlude between leaving Kosovo and moving on to Governorates in Iraq, I also had occasion to read an Article that appeared in the November 2003 edition of The Atlantic Monthly entitled 'Columbia's Last Flight.[12] In the article, the author addresses managerial problems within the National Aeronautic and Space Administration (NASA) that contributed to the February 2003 Columbia disaster. What was striking were the similarities between the corporate NASA and the corporate UN. In both organizations you can only be constructively critical of the organization outside the corridors of the organization. And in the UN, like in NASA, there too exists an 'incestuous hierarchical system with invisible rankings and a very strict informal chain of command'.[13] Admiral Hal Gehman, the senior investigating officer of the Columbia disaster speaking on the subject of NASA corporate image noted that:

It has been scorched into my mind that bureaucracies will do anything to defend themselves. It's not evil – it's just a natural reaction of bureaucracies.[14]

The UNMiK Personnel System and Mission Preparation:

Because any organization is as good as its people and the manner in which they are managed, comments related to the management and preparation of people for the Kosovo mission might be a good point of departure. I hastily add that I have never been a UN personnel officer and accordingly my comments are simply those of an informed observer of the system at work.[15] I also do not know if my comments vis-à-vis personnel administration within UNMiK relate to the UN as a whole or simply to the manner in which things were done in Kosovo.

---

unfortunate because the Vushtrri was the only Municipality in which the daily activities were meticulously recorded.

[12]Langewiesche, William, *The Atlantic Monthly* (November 2003).

[13]Ibid., p. 82.

[14]Admiral Hal Gehman cited in the November issue of *The Atlantic Monthly*, Ibid, p.73.

[15]But, as an Army combat officer, issues related to personnel and their 'care and feeding' were an essential part of our profession. A personnel officer is a personnel officer is a personnel officer – even in the UN.

How the UN determines the entry level of individuals into the system is among the greatest mysteries. Apropos UN entry level in Kosovo, for reasons that are not immediately apparent, it appeared to help if one was Brazilian. It was this former MA's experience that the process that leads to promotions within the UN, particularly as it pertains to International Staff (career and non-career UN) and local-national staff, are at the very least Byzantine. The period of time that an individual must serve in a certain grade before being considered for promotion is more a factor of personal connections than it is job performance. There were several instances in which demonstrated incompetence by career UN officers was rewarded by promotion. Some individuals progressed from United Nations Volunteer (UNV) status to P-5 in less than 4 years. Others, at least as well qualified, and in some instances better qualified, particularly if assigned to the field, seldom were promoted. Also, the apparent unwillingness to use the United Nations Volunteer UNV system as an apprenticeship through which, for the most part, young and talented individuals could be brought into the UN family deprives the UN of some of its best and most motivated officers. In one instance, a particularly dedicated UN officer was recommended for an upgrade by the individual's supervisor and, over the course of time, by three RAs. A low-level bureaucrat in the Department of Personnel Administration, safely ensconced in Pristina, overrode the recommendation. Not only do I find this curious, but also it calls into question the entire raison d'etre for Field Evaluation Reports. There are, in the ranks of the United Nations, some extraordinarily talented young people who perform far beyond their years. This should be recognized. And nowhere else has this former Administrator encountered a system in which, should one wish to be promoted, one is required to writes one's own recommendation. This I, for one, find to be just a tad disingenuous. And finally, as an MA, if I were given the option of recruiting as an additional team member a UNV, an officer on a short-term contract, or a career UN officer, my experience as an MA is such that I would relegate the career UN officers to the bottom of my list.

One wonders if there should not be some preparation for UN Administrators. I recall very vividly a meeting convened in Vushtrri in the early summer of 2000 with all of the local Municipal Staff. Erroneously thinking that the Albanian Municipal staff, like my UN team, had no real experience in running or being part of a Municipality's administrative apparatus, I asked for a show of hands apropos how many of those present had worked in a Municipality. I was astonished when some 80% of those present raised their hands.[16] I also wonder if successful service at the Municipal level should be a pre-requisite prior to an individual being assigned higher up the chain of responsibility. There were a series of decisions that were imposed on the structure of the Municipalities that were clearly taken by individuals in Pristina who had never served time 'in the trenches'.

Continuing on the subject of mission preparation, one of my Officers told me that I needed to read Nicolo Machiavelli (1469-1527). And while I have never been certain if I was being encouraged to read Machiavelli because the individual in question considered me to be 'Machiavellian', or if there might be lessons to be learned vis-à-vis local administration in a post-war environment following a careful reading of Machiavelli. Machiavelli is currently undergoing a period of rehabilitation, partially made possible by the fact that he is now understood within the parameters of his era and its concomitant political fluidity. This is something currently being pursued.[17] After all, military officers are supposed to be reading people like Clausewitz, Sun Tzu, Liddel Hart, Lawrence, Jomini, Mahan, etc. There should be something that would-be Municipal Administrators should be reading. Machiavelli might be a start.[18]

Because of the importance of 'returns', and minorities in general, in any Municipality involved with 'returns' or with a substantial number of minorities, next to the MA and Deputy Municipal Administrator (DMA),

---

[16]On the one hand, an individual who has no experience as an Administrator has the advantage of having a certain degree of intellectual freedom vis-à-vis how to proceed having no model to follow; nevertheless a basic course in local administration would have been useful. In Iraq, the Americans imported city managers from Middle America. For the most part they had never left Middle America. Needless to say, knowing nothing about the Middle East, or the fundamentals of having to build a municipal bureaucracy from scratch, they were hopelessly inadequate. To this extent UN Administrators, coming from a multitude of countries, were significantly more 'flexible' and intuitive than were their, for the most part, American counterparts in Iraq.

[17]The author was after his UN service a visiting scholar at Brown University's Watson Institute and a Senior Associate Member at St. Antony's College, Oxford.

[18]British Colonial Service Officers were given copies of a book entitled *Myself a Mandarin* by Austin Coates, available now as a paperback from Oxford University Press.

the most important member of the UNMiK team at the Municipal level was the Local Community Officer (LCO). Overwhelmingly, the LCOs were young UNV Officers. I remain concerned at the lack of any meaningful orientation or training provided to the LCOs who had among the most onerous and undefined responsibilities in the mission. The LCOs that I encountered were overwhelmingly hard-working, bright, visionary, and resourceful. They lacked at the same time, not surprisingly given their general youth, experience and self confidence. Problems related to the 'education' of the LCOs was further complicated by the fact that the overwhelming number of senior UNMiK Officers at all levels of the organization were as poorly informed apropos LCO-related conflict resolution-type experience as were the LCOs themselves. And for the most part they were considerably less resourceful.

This brings me to what is euphemistically called UN Culture and 'caste'[19] – something that I, and several of the other more effective MAs – all, initially at least, Christmas help[20] – were accused of not subscribing to, generally by individuals in the Department of Human Resources. MAs had, in some instances, almost impossible tasks to perform. Indeed the dynamics were such that if one was to be successful, it was necessary at times to bend various regulations, some of which were in any event detrimental to mission accomplishment. If, in the process of accomplishing what we were being paid to do we were to run afoul of 'UN Culture' or some obscure regulation, then I for one am not unhappy to have been accused of not subscribing to 'UN Culture' and not belonging the right 'caste'..

In this regard, it is of interest to note that virtually all of the more effective Administrators, meaning those who brought about real and meaningful change in their respective municipalities, had difficulties in

---

[19]Career UN Officers appear to the uninitiated to have far greater latitude should they stray morally and financially. At the same time anyone assigned to the Office of the Director of Personnel Administration, at least as far as this former MA could discern under the rubric of the then UNMiK Personnel Tsar, operated almost as though they belonged to an alternative organization. In Kosovo they appeared to operate entirely at the whim of the Personnel Director and were, to the casual observer, independent of the Regional Administrator or of even, one assumes, the SRSG.

[20]UN Officers on contract vice career UN Officers.

surviving the system. Those who plodded along without accomplishing very much were invariably retained within the system and prospered.

The Municipalities and the Centre

There were initially five UNMiK Regional Headquarters in Kosovo (Pristina, Prizren, Peje/Pec, Gjilane, and Mitrovica) and some 30 Municipalities. Each UNMiK Region exercised supervision and control over five or six Municipalities. A typical UNMiK Municipal team consisted of the MA, Deputy MA and between four to eight other international team members and a like number of local nationals.[21]

Of the five Regional Headquarters, Mitrovica, with its divided city and its very substantial Serbian population and other minority populations, was the most complex. During the three plus years that I was the Vushtrri Administrator in Mitrovica Region, there were inexplicably, as already noted, no less than eight Regional Administrators. Some folded their tents upon arrival. One should never have even been given a tent to contemplate opening. The most professional remained for less than a month. One interim and potentially credible RA had to divide his time between Mitrovica and his other assigned duties in Pristina. Others threw up their hands in the face of 'interference' (perceived or otherwise) from the Centre, while the few who could have made a difference opted not to remain long enough. In the long term, the Centre seems never to have understood that the solution to Mitrovica required the assignment of an individual possessed with vision, creativeness, and with the freedom and authority to operate outside the proverbial envelope. Ultimately of course Pristina assigned mainly 'safe' people, more often than not former army generals and/or senior UN bureaucrats to Mitrovica. It is a fact of life that with few exceptions, the overwhelming number of peacetime generals, and virtually all senior UN bureaucrats do not get to become either generals or senior UN bureaucrats for being 'creative'. They are promoted because of their ability to exist within their respective systems. There was, accordingly, consistently an effort to solve the Mitrovica

---

[21]Given the widely varying talents of international officers assigned to Municipal teams, it was my experience that as long as half of the international team members were professional, the team was functional. What was usually overlooked was the importance of the local staff. The difference was that one could select the local staff. The internationals simply arrived, some being more qualified than others.

problem through what might be termed 'legalistic and/or bureaucratic' means. As a consequence we never came to terms with the problems that confronted Mitrovica that were largely 'humanistic'. It was never that difficult. We simply had to demonstrate that we (UNMiK) could do more for Mitrovica than could Belgrade. We, in a nut-shell, had to make the proverbial trains run on time. We never did!

In looking back at the initial administration in Vushtrri/Vucitrn, it is apparent that UNMiK-Vushtrri/Vucitrn was far from being 'democratic'. Up until the first election in the autumn of 2000, we strove to promote social harmony. By this, generally in consultation with the Municipal Council,[22] we tried to do what we thought was the right thing for the greatest number of people that would, in the long term, have the most positive impact on the population as a whole. The promotion of social harmony, of course, is not democracy, it is Confucianism. On one occasion, when it became apparent that the activities and vision of a senior municipal employee were inimical to the 'greater good', the individual was peremptorily removed him from his position in the Municipality with little or no fanfare[23]. This, borrowing from Norman Dixon's term 'muscular Christianity' is 'muscular Confucianism'.[24]

After 38 months in Vushtrri Municipality, a decision was made to transfer me to Peje/Pec Municipality. I left Vushtrri relatively satisfied with what UNMiK-Vushtrri and the Municipality together had been able to accomplish, particularly as it related to bringing self-government to the Municipality[25] and in undertaking the 'return' of both Ashkalije and

---

[22]Given the option, at the beginning of having a 'selected' Municipal Council or an 'elected' Municipal Assembly, I, for one would go with the 'selected' Municipal Council every time. The fundamental difference was that the Council, as long as one 'selected' the right individuals, worked for the betterment of the Municipality. The Municipal Assembly on the other hand, owed their allegiance first and foremost to their political parties, often at the expense of the population as a whole, particularly in Peje/Pec.

[23]Subsequently the individual in question provided a far greater service to the community as a whole in a human-rights related position.

[24]Dixon, Norman, *On the Psychology of Military Incompetence*, Aylesbury Publications, Bucks, UK (1979) p. 293

[25]I was informally invited to return to Vushtrri/Vucitrn during the summer of 2004 by the Municipal President. The President wanted to show me the projects that had been completed. Virtually all had been initiated by the original UNMiK-Vushtrri Team. And while it was amusing to meet old friends, at the same time one could not help but notice that little new had occurred since the original

Serbs to the Municipality.[26] Because Peje/Pec Municipality was scheduled to be the focus of the 'return' of a number of Serbs to three former Serbian villages, a project underwritten by the Italian Government in 2001, based on our success vis-à-vis 'returns' in Vushtrri, I was dispatched to Peje/Pec Municipality.

In terms of complexity, the Peje/Pec Region was second only to Mitrovica. When I arrived in Peje/Pec in November 2003 I was horrified by the extent of professional indolence. One could not help but wonder what the Regional authorities had been doing for the three preceding years. And again incredibly, the Centre permitted this Region to stumble along with an Acting Regional Administrator for seven of the eight months that I was the Peje/Pec MA. This was only corrected in July 2003, when the Peje/Pec Region was subsumed under the umbrella of the very able Prizren RA.[27]

Three weeks after I arrived in Peje/Pec I formally wrote the Municipal President to inform him, that from my perspective, the Municipality was administratively dysfunctional. When the Region was approached and asked for their support in taking a harder line as it pertained to 'professionalizing' the Municipality, the Region maintained that the responsibility for the investigating and removing municipal employees rested with the Municipal Assembly. And while on the surface this may seem plausible, under the structures in place such an assumption was at best an exercise in legerdemain and self-delusion. Accordingly, Peje/Pec Municipality continued throughout the period of my assignment to be administratively non-functional and to be largely unresponsive to the needs and aspirations of its citizenry, and more importantly to directives from the Kosovo Government in Pristina.

The fundamental differences between Vushtrri/Vucitrn and Peje/Pec Municipality were two fold. In Mitrovica Region a succession of

---

UNMiK-Vushtrri team was dissolved.

[26]There are reportedly two books available that address Vushtrri/Vucitrn. The first is a published book by UCLA Press entitled *The Networks of Democracy: Lessons from Kosovo for Afghanistan, Iraq and Beyond*, by Anne Houlihan. The other book is available only in Albanian and was written by members of Vushtrri/Vucitrn Municipality. The book is entitled *A Monograph of Vushtrri*. It was locally published in Vushtrri and dedicated to Cicero.

[27]For the record, combining Peje/Pec and Prizren Regions, while cosmetically nice, in real terms made no sense.

RAs gave their respective MAs the freedom to tackle problems in their respective Municipality as they best saw fit. More importantly perhaps, UNMiK-Vushtrri/Vucitrn and the Municipal staff enjoyed an extremely close and generally harmonious working relationship. The antithesis was true in Peje/Pec. It became apparent the day that I arrived that the relationship between the Municipality and UNMiK was strained and furthermore, as already noted, the Region, under an acting RA, hid behind the chimera of 'democracy' that conveniently provided plausible denial vis-à-vis an ever-worsening political situation and absolved the Acting RA and the Centre from assuming any responsibility. Peje/Pec was 'deresponsibilization' in a nutshell.

On Government

Among the advantages of having some 'down-time', is that it affords the opportunity for reflection and retrospective thought. I find myself asking if perhaps the immediate thrust of UNMiK's mission in Kosovo, and the thrust of the mission that I encountered in Iraq, might not have been skewed at the outset. My first Daily Report written from Ba'qubah, Iraq,[28] included the following; it might just as well have applied to Kosovo as to Iraq:

> 'The immediate concern of the common people here in Iraq, not unlike that in Kosovo, Cambodia, and wherever else, is not 'democratic' government or the creation of a multi-party system. Nor is it the writing and enactment of a constitution. It is simply bare-bone survival. They want jobs, food to put on the table, security, and the other basic necessities of life, and they are manifestly disappointed that we have thus far produced few of the above.'

The imposition of 'democracy' and the writing of a constitution was all consuming vis-à-vis the Americans in Iraq. We were, to some observers, servants first and foremost to ideology. The same was true, but to a far lesser extent, with UNMiK. Perhaps we are putting the cart before the horse.

What the Centre in Pristina failed to appreciate, particularly following the departure of Dr. Kouchner's original team, was that there is more to

---

[28]Ba'qubah is in the Sunni Triangle and is located some 60kms NNE of Baghdad. The report was dated 9 Dec 2003.

'democratic government' than free elections. 'Democratic' governance can only function if there is wide respect and adherence to Rule of Law, and that those charged with 'government' understand that they have a responsibility to the community as a whole. Those charged with governance must be made to understand, forcibly if necessary, that there must be a clear delineation between their professional and their personal interests. At the outset, in addition to the imposition of law and order, the impetus should be on the rapid provision of basic services, the establishment of a meaningful degree of security, the creation of jobs, and an adequate degree of economic freedom. Concerns about 'democracy', constitutions, and other political niceties might better be tackled further down the path.

Michael Ignatieff rightly observed that it is the local political authorities who must be if necessary forced to rule in fact as well as in name. This is because, in the long term, in any struggle between the IC and the local nationals, it is the local nationals who will invariably prevail. UNMiK had both a moral and professional obligation to the population as a whole to ensure that Government, both at the centre and in the municipalities, is responsive to the needs of the population as a whole. Unless the Centre, the Regions and MAs are prepared to live up to their responsibilities and use their respective 'powers', there is the risk that the authority of the IC, and of UNMiK in particular, will be eroded and that the population will become disillusioned with the IC as an organizational entity. This, of course, is exactly what has occurred.[29] It is significant at this juncture to note that when, in July 2003 a group of former Serb residents from the village of Belo Polje, a village immediately adjacent to Peje/Pec, 'returned', Peje/Pec Municipal President defied not only President Rugova and the Kosovo Parliament, but also UNMiK's mandate and he got away with it. His opposition to 'returns' was further reinforced on 28 July 2003 when the then acting SRSG visited Peje/Pec and incredibly not only elected not to visit Belo Polje, a visit that would have given the 'return' UNMiK's imprimatur, he also pointedly informed the Municipal President that he need not concern himself with 'returns' because 'returns' was not an issue of concern for the Kosovo-Albanians but rather the responsibility of the international community'.

---

[29]Ignatieff, Opus Cit., pp. 126-127.

At the Municipal level one knew that the Centre existed, but one's contact with the Centre was, for the most part, agreeably distant. On the few occasions when MAs were summoned to the Centre for meetings, one emerged from the process wondering if we were participating in the same Mission. Fundamental to the problems in a Municipality was Pristina's failure to understand that for a host of reasons, while Kosovo-Albanians could relate to their family, for many there was no real sense of community. Building a sense of community was an essential undertaking for any Administrator. Then there were the constantly voiced concerns about Serbian parallel structures. It was for this reason that in Vushtrri/Vucitrn we developed a Municipal flag, ultimately a Municipal Song,[30] and other vestiges of Municipal 'belonging'.

In the four years that I was with the mission, Serbian parallel structures, while present at the Municipal level particularly in Vushtrri/Vucitrn,[31] were never an impediment to mission accomplishment. What was a concern was the extent and power of Albanian parallel structures particularly those encountered in Peje/Pec. While this was frequently reported to the Region and to the Centre, it seems not to have been something that unduly alarmed anyone. It is of course probable that the alternative Albanian structures played a major role in what came to pass on 17 and 18 March. Albanian parallel structures were, of course, very much a two-edged sword. In Peje/Pec, for instance, if one wanted to accomplish anything remotely controversial – like returning Serbs to Belo Polje – it was only possible with the consent/tacit understanding of local figures that had little or nothing to do with the local government, a situation that correspondingly contributed to further undermining the already dismal authority of the local authorities.

There were other issues that contributed to the general sense of malaise on the part of the residents of Kosovo that came to colour their relations with UNMiK. Some of the more significant are enumerated below:

---

[30]The original proposal sounded a lot like 'New York, New York'.
[31]It is worth noting in this regard that Vushtrri/Vucitrn Municipality initially had six Serb villages and the second largest Serbian population south of the Ibar River.

Privatization and Employment

There remains an astonishing litany of failed efforts associated with 'privatization' and putting the population of Kosovo back to work. In Vushtrri/Vucitrn Municipality the most significant commercial enterprise was the Llamkos Steel Factory, the only such factory in Kosovo. Prior to assuming the position of Municipal President in October 2002, the Municipal President was the Director of the Llamkos Factory. In this capacity he had concluded a contract with Balkan Steel, a steel-processing factory in the Former Yugoslavian Republic of Macedonia (FYROM). Under this agreement the Llamkos Factory would have been returned to 100% capacity. A considerable number of former employees would have been returned to their workplace, as would have a number of former Serb workers from neighbouring Gojbulja Village. Despite innumerable trips to the Centre, the Centre was never able to resolve problems as they related to customs fees. In desperation, a meeting was requested with a very senior UNMiK official in Pristina to discuss the impasse and a concomitant case of blatant corruption associated with the establishment of a Woman's Centre in Vushtrri for which substantial funding had already been secured. The senior official regretted that he did not have time to meet with an obscure field officer and delegated the responsibility to one of his local subordinates. Neither case was ever addressed. The Llamkos Factory continues to stagnate and the proposed Woman's Centre remains a proposal.

On the TMK[32]

Several ears after the end of the conflict in 1999, the TMK, the National Guard-type paramilitary organisation now called the Kosova Protection Corps was still without any meaningful form or direction. At the same time their considerable political and social 'influence' and grass-roots support is largely ignored.

For my part, I have spent the greatest part of my adult life involved with assorted armies, regular and irregular. More often than not, particularly

---

[32]There were several name changes associated with the TMK formerly known as UÇK. I have elected to use the term TMK/UÇK. In some circles it was maintained that the TMK/UÇK was not an army. If an organization marches like an army, lives in barracks like an army, wears military style uniforms, has an established system of ranks, carries weapons, and drives around in olive-drab military-like vehicles like an army, in all probability it is an army.

in a developing country, the army is the only institution that transcends political, economic, cultural and geographic borders. Accordingly, if properly brought into the fold, the army is an incredibly useful organization to promote social and philosophical change, indeed many of our own respective armies played a major role in the establishment of 'democratic' government. Yet we have now arrived at a point in which we seem ideologically unable to permit the military to play any role in the development of 'democratic' governance. Among the factors that led to Albania's political implosion in March 1997 was President Berisha and Defence Minister Zhulali's decision to marginalize the Albanian Army. The consequences were that when the Army was needed to restore civil order, the Army disintegrated plunging Albania into chaos. In the same vein, Ambassador Bremmer's equally ill-conceived decision to stand down the Iraqi Army in 2003 has had similar repercussions.

In the case of Kosovo, there were several options available vis-à-vis the Trupat e Mbrojtjes të Kovosës (TMK) ex Ushtria Çlirimtare e Kosovës (UÇK). The TMK/UÇK could have been disbanded. Alternatively the 'best and the brightest' members of the TMK/UÇK could have been co-opted and have become the basis of Kosovo's police and civil-defence force. We opted to do neither. And so while NATO and the International Organization for Migration (IOM) continue to strive to create an amorphous civil disaster reaction force, the TMK/UÇK, continues to transform itself into an Army.[33]

On the Missing and War Crimes
Starting in 2002 and continuing into 2003, a series of former TMK/UÇK personnel were arrested on charges of war crimes. These arrests led to demonstrations in several towns. I am not suggesting the IC was wrong to have arrested and incarcerated the individuals in question. The problem was that we concentrated almost solely on arresting Albanians while all the available evidence points to the fact that the overwhelming number of war crimes in Vushtrri and immediate region were committed not by Albanians but by Serbian paramilitaries. I no longer have access to overall figures but a substantial number of Kosovo-Albanians remain

---

[33]For more detail on the history of the UCK/KLA, see book by James Pettifer,'The Kosova Liberation Army From Underground War to Balkan Insurgency, 1948- 2001', London and New York, 2012.

missing five years after the end of the Conflict. In Vushtrri/Vucitrn alone, the total number of missing was 84. 74 of these people were arrested on 22 May 1999 by the Serbian authorities, placed in a house in Vushtrri/Vucitrn, and were subsequently never seen again.[34] The former Serbian Mayor of Vushtrri/Vucitrn and his Police Chief were members of the convened Emergency Committee at that time. Both continue to reside in Mitrovica North.

During the course of the three plus years that I was in Vushtrri/Vucitrn I appealed to UNMiK-Police, the International Prosecutors, and the American Office asking that both individuals at least be questioned apropos their possible involvement in the disappearance. As best as can be determined this never occurred. The request was made because, on the one hand, it was important to the families concerned, and because for Albanians in general it is essential that there should be closure as it relates to the missing. I also believed that it would have demonstrated a far more even-handed approach vis-à-vis the prosecution of individuals accused of war crimes, and would have at the same time made the arrest of former UÇK/TMK officers more palatable to the Albanian majority. While on the subject of law and order, during the summer of 2002, at half-time during a football match between Vushtrri and a neighbouring municipality, a senior TMK Officer, in full view of some 3,000 local spectators, beat a local physician senseless with the butt of his pistol. The officer in question, despite several appeals to the International Prosecutors, was neither arrested nor brought to trial. Several months later he was transferred to another Municipality. The failure to prosecute the individual in question hardly sends the right message to the community at large vis-à-vis the fundamental importance of rule of law in a 'democratic' society.

On Reconstruction – Funding/Banking

Vushtrri/Vucitrn Municipality was among the most devastated Municipalities in Kosovo and there was consistently insufficient funding available to meet all of the reconstruction demands in the Municipality. In the spring of 2001 I had occasion to escort a visitor from an NGO through some of the more damaged villages. The purpose of the visit was

---

[34]Some human remains recently exhumed in Serbia have been identified as some of those individuals who vanished.

to try to assess further reconstruction needs. The visitor asked if, in lieu of relying on financial support from the IC vis-à-vis reconstruction needs, any thought had been given to the establishment of a banking system that might offer low-interest, or better still, no-interest loans. When a group of local farmers were asked for their opinion, they emphatically asserted that if such an option had been in place in 1999 at the Conflict's conclusion, everything would have already been rebuilt.

On Returns

I can speak with a certain amount of authority about 'returns'. In real terms by the time of my departure in August 2003, the UNMiK teams in Vushtrri/Vucitrn and Peje/Pec had accomplished more 'returns' than any other Municipality.[35] The issue of returns was perhaps the Mission's most divisive undertaking and will be addressed in greater detail in a subsequent article. Despite the unfortunate and ill-advised comments of the then acting SRSG in June 2003, 'returns' are most emphatically the responsibility of the Kosovo Albanians working in coordination with UNMiK and with potential returnees. The mission of the IC is to create an atmosphere in which 'returns' can take place and to provide the requisite levels of funding. Without active participation of the Albanian majority, as was the case in Peje/Pec, the undertaking of 'returns' is significantly more complicated.

When all is said and done there never was any meaningful plan for the systematic re-integration of Serbs and other minorities back into the social fold. Because of this, what was accomplished in terms of 'returns', in both Vushtrri/Vucitrn and Peje/Pec Municipalities, was accomplished very much as an ad hoc undertaking. The problems related to 'returns' were further complicated by a blurring of responsibilities between the Centre's Local Community Office and the Office for Returns and Communities (ORC). And while we were consistently being informed by assorted voices from within ORC that there was an abundance of funds available to support 'returns', whenever we were presented with

---

[35] Three sets of 'returns' to Vushtrri/Vucitrn Municipality (one Serb return to Grace Village and two Ashkalije 'returns' to Vushtrri/Vucitrn) and an additional planned Serb return to Pantina Village in the summer of 2002 that did not take place for reasons that remain unclear. UNMiK-Peje/Pec was almost entirely responsible for the 'return' to Belo Polje in July 2003.

the reality of a 'return', the requisite degree of required funding was consistently illusive.

In 2001, the Italian Government provided the sum of $3 million to support returns to three villages in Peje/Pec Municipality. It was the singular inability of ORC, mainly for bureaucratic reasons, to undertake 'The Italian Project' in a timely manner that led to the planned spontaneous 'return' to Belo Polje in Peje/Pec Municipality on 14 June 2003;[36] a 'return' that was accomplished despite initial opposition from the Centre.

The fundamental differences between Vushtrri/Vucitrn and Peje/Pec as it related to 'returns' was that in Vushtrri the Municipal President and his staff embraced 'returns' and participated fully in the process. The situation in Peje/Pec was significantly more convoluted. Not only was the Municipal President not interested in 'returns', the Region discounted the importance of establishing the appropriate levels of personal contact between potential returnees and the local UNMiK Team at the Municipal level, believing it to be the responsibility of some other obscure and undefined organization. Another example of 'deresponsibilization'.

Conclusions

I suppose what I find the most disturbing about both of my missions with the UN was the stark contradictions that existed between a series of exceptionally talented and dedicated individuals who performed far and beyond the call of duty mainly in the field, and the demonstrated lack of leadership and direction on the part of the upper echelons of the UN that were seldom attuned to conditions in field. When there were hard decisions to be made, more often than not the responsible leaders simply opted out.

It is widely agreed that it is essential that responsibilities be passed as rapidly as possible to local leaders. In this context the IC has a vested responsibility to ensure that the system and works, and if this means forcibly intervening at times, the IC must be prepared and equipped to do so. There is no room for 'deresponsibilization'.

---

[36]Because UNMiK-Peje/Pec was informed of the determination of former Serb residents of Belo Polje to return on 14 July 2003, and because Italian KFOR, UNHCR and UNMiK-Peje/Pec had some time in which to prepare for the 'return', we considered the 'return' to be a planned spontaneous 'return'.

There are a series of initiatives that the UN must consider undertaking in the near term if the UN is to be able to transform itself into an organization that can effectively meet the enormous challenges that lie ahead. Included are the wide-range of activities that fall under the general rubric of personnel management and include specific mission-training,[37] and the establishment of an adequate information network.[38] There is also an urgent need for the UN to exhibit greater intellectual and philosophical flexibility vis-à-vis the provision of local government. There must also be the realization that the UN in places like Kosovo has a moral responsibility to give the population good government and not hide behind the chimera of 'democracy' when there are hard and controversial decisions to be made.

On Personnel Management and UN Culture

Among the greatest problems that face any large organization today is the increasing prominence of an entrenched bureaucracy. I am forced to wonder if among the reasons why the UN as an organization is so professionally ambivalent is because there is, among senior career UN officers, a pervasive fear of making decisions lest it impact upon their future employment within the organization. To this extent, among the first orders of business must be to reduce the apparent power of the personnel bureaucracy that, at least in UNMiK, appeared to hover over UN employees like Damocles' proverbial sword. UN officers must have the freedom and operational flexibility to adapt to situations as they develop.

In Peje/Pec of course, not having been permitted by the Region to create anything of a substantial nature, there was nothing to leave and anything that we did manage to accomplish, like the Serb 'return' to Belo Polje, was done despite initial passive resistance from both the Centre and the Region, but with the acquiescence and tacit support from the

---

[37]To this end, consideration might be given to the establishment of a trained professional cadre of individuals with proven field-related administrative skills who can be rapidly deployed. Such training should include a thorough grounding in the most essential precepts of conflict resolution.

[38]Had there been in place in Pristina an Information Bureau that maintained and collated information as it pertained to events and people, perhaps it would have precluded UNMiK supposedly being blind-sided by events like those of this past March.

leadership of supposedly the most xenophobic of the Albanian political parties. Their leadership, unlike that of the Municipality, happened to believe that 'returns' were in Kosovo's best interests.

I mention this only because in real terms there are certain trade-offs between turning everything over to the local authorities and trying to put into place a system that is viable and responsive to the population. From my perspective I believed emphatically that the mission of both of the UNMiK Municipal Teams with which I served, was to provide our respective populations a form of local government that was responsive to their needs. To this end I disagree vehemently with the view of the Acting Peje/Pec Regional authority that was unprepared to 'get involved', and as stated earlier consistently hid behind the chimera of 'democracy'.

The obvious inference is, when all is said and done, that everything comes down to people. It is people, leadership, and an equitable and responsive form of management that makes the difference between an indifferent and despondent organization and one that is ebullient and creative. There seem to be two distinct categories of individuals on most UN missions. Both are of fundamental importance to the mission. I have tentatively labelled them as 'lunatics' and 'bureaucrats'. Ideally, for any start-up mission, the UN needs the services of a gathering, or perhaps an 'asylum' is a more appropriate collective noun, of 'lunatics'. These are individuals who through sheer force of character and personal charisma are capable of extraordinary accomplishment. The responsibility of the bureaucrats, exactly as the name implies, is to oversee the smooth administrative maintenance of the organization. The difficulty of course is that the two groups are more often than not an anathema one to the other. The problem is that the bureaucrats are terrified of the lunatics because the lunatics have the capacity of upsetting the status quo and that inevitably complicates bureaucratic decision-making. In this regard, my experiences with UNMiK, and those associated with my earlier mission on the Thai/Cambodian Border with UNBRO, were not dissimilar.

Apropos the struggle between 'lunatics and bureaucrats', I have been informed by my academic friends that I have not discovered anything new. This clash between the system (bureaucrats) and its more independent actors (lunatics) is known within academic circles as 'complexity theory'. Complexity Theory argues that everything is connected. This means that every action within an organization impacts on the organization as a whole. Furthermore, it is suggested that the 'system' is in constant motion and that motion is generated by the interaction of all the parts. Hence, it can be said that the change is constant, and accordingly the organization is constantly merging into a new and different, and at times an unpredictable entity. The implications are obviously significant. Under the old Newtonian paradigm, linear, hierarchical organizations, like the UN, operate under the notion that that you can sub-divide any problem, solve it, and make it work. Reality suggests the opposite; you can never totally disaggregate a problem. Therefore any organization must, out of necessity, mirror and retain an aspect of constant motion and self-organization.

Organizational chaos occurs when the entrenched bureaucracy attempts to suppress or eliminate the more 'rogue' elements of the organization in lieu of 'responding' to them. What becomes essential, particularly at the outset of a UN-type mission, is for line managers to be at least equal, but preferably slightly subordinate, to the independent or 'rogue' elements of the organization. This is because it is the 'rogue' elements that provide both stimulus and evolution. It becomes the responsibility of the Centre to accept and nurture change in lieu of trying to suppress it, because what is most fundamental about the status quo is that it inevitably isn't.

Mission Orientation

The International Community (IC), and most prominently UNMiK, failed in Kosovo because we tried to manage Kosovo while ignoring or rejecting the most basic issues that needed to be undertaken – the restoration of services, the re-establishment of a meaningful degree of law and order, the revitalization of the economy, and the systematic return of the minority members of the population. It is essential that the IC comes to appreciate the fundamental importance of giving local leaders in post-war societies the power and the resources that they require. This must be done. Otherwise institution building will become nothing more than a growing field for new and ever worsening cycles of violence. At the same time, the IC must be prepared to be assertive, and in the words of Michael Ignatieff, be prepared to 'lay down the law in a classic imperial fashion'.

The IC must also support the development of locally-owned and indigenous means of resolving conflict, to include its causes, work towards the establishment of effective forms of reconciliation, and create institutions of political, social, and economic life, that are appropriate to the society. In an earlier incarnation I was responsible for the reformation of the Albanian Army. In that context, the greatest impediment to meaningful change was the inability of NATO (the Americans and Germans in particular) to look beyond attempting to make the Albanian Army look like any of its NATO counterparts. When, in the case of Albania, you are presented with a national army that has in excess of 300,000 bunkers, an inventory of more than 800 tanks, an astonishing array of artillery and small arms, and a population in which, at the time (1995), virtually every man and woman over the age of 17 could disassemble a Kalashnikov in their sleep, perhaps you don't need a NATO-type army at all but a militia built along the model of the Swiss militia. In order to be NATO compatible, it is not necessary to look like NATO, it is necessary only to be able to operate in conjunction with a NATO army.

In the same context perhaps, rather than attempting to tailor a particular mission to the realities on the ground and the aspirations of the people and to venture into the unfamiliar, the UN, and the IC in general continue to impose Western-oriented solutions that, in many instances are both obsolete and impotent. Furthermore, they often have little or no association with the pre-existing structures in place. Kosovo and places like Kosovo where the UN is increasingly likely to become involved are social entities. They must, to as great an extent as possible, be self-organizing. The alternative is recurring and cyclical violence. What we seem to have consistently lost track of, is that when all is said and done, what it all comes down to is people and vision and change and the readiness to assume responsibility.

Perhaps Mao was right because – 'It is people, not things that are decisive'.[39]

---

[39]Mao Zedong (Tse-Tung), *Selected Military Writings*, 2nd Edition, Foreign Language Press, Peking (1966) p. 217

Mice in the pot: International Interventions and Balkan Realities

Robert Wilton

'… Nothing hopeful or cheerful to say about Albania. All our personal kit had been stolen from the dropping ground, so that each of us started with nothing but the clothes in which we had parachuted. There was no petrol charging engine in running order, so that we were quickly introduced to the grinding labour of winding for hours on end at a hand charging engine to keep the radio batteries going. All our illusions about a colourful and lively guerilla war were punctured as we listened to… long discussions with local leaders. No one had reliable information…'.[1] Thus Reginald Hibbert's recollection of the cold night of 19th December 1943, his introduction to the hidden war in Albania.

'I leapt,' wrote Lindsay Rogers, 'into the night below. The cold air cracked me and swept me backwards in a terrific rushing. For a moment I was nowhere, conscious appreciation had gone. Then quite suddenly profound peace. The plane was far away, just a red tail-light and a low droning in the distance. Above me I saw the great white dome of the chute billowing tight, and on the horizon below the stars ending in a vast blackness. […] In a flash I saw appearing from the blackness, hills, valleys, cliffs and trees. […] I drew up my knees and held them hard together, a tree swished by and then suddenly, Crash! and I rolled over and over down a steep little hill. […] It was pitch dark. Would they be partisans or Germans who met me?'[2] 'Silence broken only by the whistling of the wind in my rigging lines', Smiley recalled; 'As we neared the ground I heard the jingling of the bells of the goats or sheep'.[3]

Deakin: 'The night was so thick that we could not distinguish the outline of the ground below. Only bright flashes of gunfire lit the

---

[1]Hibbert, Reginald, *Albania's National Liberation Struggle – The Bitter Victory*, London (Pinter) 1991 (hereafter 'Hibbert') p. 88

[2]*Rogers, Lindsay, Guerilla Surgeon – a New Zealand surgeon's wartime experiences with the Yugoslav Partisans, London (Collins) 1957, pp150-1*

[3]Smiley, David, *Albanian Assignment*, London (Chatto & Windus/The Hogarth Press) 1984 (hereafter 'Smiley'), p. 18

pervading gloom. [...] a burst of dialogues and questions started up simultaneously. Why hadn't we come before? Where had we come from?'[4]

Basil Davidson described the concept as much as the experience of the sudden dramatic translation from comfortable Cairo to uncomfortable aircraft to the weird isolation of the parachute jump to the hard bump of dropping into a different world: 'Landings are always bathos. The men at the bottom are disappointingly ordinary human beings with two legs and troubles of their own. They ought to be supermen, but they are not. You see them first when you are swaying to the ground, small grey shadows in a grey world legging it over the grass to the point you are going to hit; and once you are on the ground they rush up at your and shake your hand and thump you on the back and pull your ridiculous jumping gear off you. They are flesh and blood, of this world and not the next. You look into their welcoming faces and feel very happy; but at the same time there is a feeling of deflation. You know that the real business is just beginning.'[5] One parachutist, presented with 'a bearded character covered with bandoliers and wearing a goatskin coat', blurted out the only phrase he could remember from the Albanian he and his colleagues had been taught – a line from a fairy story, telling of a mouse who fell into a pot of hot water.[6]

The sheer alienation of life in a strange land – 'Insecurity dulled our senses,' wrote Deakin, 'blunted by hunger and isolation.'[7] – only emphasizes the courage of the men who endured it. The occasionally spirited image – Hibbert himself looks cheerfully out of the photographs, and Neel's encounter with the German butterfly enthusiast and possible military intelligence officer Brandt and his troop of Tajiks is positively nineteenth century[8] – belies the grimness of reality on the ground. The

---

[4]Deakin, Frederick, *The Embattled Mountain*, London (Oxford University Press) 1971 (hereafter 'Deakin'), pp 3-4

[5]Davidson, Basil, *Partisan Picture*, Bedford 1946, p.10. More than sixty years after the war, former motor torpedo boat crewmen who spent part of the war stationed on the Adriatic island of Vis still vividly recalled the Partisans they saw every day but were not permitted to approach – 'men, even women and youngsters with ammunition belts all over them... I was just glad they were on our side' – and even a glimpse of Tito himself (author interviews 2010).

[6]Lyon, unpublished, quoted in Bailey, Roderick, *The Wildest Province – SOE in the Land of the Eagle*, London (Vintage) 2009 (hereafter 'Bailey') p. 55

[7]Deakin p.35

[8]Described in Bailey, 287-90; compare Francis Younghusband's 1889 meeting with

lives and deaths – Faure-Field subsisting on rainwater in his scorpion-infested cave; Nicholls dragging himself across the mountains until gangrene and finally septicaemia overwhelmed him – are striking less because of the moments of real military danger than because of the harsh conditions and persistent frustrations of everyday existence. Davies's account of his brief stay in Mauthausen concentration camp is presented as a kind of macabre light relief after his weeks being harried around the Çermenika highlands.

'The Albanians are lazy, liars and thieves and personally I think we are wasting our time doing anything for them,' Field wrote from his cave; 'We hate the country and hate the people.'[9] The most depressing aspect of all of the memoirs, and of the whole SOE experience in Albania, is the fundamental futility. Put crudely, for all the heroism and endurance of the men involved, the SOE missions did little to affect the war and little even to affect Albania.

The impact of the SOE missions in Albania on the war – more particularly, the impact of the SOE missions on the dynamism of the Albanian resistance and the impact of the Albanian resistance on the German military – is of course hard to measure. With the disintegration of the Italians in 1943, more German divisions were required in Albania than would have been the case had the population been completely quiescent.[10] Albanians – principally the Partisans – were stimulated by SOE to do at least a little more than they might otherwise have done under their own steam, and they did so at least a little earlier and with at least a few more arms than otherwise. In addition to the operations of the SOE officers themselves – for example Smiley's bridge, and assorted attacks on convoys – there are clear examples of significant Partisan operations against the Germans. Arguably the most striking was the siege and eventual capture of Debar (albeit also a Nationalist base[11]) in

---

Colonel Grombtchevski in the high Pamirs

[9]Field quoted in Bailey, p. 196

[10]Bailey quotes an SOE assessment of total German losses in Albania of 6-7,000, and a lower Albanian assessment (Bailey p. 118; Barker, Elisabeth, *British Policy in South-East Europe in the Second World War*, London (Macmillan) 1976 (hereafter 'Barker') p. 183). 'The Germans had brought some first-class troops into play', Hibbert wrote of June 1944; 'A force of about 15,000 German troops had driven the Partisans off the north-south roads in south Albania' (Hibbert p. 151).

[11]See e.g. Fischer, Bernd, *Albania at War 1939-1945*, London (Hurst) 1999 (hereafter

Summer 1944, co-ordinated with arms drops and ground attack sorties by Royal Air Force aircraft, 'perhaps the largest and most successful partisan operation of the war'[12].

The German resources required to replace the Italians in Autumn 1943 – including paratroopers dropped into Tirana to forestall its loss – could have been used elsewhere. More troops were required than would have been the case had the country submitted more passively to occupation, and had the Mitrovica and Dine puppet governments been more widely accepted in the south. Perhaps the most significant indicator of Partisan impact was the German need to go onto the offensive against them in 1943 and 1944.[13] But beyond this, it is not clear how many fewer Germans would have been necessary had southern Albania been as passive as the north. The German troops tied up there – Fischer notes only three German Divisions necessary for the seizing of the country in 1943; at that time there were 19 Divisions in the whole south-eastern European theatre, 51 on the western front and 188 on the eastern front[14] – would have made negligible difference had they been redeployed.[15]

The Partisans' was an impressive success of survival, but not of offense. In 1944/5 Partisan operations did harry and hinder the Germans – not

'Fischer'), p. 214. Following common practice, the term 'Nationalist' will be used reluctantly but indiscriminately, for those who would have styled themselves Nationalist, anti-Partisan, Legitimist, Zogist or simply in favour of being left alone in their village.

[12]Fischer p. 218. There had also been notable Partisan actions against the Italians in 1943, including at Permet and in the so-called Battle of Leskovik. (Described by Smiley, p.35. See Fischer p.137; 'the Italians slowly began to panic'; by the end of February 1943 the Italians had 100,000 soldiers in Albania, incl. 55,000 regulars (Fischer pp 139-40).

[13]The impact of German pressure comes across less in statistics and more powerfully from the descriptions of men like Davies, constantly on the move between reports of encircling grey uniforms, frightened villagers and low-flying spotter planes.

[14]See http://www.axishistory.com/index.php?id=7288 for the comparative figures, and Fischer p. 161 for Albania; in March 1944 one German Division was redeployed from Albania to Russia, and another to Hungary, both being replaced by lower-quality units (Fischer p. 201).

[15]The most brutal summary was by Christopher Steel, a Counsellor in the British Embassy in Cairo, summarised by Hibbert thus: 'the scale of fighting in Albania was petty, the LNC were emphatically not in the same class as Tito, the LNC effort against the Germans had been puny and they were really more interested in fighting the BK, and Albania was not on a vital German communications link and the German anti-invasion garrison there would not be withdrawn to other fronts even if guerilla activity ceased altogether.' Hibbert p. 133

least in Tirana in November 1944 – but such activities were merely adjusting the statistical annexes of German defeat. The posture was, indeed, exactly what the northern nationalists had offered as the limit of what they were prepared to do. The war had turned at Midway, Alamein and Stalingrad, before Hibbert dropped into the pot. By the time the Partisans went onto the operational (rather than merely tactical) offensive, German armies were in strategic retreat from both ends of Europe. The growth of Partisan support in Albania was arguably largely a reaction to the weakening of German strength, rather than a factor in it. Albania was a side-show, and the fighting there had minimal impact on the direction of the war.[16]

Beyond the uncertainty over Partisan impact on the Germans is the uncertainty over how much of this limited activity was due to the stimulating, chivvying presence of British Liaison Officers. 'Now that we were on Albanian soil we had achieved the first step of our mission. The next stage – getting in touch with Albanian guerillas and encouraging them to fight the common enemy – was not to prove so easy,' Smiley wrote with typical dryness.[17] The memoirs describe specific incidents of Partisan activism, usually the result of hard bargaining over supplies and even payment, but also a general sense of frustration at the lack of it. 'I stressed the importance of denying to the Germans unmolested travel on the principal roads', Davies recalled. 'Staff cars and convoys travelled unmolested through the most perfect country for ambushes and sniping. I challenged Enver to a sniping competition […] but whenever I tried to stage the match he always had something else to do.'[18] A positive

---

[16]Is Albania's proud – or perhaps affronted – claim to have been the only German-occupied country in Europe through which no allied army passed a reflection of the uniquely independent competence of Hoxha's Partisans, or of Albania's unique irrelevance to the main axes of the war? Compare also the comment of Sir George Rendel, British Minister to the Yugoslav Government in Exile, that 'no action on the part of Mihailovic can possibly tip the scale in favour of an Allied victory, and that the war will be won in quite different areas, and by military operations on an infinitely vaster scale' (14 December 1942, FO371/33472, quoted in Williams, Heather, *Parachutes, Patriots and Partisans – The Special Operations Executive and Yugoslavia 1941-1945*, London (Hurst & Company) 2003 (hereafter 'Williams') p. 114).

[17]Smiley p. 26

[18]Davies, Edmund 'Trotsky', *Illyrian Venture – the Story of the British Military mission to Enemy-Occupied Albania 1943-1944*, London (The Bodley Head) 1952 (hereafter 'Davies') p. 80. Then 'Before I left I asked [Kupi] to attack the roads with snipers

Albanian reaction to British pressure to act against Germans depended on individual enthusiasts, brow-beating (followed by underwhelming performance; Smiley's early experiences), imminent disaster (Smiley's later experiences, with Kupi), or a convergence with local aims (defeating nationalists).

Unable to offer dramatically greater military support, the British had minimal leverage over the Albanian resistance. At best, an air-drop could pressure a çeta into a single offensive action, or the promise of future support tempt the leadership into a show of moderation towards their rivals. But the British never overcame the basic weakness of their position: an operational offer that was out of touch with the reality on the ground, and a policy that was out of touch with the reality of politics.

'Theoretical knowledge of the peoples, gathered from historical research and founded on past greatness, is not any use unless accompanied by practical knowledge of the conditions of today,' Edith Durham wrote to Aubrey Herbert in 1917, on the subject of Balkan reconstruction[19]. Fundamentally the British were not as well informed as they needed to be for the missions to have had a chance at strategic success – or, rather, better information might have made it clearer earlier that there was in any case little chance of strategic success. Thereafter, the fragmentary and delayed communication between B.L.O.s and their headquarters could not make as much impact as it should have done – leading for example to the Davies mission, which Smiley and Hibbert, who agree on little, both saw as misjudged. The imagery in the April 1942 minute by Lockhart, of the Political Warfare Executive, that action in Albania by S.O.E. would 'win the confidence of the clans' encapsulates not only the blithe optimism that underlay British intervention, but also its romantic stereotyping.[20] Churchill's invocation of the 'ancient war-

---

and ambushes, but he seemed to favour the great battle, with corps concerned and himself as the great general. A better country for guerrilla attacks could not be imagined, and, as the Albanian is a natural long-range shot, the roads should have been unsafe for the Germans everywhere.' Davies p. 84

[19]5th April 1917, Somerset Record Office DD/DRU\47

[20]FO 371/33113 of 27th April 1942, quoted in Hibbert p. 37. Both in practical terms and in terms of the colourful turn-of-the-century image it no doubt reflected in British minds, the phrase is closer to the experience in the north. Here there were groups operating as the British thought they meant when they spoke of clans, and groups who were alarmed enough by the Partisan threat to try to find some way of engaging with the British. When the phrase is applied to

like traditions' of the Albanians[21] was typical Churchill and good for the House of Commons, but the spirit of pre-mission military briefing was barely more sophisticated. Davies was told of 'this small race with a long history, very proud of themselves, very touchy, looking for slights where none were meant and, accordingly, difficult and aggravating. They could be very charming and good hosts, cheerful and amusing. In contrast, they could be very stupid, stubborn and infuriating. [… Separately] I was told that I would need a smart uniform for prestige at conferences of the Albanians.'[22] Margaret Hasluck, the remarkable 1885-born ethnographer largely responsible for the cultural preparation of S.O.E. liaison officers to Albania – including the rhyme of the mouse in hot water – had achieved considerable immersion and scholarship in Albanian affairs, but these had ended by 1939. Edith Durham before her had cemented in British minds an image of Albanians based on her experience of the northern highlanders, whose attitudes and predicament – even if understood in 1940s rather than 1900s context – were different to their southern compatriots'. Hasluck, Smiley's 'old-fashioned English nanny'[23], was understandably saddened at the impact of Communism on the Albania she had explored and loved, but there was little sign that she understood it.

Something in the British history of independent travel in Albania and the region may have produced a particular predisposition to romanticism, but the Germans were similarly under-informed for their occupation of the country. 'There had been surprisingly little preparation of a political nature and a great deal of misinformation,' Fischer judges. 'Much of the German problem in this regard stemmed simply from a lack of sources. Much of what was available in Germany in the 1930s concerning Albania was either superficial or catered to the romantic notion of the Albanians as a vital warrior mountain race, a notion that appealed to those imbued with Nazi racial theory.'[24]

---

the south, to Hoxha's dynamic, calculated, ideological movement it seems wildly anachronistic.

[21] HC Deb 04 November 1943 vol 393 cc857-8, available via http://hansard.millbanksystems.com/commons/1943/nov/04/albanian-guerillas#S5CV0393P0_19431104_HOC_199

[22] Davies pp34-5

[23] Smiley pp 8-9

[24] Fischer p. 159. See also the German frustration at trying to co-ordinate the

'The story of Britain's relations with South-East Europe during the Second World War was for the most part a story of last-minute improvisation and the undertaking of commitments without the resources to fulfill them,' is Barker's summary.[25] British objectives for the SOE missions evolved from the first efforts at a rising against the Italians in Albania, between 1940 and 1941. These efforts were casual, underco-ordinated, increasingly adrift from policy and essentially amateur. Accidentally, but perhaps significantly for future expectations and approaches, they revolved around northern conservatives including Abas Kupi.[26] For the first year or two thereafter the enthusiasm of individual politicians and officers for something new, dynamic, and low-investment was muffled by diplomatic caution about the wider regional issues of Greece, Yugoslavia and Italy. It is conceivable that a more aggressive, forward-looking position on the status of the Albanian lands, coupled with a serious investment of military effort, might have stimulated a more coherent and active Albanian nationalist resistance. But such a position was never realistic in the context of British policy. In truth, the tension between enthusiastic schemes and policy caution was never reconciled: in some cases the cautions were overtaken by new realities on the ground (the entry of Italy to the war; the fall of Greece) and, in general, inertia meant that the military activity ran ahead of the political uncertainties.

The British intent in November 1943 was to avoid intervention in civil war, assist any genuine organised resistance, and contrive small-scale attacks on the Germans[27]. It was consistent with the resources that Britain was able to invest, but politically and military irrelevant to the situation on the ground. Civil war was not a distraction that the British might somehow help the Albanians away from; it was the main thrust of the political reality in Albania. Within a month, Davies was recommending a change: civil war was a fact, and Britain should declare for the LNC. But Davies disappeared into the chaos of the Çermenika winter, leaving

---

Government they had put in place (Ibid. p. 215).

[25]Barker p. 5

[26]The first efforts – built on the enthusiasms of young gentlemen adventurers and the knowledge of amongst others a colonial policemen, an insect-collector and a chap who'd once been on holiday to Albania – are straight out of Buchan and Childers. An approach that was old-fashioned before the first world war was going to have to deal with a man and an ideology intent on transcending the second.

[27]SOE–FCO telegramme describing Davies's orders, as summarised by Hibbert p.72

British policy-makers to continue to preach even-handedness as a way to forestall civil war.

The post-war battles between the Children of Light and the Children of Darkness for the soul of British wartime policy in the Balkans presuppose a clear and coherent evolution in that policy, from prudent even-handedness to calculated support for the Partisans of Tito and Hoxha. The traditional narrative for Yugoslavia is that Fitzroy Maclean's disproportionate influence on Churchill prompted a clear shift to Tito, for Albania that disproportionate amplification of the voices of the southern BLOs prompted the same to Hoxha. But one of the persistent – and arguably unfortunate – features of Albania policy was the absence of clear and exclusive support for anyone. Smiley might well complain that more support could have been given to Kupi in 1944, but his being back in the north with McLean at that point was itself a clear demonstration that London was still trying to have it both ways; after the destruction of the Gjoles bridge in June 1944, delivery of six plane-loads of supplies to Kupi was approved[28]. London had begun to recognise the strength and potential of the LNC, but continued to despair at its fratricidal tendency, and the engagement with Hoxha was restrained accordingly. Indeed, in February 1944, McLean and Smiley had been successful in helping to stop the Davies recommendation of all-out support for the LNC. There was hardly a coherent policy, and there was hardly a policy shift.

Instead, London dithered and continued to hope for an impossible compromise, projecting onto the divided map of Albania its desire not be drawn on outcomes. 'We are ourselves creating the conditions in which reconciliation is impossible', reported Quayle.[29] Repeatedly, this dithering led it to hold back from decisive action when such action might conceivably have had an effect, and then miss the boat. In autumn 1940 British officials tip-toed around the idea of stirring up unrest in Albania, not wanting to give Italy a pretext for invading Greece, but Italy invaded Greece anyway.[30] In mid-1944, a combination of uncertainty and inertia led British policy-makers to step back from full support to

[28]Hibbert p. 165

[29]Quoted in Hibbert, p. 139. Back in 1942 the paralysis of British policy was summed up in a Foreign Office minute presenting the dilemma of having to maintain Anglo-Soviet relations while preparing to counter Soviet expansionism. (Ibid. p. 35).

[30]See Davies pp 44-5.

either Kupi or Hoxha, and let B.L.O. advice influence military support. 'The wheel completed its revolution and the Foreign Office was back to having no policy worth speaking of in relation to Albania just as the crucial point in Albanian affairs, the crossing of the Shkumbin by the 1st Partisan Division, was reached, precipitating crisis.'[31] This preserved a British sense of prudence and kept open the relationship with Kupi just in case he gained new importance, but it guaranteed the destruction of the relationship with Hoxha – even supposing he were susceptible to influence. As Hibbert wrote, 'successive attempts to evolve an effective policy in relation to Albania were overtaken by events. British actions which would have been practical and perhaps sensible two or three months earlier were out of date and counter-productive by the time they were put into effect.'[32]

Hibbert understandably describes the Davies mission as misconceived[33] – in operational terms. But that only illustrates the fundamental implausibility of the British approach, because the kind of co-ordinated strategic approach imagined in British thinking would have required precisely this more formal arrangement. Instead, Davies found himself organisationally overweight for the kind of hard mobile existence required by circumstances and terrain, and politically underweight for dealing with Enver Hoxha. His account of his unhappy first formal meeting with Hoxha is a telling insight on the inconsistencies and insufficiencies of the British engagement: trying to explain how the idea of an allied landing in the Balkáns (incidentally, one of the more credible strategic reasons for being seen by the Germans to dabble in the region) was obviously defunct now that Sicily and Italy had been invaded; trying to convince the Partisans that co-operation with the Balli Kombetar was in

---

[31]Davies p. 163

[32]Hibbert p. 166; his suggestion that Britain lost its opportunity to have with Hoxha the relatively congenial post-war relationship that it enjoyed with Tito probably overstates Hoxha's susceptibility. Distance from reality was not a solely British problem: Faik Konica told King Zog in August 1942 that 'Albanian public opinion now has become more favorable to your Majesty', which seems both unlikely and irrelevant. (Konica, Faik, ed. Destani, Bejtullah *Selected Correspondence 1896-1942*, London (Centre for Albanian Studies) 2000 p. 137)

[33]'based on several misconceptions' and 'out of touch with conditions in the field' – Hibbert p. 67

their interests when fundamentally it wasn't; trying to insist on a purely military arrangement with an essentially political animal.[34]

The pained British juggling of relationships with the Partisans and the nationalists was based on the misconceptions firstly that a unification of the Albanian groups against the Germans was still possible, secondly that British support one or both ways would make a difference on the outcome, and thirdly that an even-handed stance could preserve diplomatic influence in both directions and thus ensure post-war influence. At the end of May 1944, Deputy Prime Minister Attlee was telling the House of Commons that 'His Majesty's Government through their liaison officers in the country are, however, trying to bring [the rival Albanian groups including the Partisans and Balli Kombetar] together and to establish a united front of resistance to the enemy' at the same time that Hoxha was ordering an offensive for the annihilation of Balli Kombetar – at the Congress from which the British representatives stayed away, a posture intended to show neutrality but effectively demonstrating unreliability and irrelevance.[35]

The futility of SOE's operations should be seen not in the relative lack of impact on the war and even on Albania – they were at least trying something new in a new theatre – but in these basic misconceptions on which the operations were based. They were partly factual: ignorance about the Albania into which the operations would be launched, and ignorance about the continuing developments on the ground in which they were active. In early 1944 Cairo headquarters still saw the sides in Albania as evenly matched. As late as August that year a Foreign Office official was opining that 'we don't want to commit ourselves too deeply to one side or the other and I am against withdrawing the BLO's from Kupi'.[36] The communications challenges of wartime Albania meant that the BLOs and British policymakers were as out of touch with each other

---

[34]Davies pp 77–80

[35]HC Deb 23 May 1944 vol 400 cc572-3; available via http://hansard. millbanksystems.com/commons/1944/may/23/albania-guerilla-activities. The ensuing exchange – 'Does it not become clear that both in Albania and elsewhere the real resistance is coming from the workers and peasants? – I should think so. Albania is a country of workers and peasants.' comes close to insight on the dynamics of Albania at the time, but cannot escape the relative crudeness of British understanding.

[36]Quoted in Hibbert, p. 196.

as imperial servants and masters a century previously. For Yugoslavia, the Foreign Office line that 'while SOE was entirely free to contact anyone they wanted to work with, to do sabotage and stir up disaffection [...] the FO always had first say on contact with individuals or organizations with political ambitions'[37] implies a division of responsibility conceivable in Whitehall but hilariously out of touch with Tito.

More important were the misconceptions of attitude. SOE officers tried to convince their Albanian contacts that it was in their interests to fight the Germans. Their limited success in this was due not to lack of persistence or persuasion, but to the fact that fundamentally it wasn't true. Hibbert is understandably critical of the grandiose sweep and pretensions of the position paper addressed by Muharrem Bajraktar to Anthony Eden in early 1944, 'oblivious of the manifest obligations of Great Britain in 1944 to the Soviet Union as a fighting ally, to Yugoslavia as Germany's most cruelly devastated victim in the Balkans, and to any forces which took up arms against Germany in response to Allied incitement, whatever their political affiliations.'[38] This was and perhaps had to be the British and BLO position but, however powerful the 'incitement' of remarkable young men like Hibbert, Bajraktar was by his own lights entirely justified in rejecting it. His whole world had historically been most threatened by Serbs, and was currently most threatened by the partisans, and as any kind of threat the Germans came a very distant third. Hibbert looked askance at Bajraktar's 'most ambitious shopping list' for beginning operations in any case against the Germans, but the British were asking Bajraktar to spend the strength of his people against their least significant enemy at exactly the time that the two most significant were becoming most ominous. 'Enver Hoxha and Mehmet Shehu were not building up their military formations in order to fight Germans or Italians, but in order to gain control of Albania for themselves by force; they were not going to risk serious losses in operations which to them were only of secondary importance', wrote Kemp.[39]

The Partisans and nationalists were fundamentally at odds, in a way that the British never grasped or felt unable to grasp given their own wartime imperatives. Essentially, the British saw their clients as having

---

[37] Williams p. 120

[38] Hibbert p. 100; Bajraktar report quoted from p. 247

[39] Kemp, Peter, *No Colours or Crest*, London (Cassell) 1958, p. 120

different approaches to the same issue. In fact they had different issues. Likewise in Yugoslavia, 'Tito meant to use the war to create a socialist revolution in Yugoslavia, Mihailovic meant to keep alive the unsocialist, Serb-dominated Yugoslav kingdom […Mihailovic] wanted to preserve what the communists wanted to overturn.'[40] For Djilas, 'revolution and counterrevolution cannot hide from each other… There can be no revolution without leaders capable of combining reality with utopia. But this in turn requires a belief in inevitability and an adversary who looks to the past for that reality and ideal.'; for Tito's Partisans, the Četniks were a clearer and more definitive enemy.[41]

In Albania, the BLOs were from the start subject to manipulation and unknown currents of political interest. Hoxha was immediately trying to limit the movements and access to information of Mclean and Smiley according to his own interests. Davies was hounded out of Cermenika by a rival faction of Albanians. While producing his world-historical analysis for the British Foreign Secretary, Muharrem Bajraktar was most concerned about protecting his position against rival village chieftains. In March 1944, men of Partisan 1st Brigade sallied north into nationalist territory, demonstrating their vitality after their struggles at the turn of the year and their claim on the wider country; they exchanged fire with local men – the Germans don't seem to have come into the issue. The battle of Dibra in July and August saw Partisan forces take on the Germans, and gain legitimacy for doing so; the preparations and operational manoeuvres related to the battle involved destroying collaborators and thus local rivals. In October, the newly-arrived officers of the Long-Range Desert Group had only limited success focusing Partisan activities on the retreating Germans rather than on their campaign to secure the heart of the country for themselves. Quayle's last three weeks in Albania encapsulate the predicament: on March 13th he was invited to visit the Partisans at Gumenice; on March 20th he arrived there to face 'savage recriminations' for the lack of British support; on his departure he was shot at by Ballists for having visited the Partisans; on March 25th he had a final, fruitless meeting with the local Ballists; on April 3rd 'Major

[40]Foot, M.R.D., *SOE – The Special Operations Executive 1940-1946*, London (Pimlico) 1999 (hereafter 'Foot'), p.344

[41]Djilas, Milovan, transl. Petrovich, Michael, *Wartime*, New York (Harcourt Brace Jovanovich) 1977 (hereafter 'Djilas'), pp 96-7

Quayle was brought out [...] suffering from dysentery, jaundice, malaria, and nervous exhaustion.'[42] Well might he have been.

Something of the old warmth for the highlanders – born of romantic philosophy at the start of the nineteenth century and ethnographic experience at the start of the twentieth – seemed to underpin the British relationship with the nationalists. Hibbert noted that it was generally 'easier to establish personal relationships with nationalists than with partisans. Nationalists behaved as individuals, their friendship or hospitality, warmth or coolness, generosity or meanness having more or less intelligible roots in their personalities and personal circumstances'[43]. But the corollary was that their interests – protection of their own way of life on their own ground, and thus avoiding reprisals – were more parochial and indeed passive than the expansive and ideological partisans. 'Upheaval of any sort was not in their interest.'[44] Bailey summarises the stream of BLOs arriving in Bari 'to warn that the very basis of Nationalist society negated the likelihood of any significant rising. All testified to the lack of patriotic feeling, the insular and parochial interests and the vulnerability to reprisals of local communities, which bred disunity and an over-riding desire to seek salvation from danger.'[45] The calculation, guessed at by Quayle, in which the 'undisciplined agglomeration of individuals held together only by their hatred of communism... thought

[42]Pearson, Owen, *Albania in Occupation and War – from Fascism to Communism 1940-1945*, London (Centre for Albanian Studies & I.B.Tauris) 2005 (hereafter 'Pearson'), pp 337, 339

[43]Hibbert p. 60

[44]Hibbert p. 89. The Partisans, of course, were in the upheaval business. Heaton-Armstrong's experience three decades previously resonates: 'northern mountaineers are more loyal to their clan chieftains than to their country, and too ignorant to have any very high political ideals' (Heaton-Armstrong, Duncan, ed. Belfield, Gervase and Destani, Bejtullah, *The Six Month Kingdom – Albania 1914*, London (I.B.Tauris 2005), p. 148). Isa Boletini 'placed his country's interest before his religion' (ibid. p. 24); Hoxha was bringing a new religion of his own. The international intervention that placed Wilhelm of Wied on the throne of Albania in 1914 runs as a comic opera prelude to future interventions: the attempt to play out European rivalries on the Albanian stage; the lack of adequate military support; the failure to understand or accommodate local factional rivalries; the immediate submergence in a pool of local plotting and manoeuvring; and a figurehead who 'refused from the beginning to take advice of anyone who knows land or people' (Edith Durham, letter to Aubrey Herbert July 10th ?1914, Somerset Record Office DD/DRU\47).

[45]Bailey p. 329

that the deliverance of the Balkans could be left safely to the Allies, while they… concentrated on future and hereditary foes such as the Greeks and Jugoslavs' was of course accurate.[46]

The British approach was based in part on the assumption that, even if the Albanians didn't think it in their interests to fight, they were at least a neutral force who could be persuaded. As Williams writes with regard to Yugoslavia: 'the concept of the whole anti-Axis population in Europe being directed and guided by SOE to dovetail their activity with British war-aims totally ignored the fact that those people might have their own ideas of how to resist – or survive – occupation and of how they wanted to organise their political systems after the war.'[47] Buried among the propaganda and posturing of Arben Puto's Hoxha-era *Through the Annals of English Diplomacy* is the perceptive suggestion that 'the national-liberation movements of the peninsula were not subjects or players but only 'raw material' for the strategic plans of this or that high command'[48]. The clash of interests is most clearly embodied in the bridge over the Shkumbin, blown up by Smiley in autumn 1943 because that was exactly what BLOs and Partisans were supposed to be doing to German lines of communication, to the anger of Hoxha who had communication interests of his own.[49] Both Partisans and nationalists were more self-aware

---

[46]Quayle quoted in Hibbert p. 139. Foot's assessment that 'the decision to back the communists and jettison the anti-communists among the resisters was taken on evidence from inside Albania, coloured by some political prejudice on the part of SOE's Albanian staff, that the anti-communists were too pro-German' (Foot p.218) seems weakened by the facts that few on either side were resisting anyone, and that the nationalists were hardly pro-anything.

[47]Williams p. 243

[48]Puto, Arben, *Neper Analet Diplomacise Angleze – Planet antishqiptare te Britanise se Madhe gjate Luftes se Dyte Boterore ne baze to dokumenteve te Forein Ofisit te viteve 1939-1944*, Tirana (8 Nentori) 1980 (hereafter 'Puto'), p. 185 (author translation). He likewise criticises the tendency among British writers to present Albania as an 'unknown and almost unreachable place, cut off from the world, as if it wasn't part of Europe' (p. 188). Again, Lockhart's expectation (above) that SOE would be able simply to win the confidence of the clans doesn't imply much independent thought among the clans.

[49]Hibbert, p. 62: 'The destruction of the bridge posed in acute form the question, whose Albania was it? The Partisans were quite sure that it was theirs, and were in any case resolved to make it theirs and regarded the bridge as a vital asset. The BK intended it to be theirs, and had no stomach for damaging their national heritage by blowing important bridges and courting savage German reprisals. The British officers shared neither point of view. They wanted warlike action against

than the British gave them credit for, and had a more realistic perception of their interests that the British.

The British engagement in Albania was based on a series of delusions. They knew even less about the country than they thought they did. British policy was not as coherent as it thought it was, and its evolution was fitful and muddled. The British overstated their own capacity to influence events in the Balkans: Churchill's concern, expressed in a minute to Foreign Secretary Eden in May 1944, about whether they were 'going to acquiesce in the Communisation of the Balkans'[50] presupposes that – with Soviet forces fringing Romania, Tito emerging successfully from the last major Axis offensive against him, and Hoxha cementing his control of the only dynamic politico-military force in Albania – Britain could do anything about it.[51] The Albanians were seen as potential tools in a wider European project – Churchill perhaps still seduced by the same dream of grand strategic output from efficient operational input that had lured him into Ottoman Europe three decades earlier. There was minimal thought given to what the Albanians as a people or as a set of groups might be doing on their own account.[52] Finally, the British

the Germans and tended to regard Albania as a sort of no man's land.' The Long-Range Desert Group operation against Saranda in late 1944 was for the British a natural military operational activity on the Balkan battlefied, but Hoxha saw it as an attempt to establish political control.

[50] 4/5/44, in Churchill, Winston, *The Second World War VI – Triumph and Tragedy*, London (Cassell) 1954, p. 64

[51] Churchill's denial at the time that they were agreeing spheres of influence with the Russians (message to Lord Halifax, 8th June 1944, Ibid. p. 65) should not obscure the fact that they were agreeing – or accepting – precisely that. Tito's independent strength – and equidistance between eastern and western fronts – made Yugoslavia the no-man's land in this debate, in an interesting foreshadowing of post-war political developments. Churchill wondered in late 1943 whether the lack of adequate focus on the Balkans was due to it falling between the 'artificial line of division' between his eastern and western commanders in the Mediterranean (Churchill, Winston, *The Second World War V – Closing the Ring*, London (Cassell) 1952, p. 293); but slow progress in Italy meant that the Balkans ceased to have a significant strategic potential for the western theatre, and grew ever more firmly entrenched in the eastern as Russia began to advance.

[52] 'A Balkan union… would of course have provided an easy way of accommodating the Albanian problem as seen in the Foreign Office. Whether it could have provided a solution for the Albanian problem as seen by Albanians is another question' (Hibbert p. 35). In Yugoslavia, meanwhile, the 'plan to separate the two contending factions by moving the partisans into Croatia' (Williams p. 120) is hopelessly optimistic about Tito's willingness to be ordered around the region by

were optimistic in thinking that the Albanians would see themselves as operating in the same world and with the same priorities.[53]

Much of the English-language writing about SOE's role in Albania has been built around a debate about how much the misjudgments of Whitehall or the manipulations of left-wing sympathisers within British structures were responsible for facilitating Hoxha's success (and Tito's).[54] In effect, this thesis acknowledges that British military intervention in Albanian didn't do much to tilt the war against Germany, but suggests as a consolation that it was at least useful in tilting the civil war. But this is to replace one rather patronising model of British instrumentalisation of Albanians – handful of SOE officers can steer passive Albanians to resist Germans for greater good of Europe – with another – handful of rogue officials can distort British effort and enable otherwise avoidable Communist success. Simply put, the British were not a big enough factor to change the situation. As Hibbert suggests, 'The course of events in Albania in the spring and summer of 1944 was not and could not be determined by something under 100 tons of arms, ammunition and equipment dropped into the Partisans.'[55] Withholding supplies did not constrain the Partisans in July 1944. Enver Hoxha emerged triumphant from the chaos of wartime Albania not because the assessments of a few officials in London, Cairo and Bari led to an inequitable distribution of air-drops and moral support, but because his opponents were passive and

outsiders.

[53] All that said, post-war Communist rhetoric should not obscure the positive impact on Partisan morale of these supporters from the sky: 'We represented a symbolic link with the world outside and our physical presence was a token recognition, breaking the isolation, for the first time, of our new companions. [...] 'The news was heard in the battalions. At last we received what had long been awaited, a great moral recognition of our struggle." (Deakin, p.9)

[54] See e.g. Smiley, taken up by Foot.

[55] Hibbert p. 113. In February 1944, Steel at the Foreign Office described the pointlessness of high political expectations given 'the puny support which the present allocation of aircraft... to our organization in Albania would enable us to give' (quoted in Ibid. p. 134). See also Ibid. p. 253: The underwhelming statistics for British supply to Albania 'do not support the allegations that Britain abandoned Albania unnecessarily to communism through a feckless and over-generous arms supply policy.' Bailey highlights Hare as an officer who had experienced both Partisans and Nationalists and emerged no friend to the former, but judged that once the Partisans had survived into 1944 'Kupi and his movement were doomed to defeat and extinction whatever action he had taken' (Quoted in Bailey p. 330).

parochial while his movement was dynamic, brutally efficient, and had enough ideology to fit the time and the situation.

By way of comparison, the same combination of mis-judged intervention and then Anglo-centric interpretation of failure arose when, between 1949 and 1951, the British and Americans organised a series of infiltrations of Albania by anti-Communist Albanians – their sponsors called them pixies because of their relative lack of height – with the aim of sparking a rising against Hoxha. The traditional interpretation of the ensuing fiasco makes the principle culprit 'Kim' Philby, presumed to have betrayed the plans to Moscow: only Anglo-Saxon treachery could undermine an Anglo-Saxon plan[56]. This interpretation under-states the fundamental implausibility of the plan in the face of the practical and social realities on the ground. 'Our 'allies'', wrote one leading nationalist figure, 'wanted to make use of Albania as a guinea-pig, without caring about the human losses, for an absurd enterprise that was condemned to failure.'[57] British and American intelligence were seeking a victory against world communism, but their agents were dying lonely deaths within hours of landing in obscure corners of Albania.[58]

The Partisans were against the Germans primarily as fascists and secondarily as occupiers, but not as aggressors in Europe. They had no

---

[56]Again, see Smiley.

[57]Abas Ermenji, quoted in Bethell, Nicholas, *The Great Betrayal – The Untold Story of Kim Philby's Biggest Coup*, London (Hodder & Stoughton) 1984 (hereafter 'Bethell'), p. 194. While spotlighting Philby, Bethell gives a balanced picture of the reasons for failure: 'CIA/OPC and SIS were misled in the first place by over-optimistic intelligence […] They did not appreciate how easy it would be for the communist police, controlling Albania as they did, to gather intelligence about the operation […] They chose men of limited physical strength to do jobs better suited to trained commandos. They sent radio operators into the field without proper instruction in cipher or Morse. They gave the men no practice parachute jumps and in most cases only two or three weeks' instruction in guerilla warfare. Often they landed the men in the wrong place and no group ever got the heavy equipment that should have dropped with them.' Bethell 196-7; Bailey: 'the secrecy and security surrounding the recruitment, intentions and training of the agents were poor, and had been penetrated by Hoxha's own intelligence men' (Bailey p. 328).

[58]Even those agents who did survive to try to foster resistance did not thrive: 'As usual the story of the Second World War was being repeated. People wanted tangible proof of American commitment to Hoxha's overthrow. Once they started getting parachute drops of men and weapons, they said, they would take up arms and join the fight. The drops never came'. Bethell p. 168

interest in the neutrality of Poland, and little in the balance of continental power. They wanted to change Albania rather than to restore it, and the upheavals of war were thus for them an opportunity, part of a process, rather than an undesirable aberration from which to recover. The nationalists/legitimists, meanwhile, had equally little interest in the Germans per se: they were worried about the Partisan threat to their way of life, and hoping for a return to a comfortable status quo ante. For both sides in Albania, German defeat was an eventual necessity for the achievement of their objectives, but it was not an essential motivation. Nor was German defeat something that they themselves were likely to be able to do much about. German endurance, by the same token, was merely a delay rather than an existential problem. The idea of arming resistance organizations was flawed, Williams suggests, because it did not 'recognize the diversity of opinions and aims of the many occupied peoples, or the fact that *their* long-term objectives might differ from those of the British.'[59] Hibbert experienced a telling example of this in early 1944, when 'Something of a thrill went through the neighbourhood when one of the Lita family spread the news that the Germans were going to arm Albanians in Kosova to fight the Serbs and Tito. This was a fight which roused real enthusiasm. Our warnings against it were received in silence.'[60] A country that had endured Dunkirk, the Blitz and the Battle of Britain knew that defeating Germany was the priority. A country that had been given renewed self-government and the promise of an ethnically-defined state could afford to wonder.

For that matter, it was hardly an inconvenience – and occasionally quite the opposite – to the Germans that half of the country was forming a new social order and wanting to swallow the other half, and that the other half clung vainly to a lost hope of restoring an alienated monarchy. 'The new German strategy included occasional offensives against the partisans, which in the spring nearly succeeded in destroying the movement, although its complete destruction was never a German goal. The partisans proved quite useful to the Germans as a threat for extracting

[59]Williams p. 47
[60]Hibbert p. 99. In April 1941, there were 12,000 Albanians in Italian uniform resisting the Greek repulse of Mussolini's forces (Porch, Douglas, *Hitler's Mediterranean Gamble – the North African and the Mediterranean Campaigns in World War II*, London (Weidenfeld & Nicolson), 2004 (hereafter 'Porch') p. 97).

co-operation from Albania's noncommunists.'[61] As long as the main roads were generally clear, the German occupation could co-exist satisfactorily with Hoxha's nascent new society and Kupi's fragile highland order. It was only the British who wanted more from the Albanian situation.[62]

Between 1939 and 1945 Albania went through a significant process of political – and began a significant process of social – change.[63] What much of the rest of Europe and the world recognises as the second world war was manifest in Albania as the Italian and German occupations and puppet regimes, sometimes a threat or a hindrance to the Partisan or nationalist narrative, but also a unique opportunity to advance their own objectives. Italian occupation de-legitimised the Monarchy, and German control of the region allowed the re-conception of borders on ethnic lines that Albanian nationalists had long sought but never sustainably achieved. Germany's defeat, and the fact that Tito and Hoxha were as much politicians as idealists, reversed the latter. But the chaos of world war created a vacuum in Albania that the Partisans exploited for their own interests. Albania's war was domestic. The Italians and the Germans shaped it; the British were observers.

('The destinies of all these foreigners, cast up and crammed into this narrow, damp valley and condemned to live in unusual conditions for an unknown length of time': the Yugoslav Nobel laureate Ivo Andrić articulated most powerfully a Balkan capacity for endurance and continuity, in the shadows of an eternal intrusion of foreign meddlers[64]. *Bridge on the Drina* and short stories like *The Vizier's Elephant* are hymns to survival in the face of the bewildering challenges of existence, while the experiences of the foreign representatives in the *Bosnian Chronicle* would have resonated with the BLOs: 'Pale and alone, […the Consul] thought about it all and felt disarmed and powerless in the face of a

---

[61]Fischer p. 263

[62]'The Germans had one major motive, and that was to prevent, with a minimum of troops, an Allied landing in Albania. […Once in place,] the Germans proceeded with their plan to reduce the required number of occupation troops to the barest minimum.' (Fischer p. 261) Fischer also notes (p. 183) the relative significance of Albania for supplies of oil and chrome.

[63]Fischer: 'In the process of pursuing their own goals, the Italians and the Germans produced a profound transformation and acceleration in social, economic and political change.' (Ibid. p. 257)

[64]Andrić, Ivo, transl. Hawkesworth, Celia and Rakic, Bogdan, *Bosnian Chronicle*, London (Harvill) 1996, p. 340

whole combination of the most varied circumstances, in which he was now carrying out his duty conscientiously, exhausting himself beyond his strength, while clearly seeing that it was all futile.'[65] " Who knows what will happen with these consuls? Maybe they'll come and maybe they won't. And even if they do, the Lasva won't start flowing backwards: it'll keep on going the same old way: We're on our own ground here, and anyone else who comes is a stranger and won't be able to hold out for long."[66])

The experience of British engagement in Albania was echoed in Yugoslavia. Tito was arguably more of a threat to the Germans – or, rather, his endurance was more of a threat to the stability and efficiency of their control of south-eastern Europe. The Yugoslav Partisans' struggle for survival and then dominance was longer and more dramatic than the Albanian Partisans' 1943 winter of crisis. Tito – and Mihailovic – were more significant players in the strategic calculations of the great powers than Hoxha and Abas Kupi. But essentially the same debate was played out in the British Government, military and intelligence apparatus about the relative benefits of nationalists and communists, the same confused shifts in support policy occured, and the same arguments continued in the decades after the war.

Again in Yugoslavia came the British debate over fundamental aims: whether to support the Partisans who seemed to be more useful in Britain's life-or-death war against Germany, or to support those whose essentially conservative outlook would be more congenial to Britain's long-term regional interests. Even had Britain's impact been such as to make a difference, her dithering on the point made her irrelevant. The imperatives of war made it impossible decisively to support the nationalists; hesitancy and clumsy attempts at even-handedness lost the trust of the Partisans – whose idealism was in any case strong enough to render entirely illusory the British attempt to maintain influence with them and thereby the Russians. Williams usefully sums up the muddled thinking: 'The [Foreign Office] wanted to appease the Soviets, while keeping them out of Yugoslavia; *and* they wanted a resistance leader charismatic enough to inspire his followers, but at the same time lacking any long-term political ambitions of his own, easily bent to the British

---

[65]Ibid. p. 284
[66]Ibid., p. 3

will, and who would reunite Yugoslavia at the war's end.'[67] This would have been a high-handed and optimistic desire in any scenario: in the context of Tito's war-time Yugoslavia it was fantasy.

Weak, indecisive and ignorant, the British fell between stools. 'The plan to influence the nature of resistance had come to virtually nothing due to the problems of supplying the arms and money which had been an essential element of the scheme. The deep-seated political divisions between the two resistance movements had been imperfectly understood by SOE and other British bodies concerned with Yugoslavia: attempts to bring together these irreconcilable factions had merely served to arouse the suspicions of all sides, and the civil war was continuing.'[68] Once again, the British belief that they had the power to steer the outcome was misguided. 'While the debate on whether or not to contact and support the partisans was raging in London and Cairo, events in Yugoslavia were making this eventuality inevitable.'[69]

Reginald Hibbert got a boat out of Albania in October 1944 to re-join the second world war, with an interim for rest and debriefing in Italy in which the BLOs shared their grumbles about the shortcomings of their headquarters: 'not well-informed about the way in which events had developed or were developing in Albania. The staff had the attitudes of would-be king-makers. Policy was an extension of ideas about Albania (mostly false) rather than a construction on a reliable basis of fact. In the end all the BLO's wrote reports and left them with the staff to be filed away. With our report… [we] buried our past and turned to other things, in the first place our own individual lives.'[70] In the same month, the new Albanian government was declared in Berat, but it would not be recognised by the UK for another year; for one final time in this war, perhaps the policy-makers missed the boat.

Fifty years after the last SOE officers were evacuated from Albania, intrepid foreign soldiers began to arrive in the Balkans again, sent there

---

[67]Williams p. 114. Churchill's records (Churchill, Winston, *The Second World War V – Closing the Ring*, London (Cassell) 1952, pp 415-423) show the December 1943 – May 1944 wrangling between Churchill and Tito over role of King Petar and Partisan engagement with him; whether spurred by British conservatism or a narrow definition of stability, it was irrelevant.

[68]Williams p. 81

[69]Ibid. p. 126

[70]Hibbert p. 231

by diplomats who dreamed of stability and success in Europe. This time the challenges were inherent rather than incidental to the region, and less existential to those who intervened. Nevertheless, the interventions in Bosnia and then Kosova demanded an understanding of the difference between local and international interests, and the old lessons remain relevant.

The first lesson of SOE in Albania is that the intervention should be strong enough for the intention. To be fair, the scale of the intervention in Albania was consistent with what policymakers thought they were trying to do – it was just that the intention was out of step with the reality, and it would have taken a dramatically larger intervention to change that reality.[71] The sheer scale of the UN and NATO operations in the Balkans in the 1990s suggests resources consistent with the aspirations. In Bosnia in the nineties, more than in Albania in the second world war, the military and political tracks were broadly in step too: the seriousness and aim of the engagements on these tracks was consistent. Nevertheless, the stuttering and stillborn attempts at diplomatic solutions and military engagement in the first years of the Bosnian war reflected an intervention that only gradually came to terms with the situation on the ground. The disaster of Srebrenica, meanwhile, showed that the intervention's useable military power and clarity of mandate were not sufficient in that context to meet basic humanitarian objectives.

The intervention in Kosova in 1999 seemed to have learned from Bosnia relative promptness, and the apparent incorrigibility of the Milosevic regime. It took considerable diplomatic effort during the NATO air campaign to persuade the United States to earmark the ground troops necessary to give credibility to the threat, but when NATO did enter Kosova in June 1999 it was in numbers (some 50,000) that reflected serious commitment and the ability to dominate the

---

[71]Modern communications and the twin pressures of coalition diplomacy and coalition intervention kept the military and political tracks more easily in step in the 1990s than had been possible in the 1940s, when the military gained momentum of its own and ran ahead of the political: 'At the time when this cautious brief was being drafted in the Foreign Office, the SOE had already committed itself to an active policy of building up a network of small British missions' (Hibbert p. 41). See also the unreality of the later London debate on whether or not to pick sides: "At this stage of the war we don't want to commit ourselves too deeply to one side or the other" (quoted in Ibid. p. 196).

ground. Patience is also a resource, though, and although the draw-down of NATO troop numbers in Kosova has been broadly consistent with mission and threat, this has sometimes been as much by accident as design. Spain withdrew its troops unilaterally, and by 2010 NATO's reduction in mission size was being driven in part by the inability to attract troop contributions. Meanwhile, the failure significantly to restrain inter-ethnic excess in summer 1999 and spring 2004 suggested a mission that, although numerically strong enough, did not have the flexibility or clarity to deal with the most likely threat.

The second lesson of Albania seems to be the need for a certainty of objective: a conviction over the outcome that can drive an uncompromising engagement. SOE and the policy-makers behind it knew that they wanted to harass and draw in German forces, and that the way to do so was to rally local resistance to this end. But they discovered that in order to be able to do this significantly, they needed to reach a view on the outcome of the Albanian civil war and indeed the shape of Albania. The Germans found themselves freer on the latter, at least, and derived the benefit in the form of some stability and support. The British found themselves faced with an exam question they hadn't prepared for, and spent two years trying to fudge the answer.

There's a superficial parallel with the engagement in Bosnia, which only finally found traction when the international community essentially picked a side. But the international community had at least been clearer from the start about the depth of the fratricidal challenge in Bosnia – a challenge, indeed, that punishing the Bosnian Serb military and brokering the Dayton Accord only froze rather than resolved. Kosova in 1999 presents a clearer and apparently more successful case of side-picking: after a year of diplomatic and monitoring efforts had restrained but not changed the conflict on the ground, the Rambouillet episode allowed NATO to rule that Serbia was in the wrong and intervene accordingly. In both Bosnia and Kosova the intervention successfully met its basic motive: although the tension has continued, the humanitarian catastrophes were stopped.

Kosova, though, offered a subtler challenge for policy clarity. NATO thought it was stopping a humanitarian disaster; Kosova's Albanians thought they were winning independence at last. For the latter, the decade following the NATO campaign was a frustrated coming to terms with the cautious and limited motives of the interveners. The interveners had accordingly to manage both this frustration, and the varied attitudes and motives in their own ranks. Four of the five UN Security Council permanent members had troops in Kosova in summer 1999, and their policy divisions shaped Kosova's development for the ensuing decade.

Many of those intervening in Kosova might have argued that their goal was stability, rather than any new or particular constitutional outcome. Some would have argued that independence was the best route to stability, and those who intervened for peace rather than independence found themselves forced nevertheless to address the issue. But the quest for stability became the reinforcement of stagnation. The violence of March 2004 showed that the satisfactory prevention of humanitarian outrage had done little to address underlying tensions – indeed that the effort, born of complacency and lack of consensus, to prolong the opacity of Kosova's constitutional status was prolonging and even exacerbating those tensions. The maintenance of Kosova's constitutional ambiguity looked like a triumph for those whose focus was international consensus. For the generations of Kosovan citizens – particularly Kosova's Serbs – growing up in investment-starved economic stagnation, with shameful standards of education and healthcare, fundamental uncertainty about their identity and property, and no fully legitimised voice internationally, the diplomatic triumph felt like abandonment or betrayal. By 2010, Kosova had undergone as long a period of constitutional limbo under international oversight as it had under Milosevic.

So the intervention in Kosova saw a constant creative tension between those trying to move the country forward and those trying to hold it. Once the European Union took the lead in trying to manage the situation (arguably formalised in the summer 2010 exchanges between Secretary-General Ban and Vice-President/High Representative Ashton), this tension was manifest in the line between the 22 EU member states that had recognised Kosova's independence and the five that had not. In fact, as the Union moved to the centre of the stage, one additional aspect of the tension was between those trying to move the country forward and their own desire that this happen within the context of a unified and developing EU.

For some indeed, EU unity and development was the goal, and Kosova was irrelevant outside its ability to provide this. (Commenting on the shortcomings of the intervention in Bosnia, Simms identifies the pre-occupation with international unity on policy rather than with the content of the policy[72].) This was understandable from a wider strategic perspective, but it tended to drag the intervention away from the reality on the ground – one of the fundamental challenges of the intervention in wartime Albania.

The interveners in Bosnia and Kosova in the 1990s had better access to facts about their destination than their predecessors two generations before, and modern communications were giving policy-makers a dramatic – albeit incomplete and perhaps distorted; journalistic perspective had replaced BLO affinity – insight on daily events in the field. But the predisposition to romanticism and simplicity had not disappeared. Diplomats and soldiers read and mis-read Rebecca West and Ivo Andrić and perceived eternal inter-ethnic hatreds, rather than considering the economic basis of collapse, and headquarters analysts still emphasised the all-pervading role of Albanian clans.

In non-official analysis there was some aggressive, bordering on racist, condemnation of the structures and activities of Albanian society in Kosova[73], but the predominance of the clan also featured in official analysis and discourse[74]. The clan was one of a range of filters through which to view Kosova, and as such seemed to reflect a desire really to understand the society in which the international community was operating. But there was less sign of alternative models being considered, or of progress from a generalised attempt to grasp the dynamics of the

---

[72]Simms, Brendan, *Unfinest Hour – Britain and the Destruction of Bosnia*, London (Penguin) 2002, p. 14

[73]'But we cannot afford to ignore the features of clan-based cultures, whether in Kosovo or in the Middle East, that make them susceptible to manipulation by unscrupulous forces for nightmarish geopolitical goals.' Jared Israel at http://emperors-clothes.com/interviews/keys.htm; 'After bombing Serbia 1999 KLA leaders again changed their crime clans officially to political parties.' http://arirusila.wordpress.com/2010/02/20/kosovo-two-years-of-pseudo-state/

[74]In, for example, a 2005 German intelligence (BND) assessment that leaked. A British General working alongside the demilitarised Kosova Liberation Army noted, in a 2008 interview published on the official UK Ministry of Defence website, that 'The history of the country hardly helps here. It is fundamentally a clan-based society with a strong streak of mafia-style organised crime.' (http://www.mod.uk/defenceinternet/defencenews/defencepolicyandbusiness/britishgeneralhelpsshapesecuritystructureinkosovo.htm)

society to a specific analysis of the fault lines that were influencing Kosova politics at the start of the new millennium.

For interveners concerned to manage a latent tension between Serbs and Albanians, it was easy to presuppose an essentially homogeneous Kosova Albanian attitude, particularly to independence. But amongst other factors for diversity the division between town and country – stereotyped as bourgeois and peasant, and echoing traditions of post-Ottoman city intellectual and rural *kaçak* rebel – had influenced the spectrum of approaches in the 1990s from Ibrahim Rugova's passive resistance to Adem Jashari's patriotic banditry. After the eviction of Serbia's oppressive state structures the two traditions vied for their place in national myth, the continued discomfort of their cohabitation manifest in for example the 2002 absence of Rugova and his party officials from the commemoration of Jashari's death and the 2006 refusal of the 'honour guard' of the Kosova Protection Corps (the largely demilitarised liberation army) to parade at Rugova's burial.[75]

This is not just of sociological interest. As the BLOs found sixty years before, the fault-lines and motives of the actors influence the direction and distance they are willing to go, and the leverage that will work on them. Even Kosova's independence itself means different things to an Albanian farmer near a Serb village concerned about property title and to an educated city-dweller concerned at the habits of his new Government. Attitude surveys showed that the majority of the population were more concerned with their economy than their security[76]. But the intense international focus on domestic and regional security above

---

[75]'The gulf and the tension between the two tiers were never reconciled. Far from acting as the political or armed wing of one another, both the peaceful resistance and the armed struggle led a parallel existence until the end of the conflict.' (Bekaj, Armend, *The KLA and the Kosovo War: from Intra-State Conflict to Independent Country*, Berlin (Berghof Conflict Research) 2010, p. 37)

[76]An IFES survey published in January 2010 reported that, among those 'dissatisfied' with the situation in Kosova, the most-cited problems were unemployment (cited by 91%, an increase on two years earlier), poverty, and then general economic problems; even among Kosova's small Serb minority, likely in general to feel much more insecure, only 50% cited security as among the biggest problems, still second to unemployment (survey at http://www.ifes.org/Content/Publications/Reports/2010/Post-Election-Public-Opinion-in-Kosovo-2010.aspx). In a Gallup survey the percentage of Kosova Albanians who believed that independence had been a positive development dropped from 93% to 75% between 2008 and 2009 ('Focus on Kosovo's Independence', published August 2010).

all seemed to lead to tolerance of threats of greater concern to local people – among them corruption.[77] Only in 2010 did the international community begin successfully to challenge this perception. By autumn 2010, Kosova was the only regional state excluded from the European Union's visa liberalisation process; free movement to western Europe was a much more apparent lack for Kosova's citizens than the far more distant and clouded benefits of European Union membership. By accepting too simple an idea of the motives of politicians and population, the intervener risks a misperception of leverage; by falling out of step with their real concerns, the intervener risks seeming irrelevant.

Cynics might suggest fundamentally different motives (and the international community would surely have handled Kosova more dynamically if the global economy were powered by lignite), but there are significant similarities between the interventions in Kosova and in Libya. Whatever the palette of political, economic and serious humanitarian motives, those who intervened in Libya in 2011 essentially picked a side in an internal conflict and facilitated its victory. As in Kosova, the post-military phase was likely to be much longer and more vexed than the military. However noble its original motives, the reputation of the international intervention became dependent on the behaviour of those who benefited from it.[78] Moreover, successful engagement in post-Qaddafi Libya will have required the international community – while no doubt continuing to trumpet national unity, as both retrospective justification and optimistic exhortation – shrewdly to understand and negotiate the country's social and political currents and fault lines.

---

[77]See for example euobserver.com of 1st July 2010 (http://euobserver. com/9/30404): 'Are the EU and US more interested in making money than cleaning up Kosovo corruption?'. In the IFES survey referenced above, corruption featured as a more significant problem than security, and the proportion of respondents citing it among the biggest issues had more than trebled.

[78]In Kosova, how the Albanian majority treated the country's Serb citizens, in Libya how the National Liberation Army, the National Transitional Council and successor structures accommodated those from whom Qaddafi had drawn support. For Libya in 2011, as for Kosova in 1999, those trying creditably to understand the situation were convinced that it was all about the clans. ('As a consequence of their long experience with repression, the population is apolitical and oriented primarily toward family and clan... Libyan tribes are powerful' (Bertelsmann Stiftung transformation index for 2010, http://www.bertelsmann-transformation-index.de/134.0.html?L=1).)

Those who parachuted into Albania in the 1940s learned that those they met were not passive peasants willing to fall in with Britain's European strategy. Those who came as stabilisers and peace-makers in Bosnia and Kosova in the 1990s and beyond – as if peace and stability were things that dropped on a parachute rather than growing from the ground up – performed bravely and, in their own terms, successfully; but the local acceptance of this international order rarely went beyond the limits of local interest. The structures established in Bosnia by the Dayton Accords endure, thanks to enormous investment of money and commitment by international and some national players, but it has proved impossible to dent the determination of the Republika Srpska to entrench its identity and autonomy. Kosova continues to tick international boxes – the UN standards process, the Ahtisaari settlement plan, Europe's requirements for pre-accession and visa liberalisation, the International Monetary Fund's requirements for fiscal restraint – and to draw the consequent benefits; but her leaders continue to pursue their domestic political interests unchecked. Affection for the US and to an extent the UK, and aspiration to the trappings of western statehood, have made Kosova much more pliable and amenable than Bosnia; but its conformity with international norms and expectations, and its political and economic and social developments, occupy essentially separate and parallel tracks. The international community, with great diplomatic expertise and effort, often manages to secure the external and superficial outcomes that it desires (Tito fought Germans; Kosova adopted a multi-ethnic constitution). But its impact on underlying behaviours is minimal.[79] Interveners might argue that they are not trying to change society, merely to deal with the threats posed by instability to their own strategic interests (peace, the fight against organised crime, a stronger EU); but it is the underlying structures and trends in society that will determine how stable, what sort of soil for crime, and what kind of EU member the new state will be.[80]

---

[79]Perhaps the true modern analogue to the BLOs is not the NATO battalions but the individual advisors working with new Government Ministries and Assemblies. Mason and King (King, Iain and Mason, Whit, *Peace at any Price – How the World Failed Kosovo*, London (Hurst) 2006, p. 246) observed in Kosova the delusion 'that inside every apparently embittered militant was a tolerant, pluralist democrat waiting to emerge once favorable conditions had been created'.

[80]As Andrić recognised, the interveners come and go and the peoples of the Balkans pursue their own paths: when British former service personnel return to

The attempt to maintain a judicious distance from the local squabbling may allow the temporary occupation of the moral high ground, but it can lead to weakness and eventually moral failure. If there was ever any possibility of building a lasting relationship of trust and then influence with Enver Hoxha, it required a prompt and uncompromising decision in his failure. Instead, by the time Whitehall stumbled towards a practical acknowledgement of his pre-dominance, the attempt to have a foot in both camps had created insoluble suspicion. In Bosnia in the 1990s, Simms and others would suggest, there was for too long an insistence on the equivalence of the players, and essentially a failure to pick a side early enough.

Those on the receiving end of intervention have attitudes and intent of their own.[81] They also have their own judgements and pre-judgements of the interveners. Smiley wrote of Hoxha: 'We had naively assumed that he would welcome officers from a country at war with his enemies, who were prepared to help in fighting the Italian occupiers of his country. On the contrary, he gave the impression that he was suspicious, if not openly hostile, of our intentions.'[82] Across the accursed mountains, the Yugoslav Partisans had their own suspicions: Djilas would write that 'The British press also contributed much to a romantic, mythical notion of the omnipotence of British Intelligence. All of which gave us reason for extreme caution: we saw in Lawrence of Arabia not an idealistic hero, but the perfidious, arrogant champion of an empire.'[83]

Some of this is prejudice, some of it atavism, and some of it the recognition of genuinely different goals. But the real behaviour of the international interveners is noticed. Hoxha's Partisans protested at what they saw as treacherous BBC radio broadcasts. In 2006 the editor of the Albanian Mail brought a case to the Press Complaints Commission about a Sunday Times Magazine article that he claimed was inaccurate, prejudicial and pejorative. When European policemen are bringing

---

Vis to commemorate their fallen comrades, the stone memorial cross now has 'Yugoslavia' erased and 'Croatia' scrawled over it; and when in the democratic era a memorial was established to the British soldiers who had fought and died in Albania, it recycled stone from Enver Hoxha's monument.

[81] Puto complains at the intervention as a 'flagrant interruption of our domestic business' (Puto p. 118).

[82] Smiley p. 29

[83] Djilas p. 69

the rule of law to Kosova, it is unfortunate to have newspaper reports that some of them have been caught smuggling.[84] After the UN Office of Internal Oversight Services reported fraud and corruption in the international management of Prishtina's aiport, one local editorial suggested that 'Kosova citizens have expected much more from UNMIK, as they assumed that the international community would know how to build a democratic society. What happened in the last couple of years was far from the expectations and hopes of the citizens'[85].

Western policy-makers have a much shorter memory of their own perfidies than those who suffer them. Kosova Albanians listening to western assertions that the territorial integrity of their newly-independent state will be protected have, lurking in their folk memory, the experiences of past betrayals. The 1913 treaty of London left them outside Albania. The 1915 treaty of London between Britain, France and Russia would have carved off chunks of Albania for Italy, Serbia, Montenegro and Greece, and left the rump under Italian control[86]. A January 1920 agreement in Paris between Britain, France and Greece would have divided Albania between Italy, Yugoslavia and Greece. In a Foreign Office discussion in July 1940 it was thought that 'Albania would not be able to stand alone […] It was also conceivable that, in the event of an Italian defeat, it would be found convenient to leave the Italians in possession of Albania, in order that they might act as a counterweight to Germany.'[87] Kosova has made Europe and EU membership the centre of its political discourse, but Kosova's Albanians remember that the Albanian poet-priest Fishta – who'd been one of the impotent Albanian representatives at the Paris

---

[84]http://euobserver.com/9/30205: 'EU's Kosovo mission struggles for credibility after smuggling incident'. More unfortunate still that the policemen in this April 2010 incident were of the same nationality as the special policemen judged responsible, by a UN investigation, for the fatal shooting in 2007 of two Kosovar protesters, using outdated baton rounds (see http://www.unmikonline.org/DPI/Transcripts.nsf/0/D6DD1A2B6CE50B83C12572C000543A74/$FILE/tr170407.pdf).

[85]Blerim Shala in Zeri, April 2006, summarised at http://www.unmikonline.org/archives/EUinKosovo/upload_economic/Economic%20News%2010%20April.pdf

[86]The treaty's vision of 'a small autonomous neutralised State' of Albania might resonate hollowly to a modern Kosovar.

[87]Quoted in Pearson, p. 12

Peace Conference and therefore knew whereof he spoke – described Europe as 'the whore of the ages'[88].

Affection for America, the sinews of a global economy, and the benefits and ideals of the European Union seem to put Kosova and Albania on a course convergent with western Europe. But the interventions of the past demonstrate the imprudence of trying to fit them snugly into the world view of the intervener, believing that the country in question is merely retarded in its progress along the intervener's track rather than being on a track of its own. In the 21st century, the context is the strengthening of European institutions, and the prevailing international orthodoxy for the Balkans is that the EU is the only and ideal destination. In the late 1940s and the 1950s, when Albanian expatriates were being dropped off in isolated coves to stir up rebellion, the context was the cold war and the orthodoxy was that people would if given the chance choose to resist Communism. In the early 1940s, the context was the second world war and the orthodoxy was that right-thinking people would, if given the opportunity, fight Nazi Germany.

'It is essential to understand that there is no will to fight Germans in this land… This war which we are supposed to be waging is a complete fiction', Reginald Hibbert recorded in a cold and hungry diary entry in 1944. Nearly half a century after he was dropped blind into the middle of Albania's private struggle, he would recall 'the frictions of life in the mountains – the crowding, the dirt and fleas and bugs, the erratic food supplies, the stealing, the extortions, the hard lying – but these things would have been much more easily bearable if it had not been for the stalemate which was depriving the British presence in Albania of purpose.'[89] His experience and his testimony are ample representation of the extraordinary patience, endurance, courage and commitment of the men who parachuted into Albania and Yugoslavia, and those who suffered so greatly around them. They are also a salutary lesson for those who continue to drop into the pot.

---

[88]In 'The Highland Lute', because Europe has broken its word and carved up Albania. 'Kurva e motit' has various possible translations.

[89]Hibbert pp 98, 90

Bibliography

Andrić, Ivo, transl. Hawkesworth, Celia and Rakic, Bogdan, *Bosnian Chronicle*, London (Harvill) 1996

Andrić, Ivo, transl. Edwards, Lovett, *The Bridge on the Drina*, London (George Allen & Unwin) 1959

Bailey, Roderick, *The Wildest Province – SOE in the Land of the Eagle*, London (Vintage) 2009

Barker, Elisabeth, *British Policy in South-East Europe in the Second World War*, London (Macmillan) 1976

Bekaj, Armend, *The KLA and the Kosovo War: from Intra-State Conflict to Independent Country*, Berlin (Berghof Conflict Research) 2010

Bethell, Nicholas, *The Great Betrayal – The Untold Story of Kim Philby's Biggest Coup*, London (Hodder & Stoughton) 1984

Churchill, Winston, *The Second World War V – Closing the Ring*, London (Cassell) 1952

Churchill, Winston, *The Second World War VI – Triumph and Tragedy*, London (Cassell) 1954

Davidson, Basil, *Partisan Picture*, Bedford 1946

Davies, Edmund 'Trotsky', *Illyrian Venture – the Story of the British Military mission to Enemy-Occupied Albania 1943-1944*, London (The Bodley Head) 1952

Deakin, Frederick, *The Embattled Mountain*, London (Oxford University Press) 1971

Djilas, Milovan, transl. Petrovich, Michael, *Wartime*, New York (Harcourt Brace Jovanovich) 1977

Fischer, Bernd, *Albania at War 1939-1945*, London (Hurst) 1999

Foot, M.R.D., *SOE – The Special Operations Executive 1940-1946*, London (Pimlico) 1999

Heaton-Armstrong, Duncan, ed. Belfield, Gervase and Destani, Bejtullah, *The Six Month Kingdom – Albania 1914*, London (I.B.Tauris 2005)

Hibbert, Reginald, *Albania's National Liberation Struggle – The Bitter Victory*, London (Pinter) 1991

Kemp, Peter, *No Colours or Crest*, London (Cassell) 1958

King, Iain and Mason, Whit, *Peace at any Price – How the World Failed Kosovo*, London (Hurst) 2006

Konica, Faik, ed. Destani, Bejtullah *Selected Correspondence 1896-1942*, London (Centre for Albanian Studies) 2000

Pearson, Owen, *Albania in Occupation and War – from Fascism to Communism 1940-1945*, London (Centre for Albanian Studies & I.B.Tauris) 2005

Porch, Douglas, *Hitler's Mediterranean Gamble – the North African and the Mediterranean Campaigns in World War II*, London (Weidenfeld & Nicolson), 2004

Puto, Arben, *Nëpër Analët Diplomacisë Angleze – Planet antishqiptare të Britanisë së Madhe gjatë Luftës së Dyte Boterore në bazë to dokumentëve të Forein Ofisit të viteve 1939-1944*, Tirana (8 Nëntori) 1980

Rogers, Lindsay, *Guerilla Surgeon – a New Zealand surgeon's wartime experiences with the Yugoslav Partisans*, London (Collins) 1957

Simms, Brendan, *Unfinest Hour – Britain and the Destruction of Bosnia*, London (Penguin) 2002

Smiley, David, *Albanian Assignment*, London (Chatto & Windus/The Hogarth Press) 1984

Williams, Heather, *Parachutes, Patriots and Partisans – The Special Operations Executive and Yugoslavia 1941-1945*, London (Hurst & Company) 2003

Turkey's Balkan Policy and the agenda of the Albanian community in Turkey

Nurcan Ozgur Baklacioglu

Introduction

The contemporary literature on the linkage between migration and foreign policy use to approach migration and the migrants as ethnopolitical and demographic tools of the foreign policies of the involved states. The migrant lobbies are considered as independent variables of the foreign policy decission-making and primary actors of the public diplomacy in the involved states. They not only serve as direct conveyers of some ethnopolitical, economic and social interests and targets, but they also pose a challenge to the foreign policy identities and perceptions of the states. From this perspective the migrant communities raise as actors that transcend state-level of analysis, thus bring forward the continuity between the intra-state level and international level. In this way, the migrant communities as transborder foreign policy actors trigger farther duality and complexity in the identities, perceptions and policies of the target states. Thus, the migrants pose direct and indirect challenges to the foreign policy decission making as a process and mechanism of both political and social construction. The migrant communities might directly find place in the decission making through migrant MP's, advisors, ministers or undersecretary at various levels of the state bureaucracy, or the migrant NGO's and lobby groups might succeed in negotiating and promoting their identity, norms and interest at various levels of foreign policy decission-making mechanism. On the other hand, even the mere socio-political presence and historical knowledge and perception of a certain migrant community and its approach and narratives on a certain foreign policy issue might pose indirect challenges to the foreign policy decission making process. Unquestionably, politicaly organised migrant communities tend to find higher representation and influence in the foreign policy perceptions and narratives.

As a target country of multiethnic immigration and population exchange Turkey constitutes valuable case to examine the role of multhiethnic migrant communities in the constitution of foreign policy perceptions and practices. Turkey has been one of the prime courses of immigration from Yugoslavian lands since the 19th century. Based on common preconditions of religious (Islam) and cultural (Ottoman) belonging most of the Yugoslavian immigrations contained multiethnic character represented by immigrants of Albanian, Bosnian, Sanjak, Torbesh and Turkish origin. Under the circumstances of the post-Cold War Balkans and the spread of the ethnic conflicts and ethnic nationalism in the region, these immigrant communities have emerged as significant social actors in the constitution of Turkey's foreign policy in the Balkans.

Especially the post-Cold War conflicts in Kosovo, the minority issue in Macedonia and the financial and political crises in Albania proved sensitive focal points for regional engagement in the Turkey's regional policy in the Balkans. Weaving deep historical and social ties with the so called 'Albanian hinterland', the Albanian immigration to Turkey left deep political, ethnic, religious and societal consequences in the ethnopolitical constitution of the Turkish society and social construction of Turkey's Balkan policy. The following study tracks the historical formation and political organisation of the Albanian community in Turkey and aim to explore the interaction and linkage between the political organisation of the Albanian community in Turkey and Turkey's foreign policy decision making in regard to the Albanian issue in the Balkans. The question is to what extent and how, in what ways the Albanian community in Turkey could influence Turkey's position and foreign policy decissions regarding important issues in the Balkans, such as the war and independence in Kosovo and the crisises in Macedonia and Albania. Such a question would require examination of four important issues:

- the historical and socio-political background of the Albanian community in Turkey,
- the basic patterns of political organisation of the Albanian community in Turkey
- the basic perceptions and expectations of the Albanian immigrants in regard to the Albanian issue in the Balkans
- the main factors that defined Turkey's response and its manner of accomodation to this transnational social actor in its policy towards the 'Albanian issues' in the Balkans.

Historical Formation of the Albanian Community in Turkey

Albanian community in Turkey shares a centuries long history that extends to the early Ottoman times. There are numerous studies about the Albanian roots of famous Ottoman statesmen (Hüseyin Avni Paşa, Esat Paşa Toptani, Hasan Prişhtina), officers (Mareşal Fevzi Çakmak), writers (Şemsettin Sami, İsmail Kemal), poets (Mehmet Akif Ersoy, Namık Kemal), actors and painters/architects (Mimar Sinan, Abidin Dino), founders of the Turkish football clubs (Ali Sami Yen, Ali Naci) who left significant contribution in the political, military and cultural history of the Ottoman Empire.[1]

The establishment of the Turkish Republic opened a new era in the identity formation and political and cultural life of the Albanians in Turkey. Beside the historically established and widely-known perception of 'Turkish-Albanian brotherhood', the nation-state building policies in Turkey, Yugoslavia (Kingdom of Serbs, Croats and Slovenes), Greece and Albania had defined the minority and migrant identity of the Albanian community in Turkey. Thus, the Albanian migrations to Turkey and their demographic and socio-political background is a direct product of nationalist demography and historiography in the involved countries.

Albanian immigration in the interwar years

The recent migration history of the Albanians in Turkey begins with the interwar nationalist policies in the Balkans. There are two major routes of Albanian flows to the Anatolian lands in the interwar perriod. One comes from the Northern Greece, and the other starts from the Kingdom of Serbs, Croats and Slovenes. The Albanian immigration from Northern Greece occured under the population exchange that followed the signing of the Treaty of Laussane in 1923. The treaty devised an exchange of the Muslim population from Chamuria, Aegean Macedonia and some Greek Islands and left out the Turkish speaking Muslim population of West Thrace region. Under the population exchange Turkey received 475.000 Muslim immigrants. According to the Albanian sources most part of these exchangees are Albanian-speaking Muslims from Chamuria, called in Albanian as *Çames,* i.e. Chams. According to Hivzi İslami,

---

[1] İbrahim Hoxha, *Turqit dhe Shiptaret,* Tiran, 1994, p. 26-57; Gilles de Rapper, *Les Albanais a İstanbul,* Istanbul, IFEA, 2000, s.17-18.

there were 200.000 Cham people among the Laussane exchangees from Greece.[2] The Turkey's first official census of 1927 indicate 21.774 Albanian-speaking people who reside mainly in İstanbul, İzmir, Ankara and Bursa.[3] This number involves both the Albanian-speaking exchangees from Chamuria and the Albanian refugees who escaped the Kingdom of Serbs, Croats, Slovenes after 1919 and ended up in Turkey after the War of Independence. So what was the number of the Albanian-speaking exchangees and what is the number of the Çam Albanians in Turkey today are two controversial issues.[4] There is not available official data about the ethnic background of Turkey's population, as well as the socio-cultural, economic and political life of the ethnic communities residing in the country. Thus, the main sources of data are the civil organisations of these communities. According to the Albanian Brotherhood Association during the interwar years in 1924-1925 Turkey received 60.000-80.000 Cham Albanians. Today they constitute 10-15 % of the approximated 3.000.000 Albanians in Turkey today.[5]

After the first census there is an increase in the Albanian-speaking population in Turkey. This increase is due to the interwar Muslim immigration from the Kingdom of Serbs, Croats, Slovenes and the Kingdom of Yugoslavia.

---

[2]Hivzi İslami, *Rrjedha Demografike Shqiptare*, Pejë, Dukagnjini, 1994, p. 173-178.
[3]Fuat Dündar, *Nüfus Sayımlarında Türkiye'de Azınlıklar*, İstanbul, Doz Yayınları, 1999, p.81-2.
[4]See more at: Nurcan Özgür Baklacıoğlu, *Dış Politika ve Göç: Yugoslavya'dan Türkiye'ye Göçlerde Arnavutlar 1918-1980*, İstanbul: Derin Yayınları, 2010.
[5]Personal interview with the Secretary of the Albanian Brotherhood Association *Kamil Bitiş*, İstanbul, October 29, 2010.

The Yugoslav Immigrants according to the Turkish Censuses
Table1/a

	1927		1935	
Languages	**Mother Tongue**	**2.Lang.**	**Mother Tongue**	**2.Lang.**
Albanian	21.774	–	22.754	26.161
Bosnian	7.450[2]*	–	24.613	13.526
Serbian	–	–	4.369	–
Total Languages	29.224	–	51.736	39.687
Total	**29.224**		**91.425**	

* The Bosnian language is not available as a minority language category at the census of 1927.

Table1/b[6]

	1945		1950	
Languages	**Mother Tongue**	**2.Lang.**	**Mother Tongue**	**2.Lang.**
Albanian	14.165	17.701	16.079	–
Bosnian	13.280	9.599	24.013	–
Serbian	4.100	–	1.605	–
Total Languages	31.545	27.300	41.697	–
Total	**58.845**		**41.697**	

Source:[7]

Indeed, the interwar years constitute one of the most turbulent period in the migration history of Albanians in the Balkans. The interwar nation-building and the so called *kolonizatsia* of the Muslim lands and the nationalist land reform in the so called 'South Serbia' region forced thousands of Muslim landlords and peasants from Kosovo, Montenegro, Sandjak and Macedonia in search for refugee in the newly establishing Turkish Republic.[8] The data of the Yugoslav Ministry of Foreign Affairs registered 255.878 declarations for emigration to Turkey between 1919 and 1940. (See Table 2)

---

[6]There is not available data on the second language during 1950.
[7]Fuat Dündar, *Nüfus Sayımlarında Türkiye'de Azınlıklar*, İstanbul, Doz Yayınları, 1999.
[8]Nurcan Özgür Baklacıoğlu, *Dış Politika ve Göç…*

Table 2: Emigrants who left South Serbia on the basis of emigration to Turkey[9]

Year	Emigrants	Year	Emigrants
1919	23.500	1930	13.215
1920	8.536	1931	29.807
1921	24.532	1932	6.219
1922	12.307	1933	3.420
1923	6.389	1934	4.500
1924	9.630	1935	9.567
1925	4.315	1936	4.252
1926	4.012	1937	4.234
1927	5.197	1938	7.251
1928	4.326	1939	7.255
1929	6.219	1940	6.729
Total			**255.878**

As classified by Cevat Giray, the number of the settled and unsetled immigrants from the lands of the Kingdom of Yugoslavia who arrived and registered in the Turkish Residence and Immigration Registry between 1923 and 1940 amounts to 116.487.

Table 3: Interwar Migrations from Yugoslavian Lands to Turkey[10]

Year	Settled Migrants		Individual Migrants**	
	Family	People	Family	People
1923–33	–	–	26.120	108.179
1934	614	2.569	199	650
1935	783	3.129	109	360
1936	24	97	49	153
1937	3	17	12	48
1938	–	–	18	71
1939	20	61	23	93
1940	5	21	274	1.039
Total	**1.449**	**5.894**	**26.804**	**110.593**
			General Total 116.487	

**Cevat Geray counted the number of the families based on the average family size between years 1933-1960.

---

[9]Instituti i Historisë i Kosovës ed., *Dëbimet e Shqiptarëve dhe Kolonizimi i Kosovës 1877-1995*, Prishtinë, QIK, 1997, p.42.

[10]Cevat Geray, Appendix Tables

This difference in the emigration and immigration numbers has various reasons.[11] It is also difficult to find out the number of the Albanian immigrants since all are registered as immigrants from Yugoslavia. However, as the Albanian sources insist, the deep-rooted family networks and the memory of cultural and historical belonging to the Ottoman society draw thousands of Albanian-speaking Muslims to the Anatolian lands. Based primarily on the sources of the Belgrad Archives, the Albanian sources point out to 240.000 Albanians from Southern Serbia who moved to Turkey during the interwar years.12 This number is based on the fundamental assumption of the Albanian historical demography that claims that all Muslims in the South Serbian territory, i.e. Kosovo, Macedonia and Sancak have Albanian origin. However, the second official census held in Turkey in 1935 registered 22.754 Albanian native-speakers and 26.161 people who use to speak Albanian as a second language.13 There were 38.139 Turkish citizens who declared the Bosnian language as a native or second language (See Table 1). This data shows that the interwar immigrations from the Yugoslav lands brought significant number of Albanian-speaking population, thus had fundamental impact on the formation of the Albanian community in Turkey. Most of these forced migrants were registered as national refugees with access to state assistance and appointed residence in Anatolia.14 The Ataturk-initiated migration agreement of 1938 aimed at inclusive compensation of their confiscated property, but the death of Atatürk and the World War II interrupted the process.

---

[11]See details at: Nurcan Özgür Baklacıoğlu, 'Savaşarası Dönemde Yugoslavya Krallığından Türkiye'ye Arnavut Göçleri 1919-1935', Köprüler Kurduk Balkanlara, Istanbul:İBB, 2008, p.55-70.

[12]Hivzi Islami, *Rrjedha Demografike Shqiptare*, Peje: Dukagjini, 1994, p.194.

[13]Fuat Dündar, p.124-128.

[14]The immigrants from South Serbia and Bosnia are named 'refugees under state residence assistance. See: 'İzmir'de mukim Yenipazarlı Hüseyin ve kardeşlerinin vilayet dahilinde müteci sıfatıyla iskan ve iaşeleri', *BCA,* Fon: 272.0.0.12,Yer: 44.69..10, 8.04.1925; 'Manastır muhacirlerinden Ahmet oğlu Ramiz'in mülteci sıfatıyla İzmir'e nüfusa kayıt ve tescil edilerek iskanının yapılması', *BCA*, Fon: 272.0.0.12,Yer: 44.69..8, 8.04.1925; 'Sırbistan mültecilerinden Ramazan, Hüseyin, Şaban, Aydın, Cemal, Abbas ve Ragıp adlı şahısların Konya ilinde iskan edilmelerinin uygun olduğu..', *BCA*, Fon Kodu: 272..0.0.12,Yer No: 45.73..14, 20.06.1925.

Albanian Immigration after the Second World War

The first afterwar Albanian immigration took place between 1945-1947. Turkey provided protection to political refugees from Albania. Most of these refugees were Hoxha opponents, old Zogists, or members of the Balli Kombetare and/or Albanian National Democratic Organisation-ONDSH.[15] According to Hasani, in prividing asylum to these political refugees Turkey turned into one of the Albanian anti-Yugoslav propaganda centers. The Albanian consulates in France, Eastern Germany, Poland, Bulgaria and Turkey used to collaborate with the nationalist Albanian migrants from SFR of Yugoslavia who live in these countries.[16] Indeed, according to Sabile Keçmezi, some of the ONDSH members such as Gjon Serreqi, Halim Orana, Hysni Rudi and Hamdi Berisha had close contact with the British, French, U.S.A. and Turkish ambasade in Skopje.[17] Some of these refugees, such as General Cemal Araniti, Tahsin Strazimiri, Cevat Fişta, Hasan Koloşi took place as founders of the Albanian Brotherhood Association, the first Albanian association established in the time of the Turkish Republic.

Table 4: Postwar Balkan Immigration to Turkey

Years	Yugoslavia	Romania	Greece	Bulgaria
1946–1960	152.003	55	23.808	154.112
1961–1970	30.502	274	2.081	15.000
1971–1980	1.797	136	–	116.104
1981–1990	2.623	760	–	178.664***
1993–1997	–	–	–	77.000
Total	**186.925**	**1.225**	**25.889**	**540.880**
General Total	**754.919**			

Source[18]

***The number does not involve 133.272 returnees that left Turkey after 1990

---

[15] Şerafettin Yücelden, 'Yugoslavya Türkleri', *Türk Dünyası El Kitabı,* Ankara, Türk Kültürünü Araştırma Enstitüsü, 1969, p.1095

[16] Sinan Hasani, 'Šovinističke i Separatističke Organizacije na Kosovu i Njihova Povezanost sa İnostranim Centrima', *Kosovo, Prošlost i Sadašnost,* Beograd, Medunarodna Politika, 1989, p.213.

[17] Sebile Keçmezi-Basha, *Lëvizja Ilegale Patriotike Shqiptare në Kosovë 1945-1947,* Prishtinë, Rilindja, 1998, p. 26 ve 34.

[18] Kemal Kirişçi, 'Post Second World War Immigration from the Balkan Countries to Turkey', Foundation for Middle East and Balkan Studies ed., *Turkish Review*

The third great flow of Albanian immigrants to Turkey took place during the Cold War. The establishment of the Socialist Federation of Yugoslavia followed by tremendous ideological and political reforms in the socio-economic and cultural life of the Albanian community in Kosovo. The nationalisation of the private land and agricultural technology, the cultural reforms that required change in the manner of dressing, atheist propaganda, and the harsh disarmamanet of Albanians in Kosovo during the Rankoviç rule resulted in widespread uprisings, forceful seizure and arrests among the Albanian and Muslim community in the province. The Rankoviç rule set up the conditions of the last considerable Albanian immigration to Turkey.

Between years 1955-1965 many Kosovar Albanians moved to Macedonia in order to get immigration visa for Turkey. Some of them succeeded in emigration to Turkey, some of them not. Since the Turkish visa was available only for the Macedonian Turks, both the migration agreement of 1953 and the available official data categorizes the migrants from Yugoslavia as Turkish. This perception is widespread among Kosovar and Macedonian, or shortly Roumelian community in Turkey as well. Almost all 20 Istanbul-based Roumelian Associations and Foundations in Turkey reject any Albanian affiliation and do not define themselves as Albanians. There are only two Kosovar associations that accomodate the Albanian identity among their members (Kosovo Association and Prishtina Immigrants Association) and two Albanian asssociations that are purely based on and emphasize their Albanian identity, the Albanian Brotherhood Association and the Sakarya Albanian Cultural and Solidarity Association.[19]

The number of the Cold War Albanian immigrants from Kosovo and Macedonia is controversial. According to the Yugoslav sources the number of the Yugoslav emigrants who left Kosovo and Macedonia between 1953 and 1958 is 120.000.[20] (Table 5)

---

of Balkan Studies, 1994/95, Nr 2, Istanbul, ISIS, 1995, p. 175-80; and Bilal Şimşir, *Bulgaristan Türkleri 1878-1985*, Istanbul, Bilgi, 1986.

[19] Personal visits and interviews carried out among 8 associations during 2004 and 2010.

[20] Branko Horvat, p.94; Vladimir Ortakovski, p.326

Table 5: The Intensive Years of Immigration from Yugoslavia[21]

Year	Number of Immigrants
1955	20.076
1956	35.369
1957	32.680
1958	32.539
1959	20.612
1960	14.722
Total	**155.998**

The Turkish official sources count 155.998 Yugoslav immigrants who arrived in Turkey between 1955 and 1960 (See Table 5). Indeed, the Ministry of Village Affairs provides monthly data about the Yugoslav immigrants who arrived in Turkey between 1952 and 1967. Accordingly the Ministry registered 175.392 immigrants from Yugoslavia.[22] The highest number is suggested by the Albanian historiograph Hakif Bajrami. According to him the Albanian nationality in Yugoslavia had lost 450.821 emigrants who moved to Turkey between years 1953 and 1966.[23] Another Albanian demograph Pajazit Nushi argues that this migration wave lasted until 1972 and brought 246.108 Yugoslav Albanians to Turkey.[24] According to the Albanian sources the 75 percent of the Yugoslav immigrants were of Albanian origin.[25]

The official Turkish census data shows that between years 1950 and 1965 the Albanian speaking population increased from 16.079 to 53.520 where only 12.832 of the respondents declared Albanian as their mother tongue. (Table 6)

---

[21]Counted on the basis of Table 2. See: Cevat Geray, *Türk İktisadi Gelişme Projesi, Türkiye'den ve Türkiye'ye Göçler ve Göçmenlerin İskanı 1923-1961*, Ankara, SBF Maliye Enstitüsü,1962, p.7, Table 2.

[22]Cevat Geray, See: Appendix Tables

[23]Hakif Bajrami, Shpërngulja e Shqiptarëve prej Trojeve…

[24]Sevdije Shehu, Ferit Shehu: *Pastrimet Etnike të Trojeve Shqiptare 1953-1957*, Prishtinë, 1993, p.30

[25]Sevdije Shehu, Ferit Shehu, p.31.

Table 6: Language Census Data on Cold War Immigrants from Yugoslavia

	1950	1955	
Languages	**Mother Tongue**	**Mother Tongue**	**2.Lang**
Albanian	16.079	10.893	25.898
Total	**16.079**	**36.791**	
Bosnian	24.013	11.844	13.908
Total	**24.013**	**25.752**	
Serbian	1.605	4.654	28.961
Total	**1.605**	**33.615**	
Total Yugoslav Immigrants	**41.697**	**96.158**	

	1960		1965	
Languages	**Mother Tongue**	**2.Lang**	**Mother Tongue**	**2.Lang**
Albanian	12.025	37.144	12.832	40.688
Total	**49.144**		**53.520**	
Bosnian	14.570	37.526	17.627	37.237
Total	**52.096**		**54.864**	
Serbian	7.386	55.473	6.599	59.578
Total	**62.859**		**66.177**	
Total Yugoslav Immigrants	**164.124**		**174.561**	

According to the Turkish census of 1965 there were 53.520 Albanian-speaking, 54.864 Bosnian-speaking and 66.177 Serbian speaking immigrants among the registered 174.561 Yugoslav immigrants in Turkey. Presumably, most of the registered immigrants declared their mother language as Turkish, some others did not attend the census at all, and others concealed their mother and second languages. There is not available data about the Yugoslavian immigrants who left for Germany after the sign of the Worker Exchange Agreement of 1967, however, the Roumelian, Bosnian, Sandjak and Albanian associations there are sign of a considerable emigration of Yugoslav immigrants to Germany.[26] The Albanian immigrants of 1950's and 1960's have gathered in provinces such as Bursa, Ankara, İstanbul, Sakarya, Samsun, Tokat and İzmir. (Table 7)

---

[26]There is a wide community of Turkish migrants of Bosnian, Sandjak and Albanian origin in Frankfurt. Interview with the Board members of the Association of Sandjak Turks in Frankfurt, November 2000.

Table 7: The distribution of the Albanian Speaking Population[27]

Province	1927	1935	131945	1950	1955	1960	1965
Adana	136	–	–	–	–	119	483
A.Karahisar	35	5	4	–	–	182	2
Ağrı	–	10	4	–	–	3	–
Amasya	389	334	352	335	17	290	336
Ankara	742	588	477	336	222	207	833
Aydın	503	873	193	730	159	49	219
Balıkesir	307	340	108	105	67	66	39
Bilecik	174	121	134	15	17	16	4
Bolu	115	14	99	78	35	33	8
Bursa	1,181	1,344	516	667	549	2,315	1,928
C.Bereket	389	–	–	–	–	–	–
Çanakkale	321	177	111	48	33	20	6
Denizli	–	–	10	7	1	1	3
Diyarbakır	5	18	–	9	3	4	5
Edirne	239	198	74	323	140	87	58
Elaziz/ğ	26	484	432	281	113	12	2
Eskişehir	261	391	178	137	114	104	78
Gaziantep	268	132	51	29	17	5	11
Hatay	–	–	13	87	106	23	44
İstanbul	6,148	6,722	4,305	3,081	3,106	4,223	4,341
İzmir	2,260	2,328	1,340	1,129	1,085	691	1,265
Kayseri	748	278	84	55	442	59	160
Kırklareli	693	667	153	386	128	276	144
Kocaeli	506	1,236	973	1,451	44	42	22
Konya	737	229	132	27	56	71	75
Kütahya	269	72	146	123	41	47	34
Manisa	783	2,011	903	1,406	187	294	192
Maraş	170	143	139	15	21	28	9

---

[27]Fuat Dündar, Appendixes

Mardin	49	4	–	5	2	–	6
Muğla	163	7	75	14	12	4	–
Nevşehir	–	–	–	–	118	59	53
Niğde	1,009	20	182	316	11	15	4
Sakarya	–	–	–	–	436	850	794
Samsun	849	1,726	1,291	2,667	1,549	765	610
Seyhan		590	164	928	283	–	–
Sinop	220	241	77	126	27	15	7
Sivas	1	38	13	5	3	13	–
Tekirdağ	435	544	237	241	189	175	51
Tokat	359	83	568	320	805	734	694
Urfa	–	–	–	473	1	1	–
Yozgat	998	642	536	21	503	77	1
Zonguldak	63	75	12	5	7	4	1

The final considerable immigration of Albanian population in Turkey found place during the war in Kosovo in 1998-1999. As a signatory of 1951 Geneva Convention Turkey provided protection to 17.746 registered Kosovo refugees.[28] Almost all of these refugees were accomodated under temporary protection status *refugees en mass* in a refugee camp in Kırklareli. There were also some refugees that found accomodation and assistance through their family networks in Turkey. It is important to notice that most of the Albanian refugees in Macedonia and Kosovo objected to be sent to Turkey, instead they gave preference to be accomodated in Germany, Sweden, Switzerland, Canada, the U.S.A. and Australia.[29] Almost all of the aforementoned refugees returned to Kosovo after June 1999. Most of these refugees had family networks with Albanians in Germany, Sweden, Canada etc. For difference from the previous refugees these refugees had clearly established notion of motherland that was related to Kosovo, instead of Turkey. There is not

---

[28] *İltica ve Göç Alanındaki Avrupa Birliği Müktesebatının Üstlenilmesine İlişkin Türkiye Ulusal Eylem Planı*, Source: www.egm.gov.tr; Mahir Gümüş, 'Türkiye'nin İltica ve Göç Alanındaki Yol Haritası: İltica ve Göç Alanındaki Avrupa Birliği Müktesebatının Üstlenilmesine İlişkin Türkiye Ulusal Eylem Planı', *Stratejik Gündem*, USAK, t.y., s.14, Source: www.usakgundem.com

[29] Personal observations from a fieldwork at the Blatze and Stankovets camps in Macedonia during the Kosovo war in April-May 1999.

available data about the Kosovo refugees who settled in Turkey after
the war, but the Kosovar refugees who stood at the Kırklareli camp all
returned to Kosovo. There is data about some Kosovar refugees of Turkish
origin that remained in Turkey on the ground that there is an ongoing
assimilation and discrimination against Turkish minority in Kosovo.

Today there is not available official data about the recent Albanian
population in Turkey. The political sources cite diverse numbers that
vary from 1-2 million Kosovars[30] to 5-6 million Albanians, cited by
the Albanian sources. The fieldworks, the numbers and identification
choices among the immigrants organised under the Kosovo,
Macedonian, Bosnian, Sandjak and Roumelian associations show that
the number of the immigrants who identify themselves as Roumeli,
Kosovo, Macedonia, Bosnian and Sandjak immigrants are much higher
(represented by more than 30 associations and foundations) than the
ones who identify themselves as Albanian immigrants. There are only
two Albanian associations with two branches that place emphasis on
their Albanian origin. Indeed, the main concern of these associations is
the fact that instead of their Albanian roots, the most of the immigrants
from Yugoslavia feel and express themselves as Turks, even in the cases
when there is a known Albanian root in their family. Confirmed by the
Albanian associations, the interest of the Albanian immigrants in the
Albanian language and politics is very low.[31]

Political and socio-cultural organisation of the Albanian Community in Turkey

The recent political and socio-cultural organisation of the Albanian
community in Turkey bases on the demographic, socio-cultural, economic
and political characteristics of the Albanian immigrants from Kosovo,
Macedonia and Albania. Most of the immigrants who came during
the Cold War established in cities already known for their tradition of
immigration from Yugoslavia. According to Fuat Dündar, %69.5 of the
native Albanian speakers live in cities, while %61.3 of the immigrants

---

[30]"Deputy of Kırıkkale Osman Durmuş's talk on his Kosovo visit', *TBMM Genel
Kurul Tutanağı*, 23. Dönem, 3. Yasama Yılı, 82. Birleşim, 28 Nisan 2009.

[31]Personal interview with the General Secretary of the Albanian Brotherhood
Association Kamil Bitiş, immigrant from Macedonia who studied at the University
of Prishtina during 1970s and 1980's. (İstanbul, Bayrampaşa, October 29, 2010).

whose second language is Albanian live in the rural areas. According to the socio-economic statistics of the Institute of Statistics of SFRJ, %85 of the Kosovo population in 1948 lived in the rural areas and was involved in the agricultural sector. Similarly %62,5 of the total population, %47 of the men, %78,4 of the woman was illiterate.[32] In 1948 the Albanians constituted %68,5 of the Kosovo population, %71,2 of the agricultural population, %70,8 of the craftsman and merchants, %61,9 of the workers and 38% of the state workers in Kosovo.[33] Most of the immigrants lost their lands and properties during their emigration to Turkey.[34] The tradition of craftsmanship and commerce stil keeps its priority among Albanian and Yugoslav immigrants in Turkey.[35] Their ideological background was based on religious conservatizm pronounced in the phrase 'Elhamdülillah Türküm' (Thank Allah, I am Turkish). Most of the Yugoslav immigrants were conservative Muslims with anti-communist feelings, favoring private proprietorship and private enterprice. The azan and the flag were expressed as important symbols of their national identity during the process of immigration.

The common religion and the ties of the Ottoman culture and the historical and family networks facilitated the adaptation of the Albanian immigrants in the Turkish society. Under the perspective of the national opposition to communist/atheist threats to the Turkey's national security, the Yugoslav and Albanian immigrants were conservative democrats close to the ideology of the Menderes's Democratic Party. Moreover, as defined by Oğuz Arı, the condition of the peasantry, the common class position, the importance of education, the mosque, the Roumelian songs and culinary constituted the main common patterns that brought together the 'migrant' and the 'local' in Turkey.[36] The traditional belief in the founding role of the Albanian viziers and intellectuals throughout the Ottoman-Turkish history has defining impact on the Albanian identity

---

[32]Asllan Pushka, 'Промене у Социјално-Класној и Социјално-Националној Структури Становништва Косова", Демографски, Социјални и Економски Аспекти на Работната Сила и Вработеноста, Скопје, Македонска Академија на Науките, 1991, p.179.

[33]Asllan Pushka, p.186-187.

[34]Hakif Bajrami, 'Shpërngulja e Shqiptarëve prej Trojeve...', p. 271-272.

[35]Sevdije dhe Ferit Shehu, p. 49-54.

[36]Oğuz Arı, a.g.e., s.21.

in Turkey.[37] For example the Albanian roots of the the Turkish National Anthem writer Mehmet Akif Ersoy, the founder of the Turkish republic Mustafa Kemal Atatürk,[38] the founder of the Istanbul University Hasan Hoca Tahsin constitute only few of the highest symbols that rise the Albanian identity as a founding, superior and modernizing pattern and dynamic of the Turkish one.[39] This is the Albanian perception of the frequently declared Albanian-Turkish brotherhood, that is especially vivid in the relations between King Zog and Atatürk in the past, and Thaqi and Erdoğan in 2009. Some books and images from the 1950's and 60's talk about a temporary revival of the Albanian traces in the Turkish cultural life. The figure of the Albanian Karagöz painted by Mehmet Muhittin Sevilen in 1957 represents one of them.[40] The performance of the 'Albanian Recep: Word One, Allah One' at the Istanbul Art Theater[41], 'The Albanian Khan, 1971' written by Ümit Serdaroğlu,[42] The Birth of the Albanian Alphabet in the light of The Albanology, written in 1979 by Necip Alpan are some of the works that followed the postwar Yugoslav immigration.[43]

The centre of the Albanian social and cultural life at that time is the Turkish-Albanian Brotherhood Association established in 1952 by a Balli Kombetar member General Cemal Araniti, Albanian merchant Cevat Fişta and Hasan Kaloşi, a merchant born in Debra. The other founders are the former director of the Vardar newspaper Şemsettin Davutoğlu, Musa Şen and Tahsin Strazimiri from Debra. According to the Association Charter, the Association aims at improving solidarity, brotherhood and friendship between the Albanian immigrants and Turks.[44] After the cop of September 12, the word 'Türk' had been forbidden and removed from the names of the NGO's. Thus the name of the association turned into Albanian Brotherhood Association, that has a rather different meaning

---

[37]Sevdije dhe Ferit Shehu, p. 54.

[38]Gilles de Rapper, *Les Albanais a Istanbul*, Istanbul, IFEA, 2000, p.17-18.

[39]İbrahim Hoxha, *Turqit dhe Shiptaret*, Tiran, 1994, p. 26-57;

[40]Mehmet Nuhittin Sevilen, 'Arnavut', T.C. Milli Kütüphane ed, *Hacıvat-Karagöz Tiplemeleri Arşivi*, Ankara, 1957.

[41]İstanbul Sanat Tiyatrosu, *Arnavut Recep: Söz Bir Allah Bir*, afiş, İstanbul, t.y..

[42]Ümit Serdaroğlu, *Ağın-Kemaliye yolu Üzerindeki Arnavut Hanı*, Ankara, 1971.

[43]Necip Alpan, *Albanolojinin Işığında: Arnavut Alfabesi Nasıl Doğdu,* Ankara, 1979.

[44]*Türk-Arnavut Kardeşliği Kültür ve Dayanışma Derneği Tüzüğü*, İstanbul, Gayret Matbaası, 1971, s.1.

that calls for brotherhood among the Albanians, rather than Turks and Albanians. According to association representatives this change in the name has not changed the founding goal of the association. According to Şefik Aksoy, the primary goal of the association is to revive the Albanian identity through cultural meetings and activities and strenghten the brotherhood and friendship relations with Turkish people, thus to establish close ties between the two states and nations.[45]

According to Nafije Raqipovski, the isolationist Albanian foreign policy facilitated the assimilation of the Albanian community in Turkey. Thus until the end of the Cold War post-1960's Turkish-Yugoslavian relations provided the main ground for the development of the Albanian identity in Turkey. After the shift of Hoxha's ban on the travel of Albanian citizens abroad in 1966 the Albanian, Macedonian and Turkish literature from Albania and Yugoslavia started to enter the libraries in Turkey. Among this literature there are books about the sosyo-political developments in Yugoslavia,[46] the program of the Communist Party of Yugoslavia, the *Yugoslav Survey*, the history of the Macedonian nation,[47] the Albanian Alphabet and some Yugoslav studies on *Orientalizm*.[48] Beside these sources, since 1955 until 1980 an Albanian migrant from Italy, Vasil Antoni, provided regular acquisition of the 'Besa' newspaper, later followed by a short-lived local journal 'Besa' that could print out only few journals during 1990's. Today there is not available local journal or newspaper in Albanian language in Turkey.

After the end of the Cold War opportunities to acquire Albanian literature from Kosovo, Albania and Macedonia widened, however, the issue of 'shifting identity' stood as the most defining factor in the socio-cultural and political organisation of the Albanian community in the 1990's. The rise of the minority discourse brought the issue of identity of Yugoslavian immigrants in Turkey to the agenda of the Yugoslav immigrant community in Turkey. While the Roumeli Associations put emphasis on the common Rumeli

[45]Sevdije dhe Ferit Shehu, p. 58-60.

[46]Zvonko Spaleta, *The Liberation Struggle of the Yugoslav People 1941-1945*, Beograd, 1961; Jose Smole, *Yugoslav Views on Coexistence*, Beograd, 1961; *Historical Atlas of the Liberation War of the Peoples of Yugoslavya, 1941-1945*, Beograd, 1957.

[47]Aleksandar Stojanoski, *The Foreign and Yugoslav Historiography on Macedonia and the Macedonian People, post-war Turkish Literature on Macedonian History*, Skopje, Institute of National History, 1970.

[48]Bisera Nuridinoviç, *Bibliografija Jugoslavenske Orientalistike 1945-1960*, Sarajevo, Orientalni Institut, 1968.

identity that unites all Muslim immigrants as Evlad-ı Fatihan who left the sacred Şark-i Rumeli lands, the Albanian association emphasized the Albanian roots of the Yugoslav immigrants in Turkey.[49]

The conflicts in Kosovo and Macedonia did not lead to a 'rebirth' in the Albanian identity among the immigrants from Kosovo and Macedonia in Turkey. According to the association managers today there are not much immigrants that know Albanian or are interested in following any Albanian journals or literature. Indeed, the fate of the only shortlived Albanian journal Besa was determined by this low interest that led to financial dificulties and shutdown in 1996. By 2010 the association had only 4-5 irregular students attending the Albanian language course in the only association office in Küçük Çekmece, Istanbul. Most of the Board members do not know literary Albanian. Four of the board members of the association, graduate of Prishtina University, carry on the fundamental national, historical and cultural discourse of the Albanian brotherhood in the association. They conduct free Albanian language courses in the association centre in Küçükçekmece and in the Municipality Cultural Center of Bayrampaşa.

The regime change in Albania brought opportunity for mutual visits and exchange between the Albanian community in Turkey and Albania. However this exchange did not prove longstanding. Depending primarily on the personal contacts of the association leaders, the Albanian Brotherhood Association failed to institutionalize durable relations with parties and NGO's from Albania, Kosovo, Macedonia or elsewhere. According to the chiefs of the Albanian Brotherhood Association, today they do not have long standing links with NGO's in Albania, instead, they try to keep contact with the Albanian governments. However, this contact seems limited with mutual invitations and visits to Albanian national days and festivities. The Office of the Albanian Diaspora at the Albanian Foreign Ministry and the diaspora-supported Berisha government appears as the main contact point for the chiefs of the Association. The bilateral personal contacts with leaders and parties on power in Kosovo has moved much forward during the last years. This is because for difference from the founders of the association, most of the recent administrators and members are Albanian immigrants from Kosovo and Macedonia. As a

[49]Nurcan Özgür Baklacıoğlu, 'Türkiye'nin Balkan Politikasında Rumeli ve Balkan Göçmen Dernekleri', der. Semra Cerit Mazlum ve Erhan Doğan, *Sivil Toplum ve Dış Politika,* 77-117, Bağlam Yayınları, Istanbul, 2006

result of this membership composition the conflict in Kosovo since 1981 have had immense impact on the agenda of the Association. That is why, for difference from the associations of the Roumeli and Balkan migrants the Albanian Brotherhood Association gives priority to ethno-political activities that often transcend the Turkish borders. The conflict in Kosovo and the personal contacs with the Thachi administration brought particular transnational activity in the agenda of the Association.[50] Along with the war in Kosovo, the number of the members increased and the activities shifted from culture-based[51] festivities to political and economic lobbying and propaganda. Today, despite the low membership and low political profile, the Association shows close interest to the politics in Kosovo.

Turkey's Balkan Policy on the Agenda of the Albanian Community in Turkey

The political life of the Albanian community in Turkey has its historical roots that define the ground of the continuity or change in the Albanian politics in the agenda of the Turkey's Balkan Policy.

Short history of the Albanian migrant politics within the framework of the Turkish- Albanian Relations

The recent Albanian politics in the Turkey's history goes back to the last years of the Ottoman Empire. The Istanbul, Bucarest and Sofia based Albanian solidarity and unity associations, i.e. the so called Albanian Solidarity Society (Arnavut Teavün Cemiyeti) and the Bashkim Clubs constituted the main platform in the struggle for '*the annexation of the Albanian lands to the motherland Albania*' during 1919-1920.[52] The proclamation of the Kingdom of the Zog followed by close approach between Italy and Albania during the interwar perriod found negative reflection in the bilateral relations between Tirana and Ankara, however, it did not end up the existence of Albanian associations in Turkey.

---

[50]Sevdije dhe Ferit Shehu, p. 54.

[51]Alexandre Toumarkine, 'Kafkas ve Balkan Göçmen Dernekleri: Sivil Toplum ve Milliyetçilik', Stefanos Yerasimos, Günter Seufert at all, *Türkiye'de Sivil Toplum ve Milliyetçilik*, İstanbul, İletişim, 2000, p. 426-427.

[52]Tarık Zafer Tunaya, *Türkiye'de Siyasi Partiler 1859-1952*, İstanbul, Arba Yayınları, 1995, p.317, 395-396, 751-752.

The historical presence of the Albanian immigrants in Turkey's Balkan politics after the WWII closely depends on the Cold War mode of the bilateral relations between Albania and Turkey. Fifteen years after the shutdown of the Turkey's Embassy in Tirana, Turkey supported Albania's membership in the UN in 1955. This unilateral act did not mean a certain desire for closer bilateral realtions with the Hoxha regime, instead, the Hoxha's anti-Turkish propaganda among the Albanians in Kosovo, Macedonia and Albania continued to rise discontent among the Turkish decission makers. Yet, Turkey's diplomatic gesture rised the Tirana's interest in further approach to Turkey that found expression in Tirana's remarks on the '...*high desire to reestablish bilateral relations with Turkey...*' based on '...*the 500 years long common history of social and historical unity...*'. This short connotation on the social links, i.e. Albanian presence in Turkey was followed by Sofia's in November 28, 1956 dated diplomatic note to Ankara under formal request for protection of the 'Albanian interests' in Turkey.[53] According to Bilal Şimşir, the 'Albanian interests' here connotates the rights of the Albanian citizens in Turkey and in fact gives hints for Tirana's desire for close relations with Turkey. Yet, it is not easy to judge in this way, since the Albanian citizens in Turkey at that time are in fact anti-Hoxha, i.e. Zogist political refugees and followers of the Abbas Kupi ve Balli Kombetar. So, the time and historical conjuncture of the diplomatic note points to the Hoxha's efforts to employ the Albanian migrations in its foreign policy towards Turkey. It would be useful to note that until that time Hoxha rarely expressed clear position on the Albanian emigrations of 1950's. The Stalin's warning on non-intervention in the Belgrade's internal affairs left out few choices in the front of the Hoxha administration. For these reasons Hoxha got satisfied with few diplomatic notes to the Belgrad administration and a short public talk in Tropoja, in 1952: '...*they (Belgrade, a.n.) hope to Turkicise the Albanians and send them to Turkey...*'. The talk was completed in 1957 when Hoxha noted that '...*thousands of Albanians left their houses...*' in their move to Turkey.[54] The Hoxha's talk followed the meeting of Adnan Menderes, Fuat Köprülü and Mosha Piyade in London between October 13-18, 1952[55] and coincided

[53]Bilal Şimşir, *Türkiye-Arnavutluk İlişkileri: Büyükelçi Anıları 1985-1988*, Ankara, ASAM, 2001, p.36-50.

[54]Sevdije dhe Ferit Shehu, p.27.

[55]Personal Interview with *Kamuran Tahir*, Kosovo, August 1999.

with the Turkey's post-Korea NATO membership[56] and the initiation of the Balkan Pact [57].

By reference to the diplomatic note of 1956, it is possible to infer the Tirana's expectation for Turkey's involvement for termination of the Albanian emigration from Yugoslavia. The so far available scarce archives do not give any hints about the Ankara's perception and response to these attempts. However, some Kosovo migrant candidates of 1957 noted that Belgrad ceased the emigration procedures as a result of the Albania's diplomatic intervention.[58] The normalisation of the Albanian-Turkish relations started after the opening of an embassy in 1958 and culminated after 1965 when Tiran supported Turkey's UN position on the Cyprus issue. In year 1966 the issue of Albanian-Turkish friendship found wide place in the Turkish media. In emphasizing the common Albanian-Bosnian-Turkish defence of the Roumelian borders, the former Minister of Foreign Affairs Tevfik Rüştü Aras implied the official perception of the Albanians in Turkey as integral part of the Turkish history and society[59]. There is not enough information on the impact of the improved cultural and economic relations on the activity of the Turkish-Albanian Broderhood Association between 1966-1989. In August 25, 1971 the withdrawal of the Albanian consulate in Istanbul was followed by the arrest of Turkish citizens of Albanian origin accused in espionage and collaboration with the Albanian consulate in Istanbul.[60] The connection of the Association with this case is unclear, however, the hierarchical relation between the NGO's and the official authorities until 1990's gives hints for the inferior and passive role of the Albanian Brotherhood Association in regard to the Turkish foreign policy decission making during the Cold War.[61]

---

[56]Ercüment Yavuzalp, *Liderlerimiz ve Dış Politika*, Ankara, Bilgi, 1996, p.62-63.

[57]Duygu Bazoğlu Sezer, 'Soğuk Savaş Dönemi ve Türkiye'nin İttifaklar Politikası', İsmail Soysal der., *Çağdaş Türk Diplomasisi: 200 Yıllık Süreç*, Ankara, TTK, 1999, p. 448-449.

[58]Sevdije Shehu, Ferit Shehu, p.28.

[59]Bilal Şimşir, Türkiye-Arnavutluk..., p.39-49.

[60]Bilal Şimşir, Türkiye-Arnavutluk..., p.453.

[61]Nurcan Özgür Baklacıoğlu, 'Türkiye'nin Balkan Politikasında Rumeli ve Balkan Göçmen Dernekleri', der. Semra Cerit Mazlum ve Erhan Doğan, *Sivil Toplum ve Dış Politika,* Bağlam Yayınları, Istanbul, 2006, p.77-117.

Turkey's latest encounter with the Albanian diaspora and the Albanian issue in the Balkans has started in the late 80's, when the Kosovo associations in Turkey brought the Kosovo issue to the agenda of the Turkey's Balkan policy. The Aras's reference to the common historical solidarity and brotherhood echoed in the Association's call for Turkey's intervention against the 'Serbian invasion and massacres in Kosovo'. After Albania and Kosovo, Turkey ranges as third in number of Albanian population living in the country.[62] According to some MP's there are 1 million Kosovo immigrants in Turkey.[63] As cited above some estimate 3.000.000 Albanians in Turkey. No matter how big are the numbers, the lone fact that Turkey comprises Albanian immigrants from four regional actors such as Albania, Greece, Kosovo and Macedonia, *a priori* widens the scope and engagement in the Turkey's Balkan Policy. Crises or problems in each of these source countries brings the domestic immigrant perspective to the Turkey's decision making in the region.

The Albanian politics in the agenda of Turkey's Balkan Policy

Within the political circles of the Albanian community in Turkey, the concept of 'Turkey's Balkan policy' brings forward three major areas of interest:

- Turkey's Kosovo policy;
- The Albanian issue in Macedonia and Turkey's relations with Macedonia and
- The problems of the Cham Albanians and the Turkey's relations with Greece.

This threefold agenda reflects the regional distribution of Albanian immigrants in Turkey. The quantitative and political prevalence of Macedonian and Kosovar Albanians in the Albanian associations shifts the public interest to Kosovo and Macedonia. Thus for diffence from Kosovo and Macedonia, the political balance and stability in Albania and the situation of the Albanian minority in Greece convey particular geopolitical and strategic content. This had more to do with the degree of involvement of the Albanian associations in Turkey's Balkan policy, yet, did not define Turkey's position on the issues in the Balkans.

---

[62]IBHI, *The Albanians in the Balkan Context*, 1996.

[63]Kırıkkale MP Osman Durmuş, *TBMM Genel Kurul Tutanağı*, 23. Dönem, 3. Yasama Yılı, 82. Birleşim, April 28, 2009, p.28-29.

Indeed, the turbulent early 1990's, the war in Bosnia as well as the Macedonian dilemma in the Balkans did not leave lots of room for the civil actors in foreign policy decission making in Turkey. The 1990's discourse of the 'powder cake' threat in the Balkans shifted the Kosovo issue to the 'high politics' agenda in Turkey's foreign policy decission making process. As a yardstick of the fragile regional security, Kosovo issue was scrutinized as a high security issue where the uncertainty in the international system and the international agenda and actors had defining role over the regional and domestic factors. Moreover, the linking of Kosovo issue to the Kurdish issue caused narrowing and reservations in the decission making on the Kosovo issue. For these reasons Turkey's President Turgut Özal could not officialy support Rugova's call for recognition of the 'Kosovo Republic' declared in September 1991. The domestic, regional and international agenda had their final say in the evolution of the Turkish official approach on the Kosovo issue until Turkey's declaration of open support for the independency of the Kosovo Republic in 2008.

The Albanian question in the Balkans and the Kosovo issue kept constant place in Turkey's foreign policy agenda since early 1990's. Published in a Sanjak journal in February 1992, Rexhep Qosja's call for unification of the Albanian nation split between Albania, Kosovo, Macedonia, Montenegro and Greece, echoed in Istanbul, too.[64] Under the occassion of an international conference on the War in Bosnia[65] an U.S. senator of Albanian origin presented and commented on a documentary on the 'Kosovo Tragedy' and called for awareness of the Albanian drama in Kosovo and further Turkey's support for independence of Kosovo. Beside the officially opposite stance between Turkey's official position and the approach of the Albanian community in Turkey, the Turkish officials never seem to withold their indirect understanding on the Albanian calls for solution of the Kosovo issue. Turkish public support to both Bosnians and Albanians in their struggle against Miloshevic's Serbian invasion reflected on Ankara's approach to the issue. Turkish officials left space for public diplomacy on the Kosovo issue and oppened channels for further activities and expression of the Albanian community in Turkey.

---

[64]Rexhep Qosja, *Ligjërime Paravajtëse*, Tiranë: Botimet Toena, 1998, p.205-208.
[65]*International Conference on the War in Bosnia*, İstanbul: The Konference Hall of the Military Muaseum, Spring 1995.

After June 1991 the high representatives of the Albanian Brotherhood Association stood up as important civic actors in the Turkey-Kosovo-Albania diplomacy triangle. The association attended some official visits as well as started lobbying activities in Ankara and Tirana and entered into contact with Albanian lobies in the US, Germany and Australia. At the beginning of 1990's Kosovo Democratic Union's Deputy Prime Minister Fehmi Agani and Rexhep Boja visited Ankara in search for support in ending the Albanian tragedy in Kosovo. The visit followed by Adem Demaci's visit in October 1991 and the Albanian President Ramiz Alija's visit in November 1991. The Albanian Brotherhood Association took place as first meeting point during most of these visits to Turkey. For translation or other public diplomacy purposes, the Association used to accompany the Albanian and Kosovo delegations during this intensive diplomatic traffic to Ankara, thus it could not only observe the ongoing diplomatic effort to draw Turkey's support to Kosovo independency project, but also the Associations served as one of the main source of information in decission making bureaucracy, process and actors in Ankara.

Along the bilateral diplomatic visits the Albanian Brotherhood Association initiated numerous demonstrations in support of the Kosovar's struggle for independency. In February 22, 1992 the association organised a Concert for Kosovo, followed by joint visit to the Prime Minister Süleyman Demirel, DSP leader Bülent Ecevit and President of the National Asembly Hüsamettin Cindoruk. In the same year the Kosova Democratic Union President Prof.Dr.İbrahim Rugova, the PPD Vice President Sami İbrahimi and the Turkish Kosovar Poet Arif Bozaci participated to a conference organised by the Albanian Brotherhood Association in Istanbul. The Conference on the Future of Kosovo was a further step in rising awareness of the Albanian tragedy in Kosovo and followed by a collective visit to the Prime Minister Süleyman Demirel, ANAP Party leader Mesut Yilmaz and the President of the National Assembly Hüsamettin Cindoruk. This visit was accompanied by a visit to President Turgut Özal. The year 1992 was one of the most intensive years in the Association's struggle for the independence of Kosovo.

In September 25, 1992 the Association distributed numerous "Recognize the Republic of Kosova" posters in open call for independence. The initiation found support among different grups in the Turkish society.

Famous national singers such as Barış Manço, Emel Sayın and Arif Şentürk, as well as Kosovo folk dance groups such as 'Shota' gave their support to Kosovo through attending the concerts for Kosovo organised in Istanbul, Izmir, Bursa and Adapazarı between 1992-1994. The income of these concerts was used in printing school books for the children in Kosovo, while the Association started to publish its monthly magazine Besa, that served as a first hand source for the developments in Kosovo after 1993. In July 1995 the Association celebrated the 5th anniversary of the Kosova's independence and joined the Kosovo representatives Edita Tahiri and Edi Shukriu during their HABİTAT days in 1996.

The 'Powder Keg' debates on the potential spread of the war in Bosnia all over the Balkans through the violent clashes in Kosovo during 1992-1993 constituted the main agenda of the Albanian and Kosovar leaders during their visits to Ankara. In April 1993 Albania's President Sali Berisha declared oppen support to 'their brothers in Kosovo'. This declaration was followed by a defence agreement between Turkey and Albania.[66] This agreement was a clear sign of Turkey's position in front of Russia supported Greek-Serbian axis in the Balkans. However, Ankara's perception of the conflicts in Bosnia and Kosovo excluded any unilateral military involvement in the region. Moreover, Ankara hesitated to declare open support for the independency of Kosovo, instead, promoted further international awareness on the extensive human rights violations in Kosovo. The diplomatic efforts to keep the Kosovo issue on the international agenda and Tirana's military approach with Ankara constituted the major Turkish contribution to the Albanian issue in the Balkans during 1992-1995. Along the early recognition of the Republic of Macedonia, Turkey's emphasis on European values such as human rights, democracy and territorial unity in the Balkans contributed to the prevention of a 3rd Balkan war in the region. However, according to some confidential Albanian sources, in spite of Turkey's diplomatic self-restraint on the issue of Kosovo independency, the Turkish military used to support the Albanian struggle in Kosovo all along 1990's. This support reached high levels during the 3-year long rule of the Refah-Yol

---

[66] Miranda Vickers and James Pettifer, *Albania: From Anarchy to a Balkan Identity*, New York, New York University Press, 2000, p.156.

government between 1994-1997. After 1997, Turkey became one of the major donors in the modernisation of the military forces in Albania.[67]

After the change of the government in Turkey in 1997, the Prime Minister Mesut Yılmaz and the President of the National Asembly Mustafa Kalemli accepted the delegation of the Albanian Brotherhood Association. The Association brought to the agenda the local clashes between the UÇK and Serbian forces in 1997 and called for Turkey's support to the Albanian struggle against the Serbian invasion. During its visit the Association repeated its call for independence of Kosovo and Turkey's recognition of independent Kosovo[68]. In 1998, the Albanian Brotherhood Association initiated a Kosovo Solidarity Commitee, set up by eight associations representing the Kosovo immigrants in Turkey. The commitee aimed to rise the international awareness and draw the support of the Turkish public on the Serbian crimes in Kosovo. It launched media meetings and street demonstration in support of the Kosovo independence and called for further Turkey's involvement in the war in Kosovo and '...*further support to the Albanian and Turkish brothers in their war against the Serbian invasion...*'.[69]

The discourse on the linkage between the Kosovo issue and the Kurdish issue in the Eastern Turkey led to division in the Commitee standing on the Kosovo issue. While the Rumeli associations supported Turkey's official standing on the issue, the Albanian Broderhood Association did not join Turkey's approach on the issue of Kosovo independence. Moreover, the Rumeli associations placed special attention to the breakdown of the anti-Turkish and anti-Ottoman prejudices in the Balkans, especially in Kosovo, Albania, Macedonia and Bosnia, thus suggested the breakdown of the prejudices and avoidance of further division among the Albanian and Turkish comunities in Kosovo and Macedonia. For difference from the Roumelian associations, the Albanian Brotherhood Association called for the revision of Turkey's policy on the Turkish-Albanian relations in Kosovo and Macedonia. Through protest letters and calls for support sent to the embassies of the U.S.A., Germany, France etc. the Association started intensive lobbying in support

---

[67] *Personal interview with a chief representative of the Albanian Brotherhood Association.* Istanbul, Beyazit, November 2010.

[68] Sevdije dhe Ferit Shehu, p.59.

[69] 'Soykırıma Lanet', *Göçmenlerin Sesi*, Number 55, April 1999, p.1.

for the independence of Kosovo. Upon Turkey's decided recognition of Macedonia, the Albanian nationalist circles criticized the Ankara's self-restraint on the Kosovo independence and Kosovo Turks' neutral position during the war. The Association was also very critical in the Kosovo Turks' pro-Serbian or neutral position during the war. The Association called Kosovo Turks to join the Albanian struggle, while both the Turkish decission makers in Ankara and Turkish leaders in Kosovo advised non-involvement in the conflict between the Serbs and Albanians. This neutral position of the Turkish minority in Kosovo left deep prejudices among the Albanians both in Kosovo and Turkey.

On the other hand, the talks of the political elites in Ankara do not suggest exclusive approach towards Albanians in Kosovo. The response of the Foreign Ministry representative Sermet Atacanli during a briefing of the Foreign Ministry in 1999 provides a good example for the official perception of the Albanians in Kosovo. In response to the journalists' interest in the number of the Turkish refugees in Turkey, Atacanlı underlines the nondiscriminative approach of the Foreign Ministry: '... *we do not differentiate or count the refugees as 'Kosovar Turks' and 'Kosovar Albanians'. It is not proper to do such a thing. We know that there are many Kosovar Turks who left, but it is impossible to give you any number on that.*'[70] Indeed, some Kosovo Turks complained that in its effort to provide humanitarian and diplomatic support to the Albanians in Kosovo, Turkey left the Turks out of any support and protection. So, the main source of the well known Kosovar Albanian-Kosovar Turk separation rests in Kosovo and until the Turkish language issue in 2010 did not find reflection in the Turkey's politics.

Instead, the conservative parties such as the Fazilet Party (FP) and AKP use to unite all Balkan Muslims under a pan-Ottoman approach that bases on the reality of Muslims of Ottoman origin left in the lost imperial lands. The parliamentarian talk of the Fazilet Party deputee of Albanian origin Mustafa Baş provides a good example on that:

'...the events in Kosovo may lead to a Balkan war; indeed, they may cause the emigration and arrival of thousands of people to Turkey... when we look at the cruelty there, we see a target. What is this target? The Albanians, Bosnians, Turks...; in short, the

---

[70]'Sermet Atacanlı ile toplantı', *T.C. Dışişleri Bakanlığı Haftalık Olağan Basın Toplantısı,* Ankara, 14 Nisan 1999, Source: www.mfa.gov.tr, 2002.

purge of the Muslim people from the region. In 1946, 250.000 people immigrated to Turkey. In 1968, in 1974 thousands of people emigrated, moreover, in a period of time, 400.000 people came to the Turkish borders and emigrated from Bulgaria; during the war in Bosnia Hezegovian 312.000 Muslims have died for Islam. The target of all this is to reduce, to destroy utterly, to clean away the Muslim population in the Balkans...Look, there was only one country that recognised the Kosovo Republic: Albania!...'[71]

The pan-Ottoman perception and criticism of the FP deputy and the open call for Turkey's recognition of the Kosovo Republic was followed by the FP deputy Hüseyin Kansu who reminded the 'considerable number of the Albanian population' in Albania, Montenegro, Greece and Macedonia and underlined that the Turkish people will not stay indifferent to the tragedy of Kosovar Albanians.[72]

For difference from the conservative tradition the social-democrat parties in Turkey such as CHP (Republican People Party) and DSP (Democratic Left Party) adopt also a rather inclusive approach built upon the notion of common historical and cultural belonging of the Albanian and Turkish populations in Turkey's history. Primarily supported by Albanians and Turks that belong to the Bektashi order as well as Turkish immigrants from Yugoslavia the CHP's approach is represented by a deputy of Bulgarian Turkish origin Ali Dinçer: ' ...based on very old and deep historical ties the Albanians and the Turks are nested as the nail to the flesh, they are the conquerors (evladi fatihan) who contributed many intellectuals to the Turkish history. By reference to the Turkish poet of Albanian origin Mehmet Akif Ersoy who wrote the Turkish National Anthem, the Turkish language master Şemsettin Sami, and the ideolog of the Young Turks movement the Otoman Albanian intellectual İbrahim Temo, Dinçer rises the Albanian identity as 'a founding feature in the Turkish nation-building movement'. This approach shares a lot with the already mentioned approach of the Ablanian migrants in Turkey. The portrait of the Turkish Albanians as described by the CHP deputy also shows numerous similarities with the self-portrait of the Albanians:

---

[71]'Fazilet Partisi İstanbul Milletvekili Sayın Mustafa Baş', *TBMM Genel Kurul Tutanağı*, 20. Dönem 3. Yasama Yılı 64. Birleşim 10/Mart /1998, p.62

[72]'Fazilet Partisi İstanbul Milletvekili Sayın Hüseyin Kansu'nun konuşması', *TBMM Genel Kurul Tutanağı* 20. Dönem 3. Yasama Yılı 63. Birleşim 05 Mart 1998, p.8-9.

'…with a number close to the population of Albania, the Albanians in Turkey (are) hardworking, diligent, modest, insistent, honest, enterprising citizens who did tremendous contribution to the Turkish science, Turkish art and business…; they are the leading Ottoman conquerors who contributed the Bektashi lodges to the Turkish culture as the main centers of the Turkish Bektashi philosophy and poetry that had great contribution in the Turkicization of Anatolia…'[73]

This approach led to a new perception of the Kosovar Ablanians, Bosnians and Pomaks as Balkan Muslims who suffer ethnic cleansing and do not have a state to protect them, thus are left out of any protection. The fall of the Kosovo-supported Berisha's regime and the relative apathy of the Milo's government during the war in Kosovo oppened the platform for the international intervention. Under these circumstances, Turkey took place in the NATO operation in Kosovo and the international Kosovo peace force-KFOR. Before the conflict in Kosovo, during the so called 'Bankers crisis' in 1997, Turkey sent 500 soldiers to the AGIT initiated international peace force in Albania.[74] As summarised by the DSP deputy Şükrü Sina Gürel, Turkey cannot stay indiferent to the incidents in Albania and Kosovo, because:

'…the Albanian nation has very close historical and cultural relations with the Turkish nation. These two nations live together since Turkey (i.e. Ottoman Empire) become major regional power in the Balkans. The Turks and the Albanians today in Turkey and in the Balkans are two nations that never fall apart…'[75]

Indeed, the family networks and relatives between the Albanians in Kosovo and Macedonia and the Yugoslav immigrants in Turkey makes Turkey's interference in the Albanian issues inevitable. Eventhough the U.S. influence among the Kosovar Albanians and the contemporary Tirana-Prishtina approach and collaboration weakened this prior Turkish role in the Balkans, Turkey still constitutes the main political and military partner of both Kosovo and Albania today. Moreover, as underlined

---

[73]'CHP Milletvekili Ali Dinçer'in Konuşması', *TBMM Genel Kurul Tutanağı* 20. Dönem 2. Yasama Yılı 81. Birleşim 10 Nisan 1997, s.11-25.

[74]Şule Kut, *Balkanlar'da Kimlik ve Egemenlik*, İstanbul: İstanbul Bilgi Üniversitesi Yayınları, 2005, s.118.

[75]DSP Grubu Adına Şükrü Sina Gürel, *TBMM Genel Kurul Tutanağı*, 20. Dönem 2. Yasama Yılı 81. Birleşim 10 Nisan 1997, p.12.

during a panel on the 'History of the Turkish-Albanian Brotherhood' held by the Rumeli Foundation in 2002, Turkey is expected to give its support to the problems of the Cham Albanians, as well.[76]

Indeed, the chief of the Ankara Branch of the Albanian Brotherhood association is a Cham Albanian and many activities there are related to the problems of the Cham Albanians. The problems of the Cham Albanians entered the Turkey's foreign policy after the Kardak-crisis between Turkey and Greece. During the late 90's the Turkish-Greek relations faced with both minority issues and with a competition over the markets in Bulgaria, Macedonia and Albania. Greece's policy of deportation of the Albanian economic immigrants during the end of the 1990's found place at the agenda of the Albanian associations in Istanbul through contacts of the Chamurian Associations in Tirana. Being politicaly close to the Berisha government, in 1999, the Chamurian Associations brought Greece's bad treatment of the Albanian immigrants in Greece and the Cham issue to the agenda in Ankara.[77] There was not any official response or involvement in these issues at the Turkish side. This is because, although avoided by the Albanian governments, the problems of the Cham Albanians belong to the responsibility agenda of the Albanian governments, not Turkey. Moreover, the post-Simitis strategic approach between Atina and Ankara did not leave space for raising additional bilateral problems.

During the war in Kosovo Turkey hosted 17.746 Kosovar refugees[78] and provided humanitarian support to the refugees in Macedonia and Albania. The arrival of thousands of Kosovar refugees in Turkey during the conflict in Kosovo trigered the public interest to the war in Kosovo. During the war the Roumeli and Kosovo associations took active place in the provision of humanitarian aid to the Kosovo refugees. According to some anonimous sources some groups in Turkey provided financial and military support to the UCK during the war in Kosovo. Until the war in Kosovo, Turkey used to provide full political/diplomatic support to the Albanian political leaders in Kosovo. This support was within the frame of territorial integrity of Yugoslavia and Kosovo question

---

[76]Macit Şahinler, 'Önsöz', Rumeli Kültürü, Number 6-7, Autumn 2003, p.32-33.

[77]Kamil Bitiş, Yunanistan'ın Çam Arnavutları Üzerinde Uyguladığı Soykırım, Source: www.arnavut.com

[78]İltica ve Göç Alanındaki Avrupa Birliği Müktesebatının Üstlenilmesine İlişkin Türkiye Ulusal Eylem Planı, Source: www.egm.gov.tr

was approached primarily as a domestic problem that should be solved through restoration of the Kosovo's autonomy status granted under the Constitution of 1974.[79] In the meantime, Turkey negated any Albanian separatist tendencies in Macedonia and furthered good relations with both Tirana and Belgrade. Though Tirana expected Turkey's diplomatic pressure over Belgrade, Turkey kept its position until the escalation of the conflict in Kosovo in 1998. At the middle of 1998, Rugova expressed a somewhat 'dissapointment' in their expectation of higher support from Turkey.[80] Turkey's political and military support came under the NATO and UN peace operations in Kosovo. Turkey joined the NATO Allied Force operation in Kosovo and contributed 18 F-16s to the NATO air attacks on Belgrade, sent a fleet to the embargo meassures in the Adriatic sea and deployed 1000 troops under the KFOR mission. The Kosovo Albanians still talk about the Turkish F-16's flights over Prishtina, as the first sign of the salvation of Kosovo.

At the end of the war in Kosovo, Turkey supported the UN Security Council Resolution 1244 in June 10, 1999, thus comfirmed the sovereignity and territorial integrity of the Federal Republic of Yugoslavia but also reafirmed a '…call for substantial autonomy and meaningful self-administration for Kosovo…'.[81] This final act caused wide critiques among the Albanian community in Turkey, however, Turkey's foreign policy priorities and the choice to act within the international framework, i.e. the decissions taken within the NATO and UN did not alow any regional or local influence on the Turkey's official decission making on Kosovo. Thus the demonstrations of the Kosovar associations in Turkey could not influence Turkey's position on the Kosovo's independence. The Kosovo Albanians' restrictions on the rights of the Turkish minority in Kosovo and the affiliation of probable Kosovo's independency with debates over the establishment of a Kurdish state in Northern Iraq and its implications in regard to the fight against PKK in Turkey followed by Turkey's cautious stance based on independence recognition under resolution of the UN Security Council.

---

[79]Didem Ekinci, 'Turkey and Kosovo: A chronicle of Post-Cold War Bilateral Relations', *Avrasya Dosyası: Balkanlar Özel,* Cilt 14, Sayı 1, p.286-7.
[80]'Kosovan Leader Rugova to Seek Support in Turkey', *Turkish Daily News*, 11 August 1998.
[81]*Resolution 1244 adopted by the UN Security Council on June 10, 1999*, Source: www.nato.int/kosovo/

The Ahtisaari report and its final amendments of March 2007 in regard to the rights of the minorities in Kosovo as well as the steady progress towards independent Kosovo, found reflection on Turkey's support to the Ahtisaari's independence proposal. According to the Albanian brotherhood association the main factor that lies behing the Kosovo independence is the U.S.. According to the association representatives U.S. had defining impact on Turkey's official approach after February 2007, when the Secretary of the Ministry of Foreign Affairs Ahmet Acet visited Kosovo and officially expressed Turkey's support to the Ahtisaari plan, i.e. Kosovo's independence. Accroding to the Albanian Brotherhood Association many official institutions in Turkey tacitly supported the Kosovo independence before 2007, yet, this was usually expressed during their informal meetings. According to them for difference from the other ministries, the Ministry of Foreign Affairs has always shown more reservation on the issue.

Nevertheless, the international and regional conjuncture, as well as the domestic foreign policy decission making in 2007 provided the best conditions for the declaration of the Kosovo independence in February 17, 2008. An internet based public survey applied by the website of Albanians in Turkey called Arnavutum.com, 91 percent of the 346 respondents voted in support of the Kosovo's proclamation of independence, 7 percent declared reservations based on possibility for a new war in the region and 1.76% had no certain opinion whether Kosovo should ot not declare its independence.[82] According to Erhan Türbedar, the Turkish government took under consideration the calls and pressure of the public oppinion and the Balkan lobby in Turkey. Indeed, after Turkey's West allies, the migrant organisations constituted the second factor in Turkey's recognition of the Kosovo's independence.[83]

Kosovo's independence caused two debates in Turkey. The first was initiated over Kosovo–Cyprus connection and the second bases on the problems of the Turks in Kosovo. In recognising the Kosovo's proclamation of independence the International Court of Justice, caused debates over the status and independence decissions on Cyprus. In October 2010,

---

[82]'Kosova Bağımsızlık kararını tek taraflı ilan etmelimi? Aktif Anket Sonuçları', Source: www.arnavutum.com, (October 2010).

[83]Erhan Türbedar, 'Türk Dış Politikasında Balkanlar', *Köprüler Kurduk Balkanlara*, İstanbul: İBB, 2008, p.189

the parliamentarian debates in Ankara compared the Kosovo issue with the Cyprus issue while underlined the impact of the 'Kosovo model' on the future Cyprus debates.[84] So far, the Cyprus issue as well as the Armenian question do not seem to take place in the agenda of the Albanian associations. Kosovo and Albania also keep neutral position on the issue.[85] Turkey's strenghtening position in the Balkans finds reflection in the Albanian and Kosovar politics. Opposite to their EU and Greece-oriented opponents, both Berisha and Thachi heed Turkey and the U.S. as significant regional and global actors in the Balkans. The recent economic weakness of Greece and the EU's inconsistent approach to the Balkans seems to empower the Turkish and US presence in the region. Indeed, Turkey's and the U.S.'s military support to the strenghtening of the Albanian army constitutes one of the major factors that prevented the recurrence of the 1997 crisis during the political turmoil at the end of 2010.[86]

After the independence, the situation of the rights of the Turkish minorities in Macedonia and Kosovo found important place at the agenda of the Albanian associations in Turkey. According to Kamil Bitis, there is not another such a small minority in the world that have so much rights as in the case of the Turks in Kosovo. According to Kamil Bitis, '...the Albanians in Kosovo will hardly forget the fact that the Turks in Kosovo took place at the Serbian side during the war in Kosovo. Despite the common historical, cultural, religious and family roots the Turkish community in Kosovo did not support the Albanian struggle for independency. However, now after the war, the official representatives of this small community pretend for extensive minority rights and claim further recognition in the Kosovo Constitution... Indeed, the Albanian community in Turkey is much larger, but never asks for official language recognition, Albanian schools etc. rights that the Turks in Kosovo use to enjoy. According to them the pretentions of the Turks in Kosovo are ridiculous, since they have full right to study in Turkish, have a special MP

---

[84]*TBMM Genel Kurul Tutanağı*, 23. Dönem, 5. Yasama Yılı, 6. Birleşim, 13 Ekim 2010, p. 38-41.

[85]Falma Fshazi, 'Albanian Turkish Relations from a Contemporary International Perspective', *Köprüler Kurduk Balkanlara*, İstanbul: İBB, 2008, p.243-4.

[86]James Pettifer, *Kosova and its Neighbours: Returning Instability?*, unpublished paper, February 2011.

quota at the Kosovo parliament, have their own cultural rights at the local level, especially in the municipalities where their number reach 60%...'.[87]

This approach shows continuity with the debates among the Turkish and Albanian communities in Macedonia. The Albanian nationalists in Macedonia criticized the passive stance of the Turkish minority during the Flag crisis in 1993 and the conflict in 2001. Indeed, the second argument underlied by the Albanian Brotherhood Association touches upon Turkey's opinion on the conflict in Macedonia in 2001. The political divide among the Turks in their position on the conflict in Tetovo has caused doubts among the Albanians in Macedonia. For this reason, the Albanians opposed the participation of the Macedonian Turks during the Ohrid negotiations.[88] While the Turks in Macedonia kept somewhat neutral position during the conflict in Macedonia, the Albanian Brotherhood association in Turkey organized a press conference (May 31, 2001) on the conflict in Macedonia. The conference was followed by Turkish Minister of Foreign Affairs Ismail Cem's visit to Skopje, where he emphasized Turkey's concerns on the territorial unity of Macedonia. In June 13, 2001, the Minister of Foreign Affairs İsmail Cem, defined the conflict in Macedonia as a twofold terrorist action that not only comes from the radical Albanian gerillas, but also involves assaults on Albanians, Turks and Muslims in Macedonia as well.[89] In June 30, 2001 the board members of the Association visited the National Assembly of Turkey and Prime Minister Bülent ECEVİT and called for Turkey's support in ending '...the oppression and cruelty to Turks and Albanians in Macedonia…'.[90]

As a regional actor who gave early support to the recognition of the Republic of Macedonia, Turkey activated diplomatic initiatives for restoration of the democratic peace among the diverse ethnic communities in Macedonia. The success of the Ohrid Peace Accord shifted the centre of the politics to the favor of the Albanian minority in Macedonia. Although the AKP government emphasizes the neo-Ottoman approach and common Muslim background, the problem of discrimination in the field of education and employment persist as

[87]Personal interview with *Kamil Bitiş*, October 29, 2010, İstanbul, Sağmalcılar

[88]Personal interview with *Kamil Bitiş*, October 29, 2010, İstanbul, Sağmalcılar

[89]*Makedonya Dosyası*, Source: www.arnavutum.com, November 2010.

[90]The agenda of the Albanian Brotherhood Association, Source: www.turk-ar.org

a major problem of the Turkish minority in Macedonia. According to the Association, one of the important subjects during their negotiations in Kosovo and Macedonia is related to the problems of the Turkish minorities in Kosovo and Macedonia. However, the practice of the Association demonstrates particular efforts in establishing a sort of public diplomacy network among Albania, Kosovo, Macedonia and Turkey. For example, in October 28, 2002 the chair of the Association Halil Metin together with three board members İsmail Yücel, İsmail Sadıker and İlir Bilakaya performed a Balkan trip that involved visits to the Albanian President Alfred Moisiu, BDI leader Ali Ahmeti and PDSH leader Arben Xhaferi and the Prime Minister of Kosova Prof.Dr.Bajram Rexhepi together with the General Staff Agim Çeku. While the radical domestic political changes lead to stagnation in the regional activities of the associations, Turkey's close relations with Albania, Macedonia and Kosovo provides beneficial ground for the public diplomacy activities of the Albanian, Macedonian and Kosovo associations in Turkey. Moreover, Thaci's definition of Turkey as a strategic partner and 'big brother' capable to provide further recognition of Kosovo among the Islamic countries[91] show Turkey's role in the solution of one of the basic problems in the front of the Kosovo governments, i.e. reaching full recognition in order to (by 2010, 69 countries recognised Kosovo independence) undermine Serbian efforts against the Kosovo independence. Moreover, the Kosovo's NATO and UN membership are important enterprises where Prishtina will need Turkey's support in overcoming any potential Russian or China opposition. As in the case with Albania and Bosnia, the post-war Republic of Kosovo needed intensive military and domestic security sector modernisation that involved both the Turkish police force and Turkish arm force representation in Kosovo[92].

During the AKP government, the Turkish civic actors seem to prioritize the common cultural, i.e. religious and historical roots among the Muslims in the Balkans. Conferences organised by sivil society organisations based on solidarity among the Muslims in the Balkans and

---

[91]Rifat Sait, 'Başbakan Thaci: Türkiye bizim stratejik ortağımız', *Balkan Günlüğü Gazetesi*, 24 Mayıs 2010.

[92]'Bayrampaşa Belediyesinde Adem Jashari Parkı Törenli Açılışı Yapıldı', www. arnavutum.com, 1 Mart 2009.

the Middle East[93] promote a somewhat neo-Ottoman agenda among the Muslims in the region. These local initiatives tend to span all along the so called Albanian 'hinterland'[94] in the region. One of the main components of these initiations is the Turkey's Ministry of Education student grants/ exchange program. Since 1996 Turkey provided theological education to 539 Kosovar students. Many of these students, especially those of Albanian or Gora origin, find further financial support or attend various local associations in Istanbul, thus facilitate their interest and activism in the Balkans.[95] This program is approached as important step in expanding moderate Islam in the region. Besides, by 2010 Turkey provided scholarship to nearly 448 Kosovar undergraduate and graduate students of Turkish, Albanian and Bosnian origin. In 2009-2010 Turkey extended the undergraduate and graduate student quota for Kosovo to 130 students.[96] The primary objective of this program is to break down the historical anti-Turkish prejudices in the region; to rise positive awareness about the Turkish culture, history and politics among the Turkish minorities and the so called 'kin societies' (akraba toplulukları) in the region; to establish educational, thus cultural links between the societies in the region and Turkey. Based on common historical, cultural and religious memory and active migration linkages, Albanians are considered as one of the kin societies in the region.[97]

---

[93]The Balkan conferences organized by IHH Humanitarian Aid Fondation in Istanbul cover speakers and subjects with cultural, i.e. religious and historical sensitivities. Some of the invited speakers of the conference are Adnan İsmaili, Chair of the Merhamet Association, Hüsameddin Abbasi, Chair of Kosova AKEA Aid Association, Naim Tırnova, President of Kosova Department of Religious Affairs, Selim Muça, Lider of the Muslim Society in Albania, Süleyman Recebi, Leader of the Union of Islam in Macedonia, Tahir Zenelhasani, Admeria Association in Albania. *Balkan Sempozyumu*, İstanbul: Grand Cevahir, 18-19 Ekim 2008, See the program at: www.balkansempozyumu.org

[94]Critical of the 'Great Albania' project, the Albanian Brotherhood Association suggests the concept of 'Albanian hinterland', that according to him, for difference from the former concept has no irredentist meaning.

[95]Personal interview with Kosovar students during IHH Humanitarian Aid Conference on Asylum, 2008.

[96]Minister of State Mustafa Said Yazıcıoğlu's talk on the celebration of the 'April 23' as a National Day of the Kosovo Turks, *TBMM Genel Kurul Tutanağı*, 23. Dönem, 3. Yasama Yılı, 82. Birleşim, 28 Nisan 2009.

[97]See about the Deputy of Kırıkkale Osman Durmuş's talk on his Kosovo visit at: *TBMM Genel Kurul Tutanağı*, 23. Dönem, 3. Yasama Yılı, 82. Birleşim, 28 Nisan 2009.

There is not available fieldwork or study about the consequences of this policy. Turkey is considered as an important regional power. From this point of view, the knowledge of Turkish language brings advantages to the young foreign ministry professionals and academicians in Albania, Kosovo and Macedonia. The reflection of their experience in Turkey on their approaches and decissions is rather subjective issue, difficult to measure. However, an important indirect result of this student exchange program is related to education and training of potential state bureaucrats and political elite for the government and political life in Kosovo. There are numerous examples of Kosovo bureaucrats and elite who are graduates from various universities in Turkey. For example, the President of the Kosovo Constitutional Court Enver Hasani, the deputy prime minister of the Kosovo government Hayreddin Kuçi, the Minister of National Defence and Domestic Affairs and Kosovo Ambassador in Ankara Bekim Sejdiju are graduates from universities in Turkey.[98] Surely, the links, experience and knowledge of these political elites facilitates their contacts and communication with the Turkish officials in Turkey, however, it is not clear to what extend this student exchange policy transforms into Turkish soft power in the Balkans. The fact that one of the influential PDK designers of the new Kosovo Constitution Hayreddin Kuchi, a graduate from Bilkent University in Ankara, did not or could not promote Turkish language as the 3rd official language in the Constitution, shows that the local national, political and economic dynamics prevail Turkey's neo-Ottoman expectations in regard to the non-Turkish Muslims in the Balkans. On the other hand, this policy raises criticism among the Turkish elite in Kosovo[99]. The high unemployment among the Turkish and Gora/Bosnian youth in Kosovo raises discontent about the discriminative employment and education policies in the Albanian populated municipalities in Kosovo.

The lack of Turkish industrial investments in the country leads to low employment opportunities for Turkish and Gora minority, and equal Turkish economic power in the country. So far, Çalık Holding, Demir Çelik Company and ENKA are the main Turkish companies

---

[98]Personal Interview with the Leader of the Albanian Brotherhood Association *Halil Metin*, İstanbul, Beyazit, December 2010.

[99]Taner Güçlütürk, 'Kosova'nın Bağımsızlığı ve Türklerin Sosyo-Kültürel Durumları', *Köprüler Kurduk Balkanlara*, İstanbul: İBB, 2008, p.199-201.

in the constructing sector in Kosovo and Albania. The Turkish hospital in Kosovo and the Turkish private schools in Albania and Macedonia are important sources of prestige for Turkey. Although out of sufficient sources, TIKA has extensive programs for regional development in the health and education in Kosovo, Macedonia and Albania. Turkey's geostrategic concentration on the Middle East and Asia after the US intervention in Iraq and Afghanistan has led to a temporary uncertainty in the Turkey's Balkan policy during the last decade.

According to the Albanian Brotherhood Association there are not migrant companies with sufficient capacity to invest in Kosovo. Moreover, the limits of the Kosovo market, reduce the interest in investing in Kosovo and Albania. The Albanian migrant business in Turkey is in general small and middle scale and primarily involved in textile, plastic industry, trade etc. That is why, the migrant networks have facilitated extensive suitcase trade among Turkey and Kosovo, rather than further macroeconomic investments. Because of this, according to the association, Turkey has to promote the big Turkish investment capital towards Kosovo. After 2010 Ankara seems to initiate its second financial stretching to the Balkans through some large infrastructure investments in Kosovo and Albania.

For difference from the Roumelian Associations the Albanian Brotherhood Association does not show extensive interest in performng a role of 'bridge' for the Turkish investments in the region, insted, it heeds its role as a public diplomacy actor and bridge among the 'Albanian hinterland' and Turkey. Despite the fact that the Albanian Brotherhood Association approaches the 'Great Albania' as an irredentist idea, the notion of being a part of the Albanian hinterland in the Balkans seems important point of relation reference.

Conclusion

The political organisation of the Albanian immigrants in Turkey goes back to the last years of the Ottoman Empire. The Albanian Solidarity Society (Arnavut Teavün Cemiyeti) and the Bashkim Clubs constituted the main platform in the struggle for '*the annexation of the Albanian lands to the motherland Albania*' during the interwar years. After the WWII, the Albanians in Turkey are represented by an Albanian Brotherhood Association in Istanbul, established by a group of Albanian Bally Kombetar refugees and anti-Hoxha dissidents. The post-Cold War advance in the public diplomacy provided relatively wide space for the activities and influence of the Albanian migrant associations on Turkey's Balkan policy. For difference from the Roumelian associations that represent the majority of the immigrants from Yugoslavian lands, the two Albanian associations in Istanbul and Sakarya constitute small organisations with few members and politicaly active managers interested in lobbying and further public diplomacy practices. Differently from the Roumelian Associations, the Albanian associations insists on the Albanian roots of the immigrants from Yugoslavia, thus externalizes the immigrants of Turkish, Bosnian, Sanjak etc. origin. Similarly to the claims of the Albanian nationalists, they contend that the most immigrants from Yugoslavia are of Albanian origin. However, as declared by the general secretary of the Albanian Brotherhood Association , most of the immigrants do not want to accept/express their Albanian origin.

While rejecting the notion of 'Great Albania' as an irredentist idea, the participation of the Albanian community in the Turkey's foreign policy underlines the notion of belonging to the so called 'Albanian hinterland' in the Balkans. The notion of Albanian hinterland rises as an important point of linkage reference in the community approach to the war in Bosnia and Kosovo, the bank crisis in Albania and the crisis in Macedonia in 2001.

For difference from the Albanian community in Turkey, the fragile Balkan stability and the international efforts and consensus for building and keeping stability in the western Balkans had defining role on Turkey's policy on the Albanian issue in the Balkans. The U.S. military presence in the region during 90's, as well as the NATO and EU enlargements towards the East had enormous impact on the Turkey's policy towards crises and wars in Kosovo, Macedonia and Albania.[100] The diversity in the determinant factors, i.e. the predominance of the regional ethnopolitics in the approach of the Albanian community in Turkey and the determining effect of the systemic factors on the official decission making in Turkey, led to fundamental split in the approaches of the Albanian community and Turkey. While the Albanian community insisted on Kosovo's independence and further extension of the rights of the Albanians in Macedonia, Turkey promoted a dual strategy that on

---

[100]Bardos, Gordon N., 'The new political dynamics of southeastern Europe', *Southeast European and Black Sea Studies*, 8: 3, 2008, p.171-188

the one hand corresponded with the consensus of the international/ Western community and on the other provided opean political space for migrant lobying initiatives at the local and regional levels. Thus, in the most turning moments of the Balkan stability such as the Dayton Peace Accords, UN Security Council Resolution 1244 regulating the end of the Kosovo war and FYR Macedonia's Ohrid Accords, the Albanian community in Turkey could not show decisive influence on the Turkey's official position. However, Turkey found its place as important regional power that brought the Albanian demands and expectations to different international diplomatic platforms and agendas. It is widely accepted that the Turkish military and the Roumeli and Albanian migrant communities in Turkey did significant contribution to the NATO-oriented modernisation and strenghtening of the military sector in Kosovo and Albania. Similarly, Turkey's student exchange programs promote crossborder extention of the Turkish models of 'moderate Islam', state bureaucracy and democratisation in the Balkans. Under this perspective it is possible to talk about a source of duality in the Turkey's Balkan policy based on its traditional profile of a target country for various Muslim migrations in the region. The long history of multiethnic immigrations from the Balkans promotes elements of a new sort of neo-Ottoman identity in Turkey's Balkan policy. The policy on Turks and Kin Societies in the Balkans rests particularly on this identity background. However, the POST-Cold War local nationalism and territorial disputes in the region and the international consensus use to prevail as balancing elements in the Turkey's policy in the region.

The decade-long shift in international agenda towards the Middle East and Central Asia, the backsliding in the EU enlargement towards the Western Balkans and the progressive withdrawal of the US military presence during the last decade has been followed by Turkey's new neo-Ottoman geostrategic and geoeconomic course towards the Middle East and Central Asia and slight withdrawal from the Balkans. Russia's high-profile diplomatic and economic return to the Balkans after the independence of Kosovo[101] promotes new regional power configurations in the region. While Serbia, Bulgaria and Greece follow the Russian energy policy in the Balkans; Albania, Kosovo, Macedonia and Bosnia

---

[101]Bardos, Gordon N., 'The new political dynamics of southeastern Europe', *Southeast European and Black Sea Studies*, 8: 3, 2008, p.181-2.

and Herzegovina search for balancing Western or EU regional powers in the region. After 1990's homogenization of the national territories in the Balkans, the Albanian hinterland in the Balkans grows as an important variable in the further democratization and stability in the region. The issue of recognition of the Kosovo's independence still bases on disagreement between EU, US and Russia. Russia's return to the Balkans promotes Kosovo's approach towards Turkey during the last few years. And the signs of Turkey's return to the Balkans come near in the horizon.

A tale of two societies
Miranda Vickers

When Albania re-emerged onto the international scene, following the collapse of the one-party state in 1991, so little was known of it that to many people it was as if a totally new country had suddenly materialised. In the United Kingdom there was no diplomatic representation between Britain and Albania and there was also a total absence of any form of Albanian studies in UK universities. Albania had, to all intense and purposes, been isolated from the mainstream international world since the communist partisans and their leader Enver Hoxha came to power in November 1944. Travel restrictions meant that very few foreigners visited Albania during the period 1945 to 1991, and outside of the world's communist press, there was hardly any journalism.

Throughout those long decades of either 'lightness' or 'darkness', depending upon your political appraisal of the Tirana regime, all but the most committed and dedicated 'Albaniaphiles' chose to leave Albania ignored at the very back of the filing cabinet. These 'friends of Albania' were in fact three distinct groups of people in various parts of the world, who were positively active in all things Albanian. These groups could be identified as: Albanian émigrés and exiles in Western Europe and America; non-Albanian Marxist-Leninists, Stalinists and Maoists; and lastly non-Albanian supporters of the Albanian monarchy and the predominantly right-wing 'nationalist' forces that opposed the communist partisans during the Second World War. This essay concerns the latter two of these groups in the United Kingdom and the efforts in the late 1990s by Sir Reginald Hibbert to unite them.

It is normal for friends of a foreign country to group together to foster interest in that country and to provide a focus for relations with it and its people, alongside but outside official channels of relations between governments. In the case of Albania, however, there were two completely separate societies in the U.K. purporting to encourage relations with it: the Anglo-Albanian Association (AAA) and the Albania Society of Britain (ASB). The reasons for this duality were historical, stemming from the Second World War and the establishment in Albania of a communist regime and Enver Hoxha's subsequent dictatorship. In Albania, as in many Balkan countries, the politics of war-time resistance movements were, and to a large degree still are, very current. The ASB was formed by fellow travellers and sympathisers with the partisan fighters and the communist government in Albania. In marked contrast, the AAA would have nothing to do with communist Albania. The ideological difference between the two bodies was clear, sharp and unrelenting. One was anti-communist, the other was pro-communist.[1]

Both societies included in their membership former members of the wartime Special Operations Executive (SOE) that were sent into occupied Albania to coordinate and carry out subversive operations and to liaise with local groups fighting the Axis forces. These former SOE officers included Sir Reginald Hibbert, who was a member of the Albania Society of Britain, and the Tory MP and Foreign Office Minister, Julian Amery, and Major David Smiley, who were both members of the Anglo-Albanian Association. During the Second World War, Hibbert joined the Special Operations Executive (SOE) as a young Liaison Officer. In 1943 he was parachuted into Albania to liaise with local resistance groups. There he spent eleven months, firstly with the 'nationalists' and then with the communist partisans, who eventually emerged as the major element in the resistance forces.[2] During his time in Albania, Hibbert had concluded that the partisans were the only force worth supporting because, unlike the nationalists, they were doing most of the fighting against the Germans. He therefore remarked to various other SOE officers that had he been an Albanian, he would have fought with the partisans.[3] Towards the end of the war, the term 'partisan' had become synonymous with 'communist'. Henceforth, to many on the right of Britain's political spectrum, Reginald Hibbert was a communist sympathiser. Despite this, in his later life, Hibbert had a distinguished career as a senior diplomat in the Foreign Office serving as ambassador to Paris, he continued, however, to pursue a strong interest in Albania, often visiting the country and writing informative articles on the political situation.

[1]One Country – Two Societies, by Sir Reginald Hibbert, Albanian Life, Issue 63, Spring 1999, p6-7

[2]For a full account of these events see: R. Hibbert, Albania's National Liberation Struggle: A Bitter Victory, Pinter, 1991.

[3]R. Hibbert, Albania's National Liberation Struggle: A Bitter Victory, Pinter, 1991, p242

Simultaneously, during the War in Albania, Julian Amery, David Smiley and other SOE officers who later joined the AAA, attached themselves to the nationalists and monarchist supporters of King Zog, who lived in exile in Britain. As a result, the AAA remained strongly supportive of Zog and the various Zogist committees that existed in post-war Europe, Egypt, Turkey and America. Indeed, the wartime accounts written by Amery and Smiley were regarded by the AAA and supporters of the right in Albanian politics as the authoritative account of wartime events.[4] Despite both Amery and Smiley's books being purely eyewitness subjective narratives, they were used to establish an historical authority of how the war in Albania evolved. In contrast, in his wartime memoirs Hibbert also discusses events he had witnessed but did not just rely upon his own impressions, he analysed those events using a wide variety of primary and secondary sources in which to reach a more balanced conclusion.

Despite such differences, however, according to another influential Anglo-Albanian Association member, Nicholas Bethell, both Amery and Hibbert agreed on one important point, namely that the communist partisans were the better fighters and that, according to Bethell, the Albanian nationalists fought the Germans less than the partisans. This was not because they were pro-German, but because they represented pre-occupation vested interests, whereas Enver Hoxha represented the dispossessed and was uninhibited by the destruction that his activities caused.[5] And therein lies the key to the fundamental difference between the two societies – the AAA represented those with a vested interest in maintaining Albania as it was pre-war, whilst the ASB represented the 'progressive' ideology of post-war Albania.

The Anglo-Albanian Association

The Anglo-Albanian Association is the far older of the two societies. It was formed in 1912 by the MP and diplomat Aubrey Herbert, who vigorously campaigned on behalf of Albania, along with the esteemed

---

[4]See: J. Amery, Sons of the Eagle, Macmillan, 1948, and D. Smiley, Albanian Assignment, Chatto and Windus, 1984.

[5]N. Bethell, The Great Betrayal – The Untold Story of Kim Philby's Biggest Coup, Hodder and Stoughton, 1984, p19. Lord Bethell (1938-2007) was a writer, historian and Tory MEP, who championed the human rights of people living under former communist regimes.

traveller and tireless champion of the Albanian cause Edith Durham.[6] Following the declaration of Albania's independence, Albania remained vulnerable and threatened by her immediate Balkan neighbours. With its influential membership, which included the likes of Viscount Cecil and Sir Edward Boyle, the Anglo-Albanian Association (AAA) was able to provide invaluable help to the fledgling state by closely monitoring events in the Balkans and providing information on Albania and the Albanian-inhabited areas of the former Yugoslavia.

According to the AAA, after the Second World War, the Association concerned itself particularly with exiles from the communist dictatorship in Albania – Albanians whose lives were in many cases at risk because of the support they had given to British Liaison Officers in wartime Albania. The Association, which describes itself as a 'politically impartial body', provided them with advice and help in the process of adjusting to life in Britain. Julian Amery and fellow associates in the Anglo-Albanian Association met regularly in his home in Belgravia, initially putting their faith in Zog's son Leka to return to power as the Albanian regime began to falter in the late 1990s.

When the Democratic Party won Albania's first multi-party election in 1992, Amery and his former SOE colleague and fellow AAA member, David Smiley, decided to throw their weight behind the new Albanian president, Sali Berisha. They successfully persuaded the Foreign Office and the Conservative Party to give him diplomatic and material support. Henceforth, the Association renewed its links with Albania, and acted as a useful point of liaison for numerous aid organisations during the poverty-stricken country's difficult transition years. Julian Amery died in 1996 and was succeeded by Sir Geoffrey Pattie Tory MP and former trade and industry minister, as the Association's new head.

From 1992 until its overthrow in 1997, the powerful right-wing lobby of Zogist émigrés and the Anglo-Albanian Association provided the Berisha government with the most determined and ideological support

---

[6]For background information on both these personalities see the following publications see: Gill Trethowan, Queen of the Mountains – The Balkan Adventures of Edith Durham, the British Council, 1996, and M. Edith Durham – Albania and the Albanians, Selected Articles and Letters 1903-1944, edited by Bejtullah Destani,, Centre for Albanian Studies, London, 2001, and Aubrey Herbert and the Making of Modern Albania, edited by Bejtullah Destani,and Jason Tomes, Centre for Albanian Studies, I B.Tauris, 2011.

seen anywhere in the world. In the murky and violent political climate surrounding Berisha's attempted coup in 1998 and the assassination in Tirana of opposition leader Azem Hajdari, the AAA continued its unquestioning support for Berisha. Also, throughout the duration of the Kosovo conflict the Association also championed the actions of Kosovo's 'Prime Minister' Bujar Bukoshi, who was secretly forming a new army to compete with the Kosovo Liberation Army (KLA).

The Albania Society of Britain

The Albania Society of Britain had its origins in the cold-war climate of post-war Europe, when Albania found itself once more in a particularly defenceless situation. At that time the Albanian leadership was in a state of deep anxiety. Joseph Stalin had died in March 1953, and consequently Albania had lost her Great Power protector, and whilst the power struggle went on in Moscow, Enver Hoxha looked in every direction to encourage support for his vulnerable little country. In England he found it in the person of William Bland (1916 - 2001) a member of the pro-Stalinist wing of the Communist Party of Great Britain (CPGB) and a great anti-revisionist. In 1955 the Albanian government invited communist comrades in Britain to establish an Albania-UK friendship society. Thus, before the infamous 20th Congress of the Communist Party of the Soviet Union in February 1956 where Stalin's successor Nikita Khrushchev denounced Stalin's 'personality cult', which fundamentally altered the course of Soviet history, Bland founded the Albania Society of Britain.

The Albanian leadership meanwhile had had to swallow a bitter pill and accept the new Soviet Party Secretary Nikita Khrushchev's denunciation of Stalin, and the rehabilitation of Yugoslavia's Marshal Tito. Despite now being officially ostracized by Albania due to his continued support for Stalin's ideology, Bill Bland strove to expand the influence of the Albania Society of Britain. He organised an enormous amount of information and education on the country and in doing so became an acknowledged authority on all things Albanian. He published an English-Albanian dictionary and answered queries not only from Britain but also from around the world upon all features of Albanian politics, life, history, culture and music. Aside from his ridged ideological views, Bland was genuinely very fond of Albania and its people and was instrumental in organising that wonderful little shop on the corner of Betterton Street in

Covent Garden that contained an array of all things Albanian, including the obvious political propaganda but also imported craftwork such, as pottery and rugs as well as a rich folk music emporium at the back of the shop.

By the late 1950s membership of the Albania Society had grown to around four hundred, including many who had no real political affiliation with the regime in Tirana, but had a variety of interests in Albania. These ranged from ethnography, archaeology and music to those who were just curious and fascinated about what was then a remote and exciting land. The society's very first newsletter, published on the 28th November 1958, includes a long and detailed travel article that provides a wonderful and historically useful account of life in Albania at that time.[7]

As relations between Moscow and Bejing evaporated in June 1960, Enver Hoxha showed common interest with the Chinese and the Albanian Party of Labour duly supported China in exchange for the latter's patronage.[8] As a consequence, in Britain Maoist groups, aided by financial help from China, set up an explicit party front Albania Society, resisting Bland's call for one single united front regardless of 'narrow' party affiliation. Following Mao's death in September 1976, relations between Albania and China declined and the Maoist societies in Britain either split or disintegrated. Their remaining members were advised by Albania's Foreign Liaison Committee to join with Bland's Albania Society of Britain to form one 'United Front' of support for the Albanian Party of Labour.

Simultaneously, however, the Albanian authorities in Tirana launched attempts to remove Bland's leadership of the Albania Society, arguing that an emphasis on all aspects of life – such as music, poetry and art – was 'anti-Marxist-Leninist,' and 'insufficiently political,' and that Bland should be removed. It is testament to Bland's wide support amongst the ASB's membership, which also included non-Marxists who had a genuine interest in Albania's historic and cultural heritage, that the

---

[7] J.N.F. Newall: Notes on Albania, Albania – Newsletter of the Albanian Society, 28 November, 1958, pp4-14

[8] For more on Albania's foreign relations during this period see the following works: William Ash, Pickaxe and Rifle, London, 1974; E. Biberaj, Albania and China – A Study of an Unequal Alliance, Boulder, 1986; William Griffiths, Albania and the Sino-Soviet Rift, Cambridge MA, 1963; Miranda Vickers, The Albanians – A Modern History, I.B. Tauris, 2005, Ch.8.

attempts by Bejing to remove Bland were rejected and the Society continued to operate in its usual form until the 'revisionist' take-over of Albania by Ramiz Alia after the death of Enver Hoxha in April 1985. At this point Bill Bland resigned from the Albania Society.[9] In the late 1980's the Society continued to campaign for a better understanding of both Albania and Kosova, and some members of Kosova Albanian origins formed contacts with the Kosova Peoples Movement (LPRK), and the Society was the first organisation to publish in English its revised programme for a workers uprising in Kosova against Serbian rule. In the wake of the political upheavals in Albania culminating in the country's first multiparty election in March 1991, the pro-communist leadership of the Albania Society of Britain was finally ousted at the Society's AGM later that year and, almost to a man, the hard line membership left to join Bill Bland's new Stalin Society.

The new open tone of the Society could be judged from the contents of the Society's widely respected quarterly journal 'Albanian Life', which published articles on all aspects of Albanian life, as well as providing useful contact information, travel advice and political updates. It must be remembered that until the mid-1990s, Albania did not have a properly functioning embassy in the United Kingdom, and therefore people only had the two Albania organisations, the AAA and the ASB to turn to in order to gain any information about Albania.[10] Despite most of those in the Anglo-Albanian Association still regarding the ASB members as out and out Stalinists, the ASB membership continued to be comprised of people whose interests in Albania were not primarily political or ideological. These included historians, writers, journalists, travellers and students, who were on the whole non-affiliated leftists.

When the communist regime was overthrown at the beginning of the 1990s, it was initially thought possible to think of and discuss Albanian issues in other than the black and white terms of pro or

---

[9]Marxist Internet Archive, Bill Bland, www.marxists.org/glossary/people For information of the LPRK link, see James Pettifer, The Kosova Liberation Army Underground War to Balkan Insurgency,1948-2001,London,2012,P.340 ff

[10]There was also, in London, a very weak Kosovo Information Office (KIO) representing the Democratic League of Kosovo, which served only to provide a routine briefing sheet on events in Kosovo but otherwise, in comparison to the highly pro-active and informative KIO offices in Germany, Switzerland and the US, failed to provided information on what was really happening in Kosovo.

anti-communism. Unfortunately though, President Sali Berisha chose to make anti-communism a main plank of his political platform and anyone who opposed him was labelled a 'communist'. Instead of the politics of reconciliation and movement towards the creation of a political centre which was so urgently needed, Albania was given the politics of division. This led to Berisha's defeats in the 1994 referendum, the rigged 1996 general election, the 1997 uprising and the subsequent election of a new Socialist-led government.[11]

In Britain, the Anglo-Albanian Association openly supported President Berisha whilst the Albania Society of Britain did not. This earned the latter the reputation of being crypto-communist. The ASB, having purged its Stalinist left, now accused the AAA of perpetrating a simplistic, right-wing, nationalist interpretation of Albanian history, reflected by cheerleading for Berisha. Such name-calling had its roots in wartime Albania with the division between 'nationalists' and 'partisans'. This was translated after the war into 'anti-communists' and 'communist sympathisers', and during the 1990s into 'pro-Berisha/democrats' and 'anti-Berisha/Socialist/leftists. Thus, despite the fact that theoretically Albania was now an open and democratic country, the sharp ideological divide between the two Albanian societies in Britain lingered on, due largely to the fact that Albania itself remained deeply divided politically.

Against this factious background, in 1997 the Albania Society of Britain unanimously elected Sir Reginal Hibbert as its President. In February 1998 Hibbert wrote on behalf of the Albania Society of Britain to the Secretary of the Anglo-Albanian Association suggesting that the time had come for the two societies to consider uniting or merging to form a single society in the U.K., in order to cultivate friendship and good relations with Albania. Hibbert believed that should the two societies be combined they would undoubtedly be able to speak and act more effectively in Albania's favour, and this could not fail to be of help to Albania in confronting the difficult circumstances by which it was then beset. He believed that the old and deep antagonisms had to be overcome in Albania in view of the pressing need for national unity, and simultaneously it was time that the same antagonisms should be overcome in Britain. In the light of these reflections, it was agreed

---

[11]R. Hibbert, Albanian Life, Issue 63, Spring 1999, p6

by the committee of the Albania Society of Britain that the President should write a letter to his counterpart in the Anglo-Albanian Association suggesting a possible merger of the two societies now that ideological differences were supposedly immaterial. He duly wrote the letter, the text of which is re-printed below:

Sir Reginald Hibbert's letter from the Albania Society of Britain to the Secretary of the Anglo-Albanian Association

9th February, 1998

I write to you in my capacity as President of the Albania Society of Britain and on behalf of the Council of that Society. It is our feeling that perhaps the time has come for our two societies to consider uniting or merging to form a single society in the U.K. to cultivate friendship and good relations with Albania. It is an oddity and a weakness that so small a country should have two different societies in this country to foster relations with it. Albania has not had many foreign friends during its short history, certainly not at governmental level, and there is a strong case for thinking that overseas interest in Albania should be concentrated and not dispersed.

Politically, Albania has been a sharply divided country. That division has for most of the period since the Second World War, been reflected by divisions amongst those abroad who have professed interest in Albania. We think that the divisions are now becoming blurred and that it is time to try to overcome them. In any case, as we see it, the function of societies such as ours is to foster interest in Albania the country rather than in any particular currents which may for the time being prevail there.

We hope that your Association might be persuaded to explore the possibility of a merger with us. It would probably be desirable to start with a general discussion of the way in which unity might be approached and if this proved promising it would be possible to move on to a more detailed discussion of modalities. I can tell you at this stage that we attach no great importance to the name of our society. We do, however, value our journal 'Albania Life' highly and we would want this to survive under a new combined organisation, offering your Association an appropriate share in editorial control. I look forward to hearing whether we can tempt you to talk to us in the way I have suggested. If you can agree to have an exploratory meeting, two or three from each society might get together to see if we can find common ground. I trust that you will be able to share our view that a merger would be in the best interests of Albania. I think that the F.C.O. and the British Embassy in Tirana would also welcome it.'

Yours Sincerely,

Reginald Hibbert

There is no doubt that this letter was written by a diplomat of long standing and from the tone of the letter, it can be seen that a somewhat positive response from the AAA was thought to be forthcoming. The short reply when it came one month later was very disappointing.

Reply from the Hon. Secretary of the Anglo–Albanian Association

10th March, 1998

Dear Sir Reginald,

I am writing as Honorary Secretary of the Anglo-Albanian Society in reply to your letter of the 9th February. The Executive Committee of the Association felt it important to canvass the views of our membership, both British and Albanian. It met later to consider your proposal and after a full discussion, came to the unanimous conclusion that a merger with the Albania Society of Britain is not something which would enjoy sufficient support from our members for the Committee to take your proposal any further. Individual members of the Albania Society of Britain who are not already members of the Anglo-Albanian Association are, of course, welcome to apply for membership.

Yours sincerely,

Denys Salt

At that time, the societies shared some enthusiastic members, who subscribed to both organisations, but were not on either executive committee. There was genuine disappointment amongst these members that no merger would take place. There were, however, still too many unresolved issues including the Anglo Albanian Association's desire to take over the editorship of the Albania Society's magazine 'Albania Life'. In particular, David Smiley declined to enter into any polemic with Hibbert, labelling him a 'communist' and always refused to even shake hands with ASB member, Miranda Vickers, calling her 'the Red Lady'.

When Albania imploded into a popular and violent uprising in the spring of 1997, members of both the Albania Society of Britain and the Anglo-Albania Association threw themselves into the fray by writing and broadcasting on the dramatic events in Albania. Almost immediately the polemics became bitter and at times personal. As the uprising intensified and the southern insurgents reached the outskirts of Tirana in late March, British supporters of the beleaguered President Berisha, claimed that news reports from Albania had been grossly distorted. On 9 March, under the headline 'The Media Back the Communists as Usual,' the Sunday Telegraph carried a fierce attack on Berisha's critics, including two leading members of the Albanian Society of Britain.[12] Miranda Vickers, who wrote for the Guardian and James Pettifer who wrote for the Times. The Telegraph article was written by Anthony Daniels, an observer at the controversial 1996 Albanian elections with the self-styled British Helsinki Human Rights Group. The following day Richard Norton Taylor reported in the Guardian that: 'an intriguing sub-plot is being played out amidst the plethora of British press coverage of the deepening crisis in Albania. Two camps, originally divided by history and ideology, have been engaged in increasingly bitter verbal skirmishes over the actions of President Sali Berisha. Yesterday, their differences escalated into open warfare'.[13]

The article by Daniels severely criticised Vickers and Pettifer over the accuracy and impartiality of their reports from Albania. The article wrongly claimed that they were both supporters of the former Stalinist regime of the Albanian dictator Enver Hoxha. After legal intervention both won substantial damages from the Sunday Telegraph, which then published an apology stating that the paper: 'regretted having given

---

[12]Anthony Daniels, 'The Media Back the Communists as Usual, The Sunday Telegraph, 9 March, 1997.

[13]Richard Norton Taylor, 'Champions Go To War', The Guardian, 10 March, 1997.

currency to Mr Daniel's allegations which we now know to be untrue. Far from supporting the anti-religious and other policies of Hoxha, James Pettifer, a practicing member of the Church of England, has always strongly opposed them. Miranda Vickers is also strongly opposed to the policies of the Hoxha regime. Her association with the Albania Society's magazine 'Albania Life' began only after a new editorial board had replaced its former Marxist-Leninist standpoint with an open democratic editorial policy.'[14]

Whilst political turmoil raged in Albania and the Kosovo conflict continued, relations between the AAA and the ASB remained acutely polarised. But as time passed, and Albania achieved relative stability and Kosovo gained its independence, the decision was taken in 2001 to finally wind up the Albania Society of Britain. Its membership agreed that with the functioning of a now normal Albanian embassy in London, which could answer queries from the media and general public on matters relating to Albania, combined with the publication of increasing numbers of books and articles about Albania, the actual raison d'etre for the society had ceased. The ASB's extensive archive was given to a small society called the Friends of Albania run by Primrose Peacock, which was non-political and primarily concerned itself with the provision of aid to Albania.[15]

Albania's need for encouragement and support from all corners is as necessary today as it was during those anarchic years after the collapse of communism. But nowadays, those still actively involved in Albanian affairs in Britain do so in a more individual and tolerant manner, mindful of the past but with no ideological axe to grind. Indeed, today's membership of the Anglo-Albanian Association is almost identically representative as what the Albania Society of Britain once was. As Albania becomes more 'mainstream', rather than the quirky oddity is had been until recently, the divisive wartime legacy in Britain has mellowed, especially since the death of all the main players active in wartime Albania – Reginald Hibbert died in 2002, Julian Amery in 1996 and David Smiley in January 2009. Albaniaphiles in Britain have, for the most part, moved on from the bitter polemics that characterised their relations during the 1990s. Those who support Albania today do so largely in the spirit of inclusiveness.

---

[14]The Sunday Telegraph, 20 April, 1997. See also Misha Glenny, Now it's war among the British Friends of Albania, The Sunday Times, 24 March, 1997

[15]In 2010 this archive material was sent to Princeton University, USA.

Albanian-related events in London are now attended by AAA members together with those who were once ASB members. Twenty years after the end of the one-party state, the same sadly cannot be said about Albania itself where political extremism is rife and its politicians are as viscerally adversarial as they have ever been.

Old tradition to new reality: Environmental, social and economic impacts of tourism in Thethi, Albania

Erin Marchington and Antonia Young

A first impression of Thethi, on arrival after a bone-shattering many-hour drive over high mountains, is one of wonderment. The pristine magnificence of the surrounding mountain peaks; the purity of the fast flowing River Shala; the naturally forested quietness of this valley without motorized vehicles; the many vernacular local stone houses; and the gentle curiosity and welcome of locals, especially children, all these combine to create a Shangri-La – a vision of peacefulness and harmony, in a virtually hidden valley, at times cut off by snow from the outside world.

Given his life-long interest in Albania, Reginald Hibbert must have experienced a similar feeling of wonderment during his first journey in Albania, into which he parachuted in 1943[1]. Returning to the region many times throughout his life, and a 'brave advocate' of a country which was both physically and socially isolated for decades after WWII, Hibbert witnessed several points of transition in Albania's political history that have shaped its development: post-WWII shift to communism, end of the communist period in the early 1990s and upheaval associated with the shift to a market economy. On a national scale, these drastic political and economic changes have been well documented by many scholars, including Hibbert himself. However, it is also interesting to consider the impacts of such transitions and development on a smaller or rural scale, which could be very effective in illuminating not only economic trends, but also environmental, social, and cultural impacts of such events. Since the majority of Albania's population was scattered rurally in villages throughout the country until urban migration and depopulation of rural areas set in post-communism[2], it is relevant to investigate these impacts on the village-level.

---

[1] The Independent, Obituaries 'Sir Reginald Hibbert: Albanologist and former ambassador in Paris', 2002.

[2] Hall, D. Rural tourism development in southeastern Europe: transition and the

Thethi is a northern Albanian village, remote and isolated- a characteristic that could lead one to assume that the rural population there would be relatively sheltered from the tumultuous national political and economic changes in the later 20th century. However, upon closer inspection, various transitions have also occurred in the village as it emerges from each period and struggles to adapt to new realities. In order to understand the impacts of development in Thethi, one must understand the historical roots, or where a village 'comes from'. Thus, this chapter will first outline influential factors of rural development in Thethi pre-2009, including environmental, social, and economic or subsistence strategies; this commentary is an outcome of personal and ethnographic research and visits to Thethi during the 1990s by Antonia Young, and later in collaboration with the Shala Valley Project (SVP), during which she had the opportunity to interview families in the village from 2005 – 2007. Following this is an exploration of the effect of modern (2009 – present) rural development on these traditions, which has accompanied the periods of transition in Albania. Specifically, environmental, social, and economic impacts of tourism are discussed which is the culmination of fieldwork and research conducted by Erin Marchington in 2009 - 2010 as a part of her MESPOM thesis.

The risk in the current transition period, where tourism development is being recognized as a great opportunity for growth, is that economic growth will be prioritized over all else, which is what happened in most parts of the world during the post-WWII transition period, leading to unsustainable development.

That first impression can be abruptly changed by one of those locals pointing out that it's lovely for visitors and during summer, but not such fun if you live there year-round. Deep winter in the isolated Shala is not easy to contend with. Coping with these long and difficult winters, involves stacking wood and animal feed all through the summer in preparation for being totally cut off from outside supplies for several months on end. However, this situation is changing for most families as more and more migrate to Shkodër or further away, for the winter, returning in the spring to tend their properties and prepare to cater for tourists.

search for sustainability. International Journal of Tourism Research, 2004.

Old traditions: Influential factors of rural development in Thethi, Albania (pre-2009)

As Ethnographic Team leader of the Shala Valley archaeological Project, Young's visits with Thethi families enabled her to talk in particular to the older residents, thus obtaining memories of life in the region during the past half century. Without exception, Thethians were extremely hospitable and keen to discuss issues related to kinship organization, past and present subsistence strategies, historical data about native architecture and its change over time, as well as their thoughts about the potential and logistics of future economic developments in the region and working patterns during the past half century and more. Their interest in and concern for the development of sustainable tourism, especially as it could potentially be linked to the cross-border Balkans Peace Park Project[3] was explored, in particular there was enthusiasm for the provision of educational children's programmes.

Thethi, in the Shala Valley, lies alongside the Montenegrin border, which had been theoretically closed since the borders were drawn by the Great Powers of Europe meeting in London in 1912. In fact, it was a porous border until the Second World War, and for a short period following that War, there was discussion concerning the possibility of integration, i.e. Albania becoming Yugoslavia's seventh republic. That consideration died with Yugoslavia's break with the USSR in 1948. Thereafter, Albania's borders were strictly sealed and few Albanians were able to escape. Penalties for such attempts could bring not only death to those who tried, but extremely severe punishment to remaining family members.

Geography and environment

Thethi National Park was established in 1966, covering an area of 2,630 ha. With ranges in altitude from approx. 1,200m to 2,567m (at the summit of Mt. Radohima). At present rather little activity is taken concerning conservation, despite laws prohibiting hunting, fishing and logging.

---

[3]The UK charity envisions a transnational park spanning Albania, Montenegro and Kosova as a symbol of peace and cooperation, where communities from all three countries work together to protect their fragile environment, stimulate local employment and promote sustainable visitor activities in the region. See www. balkanspeacepark.org

Thethi's isolation is exacerbated by its very severe weather conditions and extremely poor infrastructure.

Unlike most other regions in Albania, this area received none of Kosova's half million refugees at the time of the 1999 Kosovar War, whereas on average for every seven of Albanian's inhabitants, there was a Kosovar refugee at the height of its hospitality.

Kinship and Social Organization

Like all villages in the Shala Valley, Thethi is an exogamous village since all its families are distantly related to a common ancestor, the founder of the village, Ded Nika. Therefore, the members of the village consider their community as a brotherhood *(vllazni)*. When asked to sketch a family tree, it was fascinating to find that this was traced as a single line of son-father-grandfather-great-grandfather etc., back to as many as 12 generations of male ancestors. Women never featured in these diagrams, indicating their minor importance, all having married into the village from other villages. Until the 1950's, Thethians observed this rule of exogamy amongst the villages of Shala. Usually families attributed their settlement in Thethi some 300-350 years ago as a retreat to the mountains in order to avoid a conversion to Islam.

The six neighborhoods of Thethi, named after the six original brothers, are often also organized to pool labor in working the fields co-operatively, the most efficient way to work the land both now and in the past. Up until 2009, no mechanical agricultural equipment was to be seen in Thethi. On weekdays, in feudal tradition, the particular owner pays the participants for their labor in working his fields and hosts a lunch for them. However, on Sundays such a group may work without compensation for a family in need, but again the celebratory lunch is provided in recognition of the participants' goodwill. The work is seen as a charitable religious gesture.

Each neighborhood is further divided into clusters of closely related households. This follows from the traditional splitting of extended families. The northern Albanian extended family suffered a blow during the Communist regime, especially when land was collectivized leaving only 1-2 dylyms[4] of land per each family. This led to many families dividing up, in order to retain more land. Traditionally the process of

---

[4] 1 dylym is equal to a 100 X 10 m or 1000 m2 parcel.

splitting and rebuilding involves an intricate division process that evolves over decades following the laws of the Kanun[5].

The largest household in the years 2004-2009 had 14 members with three generations residing under one roof. It has more than one descendant of the head of the household (*zoti i shtepis*). The community kin-oriented links are strengthened in a number of ways; for example, *kumbar* relationships, or the traditional first cutting of a child's hair gives the cutter the status of a non-religious godparent. Many of the rituals related to weddings such as the tradition for a new bride to be available to receive and serve a wide network of visitors during her first month of marriage also strengthen these links.

This perceived family link (however remote) has helped the people to retain friendly relations and to continue to work co-operatively. For example they still use six communal water mills to grind their corn. Even without any monetary exchange, the mills are used and maintained without dispute. However, we also found evidence of several feuds, some ongoing and others reported as ended. There were efforts made by the Communist state to uproot patriarchal ways, by breaking up large family units and by including women in the workforce outside the home. They were also successful in suppressing bloodfeuds. Nevertheless, several villagers have reported a feud incident in the past and surprisingly several were incidents within their own neighborhoods in the village. Each incident followed a particular routine in terms of settlement strategy (Mustafa and Young, 2008).

Subsistence strategies and architectural patterns of change

In characterising the three post-World War II periods (pre-1957, Communist, and post-Communist), the earliest era main economy was pastoral. During the Communist era, land and animals were collectivized and the villagers secured their livelihood through wage work for the cooperative. Currently, most households have developed their own small holdings for their domestic needs for crops and animals. Many families who have migrated return to Thethi for the summer months to enjoy

---

[5]Most families claim to be guided by traditional law, the Kanun of Lek Dukagjin for the division of property, resolution of conflicts, and for marriage rituals. Some voiced a concern for the conflict between customary and state law.

the clean mountain air, to maintain their properties, to work the land for fruit (strawberries, plums, grapes, apples, pears, cherries, mulberries) and vegetables (tomatoes, lettuce, onions, garlic and peppers), as well as the main staple crops (corn, potatoes, beans)[6]. The pastures are utilized for cows, sheep and some goats as well as hay fields for winter fodder (mostly alfalfa). All this gives their children the benefits and freedom to play and live cheaply on freshly produced food. Some take their animals with them to the outskirts of Shkodra for the winter. Several families also have beehives. Plums, mulberries, wild strawberries, walnuts and hazelnuts are available to gather freely. They grow in the wild, and people can pick them as they wish. Almost every household makes its own *raki* (clear alcoholic spirit) from grapes or plums, which is traditionally offered to guests at any time of day, from early morning until late at night. Another local product is herbs which are plentiful and in several varieties., and also used as tea. Thethi used to be a collection centre for herbs and animal hides in Communist times, but now there is no proper infrastructure for profitable collection and sale.

Residential seasonal transhumance observed in Thethi has its roots in the old pastoral transhumance lifestyle and is still practiced by some of the inhabitants who reside in Thethi year-round. In the past all families would send up some of their members to spend the summer in the high pastures, now rather few do that. The numbers of these families has dwindled year by year.

Up to the beginning of the 20th century, trade was made with Gusi, Plav, and Peja (over the Qafa e Pejes [Peja Pass] to Montenegro). Although the borders of Albania were drawn by The Great Powers in London in 1912, it seems that the effects were not fully felt until after WWII and the break with Yugoslavia in 1948, after which time access to the old markets was no longer possible. These markets were utilized for the purchase of corn, which was cheaper and more easily available in comparison to Shkodra. In turn, the Shkodra market was mainly used to sell animals and pastoral products and the purchase of salt, sugar, oil and other household needs.

The large stone houses which characterize the built landscape of Thethi have steep roofs to prevent the heavy winter snows from accumulating.

---

[6]Intercropping is a traditional practice. Beans and corn are the most common combination although grape vines may be found surrounded by other produce.

Traditional beech wood roof tiles are very picturesque, but many have found that the less attractive, cheaper, and longer lasting corrugated iron serve their purposes better. Few houses are more than 200 years old, many of them were built about a century ago. Another wave of buildings coinciding with the first couple of decades after the establishment of the communist regime. Some of the older houses were only one storey, with an additional storey added at a later date. Commonly inhabited houses kept cattle on the ground floor, a custom well into the 20th century (Edith Durham gives some very graphic descriptions of such dwellings). Human habitation on the floor above benefitted from the heat of the animals in the living area. This changed with the opening of the cooperative in 1957 and the subsequent collectivisation of land and animals. As the villagers were for the most part left with only one cow and one pig, and due to hygienic directives from the board of health that required that animal shelters should be located at least 10 meters away from the house, the first floors that once were utilized as barns were converted into living spaces. Most homes have outside toilets at some distance from the house, though each year more and more villagers are installing flush toilets.

Early forms of modern tourism

In the communist era, the government-controlled Trade Unions constructed a small holiday resort for workers' families, middle rank bureaucrats and trade union members. It was not deemed sufficiently comfortable for government ministers, especially with such a difficult and dangerous road to reach it.

Thethi remains the pearl of the Albanian Alps and is widely advertized (within Albania), as it was under the Communist regime. However, during communism advertising consisted only of pictures, stories, and the few first-hand accounts by foreign Marxist-Leninst party leaders visiting Albania at the invitation of the Party of Labour of Albania. Thethi was a symbol of Albania's wild beauty, though it was at the same time a forbidden area due to its proximity next to the Montenegrin border.

Although attempts are being made to ensure that Thethi conforms to sustainable tourism, tourism is not a new concept in the area. Between the two World Wars, Thethi was a holiday destination for rich families from Shkodër who had summer homes there, and also a place known as a cure for tuberculosis and other lung problems – though being nearer to Shkoder, the village of Razem was more attractive. It was King Zog's ambition to modernize his country, and one of his projects was the building of a dirt road from Koplik, 60 km over the mountains, north of Shkoder, through to Thethi in 1936. There was rumour that there had been a Tourist Information Centre in Thethi at the time the road was first built, though we were unable to confirm this. Several foreigners published books about their visits here in the inter-War period, so one might assume that this indicates that many more actually visited (e.g. Heseltine, Lane, Newman). The road built by Zog still remains little changed, though a portion of it has been tarmacked; it is the constant topic of conversation amongst all Thethi families, who would like to have it properly tarmacked all the way to the village, and even on down a further 20km. length of the Shala Valley. Ironically, when that happens, the influx of tourists may be the undoing of Thethi's attractiveness, which is now sharply in balance, and suffering from lack of any overall planning.

Transition: Post-communism until present (1991-2009)

It is clear that there has been a massive exodus of families since the fall of communism in the early 1990's, slower at first but particularly dramatic in the first couple of years of the new millennium. Of the 249 families in 1991, by 2005 only about 17 families were full time residents (this fell to just 8 families in 2008), although as many as sixty families that have left return to their Thethi homes in the summer. Thethi's school, built in 1957, had served hundreds of children in its 10 classrooms, but by 2004 only 20 pupils were in attendance, and teached presence was sporadic due to uncertainty and meagerness of pay.

On the other hand, as the country is opening up and Thethi is gaining in reputation as a tourist destination, some families who left many decades ago are currently returning to Thethi to take up summer residence and in particular to renovate their homes with an aim to take in tourists. While most families have relocated in Shkodra for permanent or winter residence, a good number of them have found their way to England, Greece, and Italy, and some as far as America. Lack of employment in Thethi is the major reason behind the exodus, although the villagers have voiced the need for adequate electricity, school, road, hospital, phone line, and an emergency evacuation service.

A small ethnographic museum was set up in 1985, as part of a national plan to have such museums in every village, containing artifacts supplied by the village residents. The scheme was supposed to be organized by the teachers of each village. Unfortunately shortly after the fall of Communism Thethi's museum was deceptively dismantled: uniformed men came from Tirana with false documents authorizing them to take all the contents of the museum. Additionally, considerable damage was sustained to the building during an earthquake in 2005, but the roof has been repaired. Several children promote themselves as guides to the museum and also to the *kulla* both of which stand out, on a high rocks.

Thethi has long had several advantages over most rural towns of Albania: a fast flowing river, supplying trout, a good and plentiful source of pure drinking water, lack of pollution, and until fairly recently, reliable electricity from their local waterfalls since the 'electrification of the villages' of the late 1960s and the maintenance of the communal generator. Traditionally there was natural care of woodlands by local families. Such tradition was interrupted by large scale planning under Communism, which included such in appropriate projects as planting apple orchards on the mountainside which the fierce winter weather prevented any yield. In the aftermath of Communism, economic desperation has affected traditional ways. The old electric generator (built in the 1960s) is in dire need of replacement.

Life is hard for the residents of Thethi. With little government support, pensioners receive about $70 each per month, the school has no equipment other than desks and chairs, and the building is in dire need of repair. There is no doctor or health clinic, their only medical assistance is from a male nurse with one year's training, who visits for 2 days a week from Abat (in winter he makes the journey on snowshoes, taking about three and a half hours each way). There was no telephone or radio communication until Vodafone linked up in 2007. Until 1997, by all accounts, the Albanian government provided essential food supplies that were stored centrally and available throughout the winter at minimal cost.

Thethi's Catholic church (built in 1892) was used during the Communist era as a grain store, and later as a maternity hospital. Its steeple was demolished and its bell hidden illegally by locals. In 1991 the large hidden church bell was brought out and, for lack of a steeple, it was hung in the nearest tree to the church. Shortly after, men came, claiming authority to take it to be mended, but it was never seen again. A much smaller bell was later placed in the church. In 2006 with donations from Albanian-American Catholics the church has been beautifully restored as it had originally been. Those now seeking qualified maternity care need to travel all the way to Shkodër.

On the question of women's role, most locals agree that the woman's place is to produce sone, and to sweep, clean and cook. Few discuss child rearing, so we might assume that this is considered to be something automatically happening within the communal living situation, though clearly woman tend babies. We heard more than once that women are no longer 'laden like animals as they used to be', and this was confirmed by the fact that we now see very few women carrying huge loads which were a common sight into the 1990s. It is common that young girls are prohibited from walking alone at all in the village. They work hard with domestic chores in their homes, while their brothers may go to school or swimming in the river, once they have finished their laboring work.

Since the fall of Communism in 1991, all Albanian rural areas have been adversely affected by the withdrawal of central government support, resulting in serious feuds over land ownership, often followed by high migration rates. This, as well as the search for employment away from the Valley, or abroad, led to mass migration out of rural areas of young men and even whole families.

Although many villages in the area suffer deeply from both of these phenomena, it was interesting to find that this particular village, Thethi, is unusual in its relatively lower level of internal conflict. There is a division by social status between the two ends of the village, which are beginning to be exacerbated by international financial support given to those larger homes already more easily adapted to supply home-stay tourists.

With endorsement from the Shkodër Education Authority, the Balkans Peace Park Project initiated and supported an annual Summer Programme for the local children, using Thethi School. Starting in 2007, around 100 children attended daily for two months. Classes in Environmental Awareness are taught by Albanian teachers, and English language by volunteer teachers from the UK, US and Canada. Additional activities are also offered, depending on the qualification of the volunteers (who all pay their full travel and accommodation costs). Activities offered have included sports, music, drama, crafts, civics, and most recently an international Permaculture course ran alongside the Summer Programme.

New Reality: Current rural and tourism development in Thethi (2009 – present)

From the above discussion, it is evident that there is an immediate need to initiate rural development projects in the region in order to mitigate and prevent further depopulation and economic disparity; but what project would be successful under such isolated and seemingly resource-poor conditions? It is apparent that the answer could lie in problem itself, and knowing that Thethi was used as a tourism destination in the past, utilizing the isolated yet *pristine environment* as the key resource to leverage rural development through tourism is an attractive concept for the community.

This pathway has recently been promoted by the local government and by international and local non-governmental organizations (NGOs) working in the area. However, the visitor and local community visions for tourism development, although not necessarily mutually exclusive or unique to each group, expose tension between the idea of preservation of culture and environment and the need for development and increased quality of life. Although there are many potential benefits that can result from tourism in rural villages like Thethi, the risk of negative effects are also significant. There is potential for harm to the environment, the key resource for such a development project, and to members of the local population, the stakeholders whom development is intended to aid. In recognition of such risks, there is a need to examine the form, implementation, and the actual and potential impacts of rural development strategies such as tourism.

Erin Marchington had the opportunity to conduct such an examination in Thethi, Albania during July 2009, using participant observation research methodology. Following this fieldwork, literature reviews, semi-structured interviews, and interactions with stakeholders via meetings and conference attendance were conducted from February to June 2010. The point of departure for the research was that the 'pristine environment' represents the primary resource for tourism and its enfolding activities, where 'environment' as the key resource for development encompasses both the natural and built landscapes. Following from this, sustainable tourism development (STD) in the context of the research was defined as 'tourism development that contributes to rural development, increasing quality of life for all, while preserving the key resource for development, the natural and built environment'.

Potential negative impacts of tourism could be mitigated or avoided in Thethi, pursuing sustainable tourism development more effectively. In the summer of 2010 an international Permaculture course ran alongside the B3P Summer Programme.

Current tourism development in Thethi (2009 – present)

Tourism development is apparent in many forms upon entrance into the village, where visitors are met with a large map supplied by GTZ indicating marked hiking trails in the area. GTZ also produced a walking guide, trail markings, and are working on an accommodation project. GTZ supplied grants to participating families, to renovate bedrooms and create bathrooms to meet tourists' needs, range and quality of services, signposting those homes offering such accommodation.

Although this project has been largely viewed as successful, it is also believed by some to have created tension in the village between those families included in the project and those who have not, see below under tourism impacts[7]. One community member is cited as saying '... it is ridiculous to accommodate tourists, even we, local people, do not have proper supply of water or electricity'. Some families have started to develop accommodation projects privately, independent of GTZ. It is unclear which guesthouses were funded by GTZ; and competition between families for tourists was evident; for example, one family had children approaching tourists soliciting for customers. It was evident that most encountered tourists preferred to stay in accommodation that was 'westernized' with functional toilets and working electricity and water; however, this only provided income to those families who are already relatively financially secure. Some tourists are completely self-sufficient bringing all their own food and sleeping in their own tents.

The Balkan Peace Park Project (B3P) is another actor involved in promoting tourism in the area, active in Thethi during the summer

---

[7]Information in this section primarily from Satoko Hara's M.A. Dissertation, University of Bradford (2009) and Erin B. Marchington's M.A. Dissertation, Lund University (2010).

months, operating a school programme run by international volunteers for local children annually since 2008; the volunteers stay as tourists with local families, providing some of the first accommodation opportunities for many residents

Returning to the former Communist workers' holiday resort, developers (probably from further afield than Thethi) started converting this into a medium-sized hotel during 2009; it is not located directly in the Valley, but just outside the Valley. It is unclear what the source of water, electricity, and waste disposal will be. This will result in increased competition for tourist accommodation and place pressure on existing resources.

Other local entrepreneurship supports the use and payment of local guides to hiker, and several small 'bars' and cafes have been established. The most innovative of these is a bar built very simply beside a wooden bridge over the Shala River, with a rough water mill run with plastic jugs, to turn a spit, which can roast a lamb. A single small shop opened around 2000, selling candy bars, snacks, and drinks. Another resident has begun to sell jams and preserves from her garden to tourists.

Several outdoor travel companies lead trips to Thethi and the area. At least seven travel company websites have been identified. Until recently, travel literature was very limited with little mention of the whole region. With the advent of social networks and private websites, some local residents, or people with connections to the village, are designing their own tourism sites (for example, www.thethi-guide.com).

Current and probable future impacts of tourism development in Thethi

Since tourism development is still on a relatively small scale, impacts will not be too detrimental, especially as the continual development is occurring alongside other significant changes in the region and country.

Table 1 outlines several impacts that are highly likely follow increased numbers of visitors to the region tourism develops. Impacts are organized thematically by the three pillars of sustainability, economic, social and environmental impacts, and described as a stakeholder cost, benefit or unclear, where the stakeholder is identified.

Table 1. Impacts of current tourism development in Thethi.

Sustainability pillar	Impact description	Impact occurring as a result of tourism development? [Yes, No, or Unclear] Impact is a [Cost, Benefit, Unclear] to which stakeholder? Evidence.
Economic	Influx of local, national and foreign tourists to the village.	Yes, benefit to local families and individuals able to participate. Bring income to some of those providing accommodation, entrepreneurs running small businesses (bars, cafes, local preserves, guided hikes, ethnography museum).
	External Outdoor travel companies, expeditions to region.	Yes, benefit to travel company and tourists. Bring income primarily to travel companies (aside from accommodation- indirect affects)
	Travel literature produced by private companies and individuals.	Yes, benefit to travel literature industry and tourists. Bring income primarily to private companies and individuals.
Social	Aggravation of socio-economic divides in the village.	Yes, cost to local people. Tension between families receiving benefits from tourism accommodation and those who do not, or are not participating.
	Placing needs of tourists before local people.	Yes, benefit to tourists, cost to local people. Development of tourist infrastructure before providing residents with healthcare, sufficient electricity, water, and waste management.
	Influx of tourists from other cultures or parts of Albania.	Yes, cost and benefit to local people and visitors. Bring in different ideas, and cultures to village. Some tension between patriarchal traditions, Albanian women.

Social (cont.)	Influx of NGOs (local, international) promoting tourism, researchers, media.	Yes, cost and benefit to local people and visitors. Bring in different ideas, and cultures to village, capacity and skills. Some tension with resident expectations and feeling of use, distrust in promises. Minimal disruption to daily activities via tourist observation: Church, agricultural practises, cooking, etc.
Environment and cultural landscape	Increased demand and use of resources (water, electricity, food, transportation).	Yes, primary cost to local people (and tourists while visiting). Low availability of water, electricity to some homes due to increased use; need to bring in food from outside Thethi to feed guests.
	Accumulation of solid waste.	Yes, primary cost to local people (and tourists while visiting). The presence of visitors to Thethi aggravates the waste management problem by increasing the amount of packaging and construction waste to piles around village.
	Increase in production of wastewater (sewage and grey water).	Unclear, not tested; likely primary cost to local people (and tourists while visiting). The presence of visitors to Thethi aggravates the waste management problem by increasing the amount of sewage and grey water released directly into the environment, potentially contaminating soil and waterways.
	Infrastructure construction.	Yes, cost and benefit to local people and benefit to tourists. Building: tourist infrastructure, modification of homes, road improvements, bridge reconstruction, preservation of Kula, church, 'museum'.

The majority of social and economic costs are to the local community; these can be correlated to the five common themes underlying negative impacts of tourism development: disruption to daily life (minor), disillusion with failed promises of tourism development, conflict, cultural change, and environmental degradation[8].

Stakeholders and their roles in the current tourism development process in Thethi

To address how STD in Thethi could be pursued more effectively, the impacts described above must be connected to the current tourism development process, by identifying stakeholders and their role or form of participation in Thethi tourism development. Multiple stakeholders existed, including: landowners (local, non-local); transportation providers (furgon drivers); investors (local, Albanian, foreign), Government (local, regional, national), international NGOs (B3P UK, UNEP, UNDP, etc.); local NGOs (IEP, SNV, GTZ, REC Albania); local community (distinct groups based on age, gender, year-long or part-time residents, socio-economic position, etc.); tour operators (Outdoor Albania, foreign companies, etc.); tourists (regional, foreign); and researchers (IPPE, SVP, independent).

An interesting concept to consider is the impact of geographical and timescale boundaries on stakeholder identification. This is especially pertinent when considering impacts of development on the environment, which can occur in much longer timescales than, for example, economic benefits or income, although they may occur on a similar scale to social changes. While geographical boundaries were limited to tourism development within the village, it should be noted that national and international stakeholders could also influence this process. If a sustainability approach is taken, then timescale for tourism development must be considered a few generations.

The main stakeholder of interest is the local community because tourism development is a vehicle for rural development, which is their primary objective. However, although not typically included in traditional management or organizational theory stakeholder lists[9], and

---

[8]Moscardo, G. Building community capacity for tourism development, 2008.
[9]Mitchell, R. K., Agle, B. R., & Wood, D. J. Toward a Theory of Stakeholder
  Identification and Salience: Defining the Principle of Who and What Really

excluded in IUCN stakeholder lists, Drisco and Starik have argued for the inclusion of the natural environment as a primary stakeholder, not just represented by environmental groups, organizations, or networks. It is interesting to note that although typically a community and environment are considered one stakeholder, believed to have uniform objectives and values, this is rarely the case. Thethi's community is very diverse from the point of view of age, gender, and socio-economic status. Similarly, the environment is also very diverse, in terms of multiple components and capacity to absorb impacts. The impact of tourism will be far less on the atmosphere than on the water supply.

There are multiple stakeholders and projects, all being implemented independently often allowing for little interaction between one another. Some projects, such as the accommodation project, went through a planning stage in their design; many unplanned projects lacked environmental, social, or economic impact assessments before (or after) implementation. Many also lack of monitoring and evaluation, especially in a holistic sense.

Sustainability of Thethi's tourism development process

A lack of evidence was found in evaluating Thethi tourism development for four components in sustainable tourism and rural development literature: i) functional and efficient institutional support and frameworks, ii) communication and coordination between stakeholders, iii) awareness and education, and iv) redefining the perception of development to follow sustainability principles

There are some schemes outlining stakeholder involvement and how to include the local community in TD decision-making[10]. An example is the development project 'Alps National Park' zoning. Since this model is project-based, it was compared to the development of one tourism project in Thethi. The GTZ accommodation project was selected for comparison because it is best developed, with information readily available.

In making this comparison, the GTZ project includes some relevant steps of the ideal TD process, namely stakeholder identification and community capacity building via workshops. However, their project is

Counts. The Academy of Management Review, 1997.
[10]Eagles, P., McCool, S., & Haynes, C. *Sustainable tourism in protected areas: guidelines for planning and management*. IUCN, 2002.

solely dependent on tourism without consideration of other options, its lack of strategic planning, monitoring, and evaluation, indicates a lack of sustainability in project development.

Towards sustainability: Leverage points for change in Thethi tourism development

The lack of sustainability observed above is problematic because it could act to damage the key resource for tourism development, the pristine environment, aside from aggravating already present resource management problems and social inequalities. It should be of interest to all stakeholders involved, but especially the local community in Thethi, to pursue sustainable tourism development.

Although some changes could be implemented immediately, via actions of NGOs working with the local community, many are long-term changes. Also, knowing that the activities and role of the central and regional governments are currently observed to be minimal in the region, it is unclear how effective changes in institutional structure would be in increasing the sustainability of the tourism development process in Thethi. Therefore, in the short-term, relying on these stakeholders to implement change may not be practical or useful for the local community; tourism is occurring to promote rural development for the local residents, but to do so needs to be sustainable while protecting their key resource, the environment. It is the local community that should theoretically have the highest interest in adjusting the current form of tourism to something more sustainable because they have the most to gain and lose from the development.

Thethi's local community as the main actor in tourism development

Management stakeholder salience theory is based on examining single relationships between a 'manager' and 'stakeholder' who are connected to an 'organization'. In the context of this research, there is no individual manager or an organization; rather, the manager is replaced by the person, individual, or institution who has the decision-making power in the tourism development process (landowner, local or regional government who control development, managers of individual projects, or those with access to funding) and the organization becomes the tourism development process. The 'manager' is defined as the regional government or Commune, as they by law control development, landownership, and should technically be responsible for protected area management. Second, the attributes of power, legitimacy, and urgency were defined for this research context. For the attribute of power, there were no examples of coercive power found in this research, utilitarian power was based primarily on access to financial resources, but also social connections in Thethi, materials, land, and local knowledge, and normative power could be based in deeds and contracts or institutions, such as the government or local traditions. The bases for legitimacy and urgency in the context of this research were similar to that defined by Mitchell, Agel, and Wood (1997). Results of this analysis are presented in Table 2.

Table 2. Stakeholder typology in the current Thethi tourism development.

Number of attributes	Stakeholder	Typology
3	Non-local landowners Investors: Local, Albania, foreign	Definitive
2	Transportation Investors: Albanian, foreign International NGOs Tour operators	Dangerous
		Dominant
	Local community, landowners Local NGOs	Dependent
1	Transportation National government Tour operators, Tourists Education, research	Dormant (power)
		Discretionary (legitimacy)
	Local government, Headman International NGOs	Demanding (urgency)

It is clear from Table 2 that investors (local, Albanian, and foreign) are definitive stakeholders, mainly due to access to financial resources; it should be noted that the percentage of local people with access to resources is likely low, but given their moral legitimacy, if they did have access to resources they have unquestionable salience in development. Also, non-local landowners are surprisingly definitive stakeholders because there is no management or enforcement of building activities, so they have the power to develop at will. The lack of enforcement of regulation and legislation also results in the local community as dependent stakeholders, because their power is based in land ownership, which is not defined or enforced. Similarly, local NGOs are also dependent stakeholders if they lack access to finances.

Dangerous stakeholders include transportation providers who are responsible for bringing tourists to the valley; however, as they probably have no urgent claim, they could also be classified as dormant. There are a surprising number of dormant, largely non-local and with access to finances but a lack of urgency; however, if their claims are urgent, they become dangerous stakeholders. Finally, only the local government or headman and international NGOs (if lacking funding) are considered demanding stakeholders, only possessing urgency in their claims.

Therefore, it is clear that primarily two elements differentiate stakeholders: access to finances, which results in power, and legitimacy. The stakeholders who do not have access to finances typically do have legitimacy, such as the local community, local NGOs and local entrepreneurs. The stakeholders with access to finances but not legitimacy, appear to be mostly non-local actors. However, given that contracts are not respected or enforced in Albania, and contracts form a basis for legitimacy, power overrides legitimate claims making dangerous stakeholders also definitive.

The local community could then become a definitive stakeholder in the current form of tourism development if they acquired access to financial resources; this could be through a micro-credit or small loan system operated by the government or an NGO. Currently in the EU, part of the rural development strategy is the establishment of the LEADER program, which funds small projects organized and implemented by local people on a local level. If finances are not attainable, the local community could form a partnership with other stakeholders who do possess power (utilitarian or normative) to increase their salience; for example, an international NGO that is well established has normative power and they could lobby the local government on behalf of the community to increase the communities' salience or landownership ownership, which would increase the communities' legitimacy. Partnerships or alliances could also be formed with non-local landowners, investors, and tour operators.

However, if the local community became a definitive stakeholder, or a main actor, in the Thethi tourism development process, this does not ensure that the process would change to become more sustainable; given the 'low ecological' awareness and lack of knowledge of positive and negative impacts of tourism in the community, it is likely that development would continue on its current path unless capacity building occurred to increase the sense of urgency. Remembering the other points and mechanism of change to increase sustainability in tourism development noted above, awareness and education and communication and coordination of stakeholders are also key. Therefore, in addition to leveraging the local community into a definitive stakeholder position, this must be accompanied by capacity building concerning positive and negative impacts of tourism. This could be carried out by other stakeholders; one who is invested in the development or who has an urgent claim, such as local or international NGOs. Communication and coordination between stakeholders would already be improved through the formation of partnerships, as noted above, but also the creation of a network between tourism development stakeholders would be valuable. There is indication that this may be occurring in the region through the development of LAG groups (personal communication, 2010).

Conclusion

This piece has explored the tension between environmental and cultural preservation with the need for development. If the potential of the local community of Thethi to act as leaders in the tourism development of their village can be realized and capacity building takes place, then residents will be able to achieve sustainable rural development.

Associated with the post-WW II and post-communism periods of transition on international and national scales are the feelings of opportunity and potential for growth. Reginald Hibbert surely recognized these two things during his time in Albania, and it is clear that both local people and foreigners see the potential for opportunity and growth in Thethi. There is always the concern for the preservation of tradition versus the need and desire to modernize.

NGOs, like GTZ and B3P Albania, are keen to play central roles in building capacity and knowledge within the community, watching carefully the risks of the current transition period. There is a danger that tourism development, now so advantageously recognized, could prioritize economic growth over all else.

Just as Hibbert explored Albania and learned much from his experience ('In worldly matters, Albania was to be my university'), there is the potential for those involved with development in Thethi to both learn from the experiences others have had with balancing tourism, development, and preservation of culture, but also to set a new standard for rural development in the Balkans.

Acknowledgements

AY would like to acknowledge grants supporting her work with the Shala Valley Project by the International Peace Research Association, the National Science Foundation, National Endowment for the Humanities, and Millsaps College, USA.

EM would like to acknowledge grants supporting her study in the MESPOM program by Erasmus Mundus.

Abbreviations

B3P	Balkan Peace Park Project
EU	European Union
GTZ	Gesellschaft für Technische Zusammenarbeit (German)
IEP	Institute for Environmental Policy
IPPE	International Peace Park Expeditions
IUCN	International Union for Conservation of Nature
LAG	Local Action Groups
LEADER	Liaison Entre Actions de Développement de l'Économie Rurale (French)
NGO	Non-governmental organization

PA   Protected Area

REC   Regional Environmental Center

SNV   Stichting Nederlandse Vrijwilligers (Dutch)

STD   Sustainable Tourism Development

SVP   Shala Valley Project

TD   Tourism Development

UNDP   United Nations Development Program

UNEP   United Nations Environment Program

Bibliography

Backer, Berit (l00l) *The Albanians of Rrogam*, Video produced by David Wason of Granada Television (Disappearing World Series), Manchester.

Black-Michaud, Jacob 1980 [1975]. Feuding Societies [= Cohesive Force]. Oxford: Blackwell. XXVII, 270 S.

Currie, R., Seaton, S., & Wesley, F. (2009). Determining stakeholders for feasibility analysis. *Annals of Tourism Research*, *36*(1), 41-63.

Drisco, C., & Starik, M. (2004). The Primordial Stakeholder: Advancing the Conceptual Consideration of Stakeholder Status for the Natural Environment. *Journal of Business Ethics*, *49*(1), 55-73.

Durham, M. E. (l909, l986, l987). *High Albania*, Edward Arnold, London.. Republished and edited by John Hodgson, Virago; London and Beacon Press, Boston.

Durham, M. E. (1928) *Some Tribal Origins, Laws and Customs of the Balkans*. George Allen and Unwin Ltd., London.

Eagles, P., McCool, S., & Haynes, C. (2002). *Sustainable tourism in protected areas: guidelines for planning and management.* Switzerland and Cambridge: IUCN Gland.

Eberhard, Helmut and Karl Kaser (l995) , *Albanien,Stammesleben Zwischen Tradition und Moderne,* Bőhlau, Vienna.

Elezi, Ismet 2000. Vrasjet për Hakmarrje e për Gjakmarrje në Shqipëri. Tiranë: QSDNj. 122 S.

Galaty, M., O. Lafe, and Z. Tafilica. in prep. *Light and Shadow: Isolation and Interaction in the Shala Valley of Northern Albania.* For the Monumenta Archaeologica series, Cotsen Institute of Archaeology at UCLA.

Gjergji, Andromaqi. (1963). 'Gjurmë të matriarkatit në disa doke të dikurshmë të Jëtës familjare' (Traces of matriarchy in some former customs of family life). *Buletini i Universitetit të Tiranës (Shkencat Shoqërore)* (2:284-292).

Gjeçov, Shtjefën 1989 [1933]. Kanuni i Lekë Dukagjinit. In: Leonard Fox (Hrsg.) Kanuni i Lekë Dukagjinit = The Code of Lekë Dukagjini. New York: Gjonlekaj: 1-269.

Gjuraj, Tonin 2000. Gjakmarrja në rrethet Shkodër, Malësi e Madhe. Shkodër: Qendra 'Dretësi dhe Paqe'. 131 S.

Gloyer, Gillian (2008), *Albania*, The Bradt Travel Guide, Bucks.

Hall, D. (2004). Rural tourism development in southeastern Europe: transition and the search for

sustainability. *International Journal of Tourism Research*, 6(3), 165-176.

Hanbury-Tenison, Robin (2009), *Land of Eagles: ?Riging through Europe's Forgotten Country*, I. B. Tauris, London.

Hara, S. (2009). *Peace through tourism: A case study of the Balkan Peace Park Project* (M.A. Dissertation).

University of Bradford.

Hasluck, Margaret. (1954) *The Unwritten Law in Albania*. Cambridge University Press, Cambridge. Reprinted (1981) Hyperion, Westport.

Heseltine, Nigel (1938) *Scarred Background: A Journey through Albania*, Lovat Dickson Publishers, London.

Imeraj, Petrit (1999), *Parku Kombëtar Theth (Thethi National Forest Park)*, Shkoder.

Kadare, Ismail (1990), *Broken April*, New Amsterdam Books and Saqui Books, London.

Kaser, Karl 1992. Hirten, Kämpfe, Stammeshelden. Ursprünge und Gegenwart des balkanischen Patriarchats. Wien et al.: Böhlau. 462 S.

Kaser, Karl (1992) 'The origins of Balkan Patriarchy'. *Modern Greek Studies Yearbook* (8).

Kennard, Ann (2010). Old Cultures, New Institutions: Around the New Eastern Border of the European Union. European Studies in Culture and Policy, vol. 8, Lit. Verlag, Berlin.

Krastev, Péter 2002. The Price of Amnesia: Interpretations of Vendetta in Albania. In: Identities: Journal for Politics, Gender and Culture (Skopje) 1, 2: 33-63. http://www.identities.org.mk/files/Krasztev_Cenata%20 na%20amnezijataENG.pdf [06-01-07]

Lane, Rose Wilder. (1923). *Peaks of Shala*, Harper & Bros., London and New York.

Luarasi, Aleks 2001. Marrëdhëniet Familjare (Studime për të Drejtën Zakonore Shqipatare, 1). Tirana: Luarasi. 241 S.

Mitchell, R. K., Agle, B. R., & Wood, D. J. (1997). Toward a Theory of Stakeholder Identification and Salience: Defining the Principle of Who and What Really Counts. *The Academy of Management Review, 22*(4), 853-886.

Moscardo, G. (2008). *Building community capacity for tourism development*. Wallingford, UK: CAB International.

Murzaku, Ines A. and Dervishi, Zyhdi. (2003), 'Albanians' First Post-Communist Decade: values in transition: traditional or liberal?'. *East European Quarterly*, XXXVII, no. 2, pp. 231-56.

Mustafa, Mentor and Young, Antonia. (2008), 'Feud Narratives: Contemporary Deployments of *Kanun* in Shala Valley, northern Albania', *Anthropological Notebooks*, XIV, no. 2, Ljubljana, pp. 87-105.

Newman, Bernard. (1936). *Albanian Backdoor,* Jenkins, London.

Nopcsa, Franz Baron (1910). *Aus Shala und Klementi: Albanische Wanderungen* in : Zur Kunde der Balkanhalbinsel l, Reisen und Beobachtungen ll, Sarajevo.

Pieroni, Andrea. 2008. Local Plant Resources in the Ethnobotany of Theth, a Village in the Northern Albanian Alps. Tenetic Resources and Crop Evolution [Kluwer Academic Publishers, The Netherlands), 55, 1197-1214

Pilot Productions (2008), *Treks in a Wild World: Albania,* National Geographic Channels International, UK. 'Trekking in Albania' Narrator Zoe Palmer.

Saltmarshe, Douglas 2000. Local Government in Practice: Evidence from Two Villages in Northern Albania. In: Public Administration and Development (New York) 20, 4: 327-338.

Saltmarshe, Douglas 2001. Identity in a Post-communist Balkan State: an Albanian Village Study. Aldershot: Ashgate. 246 S.

Santner-Schriebl, Silvia Ms. [1999]. Wertewandel in Stammesgesellschaften am Beispiel der nordalbanischen Hochgebirgsregion Dukagjin und der Ghettos in Tirana und Shkodër [PhD thesis]. Graz. 246 S.

Schwandner-Seivers, Stephanie. (2004) 'Allbanians, Albanianism and the Strategic Subversion of Stereotypes' in Hammond, Andrew, ed., *The Balkans and the West: Constructing the European Other, 1945-2003*, Ashgate, Aldergate, Hampshire.

Stephanie Schwandner-Sievers. (2004). 'Times Past: References for the Construction of Local Order in Present-Day Albania' in Maria Todorova, ed. Balkan   Identities: Nation and Memory, Hurst & co. 2004, pp. 103-128

Shala Valley Project, *Arachaeological and Ethnographic Reports, 2005-08*, book forthcoming www.millsaps.edu/svp.

Sheer Stanley and Senechal Marjorie (1997), *Long Life to your Childresn: a Portrait of High Albania*, The University of Massachusetts Press, Amherst.

Voell, Stéphane 2003. The Kanun in the City: Albanian Customary Law as a Habitus and its Persistence in the Suburb of Tirana, Bathore. In: Anthropos (Sankt Augustin) 98, 1: 85-101.

Voell, Stéphane 2004. Das nordalbanische Gewohnheitsrecht und seine mündliche Dimension (Reihe Curupira, 17). Marburg: Curupira. 365 S.

Waal, Clarissa de 1996. Decollectivisation and total scarcity in high Albania. In: Ray Abrahams (Hrsg.) After Socialism. Land Reform and Social Change in Eastern Europe. Providence/Oxford: Berghahn: IX, 221.

Young, Antonia. (2008), 'Establishing the Balkans Peace Park (Albania/Montenegro/Kosovo/a): Overcoming Conflicts through Negotiation on cross-border Environmental Protection', *Central and Eastern European Review*, vol 2, part l.

Contributors

Nurcan Ozgur Baklacioglu is Professor of Political Science in the University of Istanbul

Nada Boškovska is Professor of History in the University of Zurich, and has published extensively on twentieth century Macedonian history and other topics.

Shaun Byrnes was a US State Department official for his main career after military service in the US Navy. He was a senior official in the KDOM/KVM mission in Kosova in 1998-1999

Bob Churcher was a British army officer and then worked in many international community roles in the Balkans in the post-1991 wartime period. He was Country Director of International Crisis Group in Kosova between 1999 and 2003.

Bernd Fischer is Professor of History and Chair of the Department in the University of Fort Wayne, Indiana,

Michael Kaser was born in London in 1926 and read economics at King's College, Cambridge. Following the UK Foreign Service (1947-51), including HM Embassy, Moscow, and the UN Secretariat (1951-63), he was at Oxford University, retiring in 1993 as Reader in Economics and Professorial Fellow of St Antony's College. He has been General Editor of the International Economic Association since 1986 and Honorary Professor in the Institute for German Studies of the University of Birmingham since 1994. He is the author/editor of 25 books and 350 published papers, mostly on the communist and transition economies. He was President of the Albania Society of Britain 1992 to 1995 and has been awarded the Order of Naim Frashëri by the Albanian government.

Basil Kondis is a Greek historian and recently retired as Director of the Institute of Balkan Studies, (IMHA), Thessaloniki.

Charles Dennison Lane served in the US Army for many years. He was military adviser to the Albanian Army in Tirana in 1994-1995, and a senior United Nations administrator in Kosova between 1999 and 2003.

Xhevat Lloshi is an academic linguistics author, historian and translator living in Tirana.

Erin Marchington studied environmental sciences in the University of Toronto and has published extensively on tourism and the environment. She is a member of the Balkan Peace Park governing committee.

Ines Muzarku is Professor of Ecclesiastical History in the Department of Religion at Seton Hall University, New Jersey, USA, and a Visiting Professor at the University of Bologna, Italy.

Stephen Nash was a British diplomat and the first Charge d'Affaires in Tirana, Albania appointed after the end of communism in 1991-1992, and he returned as the first Ambassador to Tirana in the Kosovo war period. After retirement from the Foreign Office he is active in the Anglo-Albanian Society in Britain.

Michael Schmidt Neke published his thesis on King Zog's regime after studying at the University of Freiburg, Germany. He has published books and articles in academic journals on Albanian topics, and is co-chairman of the German-Albanian Friendship Association.

Jane Nicholov (Nee Hibbert) has studied and lived in Bulgaria and currently teaches in London.

Gani Perolli came to the United States at an early age as a refugee from Yugoslav communism, and is active in the Albanian-American community in New Jersey. He is founder of the LIBRA publishing house, and has published on twentieth century Albanian history.

James Pettifer teaches Balkan History at St Cross College, Oxford, and is author of many publications on the Balkan region. His most recent book is *The Kosova Liberation Army, Underground War to Balkan Insurgency, 1948-2001*.

Miranda Vickers is an independent scholar based in London. She is the author of *The Albanians A Concise History, Kosovo Between Serb and Albanian*, and *Albania From Anarchy to a Balkan Identity* (with James Pettifer) and other books.

Robert Wilton was advisor to the Prime Minister of Kosova in the lead-up to the country's independence, and acting Head of the OSCE Mission in Albania in 2013. He writes on international intervention, and translates Albanian poetry. He is co-founder of The Ideas Partnership NGO, and also the author of the prize-winning Comptrollerate-General series of historical novels.

Tom Winnifrith has published on Balkan topics, particularly Albania and the Balkan Vlach communities for many years while teaching in the UK at Warwick University.

Antonia Young is an Honorary Research Fellow at the Institute for South East European Studies at Bradford University in the UK. She is President of the Balkans Peace Park Committee (www.balkanspeacepark.org)